PETAR OUVALIEV
aka
PIERRE ROUVE

A Life

PETAR OUVALIEV
aka
PIERRE ROUVE

A Life

Sonia Rouve

First published in Great Britain in 2008 by
Mailer Press, 50 Comeragh Road, London W14 9HR
www.mailerpress.co.uk

Copyright © Sonia Rouve 2008

The right of Sonia Rouve to be identified as the Author of the Work has been asserted by her in accordance with the Copyright, Designs and Patents Act 1988.

All rights reserved. No part of this publication may be reproduced, stored in a retrieval system, or transmitted, in any form or by any means without the prior written permission of the publisher, nor be otherwise circulated in any form of binding or cover other than that in which it is published and without a similar condition being imposed on the subsequent purchaser.

A CIP catalogue record for this title is available
from the British Library.

ISBN 978-0-9560286-3-1

Typeset in Sabon by Taylor Thorne Print Ltd, Somerset

Printed by CPI Antony Rowe, Eastbourne

FOREWORD

I have attempted to put together a picture of the extraordinarily rich life and many experiences of a "Bulgaromane", my late husband Pierre Rouve.

He started life as Petar Ouvaliev, became Pierre Ouvaliev and emerged, in maturity and in the West, as Pierre Rouve.

In telling his story, I have drawn on the enormous range of documents that he kept so carefully: letters, articles, writings, a few diaries. To these, I have given the "skeleton" of my own recollections, noted in my own diaries and journals.

Any "memoir" of Petar Ouvaliev aka Pierre Rouve must, by definition, be incomplete; so many meetings, friends, conversations, papers... I, literally, hardly knew how to start.

However, I should emphasise that, essentially, this is my interpretation of "a life". It would be fascinating to welcome another publication which might include anecdotes, conversations etc.

I have tried to present a rounded picture. I am so grateful to all our friends for their presence in our lives. Nobody has been "hidden" by a name change.

Any errors and omissions are my fault.

ACKNOWLEDGEMENTS

Very many people have helped and encouraged me in undertaking this venture. First, of course, is Petar himself, whose memory Mila and I wanted to honour. Next is Mila, who provided memories and stories.

Of those who have shown generous and practical help, I must mention Boyan Penkov, whose encouragement and friendship – for Petar and me – has given me the strength to undertake this and other ventures. Nigel Foxell, for whose support at every stage and for the generous use of his red pen, I remain so grateful. Anthony Rudolf, whose enormous erudition and wisdom have helped me along this long path. Maria Georgieva, without whose dedicated classification of so many papers, so much less would have been easily available to me. Sima Navassardian, whose computer skills have brought to life both the oldest document and most recent photo. Assia Tabakova, for her suggestions as regards a Bulgarian readership. Nikolai Voinov, my unfailing support in every Bulgarian enterprise. And to all those who have reminded me of events and stories.

CONTENTS

In the beginning	1
Earliest days	2
The young diplomat	10
Life in London	19
And this is where I come in…	31
1959 – Our first year together and our first holiday	33
How Swinging were the Sixties?	37
1960 – *The Millionairess* and Sophia Loren	39
1961 – A house of our own	42
1962 – Our wedding	48
1963 – Mrs Ouvalieva receives permission to travel	53
1964 – Filming in Italy and Austria	60
1965 – Across Europe for the Salzburg Festival	75
1966 – Working with Antonioni on *Blow Up*	90
1967 – More films and more theatre	101
1968 – A British citizen!	109
1969 – Theatre, philosophy and art in Scandinavia	117
The Seventies – Opening up New Horizons	127
1970 – A new decade and so many new experiences	129
1971 – Pierre's first return visit to Bulgaria	137
1972 – A major theatre production	186
1973 – An addition to the Ouvaliev-Rouve family	205
1974 – Settling into a new routine	247
1975 – Back in Chelsea	263
1976 – The year of the Thracians	273
1977 – Bulgaria and Morocco	281

1978 – Istanbul, tracing Pierre's ancestors — 290
1979 – Setting up the library at 46 Markham Square — 304

The Eighties – Eastern Approaches — 311
1980 – Pierre extends his contacts with Yugoslavia — 313
1981 – Westwards, to teach in Mexico — 326
1982 – House 'For Sale' in Normandy — 337
1983 – A wedding in the family Pierre lectures in Chicago — 348
1984 – It's *1984!* — 354
1985 – Happy 70th Birthday! — 362
1986 – More celebrations — 368
1987 – Our silver wedding — 372
1988 – Salute the Southern Slavs — 377
1989 – Pierre presents Bagryana at London University — 387

The Nineties – Bulgaria rediviva — 397
1990 – A new decade, new departures — 399
1991 – Myths and legends — 405
1992 – The time of honour and acknowledgement — 411
1993 – More honours and more invitations — 419
1994 – A Bulgarian citizen – again! — 427
1995 – 80th Birthday greetings Dobrich and "Yovkov is" — 437
1996 – Dora's health deteriorates — 449
1997 – Pierre is with Dora as she dies in Paris — 457
1998 – Decline and fall Slowly, sadly towards the end — 464

Afterword — 474

ILLUSTRATIONS

Page	Topic/subject	Year
2	Certificate of baptism	
3	Entry in visitors' book at Rila Monastery	
5	Christo Ouvaliev (centre) in Fribourg	
8	School leaving certificate	1932
11	Passport for Italy	1942
11	3rd Secretary card	
12	Bogdan Filov and dignitaries at the Vatican	
13	Hungarian and Romanian visas	1943
13	Return to Bulgaria via Rousse	1945
16	Passport for France	1947
17	Visas for travel to France	
20	Order to take up appointment in Prague	1948
30	PR with '50s film camera	1955
40	PR with Sophia Loren in Italian press	1960
42	*Monsieur Topaze* and Peter Sellers	1961
52	Signing the marriage register	1962
54	"8 weeks" telegram	1963
56	The family on holiday in Grimaud	1963
60	Guina Ouvalieva arriving in UK	1964
67	On the way to Italy	
98	With Antonioni on *Blow Up*	1966
132	Sketch of PR by James Mason	1970
140	PR in Grand Hotel Sofia suite	1971
144	At his mother's house	
150	With Stefan Getzov and others	
151	At Vanyo Rumenov's home	
152	At the Hadjimishevs' apartment	
160	The 'Martell brandy' man	
184	With Baroness Budberg	

Page	Topic/subject	Year
191	*Break of Noon* with Ben Kingsley and Ann Firbank	1972
198	With Minister Goshkin at the *Aretusa* Club	
204	10th wedding anniversary	
204	Admiring Topolski's portrait	
208	At home in Chelsea with Apostol Karamitev	1973
208	Evening with Apostol Karamitev	
215	With mother and aunties	
229	Baby Mila with granny in hospital	
231	Vanyo and his Moskvitch	
233	PR with baby Mila in hospital	
236	SR invitation for *9th September* parade	
238	Baby Mila boards the plane for London	
240	SR and baby in Berkeley Square	
244	PR and SR with the Patriarch and HE A. Yankov	
246	Family Christmas at Davies Street	
255	Family at Fiquainville	1974
259	Guina Ouvalieva's permit	
262	Christmas at Pashanko's house	
283/4	A & B Diary pages Feb. 1977	1977
297	At Vanyo's home	1978
299	Anna Kamenova in Koprivshtitsa	
300	Bondo and Dora with their son Stefcho	
301	End of course book lottery	
310	At Claude's villa in Marrakech	1979
328	Milcho Leviev entry in our visitors' book	1981
329	Christo Stefanov's entry in the book	
330	Roman Jakobson with PR	
349	PR witness at Pierre-Christian's marriage	1983
350	Wedding group	
357	Sunset from *Villa Horizon*	1984
358	View of the house	
363	PR 70th birthday	1985
367	PR gardening in Normandy	
367	Christmas at the Dimitroffs	
370	Lina and Karl Ognyanov at 50 Markham Street	1986
374	A. and V. Fol and I. Marazov in visitors' book	1987
381	'Uncle Matyo' in London	1988
386	Pierre with his new Selena Vega radio	

ILLUSTRATIONS

Page	Topic/subject	Year
389	Mila cooks Easter lunch with Luben	1989
391	PR with Lina in Switzerland	
392	BBC 50 years programme (PR production 1955))	
392	BBC programme (Grigor Grigorov 1958 coverage)	
395	PR with Denis Bowen in Huddersfield	
404	Blaga Dimitrova at 50 Markham Street	1990
404	Entry in our visitors' book	
409	Mila's 18th birthday	1991
412	Blaga Dimitrova letter to PR	1992
413	PR diary pages	
414	HE Richard Thomas invitation	
415	President Zhelev invitation	
415	PR and Doctor Honoris Causa ceremony	
416	Audience at the ceremony in Aula Magna of Sofia University	
416	Vice President invitation	
422	PR and Bagryana centenary programme	1993
423	PR with Faculty of Journalism students	
428	PR with President Zhelev at Bulgarian Embassy	1994
432	PR certificate of renewal of Bulgarian citizenship	
437	Simeon Saxe-Coburg telegram to PR for 80th birthday	1995
438	PR letter in reply	
440	PR in discussion with A. Fol, D. Avramov and A. Natev	
444	'Fontcho' address to PR	
445	Yordan Yovkov celebrations and with Nikolai Haitov in Dobrich	
448	PR notes for Bulgarian broadcast topics	
449	PR article with note to Stefan Prodev	1996
452	Mila working with cat at 50 Markham Street	
454	Brian Dimitroff wedding	
456	Photo PR with Dora in Tenerife	
458	PR note on *Levski* text	1997
467	PR on phone at 46 Markham Square	1998

In the beginning

"Shall we drop in and see that Bulgarian I've been telling you about?" suggested my friend Mary as we passed No 10 Wetherby Gardens on our way home one day.

We did and that is how this – and my – story begins.

"That Bulgarian" was Petar Ouvaliev – or Pierre Rouve as he was by then known in England – and Mary had been talking about him ever since they had met. She and I shared a flat at that time (in the late 1950s) and she would often leave me messages such as "If Pierre phones, tell him…". So when she suggested that we "drop in and see…", I was certainly intrigued by the chance to meet this "mystery man".

Not only was he extremely handsome, he was also kind and hospitable and invited us in for a cup of coffee. Understanding that he was very intelligent and well-read, I was happy to share with him some of my latest enthusiasms: the plays of Ionesco and Anouilh, the works of Paul Klee…

It was not "love at first sight" for either of us, but a gradually developing relationship. A relationship, later a marriage, which lasted for forty years.

Our story now continues – and it will begin with my relating **his** story.

* * * * *

Earliest days

Depending on the acceptance of the old or the new Orthodox calendar, Petar Ouvaliev was born in Sofia on 30th December 1914 or on 12th January 1915, first child of Hristo Ouvaliev and Guina Zdravkova.

EARLIEST DAYS

Both parents were from well-respected and cultivated families: the Ouvalievs had military predecessors who fought in the struggle for Liberation in the 1870s and were from Kalofer. A fascinating document which I have had the privilege of consulting is the Visitors' Book at Rila Monastery. There the librarian showed me the entry by Petar's grandfather: "Podporuchik P. Ouvaliev ot Kalofer, 14 April 1880". It is both fascinating and touching to think that a young sublieutenant would make time while on leave to visit a historic and religious monument.

Other documents attesting to his family's military engagement are the record of a Todor Ouvaliev, born 1859 in Kalofer, and graduating top of his class at the Military Academy in Sofia in 1879. 'Kapitan Ouvaliev' is mentioned in the book *Stroitelite (The Builders)* by Simeon Radev, in particular the part played by Ouvaliev in keeping the Regent, Stefan Stambolov, up to date regarding military activity:

"Dear Stambolov
... Ouvaliev will be travelling and I take this opportunity of asking him... to inform you at length how the situation is developing.
(Prince) Alexander (von Battenberg)"

Petar's paternal grandmother was from Balat, the Bulgarian district of Istanbul. Her soups (*tchorba*) were, Petar would always proudly boast, legendary.

His father was born in 1876. He learned French and, in the early 1890s, went to study in Switzerland with a grant from Stancho Ouvaliev. He later continued his education in Fribourg and was subsequently appointed a member of the staff of the Higher Pedagogical Institute (later incorporated into Sofia University). He is the author of several articles on the teaching of French, both the principles and its practice in Bulgaria. His seminal work, published in Plovdiv in 1915, is *Obutchenieto po Frenski Ezik*, and, as he writes in his Introduction, "Taya metodika na obutchenieto po frenski ezik e, do kolkoto znam, perva u nas". ("This method for teaching French is, as far as I know, the first to appear in our country.") I have a much-cherished original copy given to me by Petar's mother and inscribed: "Na milata mi Sonia vuv pamet na skupiya ni papa. Mama". ("For dear Sonia, in memory of beloved Father".) Sadly he died in 1929 at the age of 53, the result of a minor ear operation.

Petar Ouvaliev's mother Guina, née Zdravkova, was one of six sisters (and one brother who died young), only two of

whom married and had children. Guina Zdravkova studied – under Ekaterina Karavelova – to become a primary school teacher and also specialised in French. It was when Petar's father was in Grenoble on a language course that the two met there and a short time later married.

The parents built and lived in a house on Ulitza Karnigradska (now demolished and replaced – at No. 1 – by an apartment block) with, as Petar always loved to recall, their own cow in the garden to ensure fresh milk for the children. Petar had now acquired a sister, Teodora – afterwards more commonly called 'Dora'. The house was covered in wisteria and proved a meeting place for many of the intellectuals of the time.

Both children, Petar and Dora, were early exposed to an open and international world culture and, as a result of their parents' language abilities and beliefs, were enrolled first in Italophone educational establishments: Petar in Italian Primary (Alessandro Manzoni), to be followed by French; Dora Italian Primary and Secondary in Sofia. In an article written in 1949 for the Italian review *Film*, their London correspondent Pierre Rouve wrote:

> "It was 1921 and my father – who had only one fault, but a huge one: he was wholeheartedly European – said to my mother: 'We'll need to send this son of ours to an Italian school. If one day he'll want to be a cultured person, he'll need to start by speaking Italian. Thus it was that I found myself the only foreigner in a small Italian school in a pretty small Balkan capital and, if I haven't quite succeeded in becoming what my father would have wished, it is entirely my fault".

Their mother Guina Ouvalieva meanwhile was working as a primary school teacher at the Denkoglu school in the centre of Sofia, rising to become Headteacher in 1937. All of her pupils, and several are still alive, remember her with the greatest affection and respect: firm but fair, always positive and encouraging, knowing each of her charges individually.

It was one of Petar's proud boasts, on behalf of his mother's professionalism, that she never missed a day's school, since both he and his sister were born during school holidays! Whether this had indeed been her plan for conception and deliverance can only be surmised!

* * * *

A bright young man

After the Italian primary school, where he gained a thorough, fluent and lasting knowledge of and competence in the language (and for which we can be sure that his father was proud of him!) Petar Ouvaliev was sent, for his secondary schooling, to the Augustinian Brothers' "French College" in Plovdiv (whose building now forms part of the Paissi Hilendarski University and where I, while attending a recent meeting of a European programme group, had the very strange, even eery, experience of sitting at a table in what would have been the boys' dormitory...). There the uniform, the programme and the discipline were strict: often minor infringements of, for example, the uniform code would meet with punishment, usually detention.

By this time Petar Ouvaliev was developing a passionate interest in plays and musicals. Whereas other boys, he recalled, would be kept in for punishment on a sports afternoon, the Brothers very cleverly taught him a lesson by keeping him in on Saturdays, the day when he would otherwise have returned to Sofia for the weekend and, of course, gone to the theatre!

His early youthful passions for Mimi Balkanska and, later, for Rouzha Delcheva and their performances led to an improvement in his behaviour in school!

His progress in such subjects as mathematics was subject to the teachers' insistence that the correct workings and answers be given in good French. Petar would recall how a particular teacher would listen to a pupil and then say *"Et maintenant, dites-le-nous en bon français"*! Petar had the greatest respect for one of the Brothers, Père Alain, a teacher of philosophy who, having suffered the most terrible burns during World War I, had made a vow that, if he survived, he would dedicate his life to God.

During summer holidays Petar would enjoy youth camp activities, notably at 'Lager Chaika' on the Black Sea coast.

His passionate interest in the theatre also led to youth

productions which he directed, notably of *Periferia*, as one of the cast, Angelina Ognyanova, a pupil at the American College, recalls.

Finishing his secondary schooling with the highest grades, a thorough and fluent command of French and a study prize awarded to him personally by the then Vatican nunciate

Giovanni Roncalli (later Pope John XXIII), Petar would have loved to move into the world of the arts and theatre but, as is well known, parents give advice on future careers...It was therefore, as he always maintained, that "to please my mother" he agreed to study Law at Sofia University. Less flatteringly about the subject, he would say: *"Qui ne fait rien, fait le Droit"*!

Not a lot was said about the degree programme and, apart from the fact that he completed the course, it must be assumed that he continued to spend the greater part of his time in theatres, at performances of plays and musicals. He is known to have made the Bulgarian translations of the libretti of several operettas, and a tribute paid by him to Mimi Balkanska in a broadcast on the BBC Bulgarian service was recently cited to introduce the Bulgarian TV documentary on her life and work. Generally he played the role of the elegant, handsome and sought-after young "man about town".

From 1937, after graduating, Petar started to write film reviews, published in *Balkan* (whose Arts pages he edited), *Dnes* and *Zlatorog*. He was to continue this activity, not only in Bulgaria but also while travelling and on postings abroad, for example his *Filmi ot Venezia* (published, in the form of a letter, in *Zlatorog* in 1941), for the next 10 or so years, indeed until he left Bulgaria for England in 1947. These articles have recently been collected into a volume *Filmovi Trohi* (*Film Crumbs*, Petar's own phrase) by Kostadin Kostoff, lecturer in the history of film, and published in Plovdiv.

In 1939, at the age of 24, he was awarded the Bulgarian State Drama prize for his running of an experimental theatre group in Sofia where his productions included English, French and German plays. This young "man about town", as several people recall, was one of those regularly invited to the '*soirées*' given by Anna Kamenova in her house (destroyed during World War 2) on Slavianska Street. These gatherings, one may imagine, would have seen the cream of the intellectual elite of Sofia in the late 1930s.

* * * * *

The young diplomat

But what does a young "man about town", who has completed his studies in Jurisprudence to please his mother but who is uninterested in law as a profession, do to occupy his time, earn a living and have a "proper job"? Well, to occupy his time very pleasantly he continued frequenting theatres and also VITIZ (Higher Institute of Theatre Art where, from 1936, he was an Associate Professor), but to earn a living in a way that was acceptable to his mother, he began to work for the Ministry of the Interior, in the Press section. His contacts and his excellent command of foreign languages made him very useful when official visitors came from overseas. However, not only did he work for the Ministry in Sofia but, with his fluency in languages, he was recruited as official interpreter for the Bulgarian Army Symphony Orchestra and, in 1939, accompanied the orchestra on several of their overseas tours. He always used to say that his extensive knowledge of the classical repertoire was gleaned from having to sit listening for long hours to rehearsals!

Later, in the early 1940s, Petar transferred to the Ministry of Foreign Affairs and it was in September 1942 that, appointed Legation Secretary in Rome, he made the long train journey from Sofia. It was *à propos* this train journey that he used to tell the story of how, finally, all those years of studying Latin had paid off since, as no one understands Hungarian, he found himself able to converse with a fellow passenger in Latin!

Despite the war, a diplomatic posting for a sociable and charming young man in Rome must have been a dream. Petar's Italian *carta d'identità*, issued to him as '3rd Secretary

THE YOUNG DIPLOMAT

Bulgarian Legation' on the 2nd October 1942, shows a very handsome young man.

His knowledge of Italian of course made him very useful to the Head of Mission, Boris Altinoff. Petar was present at the meeting when the Bulgarian Prime Minister, Bogdan Filov, was received at the Vatican.

The progress of the war meant that after one year of Petar's being in the post, the Allies began their push and the landings in the south of Italy meant that Rome would very soon be under attack. The 19th July 1943 saw the Allied bombing of Rome and on the 25th July there was held the Grand Council of Fascism at which Mussolini was dismissed. Diplomats were given certain options and it is clear from Petar's passport that he had applied for visas (valid for one month and issued by the Hungarian and Rumanian legations – the then, of course, 'Légation Royale de Hongrie' and 'Légation Royale de Roumanie' – in Rome on 20th and 21st September 1943) which would enable him to return to Bulgaria.

It must have been a great challenge to obtain visas at this difficult moment. The alternative option was to re-locate the diplomatic mission to Venice.

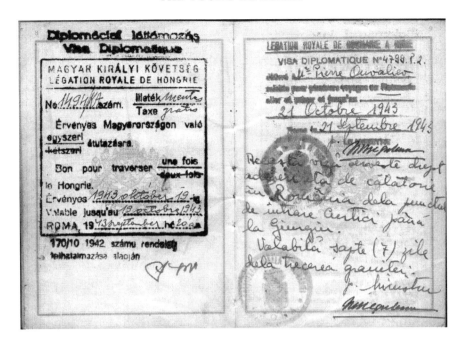

There was confusion all over Italy, yet it is clear from documents that the staff of the Bulgarian Legation transferred

to Venice (hence Petar did not use the visas which had been issued for a return to Bulgaria). Unfortunately, as is well known, Bulgaria has always chosen the losing side... and internment was to follow. Released from prison camp he returned to Bulgaria. His diplomatic passport records that he re-entered Bulgaria from Rumania at Rousse on 26th October 1945.

It is worth bearing in mind that his returning home was governed by choice rather than necessity: he held to the belief that the post-September 1944 regime offered real promise of improvements for his country.

Upon his return to Sofia, therefore, he was to resume his position as Legation Secretary in the Ministry of Foreign Affairs, and it was in this interesting and busy role that he was to meet and interview a whole range of personalities from both East and West.

* * * * *

Plans for further study

One particularly interesting person whom Petar met in the course of his work turned out to be a kindred spirit, both spiritually – for he was of Russian origin – and intellectually. This was the 2nd Secretary at the French Legation and well known writer Romain Gary. They were to remain close friends, colleagues and literary collaborators until Romain's untimely death in 1980. His then wife Lesley Blanch was also a writer, and there is reference – in a biography of Romain Gary – to evenings spent with Bulgarian intellectuals in their apartment on Hristo Botev.

Meanwhile, and one can only suppose in parallel to his work at the MFA, he continued his work with the theatre; and his production, in 1946, of Giraudoux's *Mad Woman of Chaillot* was several years ahead of the London one. This range of theatrical experience led to his appointment, at the age of 31, as lecturer in Theatre Theory at VITIZ. It is fascinating to note that, in recognition of Petar's broad range of theatrical activity, the eminent scholar in the field of ancient theatre Nikolai Fol (father of Professor Alexander Fol) inscribed a copy of his book *Teater v Antraktite*: "Na Petar Ouvaliev, edin ot maltzinata, za koito e pisana taya kniga" ("For Petar Ouvaliev, one of the few for whom this book is written"). This was indeed to prove a happy augury.

Petar's passion for theatre and film led him to a decision to pursue studies in this field and it was thus that it was arranged that he apply to study at the IDEC in Paris. Romain Gary was, of course, the person able to facilitate the issue of a permit to travel (no easy undertaking at that time) and to stay in France. All was therefore arranged and the Ministry of Information and Arts, on 11th March 1947, wrote concerning the mission (*Komandirovaneto*) of Petar Ouvaliev to France to study film-directing at the Higher Institute of Cinematography in Paris, justifying this in a letter to the Minister on the grounds of the need to develop the Bulgarian cinema industry. He was to be funded (for a period of 15 months) under the terms of the *Bulgarsko Delo* Foundation together with a stipend from the French Cultural Institute in Sofia to work as an Assistant with one of the best-known French directors. His official passport, No. 236, on which the words 'Royaume de Bulgarie' are simply scored out and 'République Populaire de Bulgarie' written in by hand (shortage of paper, printing presses and ink, personnel...?) accorded him a one-year stay "abroad" and was signed by the Director of Protocol of the time, Minister Plenipotentiary N. Volcoff. The passport, issued on the 30th June, then allowed him to seek visas for leaving Bulgaria "*prez Dragoman*", transiting "the People's Federal Republic of Jugoslavia at Tzaribrod" and a "double transit (after all, he was supposed to return to Bulgaria...) special visa" for Italy and finally a "special visa" issued by the "French Legation in Bulgaria" and signed by "the Vice-Consul B. de Warcez", granting him entry and exit and a three month stay in France, issued "free of charge" on the 18th July 1947.

He was about to leave when, as he used to tell the story, he and Professor Nikola Dolaptchiev were sheltering from the rain under the same umbrella outside the Ministry of Foreign Affairs one day and, as Professor Dolaptchiev had just been appointed

to head the Bulgarian Legation in London. In need of staff, he put the question "Do you speak English?" Petar, who then spoke French, Italian, Serbian and more, but had never had the occasion to learn English, nevertheless replied, ambiguously and quick as a flash: "Who doesn't speak English?!" This reply led to his almost immediate departure for London and, of course, once there, the need to learn English!

Travelling alone?

There was one more thing he wanted to do, however, before leaving: a favour to a long-standing friend, a young journalist called Ivaila Vulkova. What would be more logical than, if one were married, to be accompanied by one's wife...? On the 1st August 1947 Petar married Ivaila in order that she should be able to accompany him to Britain as she wished.

The request for her to travel with him was, however, refused: she was not issued with an exit visa. He travelled alone to London and took up the post as 2nd Secretary. I have since learned the not very important yet interesting fact that, travelling of course in those days by train, he broke his journey and stayed a few days in Paris with his sister Dora and her husband Luben Todorov. He was also able to breathe once again the "open (cultural) air" of art galleries and theatre productions.

* * * * *

Life in London

London suited this young, intelligent and multilingual diplomat: meetings, official gatherings, receiving visitors and other diplomats. Petar was quick to learn English – indeed very soon after his arrival he was starting to work in the theatre. Given that his original plan had been to study film production in Paris, it was no surprise for me to find in his vast archive a letter, dated December 1947, in which a friend in Rome at Scalera Film writes introducing him to the Victoria Film Company in London as:

> "not only proficient in several languages but has a vast culture linked to an acute artistic sensibility. I feel sure that you will be able to involve him in the artistic programme of your company".

It would seem that he had become interested in – and knowledgeable about – art and art history while he and his sister were in Italy, and especially in Venice where she worked on her doctorate, and in London he very soon began to write art reviews. He was also such a success in his "official" profession of diplomat that he was selected for promotion: from 2nd to 1st Secretary and in an order dated 6th December 1948, he was told to prepare "within 15 days" to travel to... Prague.

Promotion within the profession where he had proved such a success; return "behind the iron curtain"; apply to stay in the country where he was beginning to feel more and more "at home"... here, indeed, was a real dilemma; significant and lasting choices had to be made.

In the words of the title of a book by his old friend Misho Padev *Escape from the Balkans – I chose Freedom*, Petar chose freedom. Freedom: personal, professional and political. At that time, and for such a person – on the "fast track" career path – this was truly a momentous decision. Unsure what future there was for him in Britain, he wrote to the then British Minister of Foreign Affairs, the Right Honourable Ernest Bevin, the following letter on the 9th December 1948:

"Sir,

I have the honour to bring to the notice of Your Excellency that I have today resigned from my post as Second Secretary to the Bulgarian Legation in London, and that I have refused to accept the promotion offered to me on December 6th, to become First Secretary to the Bulgarian Embassy in Prague. My resignation is the natural result of my feelings of indignation towards the oppressive Communist regime in my country...

I entered the Bulgarian diplomatic service in 1938 and I am leaving it now because I want to find my place in the world of free men, fully conscious of my duty towards those who suffer under the Moscow dictatorship.

I would like to hope, Sir, that H.M. Government, following their noble tradition of tolerance and hospitality, would grant me the opportunity to live and work in England, in order that I may be able in my capacity as a writer to discharge my duty, by offering my modest contribution in the struggle for liberty and democracy.

Please accept, Sir, the assurance of my highest consideration."

Impressed by his case, the Home Office subsequently confirmed that:

"You will be able to stay... without any specific restriction of time".

Officially secure, Petar had to make ends meet. From a bedsitting-room in Kensington Court, eking out an existence on a minimum amount of money, he sought work with writers, publishers, producers and directors.

Remembering these very difficult days in the life of a political exile, he was always helpful but realistic when talking to and advising other Bulgarians who sought his opinion when they were considering the same route. As he described it, it was an extremely "lonely life". Only a few months before his death at the end of 1998, I recall being with him while he was dispensing very wise advice to a young Bulgarian lawyer friend of ours who had decided that he would try to make his life in England. Atanas often tells me how valuable was the advice he received and how kind and thoughtful Pierre was to him.

* * * * *

Cut off from Bulgaria

His decision to turn down the promotion and the move to Prague, was obviously not to remain without repercussions in Bulgaria. This, together with his application to remain in the UK, was deemed "a treasonable action". Such judgements were published in the State Gazette accompanied by the sentence imposed: in this case, of death. There were other remaining and tangled threads, some never to be resolved. He was officially deprived ("expropriated") of his own apartment, his mother suffered too, in that she was ordered to leave the family home and to return to live with her unmarried sisters; informed of the sentence passed against her son; forbidden to have any contact with him by letter or phone; left unaware, therefore, of his condition in the UK. A noble, moral and responsible woman, she never once spoke out or complained, never challenged her son for having taken this decision.

Another thread was the wife, the woman whom he had married just days before leaving for London. Ivaila, having remained in Bulgaria, obviously felt it would be better for her to be free of this marriage and her application for a divorce was granted on 2nd December 1949. Prior to its being granted, and no doubt contributing to it, was the open letter (published in the newspaper *Otechestven Front*) that she felt the need to write to the Chairman of the Praesidium, Secretary General of the Communist Party, Georgi Dimitrov.

The most kind and generous-spirited of men, Petar later forgave her for this dishonourable act.

* * * * *

Art and artists

His sister Dora, now living in Paris with her husband Luben Todorov, also a political exile, was able to give moral support and also to help with contacts – she was then working for the review *Cahiers d'Art* and its editor Christian Zervos – and, with her doctorate in Art History completed in Venice during the war, had begun to undertake some interesting and important interviews with famous artists, notably Georges Braque. Her essays *L'intérieur de l'Art (Izkuztvoto – pogled otvutre'.)* were recently published by Agata in Sofia in the Bulgarian translation undertaken by Danila Stoyanova shortly before her death.

Petar covered the London art exhibitions for French journals and also Italian ones – his fluency in both languages standing him in very good stead.

Soon his reviews of artists and exhibitions were to bring him to the attention of Dr. Richard Gainsborough, a fellow *"passioné de l'art"*, a medical doctor who launched *Art News and Review* (later *Arts Review*) in 1949. Petar's English was by then, *mirabile dictu*, of such a high level that he began writing – in his personal and inimitable style – regularly for the journal. A first, in every sense, was his review of the Massimo Campigli exhibition, occupying the important front page of issue 10 of Volume 1 (June 1949). His reviews were highly esteemed by the eminent critic Eric Newton. It is fascinating to look back and see the range of artists and of exhibitions which his writings covered:

Turner, Ben Nicholson, William Scott, Ivon Hitchens, Thrace at the British Museum... articles cut out and meticulously filed and (for the most part) dated and stuck onto the "trademark" golden yellow quarto size sheets of paper! A tradition which, my check on the handwriting shows, I continued for him when, together, we would compile the sets of articles.

* * * * *

The BBC

French, Italian and now English... but what of his native Bulgarian? Now that there are some 60,000 Bulgarians in the United Kingdom, and most, it would appear, in London, it is difficult to recall that, at that "closed" period – late 1940s, early 1950s – a Bulgarian, a political refugee, a dissident, an intellectual, was a true *rara avis*. Let us not forget that Radio London was "jammed", but the BBC – whose Bulgarian service began in 1940 – was to be Petar's "home from home". Cultural events, plays, painters, films, books, poetry... such was to be the main menu and Petar's hallmark, in fact for nearly 50 years. It was he who organised the Bulgarian contribution to the Shakespeare quatercentenary celebration, devising programmes on Shakespeare and Art, his sonnets in Bulgarian, linked Bulgarian and British cultural items, covered those events which would show Bulgarians how their culture was represented in the United Kingdom (the Thracian exhibition at the British Museum, Rangel Vulchanov and Bulgarian films at the National Film Theatre, puppet theatre at the Edinburgh Festival, Georgi Baev and Svetlin Roussev exhibitions in London galleries, translations of Nikolai Haitov's *Divi Razkazi* by Michael Holman, production of Georgi Jagarov's *The Public Prosecutor* at the Hampstead Theatre in 1967...); how British culture permeated Bulgaria (translations of Shakespeare by Valeri Petrov, Harold Pinter's plays, the poetry of T.S. Eliot, the

Royal Shakespeare Company and Voice Director Cicely Berry...).

Very few were those who may have been able to hear (able – on short wave radio; daring – to listen to the words, albeit cultural and in no way political, of a "traitor to his country"), understand and appreciate those early broadcasts. Even fewer were those who would write to him at that time. Progressively, however, as his thoughts and ideas expressed in the broadcasts were recognised as the important cultural bridge which they were, even those whom one might have expected to be the most dismissive began to express their appreciation of the high level of thought and analysis, spoken in the most rich and elegant forms of the Bulgarian language.

By meticulously maintaining his apolitical stance, by demonstrating his devotion to the country, the culture and the language he had left behind, and his desire that his listeners, deprived of most of these cultural references, should be informed, Petar Ouvaliev became something of a beacon, "a candle shining in a naughty world".

* * * * *

Bulgarian friends in London

It was at the BBC and through the contacts he made there that Petar was able to renew old friendships and these were to prove of immeasurable value in the difficult times adapting to a quite different style of life in England.

First among these was his friend of many years' standing, lost sight of since the war, Captain now in the British Army, Grigor ('Greg') Grigorov. Grigor proved a tower of strength: reviving good memories of life, times and friends in Bulgaria, introducing him to many of his English friends, of whom he had many in the literary world: John Pudney who, in 1948, inscribed a copy of his *Almanack of Hope* to Pierre; a most appropriate title! There were also Lionel and Crystal Hale... all of whom were to prove kind and helpful in presenting Petar to the intellectual and artistic life of England.

(But, while you are wondering how it was that Grigor was a captain in the British Army, let it be told that, together with that other great friend and support, Misho Padev, he made his way from Bulgaria, via Turkey to Cairo in the early 1940s. Many good tales were recounted of their adventures on the way... After Cairo, and as a serving officer in the Bulgarian Army, Grigor made his way to Kenya where he was recruited to train the troops. The story was always told of how, since the Kenyan soldiers had no reason to be able to distinguish between Bulgarian and English, it was easier for Grigor to use the commands with which he was already familiar and so it is (or may be...) that until this day, a particular unit responds not to: "Quick, march!", but rather to: "*Hodom, marsh!*")

Misho Padev and Grigor were firm friends and "battle weary" companions. The three were inseparable, especially as regards their social life, even when Misho moved to live in the USA. Grigor claimed to have been a witness at each of Misho's marriages... His own was to follow soon when he met and married the lovely director of the Royal Opera ballet, Romayne Austin, in 1960. Opera, with its many superb Bulgarian voices (Boris Christoff, Nikolai Ghiaurov, Raina Kabaivanska...) was indeed to become a central focus of the lives of Petar and Grigor.

Another Bulgarian friend in the musical world was Pashanko Dimitroff, double base player with the London Symphony Orchestra, at whose family home in Willesden many marvellous musical parties were held; Bulgarian food prepared by Pashanko, or at least under his orders, by the hospitable and one might say long-suffering "lady of the house", Margaret. Heaven forbid that anyone should forget how and when to begin the process of pickling the cabbage leaves! The painter, Georgi (Bobby) Daskaloff and his wife Nadine were also frequent guests of the Dimitroffs.

A good Bulgarian friend from earlier days in Sofia whom he

had met after his return from Italy, was Avner ('Struki') Kalev. Struki had left Bulgaria for Israel in 1948 and had subsequently served in the Israeli diplomatic service. It was, however, when he came to London to "meet" his baby son David (Struki's wife Rita had come to London for the birth), that the two old friends met up again, talked far into the night. They were to remain the best and firmest of friends until Petar's death. It is also the case that Struki, as he was universally known, was one of the most generous-spirited supporters of the Foundation set up to promote cultural activities in the name of the Ouvaliev family.

A Bulgarian writer and poet, known variously under his different pseudonyms of Ilko Iliev and, in the USA where he later settled, Gerald Dorset, was another dear and close friend whom Petar, suffering himself from home- and culture-sickness on occasions, helped enormously in his personal crises. "Geraldo" (not to be confused with the band leader!) was a sweet and unassuming person who produced and published a large body of poetry. In recognition of Gerald, I shall quote from the title of and the inscription in one of his volumes of poetry: "*An Aristocrat of Intellect* – to Pierre Rouve, a gentleman and a scholar, with best wishes from the author." Both the title and the inscription are, I believe, a perfect description of my late husband.

These were some of the "settled" Bulgarians who created their strong, supportive network. As others came, visited, stayed, in England (almost invariably in London), Petar was, in his turn, to offer friendship, conversation, solace. In the 1950s these would, for the most part, have been visiting artists, since the idea of applying for permission to stay would have been an enormous step, involving leaving one's family behind.

* * * * *

Settling in to life and work in England

Entering the 1950s finds Petar establishing himself in several fields: the reviews for *Art News and Review* become a regular feature and he is becoming the "critic of choice" for several artists and galleries. 1950 sees an early review of the work of Barbara Hepworth at the Lefevre Gallery; he is chosen to review exhibitions at the Royal Academy; he begins to write regularly about the artists exhibited at the Drian Gallery, founded and run by the remarkable Halima Nalecz; he is the first to appreciate the ideas behind the New Vision Centre, Denis Bowen's cradle for promoting abstract art. He is also contributing, as London correspondent, to the Italian *Fiera Letteraria* and to *Film* where he covers the cinema scene, not only in London but going in July 1949 to the International Film Festival at Knokke le Zoute in Belgium (about which he writes in his inimitable style: "the very word 'Belgium' has a certain calm sonority about it, evoking civic values…").

In 1956, he begins a two-year tutorial class programme – 'Appreciation of Art' – under the auspices of the prestigious Council for Extra-Mural Studies of the University of London. His concern for his students and their growing awareness of artistic styles and values is evident in his programme notes:

> "This series of informal discussions is not meant to be a systematic course in the History of Painting, Sculpture and Architecture… an attempt to pave the way to a personal… and unprejudiced appreciation of the works of art… to bridge the gulf between art and the non-specialised beholder, handicapped by fears and prejudices… whose main fear is his apparent inability to 'understand' modern art…"

This, together with his contacts in the Italian art world, led to his being elected in 1957 a member of the jury for the *Premio Lissone (internazionale per la pittura),* together with such other great names as Will Grohmann and Guido Ballo. He was to continue his contacts with the award ceremony for many years. The title of the small booklet of poems *Vorrei Essere* by the famous critic Giuseppe Marchiori and inscribed to Pierre in Venice 1959 *"con cordiale amicizia"*, again reflects his aspirations: "I should like to be".

As well as teaching and writing, he is, increasingly, becoming involved in the world of theatre, particularly the smaller, provincial repertory theatres. His first production (May 1950) ran at the Gateway Theatre. His imaginative production was *Storm Wrack*, a new play by Dorothy Hope. He was soon able to interest a range of theatre managers in French and Italian drama: at the New Lindsey theatre there were productions of Ugo Betti, with whom he had been in correspondence since 1949 and who, in a letter, wrote of his gratitude for the friendship and commitment to artistic values shown by his *"caro Amico"* with whose help he hoped to "become a friend of the difficult, serious and strong English public". At the same theatre he produced *Angelica* by Leo Ferrero; directed at the Hyde Hall, Winchester; the Tuska, Henley-on-Thames; from the early 50s he established one of his most lasting theatrical connections: working with Jack de Leon at the 'Q' Theatre. All the established and the experimental playwrights were put on stage there, from Shakespeare to Lorca, and saw performances by Michael Gough, Barbara Murray, Donald Pleasence, Patrick McGoohan and many others. As early as the mid 50s he was also a regular contributor to the De Leon drama summer schools, lecturing on 'European drama' and rehearsing students and producing scenes from a wide range of plays and, as Lewis Cranston noted in the *Evening News*, "the results were astonishing... nothing short of professional".

It was at this time that his theatrical activity moved into the world of cinema and it was to his dear friend and fellow Slav, Anatole de Grunwald, that he owed his first steps in this medium: as assistant to 'Tolly' on his production of *Flesh and Blood* starring Richard Todd and Glynis Johns; as Artistic Adviser and 2nd Unit Director on *Innocents in Paris* with Claire Bloom and Alastair Sim in 1953. In 1955 he was to be found behind the camera at the studios of British National.

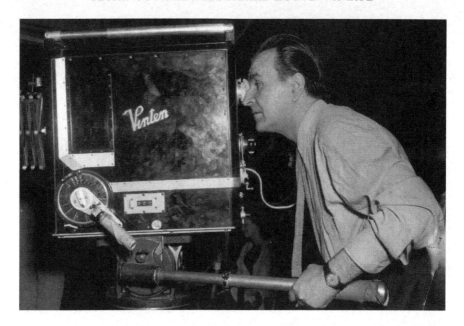

Although he continued in film production, Petar's love of the theatre led to the famous playwright Terence Rattigan's recommending in 1956

> "his taking charge of a theatre. I would like you to know that I hold him in the very highest regard as a director... a man with an incomparable knowledge of the theatre".

This was not to be as the screen continued to exercise its magic.

In between all this work, these many interests, holiday periods, particularly in the summer, see him joining his sister Dora and her family (her son Pierre-Christian was born in 1958) in Brittany.

Things are beginning to come right for Petar Ouvaliev in England: with increased stability, he takes one further step: the rental of a big apartment in a fine part of South Kensington at No. 10 Wetherby Gardens.

* * * *

And this is where I come in...

Yes, it was indeed while walking home that day with Mary past No. 10 Wetherby Gardens...

* * * * *

One could say, and it is certainly true, that my life changed from that day, that encounter, for I had met a man who was not only of quite exceptional intelligence, knowledgeable on so many subjects and multilingual, but kind, loving, generous, thoughtful and, last but by no means least, very funny (we had, shared, invented... so many jokes, a private language). I remained forever, to a certain extent, in awe of his intellectual abilities but it was he who always encouraged me to believe that I could go further, do better and who was always thrilled with any success I might have.

Having graduated in French and Spanish philology at Nottingham University (and having decided that the last thing I wanted to do was teach...) I was then working as a bi-lingual Personal Assistant for an agency in central London. Sharing a flat with two girlfriends and enjoying a good social life, I had never a dull moment. Pierre Rouve – as he was by then known in the West – however introduced a new dimension to my life: drinks with actors, dinners with writers, first night parties, travel, visits to the opera...

(About his name: from the time of the 'French College', he had been known as 'Pierre' but, when he settled in England, 'Ouvaliev' was considered too difficult. As this was also the case for Dora in France, he had the idea of dividing up the family name – more or less the only inheritance at that time – and from 'Ouvaliev' he took the first part and made 'Rouve', she the second and became 'Vallier'. As he used to say: "It was the only present I could afford to give her…")

* * * * *

1959

Our first year together and our first holiday

Reading through my 1959 (BBC External Services!) diary, I see that, from social dates in London, we also went for our first holiday together: three weeks on the French Riviera, flying out to Nice, visiting Romain Gary in Roquebrune, the small but delightful retreat that he and his first wife Lesley Blanch had chosen together. We stayed with Sasha Kardo-Sessoeff, a Russian friend of Romain's from childhood, and Sasha's partner Jane Saliaris in Monte Carlo and at their mountain villa in Peira Cava. This was an idyllic time: visiting, playing at the casino in Monte Carlo (I still treasure a small plastic token, one of those you cast onto the cloth of fortune at the roulette table. I doubt if we won anything at the tables but I can honestly say that it was my personal fortune to spend my life with this charming companion), driving through to Italy for evenings, staying in Bordighera, spending lazy days at the mountain villa. For Pierre it was also a chance to catch up, talking long into the night, with these two friends of Russian background Romain and Sasha.

A life of elegance and interest opened up for me, thanks to this kind, generous, thoughtful, intelligent man.

Back to work in London: he to film projects, I to my clients. The Padevs were in London and we dined with them, again a chance to share memories, to explore the future. In September 1959 we both passed our driving test and, since Pierre had bought an 'indulgence': a Daimler, old style, we were then able to travel around in style.

Pierre had, at that time, been working on the film *Libel* starring Dirk Bogarde and we attended the premiere at the Odeon cinema in Leicester Square in November, preceded by cocktails at the Ritz Hotel, my first experience of such a grand event, and I was certainly in awe of these famous people! (We used later to recall how, when at an evening party at the house of John Mortimer and his then wife Penelope, a novelist, I was so shy and so completely incapable of engaging in conversation with the other guests that I sought refuge and sat at the top of the staircase! This was to become the subject of some teasing.)

This was a time of attending a lot of theatre, cinema and opera and it became quite natural to complete a day's work for a client at the Agency, come home, bath, change and go out to Covent Garden.

Towards the end of the year, Pierre's great friend Bitush Davidoff came over from Israel to visit and to stay at 10 Wetherby Gardens. I accompanied him on trips and, since Bitush spoke only Bulgarian and Hebrew, it was a while before we found that we could actually communicate via my speaking Spanish and he Ladino!

What will my father say?

By the end of 1959 we had "been together" for a whole year; it was time to meet my father. We drove down to Folkestone (in the elegant Daimler!). My father, a retired Royal Navy officer, had met several of my previous "boyfriends" and so, a Bulgarian, several years older than me, was not going to be a problem... Proving that he could provide for his daughter, Pierre was accepted, although I seem to recall that he was unable to give very detailed or satisfactory answers to my father's questions about the state of the Bulgarian navy... We subsequently made several visits to my comfortable, cosy, childhood home in a quiet part of Folkestone, with its well-tended sunny garden.

(When I did enrol at the School of Slavonic and East European Studies (SSEES) for Bulgarian lessons – with Vivian Pinto and hence based exclusively on his book of literary extracts – and Pierre recruited me to do a broadcast with him, he gave me the pseudonym 'Madeleine Folkestone'.)

In this and the succeeding years, we saw a lot of Grigor and his wife Romayne. They were then living in Lord Kinross' house in Little Venice and their dinners saw music and opera performers from Bulgaria and from Covent Garden and a wide circle of friends.

During the course of the next year Pierre had to move from No. 10 and found, via a friend, a nice flat to rent at Knaresborough Place off the Cromwell Road and very near, as it turned out, to Baroness Moura Budberg, to whose apartment we were invited on several occasions; once, I especially recall, together with Sir John Gielgud. What a fantastic evening! To be in the presence of these two "greats" was rather overwhelming, but the talk of theatre and the wickedly funny stories were fascinating. I was still in my shared flat, though staying there less and less.

The question of somewhere reliable and permanent to live was a question for both of us. We were each in rented, fairly short-term accommodation. It would make sense to look for somewhere to buy. To buy – and together – was a step towards a serious commitment.

* * * * *

How Swinging were the Sixties?

1960

The Millionairess

After long – and ultimately successful – negotiations, the contract was signed for the filming of Pierre's first really "big break": *The Millionairess* starring Sophia Loren and Peter Sellers with Anthony Asquith directing. This was brilliant partnering and brought Peter Sellers (later to become very well known as a film actor, but previously better known in England for his part as Eccles in the *Goon Show*) to the general public. Pierre, with his Italian friends and fluency in the language, had already made contact with Carlo Ponti, Sophia Loren's "guide and mentor" and film producer of great renown.

All of a sudden, and as seems to be the way with films – and after prolonged initial negotiations – the shooting started and Pierre would go early every morning to the studios at Elstree.

One terrible day in May during filming, it was discovered that all Sophia's jewels had been stolen. A real fortune and, even worse, not insured (the premium, it was said, would have been more than the value of the jewels). Pierre was an absolute tower of strength for Sophia, in her distress at losing her precious jewels.

Sophia's costumes for *The Millionairess* were made by the house of Balmain in Paris and I was fortunate enough to be allowed to order a suit from the famous couture house. (A suit I later wore for our wedding.)

The respect in which Pierre's work was held is shown in this letter, written after the completion of shooting, by Asquith:

"This is just a line, dear Pierre, to tell you what I hope you know already, how profoundly grateful I am – and always will be – for the countless ways you have made my – and everyone else's – work on 'The Millionairess' so specially happy. Whatever anyone else may have contributed to it, it is essentially your film. I can guess at a few, but only you know how many burdens you never let come near my shoulders, how many headaches you suffered for me, how many dramas you kept me out of. But above all you can't imagine what a joy it is to work with someone whose judgement and taste you trust absolutely… Our unit has

Sophia Loren esce dai teatri di posa, dove ieri ha lavorato come al solito, insieme al produttore del film. L'attrice appare estremamente stanca e rattristata (Telefoto)

indeed been fortunate to have had behind it an organizer, a diplomat, a fighter...and above all a constructive artistic intelligence."

What an honest and true assessment and how Pierre would live up to this judgement!

* * * * *

1961

Chelsea is the place to be!

In 1960, and early 1961, Pierre was filming *Monsieur Topaze* – from the play by Marcel Pagnol – with Peter Sellers in Blois in France.

As Pierre used to tell the story, I phoned him one day (not so easy then) in Blois to tell him that I had found the ideal house. I had, as a matter of fact. The top floor was to be his studio, library, work place... The house was in Chelsea, No. 50 Markham Street, known to innumerable Bulgarian friends and visitors and where, indeed, 45 years later, I am sitting penning these lines! A happy, harmonious, long term house and home indeed! Writing these memories, recreating our life together, is a tribute I wish to pay for all the rich and happy times we spent – here in Chelsea and around the world – over these past 45 years.

Between seeing the house and deciding we wanted to buy it and finally moving in... there was a lot to be done: negotiating the price, builders and decorators for our choice of rooms, furniture to be ordered... March 1961 saw the contract signed, May alterations, and July, finally, we moved in to our home. To some it appears a small house and Pierre used to describe it as a *"mobiliren komin"* or "furnished chimney"! It does however have two rooms on each of four floors plus three mezzanine floors. The amount of stairs from basement (dining room and kitchen) to top (still a library, housing his precious collection of art books, and workplace with the computer which he would not have used...) keeps me active and replaces the need for a gym! It was so exciting, choosing just the right furniture for the particular contours of a traditional nineteenth century English townhouse. Pierre had the perfect eye for sizes and shapes and we invested in Victorian chairs and sofas for the sitting room (sometimes I have been heard to complain that they were not the most comfortable in the world but I have never wanted to change them, for his choice was just right). Year after year we would recline on a '*Madame Récamier*' sofa to watch our favourite television programmes! Oh, the complaints when I did buy a large comfortable three-seater sofa, but he was quite right in that it did dominate the space! Still in the sitting room (together with the dining room, the most visited by our guests), we were able to adorn the walls with paintings from Pierre's growing collection and the marvellous gouache which we were given as a wedding present by Serge Poliakoff. In the dining room (separate, then, from the kitchen, on the principle – a male thing? – that cooking was done in one place and conversation took place around the table...) Pierre recreated a version of a *'mehana'* or tavern; white, rough plastered walls, rustic pine furniture, a refectory table, icons and rugs. Innumerable bottles of red wine have been drunk around this table, many samplings of the few Bulgarian dishes that I learned to make, always in the company of friends with endless laughter, jokes and stories. On the top floor we made the perfect study for Pierre, a large room with full-length windows and a terrace, bookshelves on every available wall (it was in the mid-seventies that, the books having finally outgrown the space, we bought the 'studio' at Markham Square around the corner). A classic (though modern style Scandinavian) desk was found and, to this day, is in permanent use in the recreated office in the Foundation headquarters on Slavianska Street in Sofia. The cigarette burn-marks on the grey leather surface bear witness to a lasting habit! Some friends may recall the single bedroom giving on to the courtyard (previously, and now once again, my study). Our own bedroom bears, perhaps, the most unusual artistic witness: a painting (*'The Dragon'*), too large for any other surface, is set into the ceiling. (It is said that others often have mirrors set into the bedroom ceiling but ours is much more interesting...)

Music, films and art

Alongside these activities, we continued our social life: seeing Greg and Romayne, Yuri Boukov – over for a London concert – for drinks and dinner; Sasha and Jane – over from France; the premiere of *Monsieur Topaze* and the party at the Ritz afterwards.

Pierre was working with John Mortimer, the barrister and

very well-known playwright and creator of the *Rumpole of the Bailey* series; writing filmscripts for *Dock Brief*, one of John's plays; planning with Tolly and Carlo Ponti. By this time Pierre had formed his own company 'Prow Productions' (Prow – P. Rouve... how, again, to play on a name!) with Greg and their good friend Harry Moore as co-directors. (Harry was an American, an actor, the husband of Cicely Berry the well-known Voice Director at the Royal Shakespeare Company whom we happily lured into giving the fourth Memorial Lecture at NATFIZ in May 2004. I say "lecture", although it was in fact a marvellous "involvement" of all those present in *Hearing Shakespeare*, her title.) We went to the opera, an *Aida* with Nikola Nikolov; the opening of Tade's exhibition (one of whose "sand" paintings also graces one of the walls of our bedroom); in May the opening of the large Yugoslav exhibition at the Tate Gallery (about which Pierre wrote in *Art News and Review*); David Peretz came to visit us (he made us a present of one of his paintings; a painting which Pierre, in his kindness, lent to a fellow Bulgarian who, a Jew like David Peretz, sadly and immorally refused to return it); Ghika's exhibition opened at the Lefevre Gallery and in June Georgi (Bobby) Daskaloff at the Lincoln Gallery. June also saw us attending Covent Garden for a performance of *Boris Godunov* and July Sviatoslav Richter's concert at the Royal Albert Hall.

No getting away from teachers!

In retrospect, this was the high point of my social and intellectual life, lived alongside my work for clients at the Agency. Strangely, however, I grew conscious that I was interested in a career in teaching. I no doubt had the illusion that all my pupils would be eager to learn such interesting things from me as literature, art, music... as they related to France. And so it was that, in September 1961, I started teaching at Elliott secondary school, but only part-time, so that

I could continue, and balance, my rich and enjoyable social life. Reading my diaries of the time, I can scarcely believe that I would often go early to school, teach a couple of lessons, rush back for a lunch with Pierre, friends, film contacts, be back at school for afternoon classes, attend a staff meeting, then go home for a siesta before the opera or a film premiere with drinks and dinner after!

Pierre used to say, when I went into teaching, that he had thought that he had escaped teachers: his mother a Headteacher, his father a University lecturer, and now...his wife as well! No peace. The educational word invaded us both since, as well as teaching, I enrolled for a higher degree at London University Birkbeck College (evening courses), my topic embracing my literary and linguistic interests: *Italian influences in the poetic work of Mellin de St. Gelais,* a French Renaissance poet. Seminars were on Mondays with Professor Ross; Tuesdays was Bulgarian class at SSEES. I had, as we always joked, only started this so that I would be able to understand his otherwise "secret" phone conversations (mainly, it turned out, boring arrangements with Greg about business meetings...). However, since the first lessons in the *Conversation manual* dealt with booking rooms and checking that there were no fleas ("*A nyamate li dervenitzi?*" seemed strange...), I felt I was not likely to unravel the "secret" phone conversations. When it was not language, it was straight into the study of Vazov or Yovkov (since the only text was *Bulgarian Prose and Verse* edited by the self same Vivian Pinto). I was certainly glad that at least I recalled the Cyrillic alphabet from having started to study Russian at Nottingham University.

Pierre was now involved in various film proposals and travel: in November to Hollywood, staying at the Beverly Hills Hotel, from where he wrote me one of his amusing and affectionate letters:

My darling darlingska

I feel here very much like a nepokanen gost (uninvited guest), but am still plodding through a jungle of dull talks with crooning Pat Boone, of all people... Otherwise, life is exciting: in my 'honor', they have switched on the illuminations; two hills are burning, palms, swimming pools and all, a mile or so away from my hotel!

This letter is evidence that I miss you immensely and love you more than ever.

After Hollywood, he travelled to Rome as a big project was about to come into being.

(In all of this exciting life, you may be wondering what had become of my friend Mary, to whom, you may recall, I owed that first introduction and hence, in a way, my current life. Well, Mary had met and married Graham Dark and together they opened – in November 1961 – "Dark and Dark Antiques", specialising in early English wood furniture. Those who have visited us in Chelsea will be familiar with the dining table – a refectory table – and a splendid Cornish church column.)

* * * *

1962

Wedding plans

1962 sees us not only living at 50 Markham Street, but my thinking it might be a very good idea to get married. This, however, was subject to at least two conditions: Pierre, having had one – albeit very brief – experience of marriage, was not at all sure that he wanted to "re-tie the knot" and, anyhow, what was his legal status? Divorced? Officially (by whom, what authority?) divorced? A divorce granted in another country (December 1949) in strange circumstances, was not necessarily recognised by British law. And so it was that, in May 1962, when I made enquiries about a wedding ceremony in Chelsea, we were told that Pierre should go to the 'Decisions Office' in Somerset House (the UK records office), to check on this. He subsequently had to write to his mother in Sofia to obtain the details of the divorce which had been issued re a husband "whereabouts unknown" and being "the guilty party". Two highly challengeable concepts. The 'Resolution' was eventually forthcoming, translated officially into English and accepted. Plans could thus go ahead for our wedding.

Bulgarians take over Covent Garden

And what about life outside work? The Royal Opera House at Covent Garden in 1962 became almost a Bulgarian home from home: June saw a production of Verdi's *Otello* with Raina Kabaivanska, then a charmingly naive young beginner on the international scene, give a most impressive performance as Desdemona, together with Mario del Monaco and Tito Gobbi's truly menacing Iago and conducted by Georg Solti. Pierre was, as ever, very supportive; we saw quite a bit of her in those early days in London and my diary tells me that she and I "spoke in Italian" (so much for my progress in Bulgarian!). Raina had a great success at Covent Garden, and her Desdemona was to be repeated in 1964. It was a great pleasure to see how this young Bulgarian soprano began to make her mark. 1963 saw her as Liù in *Turandot*, with another Bulgarian, Dimiter Uzunov as the Unknown Prince and Amy Shuard as Princess Turandot. (More than 40 years later, in 2006, it gave me great pleasure to hear – and, after the performance, talk with – Serena Daolio, singing her first Liu at the Macerata opera festival. Another small but happy twist of fate is that Serena also lives in Modena where Raina has long been settled!) Boris Christoff was, of course, the great star, singing *Boris Godunov* and *Don Carlos* through into the 1970s, when Nikolai Ghiaurov progressively took over the roles.

In my new existence as a language teacher, I was now limited as regards travel, especially abroad, to the school holidays. However, after the end of the summer term I accompanied a group of students on behalf of the Central Bureau for Educational Visits and its Director Landon Temple (one of the, as the joke had it, only six members of the UK Communist Party, all of whom could fit into a telephone box...) for three weeks on a superb Anglo-French meeting in Arles in the Roman south of France. This was certainly an aspect of teaching and being with young people that I really enjoyed. These were still the days when one kept in contact by letter or postcard, not by phone (except, perhaps, for emergencies) and I gave Pierre a regular daily report on all that we did, saw and visited (and it is a tribute to our inherent archivist mentality – others might say "hoarding"... – that I now have access to so many valuable documents. Actually, I find it extremely touching that he should have kept the cards and letters I sent, from holidays and British

Council posts and to him in Mexico and elsewhere).

On my return from France in mid-August, Pierre welcomed me with flowers and dinner out. Despite having tried to get away from teachers, he was unquestionably proud of me... and, as with my higher degree studies, was always very encouraging.

September brought term time again for me, but also the on-going plans for the wedding in December. As well, we were both working: Pierre was negotiating the contract for a luxury edition of his sister's major work on Georges Braque and I was translating it.

Our social life continued to involve several Bulgarian friends: for one evening in late September my diary notes:

"Nikolai and Zlatina, Greg and Romayne came at 7 for drinks at 50 M. Dinner at 'La Bohème'. Bulgarian spoken all evening. Romayne and I spoke to each other" !

I would not appear to have learned a lot at SSEES! In late October the Hadjimishevs were in London. Friends of Pierre and his family since well before the war, Misho and Annie were not only the recognised musical and artistic directors at the Sofia Opera, but also in great demand at Glyndebourne and at the Wexford Festival. (Pierre always told how he owed to Misho his understanding of *lieder* and, in particular, the songs of Hugo Wolff). Their son Ivo was to become another dear friend and regular visitor. Rangel Vulchanov was also in London that month. At about that time news was published in the papers about our future wedding. The plans, paperwork, guests, reception etc. were by then all well advanced.

Unfortunately my father, by then in his mid-seventies, was taken into hospital. He had had continual bouts of ill-health following wounds he had suffered during his extremely courageous actions during World War 2 (for which he was decorated) and his health was now failing.

Tying the knot

December saw us – well, me mostly, as Pierre was working on film projects – organising the Register Office, the catering, the invitations for "the great day": December 29th.

Dora arrived at Victoria Station on the 27th. The Chelsea Register Office is probably no more than 600 metres from our house but... on the 29th we woke to at least 80cm of snow! Pierre, resourceful as ever, had a brilliant idea: "borrow" the Rolls Royce belonging to Richard Burton and Elizabeth Taylor. He had been working with them on the film *The VIPs* in London and, since their "liquid lifestyle" meant that they never awoke before the afternoon, he knew the car and chauffeur would be back ready for them by the time they might need it.

All was organised: I wore the suit which I had had the privilege of having had made by Balmain in Paris at the same time as the other costumes were made in 1960 for Sophia Loren as *The Millionairess*. Greg, that regular witness at all Misho Padev's marriages, was Pierre's too; my cousin Ralph, former British Consul in Iran and Macedonia , was mine; their wives and Pierre's sister Dora were also in attendance.

It was a great sadness for me that my father was not well enough to attend the wedding, but he had a full description on a visit to see him in the hospital.

After the ceremony, we all returned home where the reception had been arranged by a caterer. Among the many friends were, of course, Mary Dark with her husband Graham and Pierre's friend and colleague Anthony ('Puffin') Asquith. At one point Puffin asked us why we had not invited his own good friends and our near neighbours, Jonathan and Kathie Griffin. We told him the truth: that, however many times we saw them at the theatre or the opera, we could not have taken the initiative – after all, we had never been formally introduced! *Cela ne se fait pas!* Later on, Puffin went over to Number 12 and made sure that we would be "properly introduced"!

We spread through the house, talking, eating, drinking until late in the afternoon when the most marvellous and totally unexpected thing happened: Pierre's mother telephoned from Sofia. Hearing her and her good wishes rounded off a perfect day!

On New Year's Eve we went to a performance of *Forza del Destino* with Ted Downes conducting, after which we went to Greg and Romayne's to see in the New Year.

* * * *

1963

Permission to travel

On the 5th January, the first date of note in the New Year, Pierre and I went to celebrate one week of married life at the Casserole (famous King's Road restaurant in the "Swinging Sixties")! Later in the month my father came, together with Ralph and his wife, for dinner at home. He was enchanted. It was now my turn to be in touch with Pierre's mother and, here was a real opportunity to put those months of study into practice... so I wrote to her... in Bulgarian! I can only hope that there were not too many mistakes and that she understood!

1963 was certainly a year of a lot of changes, developments, travel... In the early part of the year, in February, we took a "belated honeymoon", just a short break of a few days in Paris, seeing Pierre's family and visiting the Bulgarian exhibition of icons which had proved a great revelation for the public. From Paris, Pierre then went on to Rome and on 23rd sent me a cable for "8 weeks of marriage", a lovely, typical, thoughtful and very romantic gesture! It also illustrated his genius for playing with words, something we always liked to share: "*Osem sedmitzi* with you may be long yoke. *Tri dni* without you is painful eternity"! ("Eight weeks... three days...").

Almost immediately afterwards, on the 28th, Dora rang from Paris to say that their mother had received authorisation to leave Sofia and travel to France. It would be difficult to comprehend nowadays what a triumph of persistence and victory over officialdom this represented... I immediately phoned Pierre in Rome, possibly interrupting important

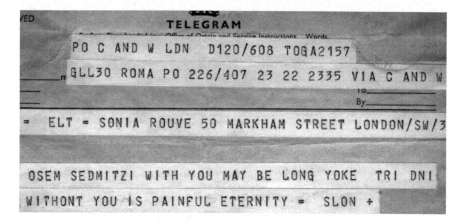

business discussions, but with the most important family news of the last 15 years! Between receiving permission to travel and arriving there were, of course, questions of time and paperwork.

With all the travelling that Pierre was doing in the course of work there was always a need to be sure that his passport was valid. Since having been accorded "leave to reside", he had been travelling with a *Titre de Voyage* (always referred to as his "dog licence"). Although this required him, for every journey, to apply for a visa – a most tiresome procedure – he clung for a long time to the idea of the "unattached citizen" and it was not until April 1968 that he took out British citizenship.

April saw the Bulgarian football team in England and, since it was a proud boast of Pierre's that, although having suffered an injury at school and not able to play football, he was, nevertheless, a very competent referee, this appeared to lead to a single minded passion for watching the game. (It is certainly true that when we did purchase our second television set, it was mainly so that he could watch football, uninterrupted by my changing the channel.) He was now going up to Wembley to watch it live! Culture had to compete and, as well as football, there was opera, the International Theatre Festival at the Aldwych, with a visit to see *The Physicists* on my birthday, followed by dinner and dancing at the Savoy; Orthodox Easter, with a party at home for Bulgarian and opera friends; the opening of Serge Poliakoff's major exhibition at the Whitechapel Gallery with drinks and lunch with him and his wife Marcelle and son Alexis (who has dedicated himself to the cataloguing and presentation of his father's work).

Mother, son and daughter together once again!

But now, it seemed, all bureaucracy had been dealt with, tickets arranged and Mrs. Ouvalieva was setting out for Paris. Pierre and I flew to Le Bourget and went to St. Cloud where Dora and her family were then living, and on the morning of the 22nd April brother and sister set out in the car at 6 a.m. for the Gare de Lyon where she was arriving on the Orient Express (still then running as far as Istanbul). This must have been one of the most moving experiences: re-united with their mother, whom they had both left, or had to leave, in an inhuman way and who, on that account, had been deprived of almost all her personal status and possessions, but never of her dignity. She had been schooled to put up with such deprivations and it took her a little while to "unwind" but, returning to St. Cloud, they then settled down and talked right through the night! As a primary school head teacher, she was soon assuming the role of teacher – as well as grandmother – to her young grandson Pierre-Christian.

Before leaving Paris we had made plans for the summer holiday we were all to spend together in the south of France. In the French tradition, it would be to take a house for the whole of August.

Back in London we continued our social life and it was at this time that I first met the Italian artist Lucio Fontana. We were at a lunch, he was absolutely charming but I was unable to recognise him in the sense of reconciling the person with the slashes in canvas and coagulations of paint in his work!

Family holiday in France

Before setting off on the "family summer holiday – French style", Pierre was determined to take some lessons in driving "on the other side" and so went down to Brands Hatch, a famous racing track, though it is not known how fast he was allowed to drive! We took the boat train from Dover to Calais and collected the hire car there. The practice paid off and we had a smooth drive down to St. Cloud where we picked up his mother and had a leisurely drive through France, with me, as he used to say, choosing stops that coincided with the 3-star Michelin restaurants that I found in the guidebook. I must say

it was as good a way of planning a route as any! We arrived in Grimaud, where Dora had been able to negotiate a sweet little house in the main square belonging to the writer Jean Grenier.

It is astonishing to think that, now that the whole coastal area around St. Tropez has been developed into pleasure boat harbours and holiday apartment complexes, we enjoyed a life of sweet old-fashioned tranquillity in Grimaud and used to go down and then across two uncultivated fields to reach the beach where there was "hardly anyone else" as I noted at the time, and which now has a name in the atlas in its own right: 'Grimaud Port'! Imagine, too, that Brigitte Bardot, whose name is now more or less synonymous with St. Tropez, was then a rather less well-known starlet whom, on one occasion, Pierre declined to accompany on an excursion!

We spent a month of lazy days, excursions, eating in and out before returning to London and to our respective jobs. In September there was the premiere of Jean Seberg's film. She was in town with Romain Gary who, since his diplomatic posting to the USA, had been working and writing screenplays for Hollywood studios. The papers were by then making much of their forthcoming marriage. Pierre was absolutely delighted to be able to spend time with this dear friend of so many years. We had lunch with them after the premiere and saw that they were very happy together. Their happiness was not, however, to last as her troubled spirit became more and more desperate.

October was a sad time for me as my father's health took a serious turn for the worse: he was in the clinic in Folkestone and, on the 9th, my cousin Ralph phoned to say that he had died. One week later we held the funeral at Holy Trinity Church in Folkestone and the impressive service was attended by a large crowd of his naval and Masonic friends and colleagues as well as family, local friends and neighbours. Our sad duty was then to close up the family house. The following day we left, by boat and train, for Paris for a second visit to Pierre's mother at St. Cloud. It was my pleasure to be able to make her a small and unusual personal gift: a bunch of chrysanthemums direct from my father's prize collection in his garden.

We stayed at the Lutétia hotel and, as well as spending many hours at St. Cloud, dined with the Poliakoffs; Pierre met and worked with Marcel Pagnol, the film version of whose play *Topaze* he had directed in 1961; we went for drinks at Romain Gary's marvellous, enormous apartment on the Rue du Bac, then for dinner on the Boulevard St. Germain – with Jean driving her Mini – and on afterwards to a jazz club where a black friend of theirs was singing; to the Boulles (Luben's niece, Julia, was by then married to Jean Boulle, the Director of Hachette publishing house) in their beautiful apartment.

A reply to His Majesty

This year, and the previous ones, saw a real development in the work that Pierre had been developing in the cinema, but it must not be forgotten that he was, concurrently, maintaining his regular weekly broadcasts for the BBC Bulgarian service as well as continuing to cover art exhibitions in the *Arts Review*. In this latter capacity, he was also a member of the International Association of Art Critics (AICA). As British representative, he regularly attended the international conferences. This year it was to be held in Morocco during December where, as well as the official visits and ceremonies, we would also be seeing our good friend Claude Castelli, French antique dealer for whom I often worked as an interpreter on his buying trips to London. We flew to Casablanca where the international group was officially welcomed by the local committee of artists, ministers and critics. We visited exhibitions and studios in Marrakesh, Fes and Rabat where, on the 18th, the group was received in ceremonial audience by His Majesty King Hassan V, who welcomed us to his country and showed his great interest in and knowledge of art, both Islamic and Western. By general consensus of those present, Pierre was ushered forward to reply to the King's speech and all were astonished that, with no forewarning whatsoever, he was able to reply in the most eloquent and elegant of terms in impeccable French. Such, no doubt, are the fruits of a thorough education in a French college and experience in the diplomatic service, combined with quickness of wit and great intelligence. He certainly received praise from fellow group members who included Carlos Antonio Arean from Madrid and Guy Whelan, Pierre Restany and Michel Ragon from France. We later had a guided tour of the Royal Palace where, as a matter of interest, I noted the antique crystal wall lights which Claude had purchased on one of his recent trips to London, and which had been installed by the King's decorator, Marc-Aurèle Bonnaud.

All good things must come to an end and the Conference did on the 22nd. After our leave-takings, there was a delay when we boarded the aircraft, and, a while later, an announcement: *"On demande Monsieur et Madame Rouve"*. What could we have done? Pierre was taken to the police; his passport (that famous "dog licence") had not been stamped; he was "illegally" on board; was he perhaps a "terrorist"? (This was 40 years ago!) However, dropping the name of a certain minister managed to clear up the confusion and we were all on our way to Paris.

Christmas Eve and the next days were spent with the family in Paris. On the 29th there was thick fog which meant that our plane was cancelled and we returned home on the Golden Arrow.

* * * *

1964

Mrs. Ouvalieva visits us in London

After the necessary paperwork, Pierre's mother received a British visa and so could visit us in England. This was, of course, an immense pleasure and we set about preparing our house to receive its first visitor.

As a family where each of us had a room as a study, this involved some reorganisation and the "creation" of another bedroom. Mrs. Ouvalieva adapted very well and quite

understood – from her own experience – the hours and days when I was in school; she was naturally relied upon to prepare delicious Bulgarian meals for us in the evenings! Otherwise, we shopped, walked in Hyde Park, visited the Victoria and Albert Museum and went for drives outside London. She met those of our friends who spoke French and also a close friend of mine, Pamela, who spent a long time practising a few words in Bulgarian! Pashanko Dimitroff's mother had also obtained permission to leave Bulgaria on a visit, and the two ladies spent some time together. When Claude came over from Morocco on a visit, he invited us all to dinner with him in the Rib Room restaurant at his hotel in Knightsbridge. That was great fun and much enjoyed by all!

At around this time, too, I had been thinking of a change of teaching post and made several applications to schools where I might extend my experience, take a more senior position, increase the amount of teaching of languages other than French (it had long been my intention to offer more Spanish and/or Italian on the secondary curriculum) and so it was that I found myself called for a very formal and official interview at the highly selective Grey Coat girls' school in Westminster. With five candidates for the post, I considered myself fortunate to be appointed. To celebrate this, Mrs. Ouvalieva and I went out on a "shopping spree"! (She was quite soon to return to Bulgaria and so certain purchases were indicated as absolutely necessary, not only for her but for her sisters with whom, having been expropriated at the time of Pierre's decision to stay in England, she was still living.)

The 8th March marked 35 years since her husband had died (1929) so tragically young, and we offered her flowers to mark the occasion and she rang and spoke by phone to her sisters in Sofia.

On the 21st there was a flurry of "last minute" packing: eight pieces of luggage for the night train (no weight and baggage restrictions as on aeroplanes...) from Victoria to Paris.

Planning to film in Italy

With the end of the Spring term in a few days' time and more travel on the cards, it was soon time to start packing for the two weeks we were to spend in Italy. The last day of term was a crowded one (but then so was my life!): after school, home to pack and off to catch the afternoon Alitalia flight to Rome. Staying at the Excelsior, we certainly enjoyed being in Rome. Pierre managed to mix business with pleasure and we spent time with our friends Ennio de Concini, the brilliant scriptwriter of *Divorce – Italian Style*, and Eliana de Sabata, daughter of the world famous conductor Vittorio de Sabata; we lunched and dined out in delightful restaurants both in and outside Rome with Pierre's dear friend the writer Paola Ojetti, with Mara Palmer Srebrova, who kindly arranged for her driver to take me on a fascinating tour of Rome; Pierre spent time at the studios and especially with Luciano Perugia; as ever, they were planning future productions. We spent Easter Day with Paola and then took the train to Naples where Pierre was to meet up with Tolly and the director Jack Clayton. What could be more fabulous than, in the search for attractive and interesting film locations, that we should walk all around Naples and visit Positano, driving via the impressive coastal scenery, and then Amalfi, staying to lunch at one of the best located hotels in the world: *Le Sirenuse*! We later headed back to Naples, via Pompeii, and spent our last hours there where, to my shame and Pierre's regular teasing ever afterwards, I did not recognise who it was when I was introduced to the "heartthrob" actor Marcello Mastroianni! (Well, I had enjoyed so many amazing visits and privileges, met so many interesting and famous people, things one can normally only dream about ... and I was still not yet 30!). Returning to Rome, the porter at our hotel informed us that we (= I) had left £150 – a not inconsiderable sum in those days – in a drawer in the hotel bedroom in Naples but that it would be brought to us in Rome.

This speaks volumes for the honesty of employees and it certainly taught me to check in every possible and unlikely place when leaving anywhere!

A *Yellow Rolls Royce*

Hardly were we back in London than Pierre was off to Austria (obliged, as ever, to obtain a visa) for the filming of *The Yellow Rolls Royce*.

Either all this travelling, or an extended interest in the teaching of a foreign language, meant that I enrolled for an evening course in the Teaching of English as a Foreign Language (TEFL) at the St. Giles' School of English in central London (this was to stand me in very good stead when, later, I began to work for the British Council on their 'Specialist Tours' and summer courses, notably in Bulgaria).

The pupils whom I was to leave at the end of the term, when I went to my new school, were some – my favourites – whom I had taught for the last three years and who, from unpromising backgrounds, had made tremendous progress in the study of French, both the language and the literature, who had come with me, during and after school, to performances of plays and to films at the 'Institut Français', who had won scholarships to study in France and who had gained places to attend some of the most prestigious British universities: Cambridge, Nottingham. We would all be leaving the Elliott school but the twelve year olds, many of whom could be quite difficult to control, would have another teacher for French. I could but hope that they had acquired some fondness for and interest in other cultures and languages during the time that they had had 'Madame Rouve' as their teacher.

For the one-week half-term holiday I naturally headed straight off for Austria and first spent an enchanted few days in Vienna, hosted by the renowned lady architect and childhood friend of Pierre's, Lyulya Praun-Simidova. She always told the story of how she and her sister Natasha were the very first to see the new born Petar Ouvaliev when she would have been about ten years old, her sister younger. I stayed (alone, since Pierre was filming in the country) at the famous Sacher hotel (no doubt consuming quantities of the famous "*torte*"...). Lyulya and her friend Shura Malinov made my visit to Vienna a real dream: we walked, visited museums, had days out, visited Schönbrunn and Krems, went to the opera for a performance of *Die Entführung aus dem Serail*, lunched in Lylula's beautiful flat. Jonathan Griffin, our neighbour in Markham Street (and to whom, by then, we had been – formally – introduced!), well-known poet, playwright (whose *The Hidden King* had been performed at the Edinburgh Festival) and translator of, among others, the Portuguese poet Fernando Pessoa and General de Gaulle, came out to Vienna for script discussions. He and I enjoyed tea at Dehmel before I flew to Klagenfurt for just one night to join the film crew. We were to stay at the Park Hotel in Portschach am Worther See and in the afternoon I was taken to visit the location up in the mountains where the stars, Ingrid Bergman and Omar Sharif were filming the adventures of this exotic Rolls Royce. The following morning, a lazy Sunday, Pierre appeared carrying a tray with a full breakfast for us to have on the sunny balcony of our room.

We both went later to the location and had lunch with Omar Sharif and others before I had to return, take the plane and prepare for the rigours of the next day's teaching... It was also the time that I had to hand in my notice to the school administrator.

Theatre time

In June our dear friends the Fadimans were in London and we saw quite a lot of them. Over from Hollywood where Bill was a scriptwriter-director and his wife Genee's family owned RKO Studios, they always liked to go to the theatre as much as possible. This time we went with them to an impressive performance of *St. Joan of the Stockyards* at the Queen's. Another theatrical highlight was Harold Pinter's *The Birthday Party* at the Aldwych, a truly electric and menacing production, with Brian Pringle and Vivien Merchant. Good things come in threes and, at the end of the week we were fortunate to have tickets for *Othello* at the National with Olivier's superb interpretation of the role; my diary observes, however, that Iago and the production in general were not of a standard equal to Olivier's performance. His Othello will surely remain one of the high points in the history of the theatre.

By this time we were seeing quite a lot of Jonathan Griffin and his wife Kathleen, who had previously worked for a theatrical agent. Through them we met other very interesting people: the actor Robert Eddison; the poet and translator Anthony Rudolf who, latterly, wrote the impressive obituary of Pierre and who accepted to give the second Memorial Lecture in Sofia in 2000; Jeremy Noble, the early music specialist; the Irish actor, writer and true inheritor of the Oscar Wilde tradition, Michael MacLiammoir whose one-man shows *The Importance of Being Oscar* and *I must be speaking to my friends* were London triumphs. Pierre, indeed, used to tell how, before he had ever known anything much about England and English, he had been bowled over by a visit of MacLiammoir to Bulgaria. A thoroughbred Irishman promotes English! As well as the Griffins there was my close friend and teacher colleague, Pamela Moore and her husband Geoffrey, Professor of American Literature at Hull University. When they were in town we would see Claire Bloom, with whom Pierre had remained good friends since the time of filming *Innocents in Paris*, together with her then husband Rod Steiger. Despite my ability to produce Bulgarian dishes, we would more often go to one of our favourite restaurants on the King's Road. Pierre and I would also make sure that we went out to celebrate his name day and my and his birthdays in style. This was certainly something I learned from him: he was a man with great style!

At the end of July I had to go and spend a day at the school where I was to start teaching in September, meet the staff, collect books and teaching programmes. At the same time there were "farewell parties" for those of us who were leaving the Elliott. It was most gratifying to receive the gifts, cards and speeches from colleagues and pupils whom I had taught. It really had been a good decision to go into teaching!

Italy this summer

Term finished on the Friday and, as usual, there was no stopping the inveterate travellers... On Saturday 25th July the car was serviced (we were taking our own this year) and on the Sunday we were off: to France to meet up with the family and head on for our month's summer holiday, this time on the Italian Riviera. We drove down to Dover, stopping for lunch in the country on the way, called on some friends in Folkestone, and boarded the ferry in the late afternoon. By evening we were enjoying the change to French air, time, food... The following day a relaxed drive, with sightseeing in Abbeville, Amiens and Rouen (marvels, all, of the Gothic cathedral builders), not forgetting a delicious lunch, brought us to Paris and St. Cloud by evening.

The following morning we collected Pierre's mother, discussed the route we should take (since Dora, Luben and Pierre-Christian would be driving with us) and left Paris for the Autoroute du Sud. It seemed to be, in our two families at least, taken for granted that the man would drive and the wife would map-read and navigate. This may have worked well in Dora and Luben's case (anyhow, she did not drive), but with us, although I am perfectly capable of reading a map and planning a route, I was increasingly keen to do some driving... it was not to be. I was, however, to be blamed for the fact that we lost the Autoroute soon after leaving Paris...

This year we were making for Italy and a delightful small

resort, Albissola, on the Ligurian coast. We headed south, and slightly east – for we were to drive via Switzerland – in perfect, clear, luminous weather. We spent the first night in Dijon at the luxurious Hotel de la Cloche. A stroll around Dijon, a delicious dinner in our best evening wear and then, after the day's drive, we were ready for bed. The next day we went first to buy books in an excellent bookshop: philosophy for Pierre and some school texts for me, and then, leaving Dijon, we continued towards Lausanne via Ornans for lunch and a visit to the Gustave Courbet museum. We began to see the Alps as we approached the Swiss frontier at Pontarlier and arrived late in the afternoon in Lausanne where Dora and Luben joined us a little later (though probably not having taken so long over extended gourmet lunches as we were wont to do...). The next day Dora was to visit a major exhibition of Cézanne, Van Gogh, Picasso...and so, while she made her "professional visit", we drove to Ouchy and walked by the lake. In the afternoon we all went to view the exhibition: "marvellous – indigestibly marvellous", my diary notes. (I have learnt quite recently, from my very good friend Alastair Laidlaw, that over-exposure to manifestations of culture – museums, music etc. – is recognised in the literature as *"Stendhal syndrome"*. Exactly where Stendhal writes of his over-exposure to culture and the effects thereof, I have yet to identify, but I certainly believe in the existence of the condition.) Stendhal would surely have approved of our later dinner at the edge of the lake!

I note that the following morning I went shopping before we left Lausanne, driving along the lake. But then our cars, being more northerly and hence unused to the altitude and the summer temperatures, overheated, and, at the last garage before the tunnel we had to wait for the engines to cool. This was, of course, an excellent opportunity to have lunch...and we later undertook the five and a half kilometres of the St. Bernhard tunnel, then the mountain *"autostrada"*, through the Val d'Aosta, arriving in Turin where we were to stay the night in the 19th century station hotel in the splendid, tall, arcaded streets. (I note, *inter alia*, that it was on this day – 31st July – that the American space rocket hit the moon.)

The 1st August, in true French tradition, we arrived to take up our rental of an apartment near the beach for the whole month. Jean and Julia Boulle, who were to spend part of their summer with us, but who were on Jean's boat, were already waiting for us in Albissola. (I was able to check with Jean that my Elliott school pupil John Hart, for whom he and I had arranged a summer job with Hachette, had in fact arrived in Paris and started work.) Our apartment building was most conveniently located almost on the doorstep of the best beachside fish restaurant, and we spent most mealtimes at Nino Pescetto's! The beach, too, was very near although, interestingly, the other side of the main international railway line (we were told that there were plans to re-route the line and now, with the enormous growth of tourism in this area, I imagine that this must have been done). As always when arriving in a rented property, we spent some time re-arranging the furniture to our liking.

The days then passed, as they do in "memories of times past" (and here, I am certainly *A la Recherche du Temps Perdu*...) in tranquil, hot and sunny anonymity and the enjoyment of relaxation after work and driving, in the company of friends and family, spending sunny days on the beach, going out on Jean's motor boat, exploring the local markets...

An operatic excursion

Until, on the 7th, up bright and early, the car washed and serviced, we set out: our destination Sirmione but taking in some fabulous places on our way: first Genoa, then Piacenza with its beautiful square and Piazza del Comune; then Cremona and its Duomo piazza where we took coffee. Then on to Mantua, which was mostly lost on me – unfortunately – because of the heat (I recall lying down in the stone cloisters). Mantegna and the "*Camera degli Sposi*", what a beautiful town! We then drove on to Sirmione where we were to meet up and spend time with Nikolai Ghiaurov, his wife and son. That evening we dined alone with Zlatina as Nikolai had gone fishing with Vladimir, who was then about ten. (I recently saw him again, after an interval of 40 years...conducting the splendid first performance of Verdi's *Macbeth* at Sofia opera house.) They arrived back late, and it was then that the Bulgarian talk really began! The specific aim of our visit, apart from the pleasure of spending time with these friends, was to attend a performance at the opera festival in Verona. The following day we spent the morning in the beautiful surroundings of the "ideal village" and the lake where Zlatina and I swam until midday. We joined Pierre and Nikolai on the terrace for drinks, then lunch, after which we walked, with Vladimir, in the village. Getting ready, dressed and coiffed, for such an occasion, then took some time, but we were ready to leave for Verona at 7 p.m. Zlatina collected the tickets, we had drinks and then... the magnificent "*spettacolo*"! The candles in the dark night all around the arena and... the performance of *Mefistofele*, superb! A truly unforgettable evening!

It was late before we arose the next day – and even later when we lunched, then played a few games of table tennis with Pierre as it was too cloudy and cold to go swimming or water skiing. Finally, we all listened to a new recording of *Carmen* – with Maria Callas and Nicolai Gedda. Never very far from work for Pierre, he had a phone call from Tolly, then in Paris on film business. Nikolai and Vladimir spent the late afternoon fishing in the lake and then we all went for a relaxed supper at a local pizzeria.

Sad to leave this idyllic spot the next morning but we drove, together with Zlatina, to Milan where we all had lunch and afterwards, with Pierre, continued towards Genoa (at the same time looking for a garage – really, these British cars are not happy in the Mediterranean climate!), arriving back late in Albissola to tell of our adventures!

Our base there had become something of a centre for friends to come and visit, mostly Italian artists and film people, so it was a lazy continuation of beach, talk and lunches. One day we drove along the beautiful '*Riviera dei Fiori*' to Imperia and then up into the hills to a peak-clinging village where the music critic Luigi Rognoni and his family were transforming a 16th century house. Although Dora had sent a telegram (what primitive means of communication in those days!) it had failed to arrive and so we were not expected, but were received warmly for lunch (I remember there being loads of delicious figs within picking distance) and lots of talk. We were given a bottle of their own pressing olive oil on leaving. Other days I recall were spent out on Jean Boulle's boat, at a performance of a delightful opera by Pergolesi at the Villa Farnese, visits, shopping, an exhibition – including work by Lucio Fontana... in other words a perfect balance of activities and relaxation: the ideal August summer holiday. It was also the "ideal" family unit: grandmother (Mrs. Ouvalieva) taking care of, keeping an eye on, teaching... her grandson, Pierre-Christian; he practising on his new bicycle; other family members and friends talking – and arguing – about so many things. August was drawing to a close and we made last minute visits: to Fontana and San Lazzaro; did quite a lot of shopping (remembering that Pierre's mother was to return to Sofia). One day we were astonished to see a Bulgarian registered car (this is the mid-sixties) to whose driver Luben spoke in Bulgarian as he overtook and, for whatever reason, they fled!

On 31st August, true to the holiday period, we left Albissola for the long drive back (first to Paris) via Turin, Vevey, the Château de Chillon with thoughts of Byron's poem *The Prisoner of Chillon* honouring François de Bonnivard who, in 1530 and for his support of Geneva, was imprisoned in

> "Chillon's dungeons, deep and old"
>   ... consigned
> To fetters, and the damp vault's dayless gloom".

Through France, leaving *"maman"* in St. Cloud; on to Montreuil where we spent a night in a charming hotel before leaving from Boulogne the following day.

The next week London life resumed to its full: friends were back, Pierre went to the film studios and term started for me at my new school on 9th September. I kept in touch, however, with all the friends from the Elliott, visited, had lunches. At about this time, Pierre had an agreement to meet up with 'Gerald Dorset' (Ilko Iliev) and go out together somewhere, but he wrote and, as my diary notes, "has 'fled' once again". A dear, troubled person with personal, political and family problems, he later settled more permanently in New York, publishing his poems over there.

I start a new job

My new job involved more preparation for the highly academic girls whom I taught: juniors, setting out on learning French, and seniors, who were preparing for their university entrance exams. I also introduced Spanish at Grey Coat for a small group of girls who had been successful in their early language learning. This job was very enjoyable and challenging in a different way. It is interesting to note that I am still (40 years on ...) in touch with some of those seniors whom I taught at both schools; this gives me real pleasure and satisfaction (especially the fact that one of the girls from Grey Coat, Evelyn Gregory, is now a Professor herself and, in her inaugural lecture, paid tribute to my having first awakened her interest in the concept of language!). Another senior from Elliott, Ian Buckley, kept in regular touch as he was preparing for his Cambridge entrance and for a long time thereafter.

Our social life also continued, around Pierre's film work. He was at this time negotiating with the Chaplin family and going over to Switzerland. This was to result in hiring Geraldine Chaplin for a star part opposite James Mason in the next film: *Stranger in the House*, a version of a Simenon novel. This was a Dimitri (brother of Anatole) de Grunwald production and as well as directing this film, Pierre co-scripted the novel with John Mortimer. Mention of Pierre's being in Switzerland reminds me of one of the many times when he would bring back presents, always something specially chosen, with a funny message. This time it was several small gifts and a card announcing: "*Plusieurs petits suisses*", again a play on words.

A short holiday in Holland

Travelling together was thus limited not only by his filming commitments but also to the school holidays. For the half-term week in October 1964, we decided to go for a short six-day trip to Amsterdam. Hardly had school finished on Friday afternoon than we were off with KLM, checking into the Hôtel de l'Europe with a lovely room overlooking the canal and the Mint Tower. Neither of us had been to Amsterdam before and it was just the right choice: near enough, a vast array of things to do and see, canal trips, museums and shopping...(for once, no Bulgarians to meet up with...). We wandered along the greyish, misty-gold canals, then took a river boat tour of this 'Venice of the North', and went, of course, to the Rijksmuseum for the imposing collection of Rembrandt, Vermeer, de Hooch, Frans Hals; later had dinner (remembering Holland's colonial past) at an Indonesian restaurant. Another day we went out to the Stedelijk museum and gallery where I concentrated on the four magnificent Van Gogh rooms (three of paintings of all periods and one of drawings and sketches) although Pierre visited all the other parts. The remaining few days of this brief but delightful holiday were spent walking, visiting shops and galleries and the 'Tropical Museum'. We flew home, again with KLM, after five interesting, relaxing, invigorating days.

The time remaining until Christmas was dedicated to work, plus, of course, the occasional theatre visit and gallery opening for Pierre who, while very busy filming, was still able to write the occasional article covering one or other major exhibition. The 29th December marked our second wedding anniversary and we planned a small party (important to mark the date and, after all, how were we to know then that we would be celebrating almost 40 years of married life!) at home with close friends: the Griffins, actor Robert Eddison, Michael Ayrton (the artist) and his wife, Pamela and Geoffrey Moore (Professor of American Literature), the conductor Edward Downes and his wife. This was the festive season and, true to form, we had a full social programme for these last days of the year: on the 30th the premiere of *The Yellow Rolls Royce* at the Empire cinema in Leicester Square with a reception at Claridge's hotel after; on New Year's Eve we had tickets for Michael

MacLiammoir's one-man show *The Importance of Being Oscar,* after which we dined at the Mirabelle where the New Year was appropriately "piped in" as we took our leave of a busy and exciting year in our lives!

* * * *

1965

Films, theatre, opera...

After such a busy year in 1964 we might have thought that 1965 would be a quiet one. Well, every year with Pierre was different but equally exciting in its own way.

It started on New Year's day when, having been to the *Oscar* show the previous evening, we could hardly believe our eyes when we saw the great MacLiammoir coming out of the Griffins' house opposite (with whom he was great friends) and setting off towards the King's Road. We guessed that they were probably going to lunch at one of the nearby restaurants and so we jumped into our clothes and very casually (by accident/on purpose...) walked into the Unity. We were immediately invited to join the threesome. (I don't think they ever did guess our subterfuge...) I was invited to sit next to MacLiammoir and the marvellous man entertained us with stories until mid-afternoon. This was surely a good augury for the New Year!

Indeed, 1965 seems to have been marked by a lot of theatre, art and music. One of the very first dates, however, was Pierre's 50th birthday on 12th January. We had drinks at home with friends before going to the Mirabelle for dinner where he opened his cables, cards and presents. A half-century full of movement, excitement, fear, memories and now, building on all that experience, a happy, busy and fulfilled life in his adopted country.

The next day provided an example of this new, amazing, crazy life: Pierre left in the morning for Switzerland to attend a dinner with Charlie Chaplin and Sophia Loren, who were to discuss his plan for her to star in *The Countess from Hong Kong*, one of Chaplin's long cherished projects. Pierre was to be involved in the direction. He phoned me in the evening from Montreux when on his way, and returned to London the following day. Meanwhile, around school, I was planning for the next day when we would have Catherine and Jack Lambert (the theatre critic) and the Steigers (Claire Bloom and Rod, American actor) for dinner.

In February we saw the second of Michael MacLiammoir's one-man shows: *I must be talking to my friends* at the St. Martin's and, after a wonderful performance, went to his dressing room to congratulate him. London-based for a while, we saw *The Crucible* at the Old Vic, *The Shoemaker's Holiday* at the Mermaid, *Happy End* at the Royal Court (our "local" theatre at Sloane Square) with the Griffins, after which we went for dinner with Jean Desailly. What a pleasant evening! Jonathan, who had been at the British Embassy in Paris, knew "everyone who was anyone" in the French literary and artistic world. To mark my birthday Pierre had managed to obtain tickets for *Le Soulier de Satin* (in the International Theatre Festival season) at the Aldwych. A most effective three and a half hour performance of this key Claudel play. (A production of Claudel's *Partage de Midi* was, a few years later, to give Pierre and Jonathan another opportunity of working together.) The following day I met with Jonathan in the King's Road and we talked at length about the production. Continuing the International season, we also saw Pirandello's *Sei personaggi...* and *The Birds* by Italian and Greek companies and, later, John Osborne's latest play *Inadmissible Evidence* at the Royal Court, where Nicol Williamson gave a remarkable performance.

Opera that season was, for us, performances of *Elektra* with the title role sung by Amy Shuard and conducted by the great Rudolf Kempe; *Il Trittico* with Tito Gobbi in the role of Gianni Schicchi; Benjamin Britten's quintessentially English work *Billy Budd*, with Peter Glossop in the title role. It was as a winner of the International Opera Competition held in Varna that Peter

Glossop first made his name and we were to hear him sing again that season, as the Count of Luna in *Il Trovatore*. In July there was a rare performance of Schoenberg's *Moses and Aaron*, perhaps more properly called an oratorio conceived for the operatic stage. A challenging work for both audience and performers. It was unusual that, for most of the season, there were not Bulgarians "guesting" at Covent Garden, but that was rectified in December with the appearance of Boris Christoff in the title role of *Boris Godunov*. His was, as ever, the classic performance. I should add here that for all opera productions at Covent Garden the ballet mistress was Greg's wife Romayne Grigorova.

The Whitsun holiday provided me with the opportunity of a one-week visit to Rome. Pierre had gone some days before with Anatole for discussions of film projects. As it happened, I discovered that Carlo Ponti, whom I had seen at the air terminus, was on the same flight as me; I was obviously destined to be among film people! Once in Rome I went to join Eliana de Sabata at her apartment. We had a lovely relaxed time and then, as it was fine summer weather, decided to go to their summer beach place at Fregene, south of Rome where we spent a couple of lazy days on the beach, leaving the men to work on scripts, contracts etc. At the weekend we went out for dinner with Peter Sellers and his then wife Britt Ekland at their villa on the Via Appia. This was a fun evening, ending with the men talking business and the women gossiping happily! Pierre was not long back in London before going off again, this time to Geneva to see Chaplin with Ponti about the *Countess from Hong Kong* project; I, however, had to go back and teach! My diary tells me that "I mended P's pockets". This must have been a noteworthy event and, since I was forever being told that I "was incapable of sewing on a button", may well have been one of the only times that I picked up a needle and thread!

In mid-June Pierre was to go to Ljubljana for the AICA Congress and the exhibition. In succeeding years he was to develop a major role in connection with art in Yugoslavia, not only in Slovenia (although he was also closely involved with the Rijeka annual events) but also in Zagreb, in Tuzla and in Belgrade. In Belgrade he always maintained contact with his and Dora's good friend, the art historian and writer Katarina Ambrozić (and it was she whom I had invited to come to Sofia in 2003 to give the fourth annual memorial lecture but who was unfortunately in hospital at that time).

July saw, for me, a slight chink in Anglo-Bulgarian relations in that, at our low level of teacher visits, I was able to meet and welcome a teacher of English with whom I had been corresponding: Radka Strahilova was coming to Britain to attend a British Council summer school in Newcastle. After the, then, obligatory visit to the Bulgarian Embassy, we then "kidnapped" her and took her out for dinner; I took her the next day to school where she came to classes with me and later we did a walking tour of central London sights.

The end of the school term meant time to travel: a small and a big holiday this year. First I drove down to join my friend Pamela and her two children who were staying by the sea on the southwest coast in Devon. These few days were taken in late July, as soon as term finished! We had a great time, rowing, walking, swimming...

This was followed by the "traditional" August holiday (extended, this year, through into the beginning of September) and, although we were to meet up with friends on the way and at our destination, this year it was just the two of us. This summer, instead of going south, we had decided to explore Germany and Austria with, as our final destination, a week or so in Salzburg for the festival. Travelling by car, our aim was, insofar as it was possible, only to follow the course of rivers. (I was much later to recall this journey when, in my acceptance speech for the award of Doctor Honoris Causa of the University of Rousse in October 1999, I spoke of the flow of culture along waterways, referring in particular to the river Danube. It was an extraordinary thing but when, in the course of this speech, I mentioned Pierre's name there was a huge clap of thunder. Everyone in the Aula was astonished but I somehow knew he was there.)

All across Europe...

On the 2nd August we crossed from Dover to Ostende, spending one night there before driving on to that most beautiful of Belgian towns: Bruges. With my genius for finding us the best hotels with the best locations and restaurants... we not only enjoyed the museums and parks but dinner on the riverside terrace and, later that evening, a pageant of Light and Sound in the courtyard of the Gruuthuse palace. The next day we drove to Ghent, visiting the belfry, the old town and the castle and, of course, the cathedral with its superb van Eyck triptych the "*Adoration of the Mystic Lamb*". (A friend of ours, whose command of English was less than perfect, was once heard to refer to it as "*The Mysterious Mutton*", and this became our private name for it.) On to Liège where we spent the night before crossing into Germany at Aachen, and there we were lucky enough to catch the impressive Charlemagne exhibition at the cathedral and the town hall. We went on to Koblenz, to start our "river tour" and, already beginning our "musical tour", met up with a dear and longstanding Bulgarian friend, the tenor Christo Baev, who was now the owner of a delightful guest house on the Deutsches Eck confluence of the Rhine. We dined, he and his staff entertained us to a marvellous concert and the next day we started out, following the Rhine, with sensational views at every turn, recalling the tale of the Lorelei on the opposite bank, as far south as Mainz. We then cut across, on beautiful minor roads through rich green sunny country, making for our next river, the Neckar, a gentler, more peaceful river than the Rhine. We made an overnight stop at Heilbronn and visited the Kilianskirche with its tower, the first in Renaissance style to be built north of the Alps. With our taste for luxury we would have liked to stay in one of the 'Castle

Hotels' but, to our disappointment, all were fully booked. Nevertheless, we stopped for a while to admire the view from the one of our choice: Götz von Berlichingen.

On our way to Nurnberg we made many delightful diversions: we had heard about a beautiful painting by Grünewald and discovered it in a very simple chapel in the church at Stuppach (we had to drive through a forest to reach the village!). In the afternoon we came across a charming small baroque castle, Schloss Weikersheim, in a little village; this was the residence of the Hohenlohe family. Here a performance of *Fidelio* had been given the previous evening. In Nurnberg we settled in to the Grand Hotel and immediately set about trying to get tickets for the next day's performance at the Bayreuth Opera Festival. No easy task! Pierre asked the hotel porter (always a good tactic) and was told to go back at 12h30 and, if unsuccessful, we could perhaps "bargain" with some of the Japanese! Meanwhile we went to visit the St. Lorenz cathedral, entirely destroyed during the war (although fortunately the 15th century altarpieces had been removed) and now rebuilt.

We were in luck! The porter had been able to obtain two tickets for *Tannhäuser* and they would be waiting for us with one of his colleagues in a hotel in Bayreuth. This was a bit scary and last minute but turned out perfectly. Getting to Bayreuth was, in itself, a challenge. Organising the tickets seemed the easy bit when compared with tussling with the German *"autobahn"* system! Each time we should, I thought, have come off the motorway, we seemed to be going around in a circle... there obviously is a logic to it but it defeated our joint talents of driving and navigating! After panicking about arriving on time, we finally made it for the 4p.m. start. This really was an experience to savour: a Wagner opera, in Bayreuth at the famous Festspielhaus, all the audience in evening dress. Conscious of the privilege and also with the intense concentration of trying to follow everything in German, I am sure I paid more attention then than on many other occasions! Wolfgang Windgassen, whom we had heard in the *Ring* cycle that same year at Covent Garden, sang the title role, Hermann Prey (whom I had not heard sing before but for whom I developed an immediate passion) sang von Eschenbach, and the great Finnish Martti Talvela sang Landgraf Hermann. This was truly a marvellous experience.

The next day we visited the Germanisches Nationalmuseum to see the mediaeval tapestries. In many respects the extraordinary iconography of the tapestries reminded us of the Boyana church murals. We left for Augsburg later in the day. My particular gift for navigation and map reading, which had already proved untrustworthy on the autobahn, led us along a narrow farm track. I was insistent that I was right until we got to the very edge of a quarry! I never heard the end of that! Arriving finally in Augsburg we visited the Mozarthaus, birthplace of Leopold Mozart, with its music room and portrait of the family. After a day and night in this elegant town, indulging our luxury tastes with a suite at the '*Drei Mohren*' hotel, we continued towards Munich. Once again risking my map reading skills, we decided to make a detour via the Ammersee. Finally we came upon it and followed the lakeside to Hersching, a delightful resort about which I have often heard from dear Lina Ognyanova as her father the Minister Grigor Vassiliev would take the family there for holidays in the early part of the last century. She told me that it was also a holiday place for the family of Ivan Penkov, the artist, and where she first got to know his two sons Boyan and Jonny. Pierre and I enjoyed a drink at a lakeside café unaware, at that time, of the Bulgarian background!

We arrived on time in Munich where, after dining with Pierre's dear friend Stefan Popov, the historian and philosopher, and his wife on our first evening, we spent time at the Schatzkammer, coveting the treasure, and in the Residenzmuseum. In the evening more opera awaited us: in the National Theatre, completely rebuilt after its destruction during the war, a performance of *Der Rosenkavalier*, a delightful production, with a full German cast of singers; we thus felt completely immersed in the culture. The following day Carlo Ponti phoned for Pierre and they went together to see the "*2,000 year old Sofia*" exhibition while I took the car and drove out to visit the beautiful palace at Nymphenburg for the afternoon. Back at the hotel, Ponti and several Italian friends and colleagues came to join us and we all went to eat in an Italian restaurant. After dinner, they all seemed to want to go to a nightclub and so, cramming into two cars, we set off in search of one. At last, finding one called '*Eve*', Pierre and I stayed with them until 1h, making our own way back to the hotel!

The next day, relatively early, we left Munich, driving on towards Salzburg, our destination. On the borders of Germany and Austria we visited a delightful little church in die Wies; mid-18th century, built by Dominikus Zimmerman, the exterior would not necessarily draw attention to itself but... the interior is not only Zimmerman's masterpiece but the summit of German ecclesiastical architecture of the Baroque period. Absolutely breathtaking! But it is not only the church architecture and decoration which are of an extraordinary richness in this part of south Germany; there are also the castles, and one of the most amazing, and best situated, is that of King Ludwig II ("the mad") of Bavaria, Königschloss Neuschwanstein. We could only view it from afar as there was no possibility of visiting, but it conjured every childhood memory of a fairy castle!

Mozart and more Mozart

Anyhow, it was time to press on to Salzburg, for the "*Mozartfest*" we had been promising ourselves. We entered Austria through the Fernpass, stopping for tea on a terrace right opposite the Zugspitz, with the deep turquoise waters far, far below. We had booked into what was described as "a delightful 'country style' hotel, the Kaiserhof, just outside town and surrounded by a lovely park". Besides that, all we knew was that it was in Morzgerstrasse. Naturally, on arriving in Salzburg, I lost the way. We went to the centre to buy a street plan: no Morzgerstrasse! Pierre went to the Post Office but even there they did not know it. Where on earth could this "delightful country hotel" be? Finally, on an even larger map, we found the street. It was anything but promising, a semi-rural suburb. Our thoughts turned immediately to: "Where might we find a room in a nice hotel at any price?" But...when we arrived, we discovered a truly enchanting country house with a drive, a huge garden. Exquisite! Quite a paradise (and quite "lost"!). Far more relaxing than anywhere in the noise and bustle of the centre. A particular joy was that Sviatoslav Richter was also staying there and so, as well as formal concerts, we had the informal practice! Another fact that recommended the hotel to Pierre was the excellent *"Serbische bohnensuppe"* which the restaurant served.

Here we were not only in the heart of central Europe but also, it seemed, of the Balkans for, on our very first evening, 16th August, we attended a performance of *Boris Godunov* in the Grosses Festspielhaus with an almost completely Bulgarian cast! Nikolai Ghiaurov in the title role; Nikolai Ghiuselev as Pimèn; Dimiter Uzunov as "the false Dimitri"; Nadezhda Dobrianova as Xenia; Anton Diakov and Milen Paunov as Varlaam and Missail and also Aleksei Maslenikov and Gregor Radev. This excellent cast was conducted with absolute mastery by Herbert von Karajan. Certainly a fantastic start to our "festival week"!

The following day Pierre and I went for a walk in town where we met Nikolai with Lubomir Panchev, a singer who had settled in Vienna, and young Vladimir Ghiaurov. Walking to the opera house, Pierre discussed the previous evening's performance with Nikolai. Once there, Vladimir told me all about his father's car, a Jaguar, while several people came asking Nikolai for his autograph. That evening Pierre spent talking with friends and I went to a performance of the *Goldberg Variations* in the Schloss Mirabell.

But the treats went on and on...the next day exploring Salzburg and visiting the Mozart family house, relaxing at our hotel and on the Wednesday, again in the large concert hall a concert given by the Vienna Philharmonic Orchestra, conducted by Zubin Mehta and with Daniel Barenboim playing a Mozart concerto. Great names even then, how much more so as they have matured; it was exhilarating to be "in at the beginning"!

When we were in Munich Pierre had tried several times without success to reach his good friend the poet Christo Ognyanov by phone, hoping to see him and his wife Inge in Salzburg where they lived. As chance, and good luck, would have it, while walking in Salzburg on the Thursday morning, we bumped into them in the street! They were on their way to the theatre and so Pierre arranged to meet them after his dinner with the great critic Bernard Levin. (I can only imagine the very lively conversation that there must have been!). His evening continued with Christo and the actors from *Faust*. I note in my journal: "P. back in the small hours"! What treats though: music, theatre, Bulgarian and other friends and colleagues, a lovely country hotel!

Friday we took the car and went for a drive up into the surrounding hills before returning for a concert. All these social activities had necessitated visits to the hairdresser (for me) and several changes of outfit (for both of us); luckily we were travelling with our car! We set out that evening in search (and indeed, it was a search) of the Mozarteum for a chamber concert with the string quartet of the Vienna Philharmonic. Perhaps tired, Pierre was not initially enthusiastic but as soon as the music started he was enchanted by this exceptional quartet. Although there were many other Festival offerings, and Pierre attended both parts of *Faust*, it was principally on Mozart that we feasted and, in the Kleines Festspielhaus, attended a delightful *Così fan tutte* with, amongst others, Christa Ludwig, Graziella Sciutti and my much admired Hermann Prey, conducted by Karl Bohm. Another delightful, and very rarely performed opera *Die Gärtnerin aus Liebe* was performed in the Residenz, again with Graziella Sciutti in the role of the maid Serpetta. A deliciously Italianate *"divertissement"*. A set with several enormous croquet hoops and flower-decked costumes.

Before leaving Salzburg, we had decided to host a lunch party at our lovely hotel. The day proved cloudy and we ate indoors. At midday Zlatina and Nikolai Ghiaurov arrived together with Lubomir and Evgenia Panchev and we settled down to a delicious, and very talkative, lunch. From my place at the table, I saw Sviatoslav Richter come in after his morning walk in the park. I told myself that although Nikolai and Zlatina knew him, they would not expect to see him at the hotel. Five minutes later (and for the first time!) he came into the dining room as he, too, had invited guests for lunch! It was introductions all round and thrilling talk of music until 4 p.m.

On our very last day I thought I had lost Pierre. After a concert I went back to the hotel where I expected him for dinner. He got back at about midnight and told me how he had spent the evening. He had gone over to say goodbye to Zlatina and Nikolai and had found them in a terrible state. Nikolai had two contracts for work which "overlapped": he was supposed to record for Decca in London and, at the same time, to sing in Sofia (on 9th September). Pierre had had to try to calm them down, explain a thousand things, and act as their lawyer, phoning to Decca in London and New York... In the end everything was settled. However, as the kitchen in the hotel was closed by the time he got back, he had to go hungry to bed!

All good things must come to an end and after our 10 days in Salzburg we set out again. These ten days, however, remain with great clarity as one of the highlights of our early married life: fun, friends, music, visits. We continued our "river route", this time following the course of the Danube (little did I then know the part this river would play in my academic life and contacts with Rousse university). Rounding a bend in the river one comes across one of the wonders of church architecture: Melk monastery, painted a soft yellow and dominating the river and the surrounding plain. Returning via Vienna we spent time with Lyulya Simidova, visiting friends in the country, and later continued to Munich where we indulged our gourmet tastes with a delicious dinner at the luxurious Humplmayer. Making our way to Heidelberg we sought out a hotel with a view of the Neckar from which we explored the charming old town with its famous university dating from the Renaissance. We certainly favoured the Neckar over other rivers and proceeded first along the valley, then among forests and quiet green hills on winding roads as far as Miltenberg. Following the Main we drove to Frankfurt where, that very evening, we were able to continue our "European opera tour" by attending a performance of *The Queen of Spades*, a strong and moving production with Mariana Radeva as the Countess. The following day we visited the atmospheric Goethe house with his desk, pictures and books. Just the kind of surroundings that I knew Pierre would love to create for himself and which, in a minor key, he had begun to create in his study in Chelsea.

We were already at the beginning of September and overstaying the traditional August summer holiday; with term time impending, we rushed towards Aachen. As the hotels were all full, just for the fun of adding Holland to our itinerary, we slept in Maastricht before taking the ferry once again at Ostende. Back in Kent, I went to see friends and a very dear teacher, then Pierre and I walked on the cliffs, remembering my father and the house in Folkestone until it was time to drive back home to London, full of the most marvellous rich tapestry of experiences, places visited, friends seen. It had truly been a summer to remember!

Pierre was soon caught up once again in film projects and in particular with the possibility of a Mosfilm co-production for a film on Tchaikovsky. Despite a full schedule at school, I note that I left on Friday afternoon at the beginning of October to spend the weekend in Paris. Saturday was spent strolling in the Latin Quarter and visiting Dora in St. Cloud, returning to London on the Sunday. In retrospect, the active, busy, travelling life we led absolutely astonishes me! We packed in so much and, apart from occasional references to a "siesta" in my diary, never seem to have got tired.

This year at school we had a German language *"assistant"*, Sieglinde Pfarbigan from Linz, and, as her first name might indicate, she was a passionate opera fan. This also meant that, as she only taught a light timetable, she had time to go and queue for tickets at Covent Garden! The first time we went together was for *Siegfried* with Hans Hotter, a marvellous Wotan, and Wolfgang Windgassen in the title role.

Lest it be thought that our life revolved entirely around opera, it should be said that Pierre was committed not only to film projects, but also to his regular weekly cultural broadcasts for the BBC Bulgarian service. These he recorded on a Saturday and our activities, visits etc. certainly gave him many subjects about which to speak: the International Theatre Festival, Bulgarian singers in London and at the different festivals we ourselves attended. There were, of course, many gallery openings and exhibitions and, in mid-October, he flew to Belgrade for the inauguration of the Museum of Modern Art. This was obviously something very special in that he was in his beloved Balkans with friends, artists, critics and writers for the most stimulating events. His intellectual span and brilliance were only later to be truly acknowledged in Bulgaria. *"Nul n'est prophète"*. His artistic contacts with the then Yugoslavia were to remain both close and deep.

I note in my diary that in late October we attended "a reception at the Bulgarian Embassy for Minister of Education Ganev. Met all the usual…" (Who, I wonder, were those "usual" people? Amongst them, probably, would have been Mercia MacDermott and others of the Anglo-Bulgarian Friendship Society.)

The following day Pierre had a "film business" meeting with Antonioni, then planning his next film and keen to work again with Pierre. Sieglinde had, meanwhile, organised that she be the "London correspondent" for her Linz newspaper and we sat together in the Press Box for a fabulous performance of *Il Trovatore* with Giulini conducting and splendid singing, especially from Carlo Bergonzi as Manrico and Fiorenza Cossotto as Azucena. Afterwards I joined Pierre for dinner at the King's Road restaurant Alexander's (underneath the famous boutique 'Bazaar' where Mary Quant launched the "mini skirt" and Sixties fashion) with Colonel Kendall (a retired diplomat with experience in Bulgaria), Minister Ganev and Jennie Lee (our parliamentary spokesperson on education). This was obviously to be my early introduction to the Bulgarian education system…

Had we perhaps had too much travel? I notice that in the October half term week we stayed in London, *mirabile dictu*… Certainly Pierre was very busy with Antonioni, often out all day organising photographers and painters. At about this time they were also in regular contact with Carlo Ponti who, as a producer, made up their "Italian 'A' team"!

After the performances in Europe earlier in the year, I was keeping an eye out for recitals to be given by, for instance, Hermann Prey. I was not disappointed as, in November, he came to give a recital at the Royal Festival Hall. Before that, and on the recommendation of one of my "opera fan" pupils, Janet Ennis, I had also attended the recital given by the world famous Dietrich Fischer-Dieskau: Beethoven songs, a truly magnetic atmosphere and a most beautiful interpretation. Two German idols!

Early in December, and continuing the musical theme, Pierre and I invited Grigor and Romayne for dinner at home together with Ted Downes and his wife Joan and, a real surprise treat for her, Sieglinde. This was opera in a social setting! A few days later I attended a performance of *Simon Boccanegra* (produced on this occasion, as well as sung, by Tito Gobbi) with her and on the 13th the dress rehearsal of *Boris Godunov*. As these treats were all on weekday evenings I had to make a great effort to be up bright and early for school on the following days! But not only in the morning, for I note that on the 15th, prior to the first night of this production of *Boris Godunov*, I went in the afternoon (after lessons, I imagine) to have my "hair up"! We attended this first night (of what was the 50th performance at the Royal Opera House) with Grigor. My diary says: "Fabulous Boris (Christoff) in fabulous *Boris* and rapturous applause". We went again on the Saturday and noticed certain minor variations but "Boris again marvellous, went to see him after, and Jo" (Joseph Rouleau as Pimen). We went on to dinner at one of our favourite restaurants, the *"White Elephant"*.

The year was drawing to a close and, with our December visits to Covent Garden, we had had two of perhaps the best ever imaginable operatic experiences: two productions of *Boris Godunov,* the one in Salzburg in the summer under Karajan, starring Nikolai Ghiaurov and with a prime Bulgarian cast, the second in London under Edward Downes with Boris Christoff and the very best of a British and European cast (Alberto Remedios as the Pretender, Yvonne Minton as the Polish princess and Otakar Kraus as Rangoni). It was a year filled with music. But not only music: the same weekend as Covent Garden, Pierre and I attended a lunch at the Ritz, hosted by Dimitri de Grunwald, for Jacques Tati with whom we later attended the gala presentation of his film *Les Vacances de Monsieur Hulot* at the Prince Charles cinema.

The Christmas holidays (term had by now ended) were spent in London and in the quiet and welcoming family surroundings of Pashanko and Margaret Dimitroff's lovely house in Willesden. This was, indeed, the first of many Christmas days to be spent with them and their family and friends. The end of the year marked our third wedding anniversary. What a full, busy and exciting twelve months!

※ ※ ※ ※ ※

1966

In a way, the year started with the celebration of Orthodox Christmas in early January, with presents for Pierre's mother, lunch out at a local restaurant and then a visit to the Bonnard exhibition at the Royal Academy; a huge show with some really beautiful pictures and variations on one or two main themes.

The appreciation of artists

This year saw an increase in Pierre's art critical writing activity and for me it was always a pleasure to be able to accompany him to galleries and to see (and, of course, to learn from him) the work of a vast range of interesting artists, both established and *avant garde*. Pierre also added to our personal collection of works of art, either by purchasing from an exhibition or studio, or by receiving a work from an artist about whom he had written. We thus have important and interesting work by, for example, Bernard Stern, Denis Bowen, Anita de Caro, Vieira da Silva, Nick Danziger, Paul Feiler, Doru Marculescu, Niko Ghika, Mary Newcombe, Serge Poliakoff. We also have works by Bulgarian artists Detchko Ouzunov, Svetlin Russev, Ilia Beshkov, Luben Dimanov and others, collected, it has to be said, at a much later date.

The unceasing planning of films meant that, in January, Carlo Ponti came to London as did Ennio de Concini and Eliana. I note that I

> "rushed home after school, went to the hairdresser's as it was to be an elegant dinner chez Tolly (Anatole de Grunwald); the men talked business".

Ennio and Eliana were staying at the Carlton Tower hotel in Chelsea and so she and I had some social and shopping time. The 14th seems to have been a busy day:

"At school until lunch time; dashed home to leave things; on to the Carlton Tower for lunch; Pierre and Ennio there already, also Beatles' (yes!) PR girl; Ennio to see the Beatles in p.m. re possible film project; Eliana and I then to hairdresser via the shops; home to change; then all to David Warner's fabulous 'Hamlet': ugly, youthful, graceless, gawky... marvellous; then on to dinner at the Savoy until 2-ish".

Lucky for me that this was a Friday! On the Saturday, Ennio came to our house to watch (and discuss) football on television with Pierre (a not uncommon event...).

On 28th January we attended the first performance of a new (and, in the event, rather startling) production of *The Flying Dutchman*. This opera had last been given at Covent Garden during the 1950-51 season. The production, by Clifford Williams (doing his "Wieland Wagner"!), was absolutely bare; new, and rather horrifying for Covent Garden, though really we found it to be very acceptable if not outstanding. Solti and the orchestra were excellent and David Ward a superb and noble (although casually attired) Dutchman. Gwyneth Jones was also excellent as Senta and Gottlob Frick as ever the true professional as Daland. We met several of our friends both during the interval and after the performance and went on to dine at the appropriately named *L'Opéra* restaurant, where we joined up with David Ward. A truly marvellous evening!

Another day we dined, and this time in a literary (and, indeed, political) mode, at Pashanko's with Robert Conquest. I have in my hand as I write, his *Back to Life – Poems from Behind the Iron Curtain* published in 1958 (and containing an extract from *Fear* by Todor Genov) and it is fascinating to recall, now and in another age and climate, the intensity of debate and the challenge of talk in those days.

Films and furs in Rome

For the February half-term holiday I had arranged to go with Pierre to Rome. It was the usual last-minute dash: to the bank, the hairdresser, writing school reports... and then by car to the airport for a flight on East African Airways (final destination Nairobi) via Paris, flying first class, very luxurious and relaxing! A most excellent journey after which Pierre, for reasons of visa – or, more precisely, of non-visa – was kept for about an hour by the police. Finally we were able to take the Ponti car to our hotel, Parco dei Principi, and Pierre went out with Topaldjikov and I to bed. The following morning, on drawing up the blinds, a sensationally beautiful – most Roman – view: a vista of pink *palazzi*. Roman domestic architecture at its most pleasing: terraces, tall windows, flowers and, ahead, the park stretching for miles; down below, the Zoo with two zebras. I met Eliana at the furriers where I had already selected a style for a jacket. She was in search of a dovecote. Not a single one was to be found in the whole of Rome, but Tolly, who was with us, bought several antiques. We went to Ennio's for lunch, together with Mastroianni's agent. Eliana and I did more window-shopping after a siesta, and had tea at the Caffè Greco. Later, at Ennio's flat, Topaldjikov was quite bowled over at the sight of the magnificent collection of icons.

The next (another soft, hazy and blue) day, Pierre was to work and so Eliana and I left Rome, following the Tiber, to go and visit her mother at her house outside Filacciano. The house was on a rise overlooking villages, churches, castles... the most splendid vista. (I note from my diary that I thought it would be "bliss, but how impractical, to have a similar property". I expect it would have been... and this was twenty years before we did buy a property in an idyllic location, not near Rome but on the French coast!) After deciding on places to plant trees etc., we went for lunch to Filacciano, a feudal village with a castle-fortress and a real *"principe"* living there. I learned that it had been used for the set of the famous film *8½*. After lunch we went to Ponzano, another delightful mediaeval village on a hill with narrow, steep, angular cobbled streets. We were going to visit a woman who knitted: dresses, coats etc. It seemed that she lived in one room with an enormous knitting machine! Once back in Rome, they dropped me off at one end of the Corso, to meet me later at the Piazza del Popolo. The temptation of the elegant shops soon overcame me and I bought shoes and gloves and coveted several other things, including a lizard bag (this was well before the days of ecological concern...). It was then back to the hotel to change as Mastroianni had managed to get tickets for his very popular show *Ciao, Rudi!,* a musical of the life of Rudolf Valentino. Pierre, however, had organised a "Bulgarian evening". I do remember thinking that it might well have been the last time that I went to the theatre in Rome: a converted 1930s Mussolini-type cinema; an audience that never stopped talking all the way through; smoking in the auditorium all the way through... I do actually wonder if things have changed even now...

On Sunday I went and had a fitting for the fur and then, with Eliana, went to the Porto Portese open market, but found nothing of worth to buy. Pierre was with a very dear friend, fellow art critic from London, Kenneth Coutts-Smith, and we three had lunch at Bolognese. After lunch and a very short rest, we were ready for the car that Ponti sent for us at 4 p.m. to take us to visit him at the house in Marino where he was living with Sophia Loren. That was very grand: I did enjoy getting into the Rolls Royce at the hotel and driving in it along the streets and the Appia Antica among the post-siesta Sunday crowds! In Rome, as I note in my diary, "a Rolls, especially chauffeur-driven, still has immense novelty value". (Perhaps no longer now with the general debasement of style...) The beauty of

Ponti's house struck us as incredible. I remembered a little of it from an article in a colour supplement, but the idea of this beautiful '*palazzo*', with its hand-painted walls and ceilings and several '*salotti*', Ponti's "travelling altar" and Sophia's study, was almost impossible to describe. "Out of this world". From the main reception room there was a view down over the lawns and statuary and a guest house. A maid, in "English style" uniform served us tea from a silver service. We were later joined by other film colleagues, delayed by traffic jams (no change there...), and we had to leave just after 6 p.m. as we were to go to Michelangelo Antonioni for dinner.

The jams were as bad on the way back and we arrived late (still in the luxurious Rolls!). We went to his fabulous top floor maisonette: two floors for two people, which Pierre coveted. A penthouse, overlooking the Tiber and the whole of Rome. We had drinks and met Monica Vitti (his partner), admired his collection of paintings and then went to meet other friends and to have dinner. Everyone was talking about Monica's programme on the television the previous evening (which we hadn't seen!). In the face of many Italians talking a lot, I was almost completely silent (not for any inability to speak Italian, but a sense of being overwhelmed!). We later went on to a party in another amazing flat, owned by an old friend of Pierre's from the BBC. What I describe reads rather as if we were living scenes from *La Dolce Vita*... as indeed we were!

On our last day we both went to visit Pierre's dear friend Paola Ojetti and he went on to see the artist Sergio Vacchi. I find his work, especially the "*Studies for the 'Concilio'*" in the Ponti-Loren collection, not unreminiscent of Francis Bacon's "*Popes*". I collected my fur and we made our way to the airport at the end of our four fabulous, concentrated (holi)days!

Never would it have been more appropriate to quote the famous lines of Alphonse de Lamartine:

> "O temps, suspends ton vol! et vous, heures propices,
> Suspendez votre cours!
> Laissez-nous savourer les rapides délices
> Des plus beaux de nos jours!"

In March, back in London, we had the pleasure of a visit from Pierre's very great friend of many years, an even more committed pan-Balkan activist – in this case in the interests of Macedonia – Christo Ognyanov and his wife Inge (who also devoted herself recently to the continuing promotion through publication of her husband's work and memory and very sadly died a short time ago. I just feel so happy that I had the chance to have a long conversation on the phone with her before she died. One all too often finds the time has slipped by and it turns out to be too late...). Long talks were held over long lunches. There were also other friends visiting us: Ennio and Eliana on film business, Claude from Morocco on buying trips. This was, however, the year in which, having introduced the teaching of Spanish at my school, I took my first group of 17-year-old pupils on a study visit to Madrid. This was great fun for all of us: one of the best things was that we left school one week before the end of term, replacing lessons in London with classes in Madrid! Although the Headmistress had insisted on the girls wearing school uniform for the journey (she came to Victoria Station and checked...), this was soon discarded! We travelled by train, making connections, practising Spanish. The two week course was full of interest and the girls were all tearful as we took our leave to travel back... to a snowstorm in Dover! Due to the weather, I missed Pierre who was to meet me at Victoria, went home and discovered him across the road with the Griffins!

The increase in Pierre's coverage of art exhibitions, as well as his regular weekly broadcasts for the BBC Bulgarian service, meant that he was building up an extensive file of published articles and it was my task to collect and date these, again using the golden yellow paper. Many of these, for example on Lucio

Fontana, Ben Nicholson, Ivon Hitchens, Barbara Hepworth, Henry Moore and others, have been included in the artists' bibliographies. (Pierre, I discovered fully only recently, was one of the best and most dedicated of archivists: documentation of his life and times and of Bulgaria surrounds me as I write.) It was also at this time that Kenneth Coutts-Smith was appointed associate editor of *Art and Artists*, a highly innovative monthly journal appearing in both London and New York, and in whose first issue Pierre published an article on Dubuffet. In October he wrote an extensive article for the same journal: *Discovery of Lissitzky* (strange, now, to think that he needed "discovering" though, as Pierre wrote) :

"Only now the first rays of poised recognition begin to fall upon Lissitzky's relics scattered along the convulsed paths of European history. Now Eric Estorick, long-sighted ambassador of the glory that was Russian Art, shows a most telling selection of Lissitzky's manifold legacy".

Paris in the Spring

Pierre must have taken pity on me having to go almost straight back to school after the Easter holiday because, on the following Saturday, while he was at work in the film production office and I was at home, he rang (I recall that I nearly didn't answer but luckily I did...) and said: "Do you want to go to Paris?" No sooner said than organised: I raced around for tickets, a hotel, packing and at 4.15 p.m. Pierre was home. "The mad Rouves" ran over to have a chat with Jonathan and at 5.30 p.m. we were off! A no-time-at-all Caravelle flight and we were in warm and sunny Paris. Pierre had good reason to be in Paris anyhow: he was meeting a college childhood friend, Kolya Christov, who joined us at our hotel and we all went to eat at the '*Rotisserie Périgourdine*' with the most enchanting view of Notre Dame lit up in the dark. After dinner we all took a marvellous, atmospheric walk back to the Pont Royal hotel, along the quays, through the small streets of the Latin Quarter, stopping after midnight for a drink at *'Les Deux Magots'*. I got to the hotel at 0h30 but Pierre and Kolya stopped off at the *'Escurial'* for more drinks and talk until 2h! What an evening!

The 1st of May, what a glorious day to wake to sunshine in Paris. Pierre was going to Kolya's hotel to see him and dropped me off to enjoy a walk to Notre Dame and along the quays; later, together with other Bulgarian friends, mostly singers, we all had lunch by the Seine, walked in the Tuileries gardens enjoying the sun and being in Paris and, later on, went to Orly for our return to London. For me, the very next day; it was back to school and the exam period. What fun it was to be with Pierre, to be a part of his life (of all his lives!), to do such marvellous, crazy things!

Blow Up is on!

Pierre was kept very busy with film plans and, suddenly, it seemed, after all the discussions about casting, location, budget etc., with the shooting of what was later to be titled *Blow Up*. (The original production plan and "picture estimate" for set, make up, lighting etc., are simply called *The Antonioni Picture*.) *The Millionairess*, with a star cast, a marvellous script and a huge box office success, had launched Pierre "big time", but working on *Blow Up* as Executive Producer with director Michelangelo Antonioni, was a real high point.

This was truly the breakthrough film, with the young David Hemmings in the role of the photographer and also starring Vanessa Redgrave. The pace was fast, the demands great: parts of Stockwell and a whole road to be painted red; the cast and filming from early morning. But Pierre and Antonioni worked brilliantly together, with Pierre's organisational skills complementing Antonioni's creative genius. His first film

outside Italy, and in English, this was truly a triumph. *Blow Up* is acknowledged to be the "icon" film of the Sixties. (Very recently, in June 2006, there was a '40th anniversary' celebration arranged at the Photographers' Gallery in London and I am happy to say that I have been able to contribute many photos and documents to a book to be published about this ground-breaking film. Sadly, Antonioni was not able to attend.)

On the 12th June Greg and Romayne celebrated their sixth wedding anniversary with a dinner where we were together with Nikolai and Zlatina Ghiaurov who were in London for the performance of *Don Carlos* which we had attended at Covent Garden.

This summer I was planning a quite different holiday: I was going to France with Pamela Moore and her two children. We were all going to travel in my car and we spent several days planning a very interesting itinerary with the guidebooks and the maps spread over the table in her kitchen. Before that, however, Pierre was to go to Paris as his mother was due back in Sofia at the end of June. It had been a marvellous time for us all, being able to have her with us in France and in London, living with us and coming on holiday too. She was also able to help Dora by being with Pierre Christian, reliving her days as a primary school teacher! I believe it must also have been a most moving experience for her since she was able, through extraordinarily difficult circumstances, to be once again with her two children and their families. She certainly deserved these moments of happiness.

During the summer, when Pamela and I were touring, Pierre stayed in London to work on film projects, especially the completion of *Blow Up*. The BBC and exhibitions also kept him busy. I recall that I sent him a postcard, or sometimes two, from each of the places we visited and also put in phone calls several times (no direct dialling in those days!). On our way back through France we called in on Dora and Luben in Portbail and when I got back home I saw that Pierre had, in fact, been organising a lot of improvements: painting, floors, decorating... perfect!

September obviously saw another small chink in our international relations since I note that on the 8th September we went for "cocktails at the Bulgarian Embassy". It was no doubt beginning to be recognised by "the powers that were" that Pierre was a most worthy, important and dignified representative of Bulgarian culture, sought out by many of those who were in a position to travel to Britain. Why the 8th and not the 9th, I am not sure. At any rate it was the occasion to meet the newly appointed Ambassador, Petar Voutov. This improvement in British-Bulgarian relations was something on which Pierre was to reflect over the next months and which was to form the core of a very significant broadcast that he made on the BBC Bulgarian service on 1st January 1967.

In the autumn the British Film Institute organized a Week of Bulgarian Film with screenings of, among others, Vulo Radev's excellent 1964 release, *The Peach Thief*. Bulgarian cartoons were also favourably received.

December saw us planning for our Christmas break which we were to spend in Morocco. But before that there was the annual dinner of the International Association of Art Critics at the Arts Club in London, an important event, especially as Pierre was very active in the Association. Having been to Morocco for the AICA conference in 1963, we decided we would spend our holiday at the luxurious Mamounia Hotel (favourite of Sir Winston Churchill) in Marrakesh. Needless to say, on the very last day of my school term, having rushed and packed, we were off on the 6p.m. Royal Air Maroc plane to Casablanca! There we were met by Claude Castelli, who later drove down to join us in Marrakesh. This was indeed, in every way, an ideal holiday: warm, sunny weather, a beautiful hotel in a glorious sub-tropical garden, the view of the snow-capped Atlas mountains as well as the ever exciting surroundings of the souk and Djema el F'naa square. We certainly enjoyed every moment of our stay! At the gala Christmas and New Year dinners all guests were at their most elegant and we were entertained by the famous French "*chanteur*" Charles Trenet, whose rendition of '*La Mer*' was applauded long and loud! But in between, on the 29th December, we were to celebrate our fourth wedding anniversary. This too was a lovely occasion spent with friends. We also took the opportunity to visit artists and writers whom Pierre had met during the AICA congress, Aicha and Taieb Lahlou, Farid Belkahia and others.

* * * * *

1967

Pierre takes on work at the 'Q' theatre

A Good Beginning

All good things must come to an end... and we flew back from Casablanca on 3rd January to a cold Paris where we stayed for a couple of nights, visiting Dora and viewing with her the charming 18th century apartment in the rue de Babylone which they were to buy, moving from St. Cloud where she and Luben had lived since settling in Paris. The new flat is well known to many of our Bulgarian friends who have, subsequently and increasingly, visited the Todorovs and enjoyed their hospitality: Karl and Lina Ognyanov, poet and writer Lubomir Levchev and his artist wife Dora Boneva, ex-Ambassador Boudinov (who invested in studio space for visiting Bulgarian artists such as Soon and Marin Varbanov), art critic and historian Dimiter Avramov, television programme maker Toma Tomov and many, many others.

In Paris, Pierre met up with one of his Yugoslav artist friends Ivan Piceli, with whom he later enjoyed a lasting relationship with regard to the promotion of Yugoslav art through the annual exhibitions and prize competitions held in Rijeka, Ljubljana and Tuzla, Pierre serving as a member of the prestigious international jury.

The 4th of January was a momentous day in the family life as Dora and Luben's son Pierre-Christian was to start his first day at the top-ranking *lycée Henri IV*. Not only was this his "local school" but, as it happens, one of the very best and most historic educational establishments in the whole of France. Pierre-Christian (or 'Pierre' as he now prefers to be called) certainly went on to make the very best of every opportunity: from school to one of the top "*Grandes Ecoles*", then to the "*Ecole Nationale d'Administration*" (ENA), becoming a *Conseiller d'Etat* and recently a Managing Director of the international '*Accor*' group. Bulgarian by blood, a Frenchman by way of life.

Meanwhile, in the studios of the Bulgarian Section at Bush House, the New Year broadcast which Pierre had prepared was put out on the airwaves. As previously mentioned, this not only contained significant content but it evoked a lengthy and serious comment in the Bulgarian press. Pierre (though he remained anonymous) spoke of:

> "...that indefinable emotion which has lingered in the background of these attempts to build an intangible bridge over the visible and invisible precipices along which Bulgarian successes would reach the world and world famous achievements would filter into Bulgaria...
>
> The faith in this cultural coming of age of Bulgaria spurs these dialogues. The past year will remain memorable in the chronicle of cultural links between Bulgaria and the West. The road to London was cleared of rocks... the President of the Union of Bulgarian Writers was invited by the British Council... an act of deference, not only to Georgi Jagarov but also to Bulgarian literature as a whole... Publishers showed an interest, writers offered to revise English translations.
>
> Well known critics praised the films and cartoons shown at the Week of Bulgarian Film organized by the British Film Institute.
>
> In music too... for the first time a Bulgarian conductor was invited to work with a British symphony orchestra. Constantin Iliev had concerts in Bournemouth and Birmingham... Marin Goleminov's opera *Ivailo* was broadcast by the BBC.

> An open and unprejudiced approach...were the qualities shown by the impressively well informed young critic Julia Krusteva. Yet another guest of the British Council was the poet Christo Radevsky, living historian of Bulgarian revolutionary literature...
>
> ...a tolerance...in the cultural links between this country and Bulgaria"

This was a New Year message reflecting the increasing openness of cultural relations and it must be remembered that Pierre only ever used this broadcast vehicle for cultural debate. It was welcomed a few weeks later by at least one person who had listened to the broadcast and appreciated the general tenor of increasing openness. This was the front-page article by '*Litfront*' (as unsigned as the un-named broadcaster) in the 16th February edition of *Literaturen Front*, entitled *A Good Beginning*, a neat play on words. The article showed that the broadcast had been appreciated:

> "Though Bulgarian culture enjoys friends in Western countries, we must confess we are far from being spoilt... This is why the January broadcast of the BBC dealing with Bulgarian art and literature echoed as a hopeful symptom of further development of cultural relations between our two countries.
>
> ...The broadcast makes a good impression with the definite tolerance of its tone...and sounds so full of hope...and goodwill...A bridge is best built when work proceeds from both sides...the bridge in question is a bridge of friendship."

It is very rewarding to reflect, forty years later, that Pierre had started that process of "building bridges", at the same time pushing open a few doors!

The broadcast had gone out while we were still in Morocco and the article in *Literaturen Front* did not reach him from the BBC until the middle of February.

Back in London we learned very sad news on the 8th January: Pierre's very dear friend and film production colleague (and perhaps even more importantly, fellow Slav) Anatole de Grunwald (Tolly) died suddenly at the early age of 56. Born in St. Petersburg, Tolly played a leading part in the development of British film over the previous twenty-five years. In 1943 he became a producer and writer for Two Cities Films. He was producer of one of the most successful British war films *The Way to the Stars* which Anthony (Puffin) Asquith directed and which starred Michael Redgrave and Trevor Howard. In 1953 he wrote and produced *Innocents in Paris*, the first of the many productions on which he and Pierre would later work together. Tolly went to work for MGM in Hollywood in 1959 and, for them, working with Pierre, made *The VIPs* with Richard Burton and Elizabeth Taylor and *The Yellow Rolls Royce* with Ingrid Bergman and Omar Sharif. MGM's films were made at the Boreham Wood studios outside London or on location.

As I noted in my diary of the time:

"Sweet, kind, mad, extravagant, colourful, generous, proud, vulnerable, sociable, lovable, foolish, impetuous... dear Tolly. A part of Pierre's life, of our lives. Part of a way of life. *Toute la folie russe*".

Stranger in the House

In February there was a first projection of the film on which Pierre and Tolly had been working these last months: *Stranger in the House* starring James Mason and Geraldine Chaplin (whose father Pierre had visited some time previously).

The film, based on a novel by Georges Simenon, was a de Grunwald production and directed by Pierre for Rank World Films. The gala premiere, attended by the stars, was in May. Pierre was by now very highly thought of in the film world and reviews of his film work were very positive:

"Rouve is a strong, non-conformist personality who has thrived in the British cinema world ever since he joined de Grunwald Productions in 1950"

wrote *The Daily Cinema*.

Before that, however, we had a short break together in Madrid. I was on a course for teachers of Spanish organised by our Education Inspectorate and those attending were all staying in a pleasant, but basic, "*hostal*" in the centre of Madrid. When Pierre arrived, not only did I skip some of the lectures but we made sure that we tried out several of the good restaurants, visited the Prado museum and, since, as a film executive, Pierre was staying at the Ritz, I secretly (not wishing to offend my colleagues) moved there for a few nights! There is certainly little to compare with the luxury of the Ritz Hotel in Madrid!

In early May our car, which had carried us so faithfully all along the course of rivers in Germany and to Italy and Switzerland, was stolen in London. This was a blow and it was some time before we bought another to replace it but, as our friends were arriving from Morocco on a visit, we had little choice.

Relations, at least on the cultural front, were obviously improving with Bulgarian officialdom (or perhaps it was because the people with whom Pierre had spent many pleasant hours during his youth in Sofia were increasingly able to visit London and were keen to see him), since I note that on 6th June we were invited to a dinner at the Bulgarian Embassy by Ambassador Voutov. Soon afterwards we spent a brief but busy weekend in Boulogne. Even though it is just across the Channel, we would not normally have thought of going there had I not wanted to spend some time planning in detail for the school trip I was organising for the end of the summer term. Our stay obviously involved some sightseeing of the Old Town, my making out a quiz sheet for the pupils to complete and visits to shops for some tasty purchases.

Working at 'Q'

Pierre's work in the theatre, alongside his film work and his writing, had been developing with the regular summer school classes that he initiated for drama students at the De Leon Theatre School at the 'Q' theatre in Richmond. This year, together with actors Dirk Bogarde and Barbara Jefford, he was also a member of a Brains Trust panel, organised by the De Leons and very well attended. The performances which he achieved with the students were, as Lewis Cranston noted in the *Evening News*, "astonishing...nothing short of professional".

That summer we had two holidays or, I should rather say, we had one in Rome together and I had another visiting friends in Morocco. At the Parco dei Principi hotel it seems that I spent a lot of time in the hot weather at the swimming pool ("Down to pool for lazy day, Pierre out for work, we lunched later at the hotel") while Pierre was holding meetings about film projects. One evening we went again, with Ennio and Tonino Guerra the scriptwriter, out to Marino to dine with Carlo Ponti. Sophia, however, was not there that evening and the men tended to talk business; later we viewed a film *C'era una volta* in their own delightful cinema. Around the pool I had met and made friends with a nice Persian couple, he was at the Embassy (this is before the days of the Ayatollah's revolution and the Bayats may still be living in Italy, but now in exile...). Ronald Harwood, the playwright, was also at the hotel and so more projects were to ensue. Rome, as ever, was truly impressive and, on the last morning, driving to the airport, we had a last sunlit view, driving past St. Peter's, the perspective constantly changing as each pillar, and the double line of pillars, slid past.

Before I went off again towards the end of the month, Ennio de Concini came to London and, although on film business, we managed to enjoy some lovely days: talking Italian translations of T.S. Eliot's poetry with Jonathan Griffin, driving over to lunch by the Thames at Bray, visiting Hampton Court Palace, spending time with Pamela and Geoffrey Moore and their children as well as discussing literature with Geoffrey. At about this time Jonathan and Kathie moved away from their house opposite us in Markham Street and up to Regent's Park (a bigger house could accommodate all his books!). Although, of course, we continued to visit each other, go to the theatre and opera and to have dinners, it was no longer just a question of popping across the road...

October saw me starting a higher degree course, on secondment from teaching at school, at the London University Institute of Education. This meant a lot of reading, study, attendance at lectures and seminars, but proved fascinating as I had become increasingly interested in the philosophical underpinnings of educational thought and practice. This met with Pierre's enthusiastic approval: he had always encouraged me to take a deeper and broader interest in theory. He was, as one may imagine, a tremendous support in this new venture and, as with so many things in my life, I have to thank him for all his knowledge, support and encouragement.

Diamonds for Breakfast at Blenheim Palace

He, for his part, started the filming of *Diamonds for Breakfast*, a most glamorous production, starring Marcello Mastroianni and Rita Tushingham and filmed almost entirely on location at Blenheim Palace. Pierre was co-producer (an exacting administrative role) with Carlo Ponti and he also co-wrote the screenplay with N.F. Simpson and Ronald Harwood (all those hardworking days in sunny Rome had paid off!). Friends who have visited us either at the house in Markham Street or, later, at Pierre's studio in Markham Square, will remember the larger than life-size reproductions of icons which were created as stage sets for this production and which we were allowed to keep after completion of the film. Filming on location meant that Pierre either stayed in the nearby Oxfordshire village of

Woodstock or came home very late. It did, however, mean that I could go and spend weekends in the country!

December was perhaps notable for two events: there was the major Turner exhibition at Agnew's gallery in London, a first stimulus maybe for the important study which Pierre was later to undertake; then, on the 21st, there was the memorial service at the National Film Theatre for Anatole. This was both a sad and also an inspiring occasion. Much to my surprise, we would appear to have spent Christmas and New Year in London!

* * * * *

1968

Vanyo visits

One advantage of being in London was that I was able to attend the annual New Year conferences of the Philosophy of Education Society. These had become a steadily growing interest for me, in which I was much encouraged by Pierre, who often joined me and my colleagues for discussions (to which he brought a valuable continental philosophical flavour and a particular interest in metaphysics). My teachers and "gurus" at London University were Professors Richard Peters and Leslie Perry, whose classes I was later to share. Pierre and I also enjoyed the stimulating company of Professor Louis Arnaud Reid and Ray Elliott, both working in the field of aesthetics.

Towards the end of January we had the enormous pleasure of a visit from one of Pierre's oldest friends, Dr. Ivan (Vanyo) Rumenov, the famous oncologist. In those days Bulgarians were not permitted to travel abroad accompanied by their wives or other members of the family (lest they should decide to do the "unthinkable"...) and it was therefore some time before I was able to meet his kind and supportive wife Jeannie, a well known pediatrician and their son Vladi, then a schoolboy, now a member of the artistic and restoration team of the Icon Gallery in the crypt of Alexander Nevski cathedral. With Vanyo we did the full sightseeing tour of London and Hampton Court, visited the medical bookshop of London University for texts that were not available to him, and spent many happy days together. This hospitality was returned when Pierre and I visited the Rumenovs in Bulgaria and were taken on many excursions around the country. Vanyo stayed with us for a whole month and left by train for Paris on his way back to Sofia in February. He wrote to us on his return:

"I am already two weeks home. Many operations, many things to do, but my London days with you and Petyo are unforgettable and I dream for them. My love to you both, yours Vanyo."

With my studies for the higher degree and Pierre's increasing interest and involvement in the groups of students to whom he was lecturing, both at the 'Q' theatre and at Art College, we were both thinking at about this time about applying for jobs: I to move into higher education and he for a post in one of the Colleges. A full-time lecturing post would of course have limited his possibilities for taking on the interesting challenges of film production and direction as well as of theatre production and we discussed our future directions in some detail at this stage. I made an application to a Teacher Education college where I felt I could put my experience of teaching in school to good use in the preparation of future teachers of foreign languages, at the same time looking at the underlying principles of education. Pierre was attracted to posts in the major Art Colleges: the prestigious Royal College and the Chelsea College of Art.

At this time Pierre's very dear friend and film director colleague Anthony ('Puffin') Asquith, with whom he had worked on *The Millionairess,* died. The memorial service, held in St. Margaret's Church, Westminster, in March, was a fitting tribute to this cultured member of a class of *"la vieille Angleterre"* whose ancestors had made a notable contribution to British parliamentary debate. Yehudi Menuhin played Bach's Partita in D minor.

A British citizen!

For twenty years Pierre had lived in England as a "stateless" person (he felt sad at having been deprived of one citizenship; perhaps not, until now, feeling ready, confident, worthy of taking the new...). "Pierre Ouvaliev known as Pierre Rouve" now made application "to one of Her Majesty's Principal Secretaries of State for a certificate of naturalisation" and, as a result, the "Secretary of State declares that upon taking the Oath of Allegiance he shall be a citizen of the United Kingdom". The Certificate was issued by the Home Office on 8th April 1968:

> "The Secretary of State, in pursuance of the powers conferred upon him.... grants to the said Pierre Ouvaliev known as Pierre Rouve this Certificate of Naturalisation".

The Oath of Allegiance:

> "I, Pierre Ouvaliev known as Pierre Rouve swear by Almighty God that I will be faithful and bear true allegiance to Her Majesty, Queen Elizabeth the Second, her Heirs and Successors, according to law"

was then signed by him on 11th April before a Commissioner for Oaths.

Thus a new person came into being, and a new life opened up. But only in the administrative sense: Pierre had already, over the last twenty years, made a "self" for himself, never, however, forgetting his previous existence which persisted through his broadcasts on the Bulgarian service of the BBC, his occasional contacts with old friends from Bulgaria and his continued devotion to the best of Bulgaria. Here I think it appropriate to quote at some length from one of the many letters sent to the Bulgarian section from listeners:

> "...these few lines concern the short talk you broadcast every Sunday on cultural matters. I do not know the name of the commentator but follow each of his talks with mounting interest and am pleased and delighted by the way in which he analyses everything he talks about... the style and language with which he presents everything in such an original manner; he brings out national nuances for which we must be grateful to him.
>
> To him we owe the fact that we have got to know the works of T.S. Eliot and many others... regretfully we have to wait a whole week for a 10–15 minute talk: much, much too short! Could you not lengthen the talks to 30–40 minutes or else broadcast them three times weekly?
>
> He has good diction, a well balanced and intriguing voice which is partly the reason for his success."

This delightful testimony was sent by 'Alexander N. Terziev, a student from Plovdiv' and, more than 40 years later, it would be good to have news of him!

At the same time we were continuing our social life: a dinner at the house of the famous actress Louise Rainer and her husband the publisher Robert Knittel, an invitation from Ambassador Voutov to a reception at the Bulgarian Embassy, Dora visiting us in London while seeing her publisher for the book on Georges Braque, a dinner with the Bulgarian sculptor Lyuba and her husband Ernesto Wolf, visits to the International Theatre Festival. Pierre was also invited to participate in an important symposium at the Institute for Contemporary Art (ICA). This season Misho and Annie Hadjimishev were in England for his production of *Eugene Onegin* at the famous Glyndebourne Opera House. It was a joy to receive these old friends of Pierre's from the days of his youth and to share with them their artistic and musical activity. We attended the dress rehearsal together with the Griffins and dined with Misho. Two days later, dressed in our evening finery and cutting an exotic picture, we took the train from Victoria station to attend the first night. This was a great event: the music, the production, the countryside location, the opera house... Some days later we had the Hadjimishevs and the Griffins to dine with us in Chelsea. This was indeed an evening of shared experiences and memories of music, performances and singers.

Meanwhile, having been successful in my application to join the staff at the Teacher Training College, I was to start there in September and so was completing assignments for the course. I had so enjoyed the philosophy and the aesthetics aspects that both Pierre and I were happy to be able to spend time with the professors, who had now become friends and were, indeed, to be instrumental in my continued progress towards teaching at London University. "May '68" was felt in England as well as in France among the student body and I attended some fascinating "talk-ins" with students both at the University and at Hornsey College of Art, where the challenge was to the type of teaching, the subject matter and to the exams.

Festive music in Aldeburgh

This year, with all that was going on and needing to be prepared, we had no long overseas summer holiday. We went, for the first time, to attend the Aldeburgh Festival, Benjamin Britten's musical creation by the Suffolk seaside. The marvellous converted Maltings at Snape provided a first class concert venue, the Jubilee Hall in Aldeburgh a smaller, more intimate one. Joining the Griffins (regular attenders of the festival, with a cottage on the seafront) on our first day we saw Haydn's *The Seasons* and, later, Britten's opera *Gloriana*, a tribute to Queen Elizabeth I. Other concerts were given in the magnificent Suffolk churches, built in the Middle Ages by rich wool merchants, and we also took the opportunity to drive around the countryside visiting some of them. Back in London, there was the Alfred Wallis exhibition at the Tate followed, in July, by the major Henry Moore exhibition. At St. Paul's

Cathedral there were performances of three of Benjamin Britten's religious operas: *Curlew River, The Burning Fiery Furnace* and *The Prodigal*, very impressive settings. At the end of July Pierre went to Rome and I joined Pamela and her children for another lovely, restful holiday in Devon. August saw the first performance of a new play by John Osborne *Hotel in Amsterdam*, in which Paul Scofield was superb, though we were less impressed by the play.

A Pirandello production

Upon his return, Pierre was drawn back to the live theatre and became fully involved in a new project: the production of a Pirandello play in Guildford. He had been invited by the director of the Yvonne Arnaud Theatre to direct the challenging question of personal identity: *As You Desire Me (Così è, si me vuole)*. He assembled a star cast of Barbara Jefford and John Turner. So August and September were taken up with planning and rehearsals as the play was to open in October. It was a great success and received excellent reviews. It is interesting to note that, some 35 years after the production, I recently had a letter from Barbara Jefford who wrote:

> "(your letter) reawakened memories of your talented husband and of the time that we worked together on the Pirandello play... our chief memory is the pleasure of meeting the charming, erudite and deeply civilised man that Pierre was. As a director he was helpful, informative and supportive in a way that all should be (and very few are, unfortunately) and that the rehearsal period was painless and constructive in equal measure. One could not bestow a higher accolade!".

Later we did manage a weekend in Aldeburgh for their "Bach weekend": a choral and orchestral concert at The Maltings with the English Chamber Orchestra, conducted by Benjamin Britten, with Peter Pears (for whom Britten had himself written so much) in Cantata 73. On the Sunday Rafael Puyana gave a harpsichord recital and later Philip Ledger performed organ solos in Aldeburgh church.

Now it was time for term, and my new job, to begin. To my surprise and delight, Leslie Perry had asked me to contribute to the Diploma in Art Education course at the Institute of Education at London University. The appointment, for one half day per week, had been confirmed by Professor Peters, head of the Philosophy of Education department, and so I had two new jobs! Very exciting, but also very challenging. In addition, I had to make sure that I was able to get from one building to the other across London!

Those doing the Diploma were all practising teachers of art who wanted further to explore the different aspects of their work. We had a thoroughly enjoyable and stimulating time considering the philosophy of perception: Bertrand Russell, Bishop Berkeley, Warnock, Solti and Sartre. I later went on, with Pierre's help and guidance, to develop a module on the teaching of History of Art.

October 1st was the opening night of the Pirandello: a group of friends set off from Waterloo to attend what was a critical and artistic success:

> "His production... thoroughly justified the modern treatment of Pirandello's lines".

The production enjoyed good audiences during its two-week run. November 7th saw the premiere of *Diamonds for Breakfast* at the Plaza cinema. Theatre and cinema were coming together. Music was added in December with a concert and dinner with Andre Boucoureshliev. This must have seemed, even then, a busy schedule as, on 6th December, I note: "evening at home with Pierre!". Probably a relatively rare event!

Luxury at the Mencey

We had not, however, given up the habit of spending the Christmas holiday period in the sunshine and, this year we chose the Canary Islands for the first time. On the 19th we flew with Iberia to Tenerife, staying at the luxurious Mencey hotel, recommended by our travel agent. This was certainly the best kind of holiday: a hotel with garden and swimming pool but located in the centre of a delightful Spanish provincial town of 19th century charm, Santa Cruz, with bookshops, market and a lovely theatre. It was sunbathing and swimming in the garden, lunch at the hotel, siestas, then exploring the town, the shops, the port, taking coffee at what became one of Pierre's favourite cafes, the Bar Atlántico. On Christmas Day there was a gala dinner at the hotel. We attended performances at the Teatro Guimera and on the 29th celebrated our 6th wedding anniversary. Another day we took a taxi for an island visit: a most beautiful drive up through pine woods that sloped down to the sea on both sides. Up and up to the foot of Mount Teide with its lunar landscape; we lunched at the Parador and then down, through the clouds and mist to the "*jardín botánico*" and to the rather over-developed resort of Puerto de la Cruz (now, sadly, the rest of the suntrap south of the island is much more commercially exploited). Back at our hotel we relaxed and on the 31st, New Year's Eve, dined at a restaurant we had discovered. On our last day we shopped and had coffee at the Atlántico before flying back to chilly England at the conclusion of another busy, fascinating year full of friends, music, work and fun, ready to start another.

* * * * *

1969

More theatre and more philosophy

The beginning of every year now seemed to be taken up by attendance at conferences: immediately upon our return from Tenerife I went to the Philosophy of Education weekend. At least it was held at a London college so I could go home and relax each night! Pierre often joined me and my colleagues for presentations and discussions since he was also so interested in the subject. There were only a few days to go before term began, and, in my two different jobs, the pressure was on: preparing lectures, seminars with students... for both the Diploma in Art Education students and the future French teachers at the College. As well as the teaching there was the regular attendance, together with my friend Pamela, at philosophy and linguistics lectures and seminars, time in the library, preparing presentations and writing up... for our higher degree. Looking back on those days I wonder how I found the energy, not only to complete, but also to enjoy, such a full schedule!

Socially, we spent time in early January with the Bulgarian artist Georgi ('Bobby') Daskaloff and his wife Nadine, dining at Pashanko and Margaret's house, where Nikolai Ghiaurov also joined us. Bobby had an exhibition opening at the Ewan Phillips gallery later in the month, one of the first about which Pierre wrote and broadcast. Here I should mention that his collected texts were, at Svetlin Roussev's suggestion, recently published as *Bessedi za Bulgarski Houdozhnitzi (Writings on Bulgarian Artists)* by Anubis in Sofia.

At the end of the month we attended a fascinating lecture by Roland Barthes, one of Pierre's great inspirers, at the Institut Français.

February saw a most welcome return to London of Misho Hadjimishev, this time accompanied by his son Ivo, already a very promising photographer, who was later to undertake postgraduate specialisation in England and to become a member of the Royal Photographic Society. They were to spend quite some time with us and, of course, with our operatic friends the Griffins. Many talks and dinners were enjoyed with this group of dear friends! Another Bulgarian friend of long standing who was then over from America was Misho Padev, so the Chelsea house was certainly becoming the first port of call for many Bulgarian visitors!

The theatre, in all its manifestations, was beginning to take up more and more of Pierre's time: he was invited to give talks at Jack de Leon's 'Q' theatre in Richmond; he was planning a production with the famous French mime artist Marcel Marceau; we went to the opening night at the Yvonne Arnaud theatre of *The Cardinal of Spain* by Henri de Montherlant in Jonathan Griffin's translation and there was talk of a production of Sartre's *The Prisoners of Altona*. Art, too, occupied us: there was the opening of the Magritte exhibition at the Tate Gallery and Manzù at the Hanover Gallery.

April brought the Easter holiday time. This year we went back to Munich for a week and saw Stefan Popov. We walked, rediscovered our old haunts and visited the Alte Pinakothek for the Cranach, Altdorfer and Rubens, dining at Humplmayer. On a fine and sunny Good Friday, we walked to the Peterskirche, to the river, lunched at the hotel and went to see a German horror film. Another day we walked to the Haus der Kunst for the Miró exhibition and to the Stuck villa for the Art Nouveau and an exhibition of Jugendstil glass. In the evening we went to the Popovs and dined at a Bulgarian restaurant. It was always such a pleasure for Pierre to meet up and talk with his friend Stefan. On Easter Monday we attended a performance of *Tristan und*

Isolde with Wolfgang Windgassen (whom we had heard in so many *Ring* performances at Covent Garden), at the Residenztheater. Tuesday saw us doing last minute shopping, packing and flying back to London where Pierre went straight to the office and I prepared for the next day when, after dropping in at the University, I went to Kent to attend the Easter School of Philosophy. This year the theme was *Reason and Feeling*, the keynote speakers being Professors Dilman (from the USA) and Vesey, who spoke on David Hume. I found myself allocated to Professor Peter's group for seminars, which was very stimulating. One afternoon I drove over to visit my friend from schooldays, Rosie, and her husband and children (to one of whom, Johanna, I am godmother). This, together with occasional drives into the country and the sea, compensated for what otherwise might have become an overdose of intellectual activity! However, the walks and talks, with Dilman (whose lecture was on *Faith and Reason*), Peters, Hirst and Arnaud Reid were something to treasure! The social, the "colleaguely" and the academic elements of these gatherings, taking place in the midst of the beautiful Kent countryside, were certainly things to recall with the greatest pleasure.

Philosophy was to continue to be prominent as, in early May, B.F. Skinner was to lecture at London University. His title *Freedom, Dignity and the Abolition of Man* was designed to be controversial as, with his Behaviourist views, Skinner always is. Contrastingly, Noam Chomsky (a week later and in the same lecture hall, as he himself pointed out…!), spoke three times on *Problems of Syntax and Semantics*. To hear two of the key figures in the field of psychology and of linguistics (from Skinner's *Verbal Behavior* to Chomsky's *Language and Mind*) was a rare privilege.

Pavleto and the mini-skirts

At the same time Pierre and I were seeing many of his Bulgarian friends: at Liliana Brisby (Daneva)'s house there was a dinner party for her father, a previous Minister of Foreign Affairs, who was visiting England. The writer and poet Pavel (Poli) Spassov and his wife Vena visited us in London and we introduced them to many of our friends: they came with the Danevs to dine and Pierre also took them on a visit to Stratford on Avon. Pierre was also able to spend time with three well-known Bulgarian artists: Pavleto, Georgi Kovachev and his wife Milka Peikova who were on a visit to England. In his recently published memoirs, Kovachev recounts their meetings in Chelsea and Italian restaurants, their talk of art and...of *"mini-jupes"*! Another day we went to Pashanko's to dine with the violinist Gavrilov.

Life, and music, in Venice

Term at the Institute of Education lasted till the end of June. I then immediately flew to join Pierre who was in Venice, again on film business. Taking a late plane and arriving at 2.30 a.m., I had the most amazing first impression of Venice: Pierre had come to meet me and we took a *motoscafo* for a night water drive to the incredible Daniele Hotel, where our room was full of roses! The next morning the view from our balcony, out over S. Giorgio and Sta. Maria delle Saluti, in the brilliant sun, was out of this world; a light that made three dimensions seem four and more! Later, a *motoscafo* along the Canal Grande, a walk back from the Accademia over canal bridges, lunch on the hotel terrace, drinks in the evening in St. Mark's Square and then dinner with Giuseppe Marchiori (President of the Italian section of the AICA) at an artists' restaurant. The next day was clear but with a strange grey light and we walked, via St. Mark's Square, to the Rialto (shades of *The Merchant of Venice*!), bought tickets for a concert at the Fenice theatre (later burnt down), had lunch at the hotel with Amy Shuard. Pierre then had to work on scripts and I went shopping. The concert, in the most beautiful theatre, was a dream: Berlioz, *Harold in Italy*, with its superb viola solo, one of my favourite pieces, and Stravinsky. Sunday "a clear day dawns, sunny across the water, greys and blues. Perfect Venice from the Daniele", as I noted. We visited the Palazzo Ducale, all the grand rooms and 14th century frescoes, the prison and the Bridge of Sighs ("A palace and a prison on each hand..." as Byron writes in *Childe Harold*). In the afternoon, we were taken by Marchiori and his wife Laura to visit the island of Torcello. A lovely *motoscafo* ride across the lagoon and when we arrived in this paradise... what a jewel: the churches, then Sunday lunch in a garden restaurant, Venetian style. Truly a dream holiday!

A Scandinavian Saga

In July Dora came over to London with her son Pierre-Christian, then a young teenager and on holiday It was fortunate that we could be with them, Pierre and I being in London for this early part of the summer holiday, and together we visited many of the sights of London. In August we set out to take the Harwich ferry to Copenhagen, via Esbjerg and the islands, where the AICA congress was to open. During the ten days of the congress we visited all three Scandinavian countries. On arriving, having registered, we went to meet Dora and the French art critic Jeanine Warnod who were arriving by train from Paris. Katarina (Katya) Ambrozic, the art historian, was also attending, in her capacity as President of the Yugoslav branch of AICA. The congress opened in the evening with a reception at the Radhus. The next day we were taken by coach to visit the Louisiana Museet, its marvellous collection and an exhibition of Calder's "mobiles" in the gardens! Afterwards we went on to visit Elsinore Castle (shades, here, of *Hamlet*!) and on through the countryside to visit a sculptor (who gave me a souvenir piece which I still have at home) and to eat a roasted ox in the garden. In the evening Pierre and I visited the famous Tivoli gardens. The following evening we were to transfer by plane to Stockholm, the second congress venue, but in the morning we attended a presentation and then went to the Glyptothek to see the Matisse, Impressionist and Gauguin paintings. After arriving we walked, exploring Stockholm with a map, and then dined at the *Operakallarer*. On Monday, at the reception and discussions in the conference hall of the National Museum, Pierre was called upon to interpret. I visited the Old Town, shopped, saw the changing of the guard at the Castle; together we visited the splendid Modern Art museum with its collection of Braque, of special interest to Dora. With Jeanine, who is very well organised, I went to a store where one could buy tickets for an opera performance at Drottningholm, an unforgettable experience! Handel's *Il Mondo della Luna*, all in period: costumes and set. We returned afterwards by boat in the twilight. The following day, before flying on to Oslo, we made more visits and I took a boat trip with Dora, Jeanine and Katya around the islands, which was lovely. In Oslo Pierre organised the translation of one or two of the presentations and we visited the extraordinary Munch museum where we not only saw those works that were on display, but also had the privilege of being shown some kept in store. A visit to the Vigelund sculpture park was impressive as was the reception at the Henje-Onstad Centre (the donation of the famous Norwegian skater). We had wanted to take a boat trip along the fjords, but it was too late. Dora, however, decided to complete the Scandinavian experience by taking a trip up to Bergen while we flew back to London.

Puppets and other topics

In September Pierre went to Edinburgh for the performance given by the Bulgarian puppet theatre. It is perhaps appropriate at this moment to give an idea of the range of coverage of his broadcasts for the Bulgarian service of the BBC. I have in front of me now his diary for 1969 and his topic is meticulously listed for every week. On the 14th September it was *Bulgarian Puppets* and on the 21st, *Edinburgh*, taking in the broader canvas of the Festival. However, a glance across the year shows that he spoke on E.M. Forster, Shakespeare films, Daskaloff (the exhibition), Bulgarian culture, Chaplin, Milev's translations, centenary of Stamatov's birth, Gladstone, Congreve, provincial theatre, Bogomils, art and science, Sunday in August, J.B. Priestley, mass culture, Jean-Louis Barrault (to coincide with his visit to London and the performance at the Royal Court theatre of Samuel Beckett's *Oh, les Beaux Jours*), art and revolution, Vera Mutafchieva, film theory, Nikolai Haitov (twice)... and this is just a selection of the topics on which he spoke between January and December that year!

Also in September there was the conference of the International Association of Applied Linguistics in Cambridge, and I attended with several colleagues. This was an opportunity to hear prominent speakers: Hartmann, Halliday, Wilga Rivers, Peter Strevens, Glanville Price and to exchange experiences regarding teaching and research with those in other universities in the United Kingdom and abroad. Cambridge was also extremely attractive, though we could have done with fewer lectures, but I had time to explore a range of country pubs with my close friend and research colleague Vaughan James of Sussex University.

A moving tribute to a great friend

September 19th was a sad day as Pierre's great friend and early mentor in the field of art criticism, Dr. Richard Gainsborough, founder of the *Arts Review* had died. We went to the funeral ceremony at Golders Green where Pierre gave a most moving tribute to this tireless supporter of the cause of art:

> "We are gathered here to part from a man who meant much to all of us; to draw a final, irrevocable line between

his presence and his absence; to confess in the silence of our hearts what he was to us and what he will be.

...But words fail me precisely because I shall try not to fail him. They may soil with routine rust the purity of the feelings that flood all of us: respect for his integrity, admiration for his unselfishness, gratitude for his generosity. They make the pure seem pompous and the true, trite. And yet we have nothing but these words to repay him for his deeds: a devalued currency that will leave us forever in his debt.

...And because I owe him more than most, I fear that I may not be doing enough to honour his memory: private emotions may drown the public eulogy. But even they mirror the vocation of Dr. G. to help and to heal.

...In accepting me among the very first contributors to his magazine, he helped me to find new bearings in a foreign land. In inciting me to dive into an alien language, he healed the loneliness that cripples and destroys exiles. With patient kindness he guided my first steps on my way to a new life. It is hard to talk about his last steps on his way to eternity.

...He served art with unfailing devotion: Dr. G. served it where service is most needed: in the muddled mass of striving and starving artists, unknown but not untalented, unsold but not unworthy.

...Dr. G. was what few have ever been: a man born to give."

Later the same day, and perhaps appropriately, we both attended a meeting of the British Society of Aesthetics, where one of my colleagues, Ray Elliott, gave a paper on *Interpretation*.

After a feast of philosophy, there was to be a feast of theatre in October seeing several productions at the Old Vic: *Rabelais*, a fantastic show; a brilliant *Partage de Midi* with Jean-Louis Barrault (and we joined Jonathan for dinner with him after the performance); Tom Stoppard's fascinating *Rosencrantz and Guildenstern are Dead*; a modern play *The National Health*; a Feydeau farce *A Flea in her Ear;* the classic restoration comedy *The Way of the World* and the highly dramatic *The White Devil*. On the 6th, a Monday and hence a working day, we took a plane to Paris in late afternoon for the Paris gala mime performance given by Marcel Marceau and stayed overnight at a hotel beside the airport and I took the 7 a.m. plane the next day and went straight in to work!

December saw quite a few social engagements: on the 1st a reception at the Bulgarian Embassy for Ambassador Voutov; on the 6th the wedding of Tolly's son Alex in the Russian church in Kensington with Father Anthony Bloom officiating. I organised an end-of-term party for my Diploma students at our house and on the 19th there was a performance of the rarely produced *Pelléas et Mélisande* at Covent Garden. Christmas this year was spent with our friends the Griffins (and their several cats!), talking, reading poetry, opening presents… at their house in Primrose Hill, after which, and for the New Year, I went to York for the Language Association's annual conference.

* * * * *

The Seventies – Opening up New Horizons

1970

Into the next decade

The start of a new decade and one during which several momentous changes were to take place in our lives: a return, finally, to Bulgaria for Pierre in 1971, my first visit there in the same year, the birth of Mila Georgina for us in 1973... but I am running ahead.

At the beginning of January 1970 I was in York where, as well as the Languages Conference, I did a broadcast for French radio about the Minster's stained glass windows and their restoration. That same day I drove back down to London and, in the evening, on to the Philosophy of Education conference. After the linguists the philosophers! Quite an intellectual challenge to start off the New Year!

At the York conference I had met up with my colleague and friend Vaughan James and he had with him an invited guest from Bulgaria for the Russian language section: Professor Simeon Rusakiev. On the 7th January we arranged to spend a day together in London during which we took in all the sights and ended by going to an excellent performance of *Don Giovanni*. A couple of days later Rusakiev was again in London and Pierre went with him to buy books, difficult to obtain in Bulgaria, at Colletts.

Bulgarians, Bulgarians

We were seeing more Bulgarians now: friends coming officially (those whom Pierre had known in his younger days who had now risen to important positions and who wished to renew their contact with him), and friends on cultural visits. In addition, it was obviously realised in official circles that Pierre was a very important contact with regard to the wider diplomatic brief: he could open doors, bridge gaps which other severe restrictions had often made impossible for Embassy officials otherwise to close. Perhaps one of the most interesting examples of this was the developing relationship between us and the then Cultural Attaché, Chavdar Damianov. Chavdar was an absolutely charming person for whom, on the professional level, Pierre facilitated official cultural contacts with theatre directors, gallery owners and, indeed, his own opposite number, Brigitte Marger, the French Cultural Attachée and a good friend of ours who was later to work closely with Pierre Boulez. In February we invited Chavdar and his then wife Emi, a ballerina, to dine at home with the philosopher Lubomir Dramaliev.

At about this time a story regarding our Bulgarian evenings would assume the status of legend between Pierre and myself: I would be with the guests for drinks, dinner and coffee afterwards; then I would make my polite apologies and retire to bed, leaving them to continue talking in Bulgarian – and smoking – often until about 3 a.m. I must say at this point that whereas Pierre himself would always claim not even to be able to boil the proverbial egg, he was a superb washer-up of dinner dishes and cutlery! These were the beginnings of closer, but positive, relations with Bulgaria and a time when it would be unusual for a Bulgarian visiting London not to seek Pierre out. Although always busy, he was unfailingly generous with his time, welcoming a wide range of people (not all of whom, sad to say, returned, or even acknowledged, his kindnesses and endless hospitality).

This was also a time when there was a particularly active programme of events at the Institut Français in South Kensington and when we were seeing many visitors from

France, dining with Brigitte Marger or Andre Zavriew of the Cultural Services, following Jacques Derrida's or Jean-Marie Benoist's talk at the Institut; dining with the Gimpels, owners of the Gallery of the same name, after an opening. I was also regularly involved, every Tuesday, in the university courses in Metaphysics and Philosophy of Mind and Pierre was active in the Aesthetics group. He came several times to talk to our group of Art Education students and we would lunch afterwards at the Blue Dolphin, one of the Greek restaurants in the area. He was also increasingly involved in the artistic events in Yugoslavia, meeting artists when they were in London, covering exhibitions and going regularly to Slovenia, Croatia and Serbia.

April was the time for the International Theatre Festival and this year we saw *Mandragola* and *The Government Inspector* given by the Czech company; *Krapp's Last Tape* by a German group; *Amphytrion* and *Dom Juan* by the Comédie Française, after which we dined at the French Embassy, and *The Seagull* presented by the Moscow Arts Theatre. In music, we enjoyed Pierre Boulez and Andre Boucoureshliev, both of whom gave concerts at the Royal Festival Hall. The Boucoureshlievs came to us for dinner a few days later and there was lively talk about music.

At the end of May, and for the short holiday, I joined Pierre who was already in Rome on film business with Carlo Ponti. Whenever he was free we would walk: the Villa Borghese, Via Veneto for shopping and coffee, Trinità dei Monti, the Colosseo…, and visit friends. One day we had lunch with James Mason (whose line drawing of Pierre so exactly captures his expression), with whom Pierre hoped to work again on another film, and another day we met at Ponti's office in the Piazza Aracoeli and lunched with Tonino Guerra the scriptwriter. Back in London, we were just in time for a performance of *Don Giovanni* with Nikolai Ghiaurov.

The end of June brought the end of the university term and many jolly parties for staff and students. Pierre had, as always,

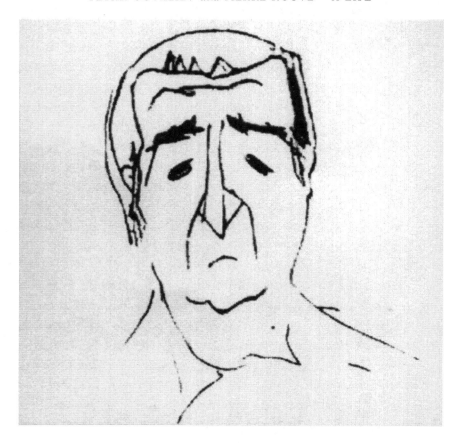

been extremely helpful with regard to seminars and discussions on a range of topics to do with art. Much appreciated by the students, he was to be invited in many of the following years. But July was hardly holiday for he was, as usual, involved with the summer school at the 'Q' theatre and also as a member of the Brains Trust panel, which always elicited many interesting questions from the audience and which Pierre enjoyed a lot.

Belgrade beckons

On the 3rd he took a few days off from London work to go to Belgrade to attend the exhibition of *Yugoslav Art at the*

Belgrade Triennale and about which he wrote in a full-page article in *Arts Review*:

> "The quests and queries of Yugoslav artists over the last three years may seem much too esoteric to be of any relevance to the British art scene...Nonetheless...man's power to assert his fractured identity confers a particular dignity on the Belgrade show...Branko Ruzić enriches his rough wooden carvings...Jagoda Buić achieves a minor-miracle in her tapestries...the work of Stojan Celić and Miodrag Protić, two painters who are thinkers as well as makers."

Hardly was he back from Belgrade than, on the 17th, he flew to Zagreb for a week.

Misho Hadjimishev was back in England for the summer opera season at Glyndebourne and Vanyo Rumenov had been able to visit England with a tourist group and we had an all too short six hours with him on the day the group was in London! Our American friends Bill and Genee Fadiman were also in London and, together with the Griffins, we attended the opening at the Old Vic of Christopher Fry's new play, *A Yard of Sun*, dining together afterwards. We also saw Gunter Grass' *The Plebeians* together and later in the month Stefan Popov came over from Germany.

On the 1st September I had to hand in my thesis at the Senate House, one of the reasons for not going away on an extended summer holiday this year! This was followed by the Aesthetics conference where both Pierre and the art critic Paul Hodin gave papers.

Bulgarians abound

October brought more Bulgarian visitors: one day, after lectures at the university, I joined Pierre and Hans Keller, the eminent musicologist, at the *Blue Dolphin* restaurant. Pierre had brought with him Georgi Markov who had recently arrived in England from Vienna, whence he had written to Pierre asking him to help him in finding openings and opportunities. Then a struggling and hardly known writer who had "left" Bulgaria, Georgi had difficulties in finding work, but Pierre, generous as always with time and advice, helped him in every respect to gain the beginnings of a footing in London. Another day we had Chavdar Damianov and George Ganchev with his then wife Wendy for dinner. Ganchev was also trying to find some work opportunities to maintain himself in England. He was, as ever, cheerful and eminently sure of himself and of his ability to succeed. He was also, reportedly, a good sportsman, specialising in fencing. Pierre was able to offer him some advice and introduce him to some contacts in the film world where Ganchev was hoping to work.

Other Bulgarians who were in London in October that year, ones who had already made a name for themselves, were Julia Krusteva together with her husband Philippe Sollers, for lectures at the Institut Français. With them we dined at the Zavriew's house. Tzvetan Stoyanov and his wife Antoineta Voinikova also visited us during their stay in England and they, together with the film director Georgi Stoyanov-Bigor, were friends whom it was always a pleasure to see.

In November, there was a series of top-level lectures at the Institut Français, inaugurated by Claude Lévi-Strauss. He was followed by Tzvetan Todorov who gave a lecture on *Littérature et Langage*, and Jean-Marie Benoist speaking of *Descartes et Freud*, after which we all dined at the Aretusa club restaurant, which many of our Bulgarian friends will remember. (Dining in good restaurants was very much a part of our life but such an outing was obviously not the reason for my awarding a "Special Medal for Domestic Excellence to P. Ouvaliev on 8th November" – most likely for his having done all the washing up and even, perhaps, having hoovered the carpets...)

The year was drawing to a close and we had decided to go

again to spend Christmas in Tenerife, again at our favourite hotel, the Mencey in Santa Cruz. We left a foggy London on the 12th December and found a warm climate. The day after we arrived Dimiter (Mitko) Grantcharov came over to visit and took us on a lovely drive down to the south of the island exploring the as yet undeveloped bays and villages. On our previous visit we had already discovered some of the interesting things to look out for, so we made sure to get tickets for *200 years since the birth of Beethoven,* a concert at the Teatro Guimera, which made us really feel part of the community. We dined afterwards at the restaurant where we had celebrated New Year on our previous visit. The following day we went to a Moliere play at the theatre, as well as shopping for Christmas presents and sending cards. Another day we dined aboard one of the many ships at anchor in the port of Santa Cruz, the *Jedinstvo,* to create an East European climate! The purser showed us all over the ship, but after coffee we had to leave as the ship was due to sail at 10.30 p.m. Mitko, whose usual base was in Germany, was working for a property development company and drove us up in the mountains, to the university town of La Laguna and over to Puerto de la Cruz and to the *Romántico* development of apartments which the company was building. We had an apartment on the cliff face; very dramatic, with the Atlantic waves and, in the clear morning light, a view out towards America! We ate, talked, enjoyed ourselves, relaxing in deckchairs by the pool and later returned to Santa Cruz. On the 22nd there was a phone call for Pierre from *Radio Nacional de España* and from the local paper *El Día,* wanting to interview him. I later joined them on the terrace when Pierre was already in full swing (in Spanish!). The radio interviewer then rushed away to broadcast the talk and the next day Pierre was all over the newspaper. The radio and the paper had been tipped off that Pierre was in discussions of a new film with Sophia Loren and the fact that the director-producer was staying in Santa Cruz was indeed interesting news!

> "The producer-director of the Antonioni film 'Blow Up' is in Tenerife. Pierre Rouve told us 'Perhaps, with Sophia Loren and Carlo Ponti, we'll shoot a film here about the kidnapping of diplomats in Latin America.'"

Christmas was spent at the hotel and in the evening Mitko came over to join us for the gala dinner, with music and a show, until the early hours.

The very next day we were to return to England and, as the plane landed late at Gatwick, we took a car home through the most marvellous winter wonderland of snow weighing down the branches of all the trees on the route.

This marked the end of another wonderful year spent with Pierre, memories which, as I write, come flooding back: major events, important meetings, marvellous visits, interesting discussions but, as well as the major events, the small, personal memories, his thoughtfulness, kindnesses, friends... all the things that make for a rich life together.

As this year ends and leads into the next, I conclude this first part of my memoirs. 1971, as I earlier indicated, marks a very important event for Pierre: born in Bulgaria, living for many years in England, making his life here, taking British citizenship but never for one moment forgetting the ties which bound him to, and the love he had for, his native Bulgaria. This momentous year sees him make the decision to accept the many invitations that he had been receiving and to return on a visit to Bulgaria. This next stage in his life – our life together – is the subject of the next part of these memoirs.

* * * *

1971

Pierre's first return visit to Bulgaria

Bulgaria beckons

Even Pierre's closest friends and relatives would have the greatest difficulty in grasping the range, depth and mixture of emotions which Pierre experienced on returning to his homeland after a quarter of a century.

While it is true that he had received many invitations from longstanding friends, it was this carefully planned visit which was to convince him to take what was obviously a momentous decision: after all, the death sentence for treachery (passed for having abandoned his Legation post and his country) was still on the statute books.

However, although the visit took place in 1971, there were many days of planning and other activities which occupied us in the first months of that year.

* * * * *

It had been decided, on the basis of the different invitations from his friends, family and colleagues from earlier days, that the most convenient time for the visit would be March (when Baba Marta would, appropriately, be ushering in a new and less cold season...).

The year began with the usual combination of activities: the Philosophy of Education conference, the beginning of term for me, part time at College where I was still teaching languages and two days a week at the Institute of Education for Philosophy and Art with a great group of students: artists themselves as well as being art teachers. For me this represented a fascinating mix of activities and academic challenge. In this I was always encouraged by Pierre, to whom I owe so much in terms of my academic advancement and developing interests.

There was Pierre's birthday and, for him, a trip to Switzerland regarding a film project which was to develop later in the same year. There were lectures: Foucault at the Institut Français; concerts: Hermann Prey at the Queen Elizabeth Hall; opera: *Turandot* at Covent Garden with our dear friend Aldo Ceccato conducting, and film: a season of Soviet films at the National Film Theatre.

March arrived and, appropriately perhaps, the opening of the first London exhibition of "wrapped" works by Christo (Yavashev) at Anely Judah's stylish gallery. Indeed, it was about this exhibition that Pierre made one of his broadcasts, the first line of which reads: "The best known Bulgarian artist in the world is the least well known in Bulgaria". We must remember, of course that, at that time, almost all knowledge of what was going on in the west as far as culture was concerned, was to be gleaned from such sources as Pierre's broadcasts for the BBC Bulgarian service. The 1971 article on Christo, one of three he wrote following Christo's successive *"wrappings"* of the Reichstag in Berlin and the Pont Neuf in Paris, *"surrounded"* islands and umbrellas in Japan, have since been included in *Bessedi za Bulgarski Houdozhnitzi*.

He's off!

And finally...the paperwork completed, many concerns addressed, setting his mother's mind at rest, shopping (tea, coffee...) for the exigent aunties...the worries, planning, nerves, hardly suppressed excitement...and on the 13th March (a Saturday, luckily, not a 'Friday 13th'!) I drove him to Heathrow for the 13h45 Balkanair flight via Brussels to Sofia. A story I remember he used to tell about that flight was that, as always a smoker (and smoking in planes was still allowed then), he asked the flight attendant for a packet of cigarettes, no doubt Benson & Hedges or another of his favourite brands, to which the reply was: "I'm sorry, sir, but would you like one of our 'Stewardesses'?" More than one interpretation possible regarding this offer!

To take my mind off his journey, arrival etc., I drove over to spend the afternoon with my friend Pamela. However, the following day Pierre rang (no easy task to get a connection in those days) to let me know that "all was well"; giving me his impressions; telling of some of his encounters; the visit to his mother (which must have been so emotional) and that he was well settled in at the Grand Hotel Sofia (the 'real' one...).

It's my turn

One week later, full of a mixture of excitement and trepidation, I took the same flight to Sofia where I was to join Pierre for two weeks.

It was hard to believe that I was on my way to Sofia! A very bumpy flight from London to Brussels and of course I had forgotten my *Nautamine*. The smiling stewardess gave me the Bulgarian version and, after some sleep and brave attempts to read *Otetchestven Front* etc., the plane was flying over snowcapped mountain ranges, the outskirts of a big town... and, suddenly, over the illuminated Alexander Nevski, set like a jewel amid large yellow buildings. At 7 p.m we landed. How strange it was to see 'SOFIA' (in Cyrillic) on an airport building! The chap took a long time over my passport (now all is swiftly revealed by computers reading the information!).

Going through for the luggage I caught sight of Chavdar Damianov, whom I thought was in London, and then, without any Customs formalities, I suddenly saw my "reception committee": so many friends, all with flowers: carnations, red and pink; hyacinths, white and blue; red roses...to meet me. A royal reception! As well as Pierre there was his mother, aunt Vena, Vanyo and Jeannie Rumenov, Annie Hadjimisheva, Karl Ognyanov, Chavdar and Emilia Damianov. Ordinary passengers, British and/or Bulgarian, must have wondered who and what...! Such a welcome! It also, of course, gave me the chance to realise that Pierre had been able to be in touch with so many of his close friends and family.

Chavdar had already put my cases (note the plural; not only all those clothes and shoes for two weeks...but yet more coffee and tea...and presents for all friends and their children) in his car, but Pierre had one too, and we drove to the hotel with him

explaining where and what places, buildings, views. We soon arrived and had the luxury of an apartment on the second floor with a superb view of Alexander Nevski and the Parliament building directly in front. I began to unpack in the spacious apartment and then the phone began to ring as, indeed, Pierre said it had been doing almost all of the previous week with people wanting to meet him.

Friends reunited

This evening was for us and his friends. First came Ancheto Fadenhecht (mother of the three Sertchadjiev boys), then the Poli and Vena Spassov, Vanyo and Jeannie Rumenov, Emi and Chavdar and another diplomat. After drinks in the mezzanine bar we went up to dine on the fifth floor 'Panorama' restaurant with a big table in a window alcove offering a perfect view over the cathedral. We were joined for coffee by Lina and Karl Ognyanov; he had just performed a caesarean operation. Karl had been to London but his wife Lina I had not previously met. She was to become one of my closest and dearest friends whom I would call 'Mamche' (as mine had died) and who would call me 'Bebche' (she had not had children).

(I was later to learn that through an insignificant door at the back of the restaurant on this floor were to enter those who had been to London and who were thus "invited" to relate their experiences, meetings and visits to us and no doubt to other "doubtful" people...) None of these kinds of thoughts, nor this knowledge, was to spoil this, my first and quite exceptional evening in Sofia.

Despite the excitement and the activities of my day of arrival, we drew the curtains at about 9 a.m. the next day, to be greeted by blue sky and the sun pouring in. We had in fact been woken by the sound of the bells of Alexander Nevski and I could imagine myself on the set of *Boris Godunov*! While Pierre took the many phone calls, I just sat and looked out of the window:

groups of people on day trips, a group of singers and dancers in costume formed up in a horseshoe shape for a photo...every single spectacle for the 'newcomer' from the west! It would have been too late to go to the service so we had a lazy breakfast in the suite and I then contemplated the amount of 'wrong' clothes I had brought (it is a regular feature with me, to have the wrong clothes for events, the weather, the place...) as it was so much warmer than the −3 deg. that I had been expecting.

Sofia scenes

We went out, simply to walk about in Sofia. For me an absolutely fascinating, and long imagined, experience but for Pierre a totally unique occasion, something I could never entirely share: re-discovering the days, the streets, the places... of his youth. The unique circumstances: after 24 years, to be invited back – and after having been sentenced – by those for whom, officially at least, he was distinctly *persona non grata*. The BBC has never been against Bulgaria, rather the opposite and, since Pierre had always and only ever spoken positively and on cultural themes, he is surrounded by such a positive aura. Everywhere people greet him: from all sections and ages, in the street, ringing up... it is the news of Sofia. He is invited, feted, left and right, by colleagues, family, ministers. My impression at the time was that we would no doubt come back again but that this time will have been unique.

And so... we walked along Boulevard Russki with Pierre showing and explaining to me: the headquarters of the Bulgarian Academy of Science, the Military Club and, on the left, Grand Hotel Bulgaria and the Mausoleum. A voice called out "Petyo"; it was Ivan Slavkov in his car with a friend and we all went back to the hotel for coffee (no problem in those days to park outside; indeed so few cars in Sofia...). In the coffee lounge we immediately met several people whom Pierre knew.

It was almost as if he were "holding court"; as much so as the "Prince Consort" with whom we had arrived!

'Mother's Day' with his mother

Ivan then very kindly drove us to see Pierre's mother and to have a magnificent Bulgarian "Sunday lunch". This again was a most moving moment for me (in my 'western calendar' diary it was 'Mother's Day'!). Through the garden we came upon the lovely old family house, now long lost to us – to Pierre, his sister Dora and our descendants: another branch of the family acquired it through mean-minded machinations and by dubious legal means. We went up to the second floor flat occupied by his mother and the aunts, Vena and Bogdanka. The flat, like so much in Sofia, is Vienna, Madrid, Paris… Never has real life felt so much like a novel: the 'old style' family flat, the family photos of the prodigal son, the different personalities: the aunts, one a lawyer, the other a medical doctor; everyone intent on putting his or her point of view; gathering around the family table for the meal to greet the return of the prodigal, together with his (strange, western…) wife. Pierre was understanding of his mother, sardonic with his aunts… trying, no doubt, to find just how to be with the family whom he had left when so young and not seen for so many years.

Later in the afternoon Vanyo Rumenov and his hugely tall son Vladi, then 15 and already speaking a fantastically fluent English and now, of course, a grown man and, more importantly, a much respected restorer of icons in the marvellous national collection housed in the crypt of the Alexander Nevski cathedral, both came to the hotel, offering to drive Pierre and me to Vitosha. Pierre stayed at the hotel to see (as I then described it) "who-knows-whom…" and, indeed, which of his many friends may have come to see him while I was to discover how amazingly close to the centre of Sofia was this staggeringly impressive mountain. This has, of course,

always been a "selling point" for this lovely human-scale but surprisingly little visited capital city. We drove quite far up – now no longer permitted, especially at weekends – and saw that there were many strategically placed boulders to facilitate hill starts; very useful for old Moskviches!

People were walking back down the mountain slopes as it was by then quite late and we were still following the winding road. Melting snow was streaming down although there was still skiing higher up at Shtastlivetsa. Sofia could be seen through a haze. This must have been the coal, wood and heavy industry smog of the times, and has since increased enormously with car and bus exhaust pollution. I filmed, with my ancient 8mm camera, while Vanyo took photos near the ski slope. He met several of his friends and colleagues; many doctors belonged to the volunteer brigade of mountain rescuers. We drove, as it seemed, around the other side of the mountain. No flowers were out except a few yellow-green aconite and pussy willow on the branches. We came across a big stone *"metchka"* (bear) and young Vladi was amazed by my rendition of *"Gladna metchka..."*, one of those little ditties I had learned either from Pierre or at the School of Slavonic Studies!

We drove on (it now seems inconceivable...but so much better for the preservation of the mountain ecology...) to yet another splendid panorama, being admired by a coachload of Russian tourists, Bulgaria then being the holiday spot of choice for Russians and East Germans. We went back via Boyana for a late tea at the Hanche: hot *pitka, sirene* and *chubritsa* plus Turkish coffee. It is a source of amazement to me how much food we were plied with and seemed able to consume! Sitting at a table in the window corner we again had Sofia at our feet! On the way out every dream was fulfilled by a bagpiper player – a real, nutbrown, old, country man – playing plaintive and magical arhythmic melodies; it was as if we had ordered him to be there, just for us!

Sofia stories

We had to hurry back to the hotel as we had a dinner to attend. At 8p.m. and only round the corner (although I am quite sure we were taken by car...) we went to Chavdar and Emilia Damianov's flat, in a proper, solidly built, four storey block on Tolbukhin, now Levski; a block now given over to Philip Morris and, more recently, the Azerbaijani Embassy; tobacco and oil, the current ruling powers... Their flat was large and not divided up like Pierre's mother's flat to provide space for people seeming to have some claim to a living area in central Sofia. It had a '30s feel about it or, to me "turn of the century", and was cluttered in that strange way with enormous pieces of furniture and *vitrines* containing souvenirs from world travels. Pierre and I wrote a letter to the famous musicologist, our friend Hans Keller, about another dinner guest, a certain Asparukhov, who must have been a musician – or so I deduce from my notes of the time. Chavdar was to return to London, to the Embassy and for the cultural agreement, the next day and so, before midnight, we walked off the dinner and homemade red wine, returning to the hotel. A day full of activities, meetings, emotions, food... was to be followed by so many more!

The next day, Monday – a normal weekday working day – was nevertheless given over by our dear friends the Rumenovs to taking us on an excursion to Rila Monastery. At 9a.m., after picnic-cum-Himalayan excursion preparations, and not forgetting all the cameras, we set off. We drove out via an oldish and shabby district with, all the same, some beautiful *"Sezession"* type buildings with Pierre and Vanyo describing some of the most important. Vanyo filled up the Moskvich with petrol. This, his "donkey" – the ultimate beast of burden – was known affectionately as 'Daisy' and he told us that he had been asked: "Did you build it yourself or did someone help you?" which, now that I still see Trabants in the streets of Sofia, must say something about the automotive industry, then and now. We drove on through quite beautiful countryside, mountains on each side, stopping by a drinking fountain for a coffee in the car, surrounded by views of distant mountains: all was still, mauve-grey-brown and hardly green at all, except for some forsythia. Vanyo's driving, with which this was our first encounter, was strange and erratic (something I would experience many times again) but, about noon, round a bend, there was the majestic sight of Rila Monastery. Pierre, of course, must have visited Rila several times as a young man and he and Vanyo did their tour and Jeannie took me everywhere: the monastery, the church and the museum with the extraordinary carving of a crucifix and all the scenes of Jesus' life. We took many photos, had lunch in the Balkantourist hotel – a somewhat limited menu choice – and walked around the site, admiring the mountain views and the determination of those builders, preserving their faith in the mountain fastnesses, and also the limited extent to which the faith continued to be sanctioned, in the time of the 10th Congress of the Bulgarian Communist Party.

A perfect day: with good friends, visiting a national treasure set in breathtaking country scenery, continued with tea taken back in the Rumenovs' flat in Sofia before Pierre and I went back to the hotel to prepare for the evening's event: a very grand, yet warm and friendly, reception organised at his house by the great painter Detchko Ouzunov and his wife Olga. Again, this was something arranged in honour of Pierre; his dear good friends the Ouzunovs, in their amazing, art filled house. My diary tells me that the other guests were "ministers etc.". I wish I could remember which or who exactly... but certainly the arts and culture were represented. At another level altogether, there was a touching moment, I recall, when the butler, who had worked at the Ministry of Foreign Affairs at the time when Pierre was a diplomat, recognised him and the two men greeted each other so warmly! This was a marvellous evening, everyone keen to talk to Pierre, who felt truly welcomed and acknowledged in his home country by people he had grown up with and with whom, having never grown distant, he could now be close again.

Tuesday just had to be more relaxed... Pierre and I walked around Sofia in the morning and towards midday Ivan Slavkov came to collect us at the hotel where, by chance, we saw Mr. Tsenko, the 'Illusionist', who was pleased to show us several 'tricks'. After the "illusions", we drove, together with Olga Ouzunova, to the 'Writers' House' at Borovetz, a lovely location for inspiration to be called up... later to be turned into some kind of 'sleepover' place and, more recently, I believe, given over to a more capitalist venture. Pierre had the pleasure of talking with some of the writers who were then in residence. We lunched in the village with Ivan and Olga at what was then considered to be a rather large hotel, and the best, the *Eidelweiss*, now completely outsized by the mammoth new ones in this ski resort. Lunch on the terrace in the spring sunshine was perfect. On our return to Sofia we visited

Samokov and had a chance to see the lovely mosque. An evening with Pierre's mother and aunts followed when, again, we were treated to the very best that their modest means could prepare. Kind, generous, unstinting people who had, of course, suffered not a little from Pierre's leaving his diplomatic post in London.

A late-ish morning on Wednesday as, at 11h30 Ivo Hadjimishev, young (then) son of our dear friends Annie and Misho, came to the hotel accompanied by Pierre's first wife Ivaila Vulkova (yes, Pierre was a very generous spirited person...) and we all went for a walk, meeting people en route, before going for lunch at *Budapest*, until quite recently a splendidly old-fashioned place to eat; now surely a less "Happy" place to "Eat" than before?

A proper siesta followed the excellent food and excited talk and it was not until about 6 p.m. that we went to Alexander Nevski with Karl and Lina Ognyanov and then had coffee and cakes with them. Lina made sure to tell my 'fortune' in the coffee grounds. However the fortune then foretold turned out, it was a fascinating life that I enjoyed with Pierre. We later went by car, invited by Pavel Matev – concerned for "Bulgarians Abroad" – to dine on the slopes of Vitosha at the *Vodenitza* restaurant.

My diary tells me that, on Thursday morning, Pierre was "with people". He mostly was but, in this instance, nobody in particular is specified. No secrets, for sure, just that I probably could not remember all the different people, positions and names... I seem to have gone walking in Sofia, taking photos until midday. When Pierre got back we went with Karl and Lina to Boyana where we were able to visit the church. How lucky I was, since it was subsequently closed for so long, to see something of the extraordinary 13th century wall paintings, now so beautifully restored. We had a relaxed lunch at the delightful *Boyana Hanche* and I feel so privileged and happy that I was able to have such warm and empathetic relationships with these people, friends from Pierre's youth, some of whom I had already met during their visits to London: Karl, Vanyo, Ivo ... and now meeting their families. Mid afternoon saw us making our way back to the city centre for Pierre to visit his mother, while Annie Hadjimisheva came to take me for tea at their flat – another perfect period piece: furniture, pictures, piano... Pierre joined us later with Vera Netkova, whose painting he much admired. She recently had an excellent exhibition at the National Gallery in Sofia which I had the pleasure of seeing. It is also good to know that, at the suggestion of Svetlin Roussev, her workplace apartment has now been transformed into a "House Museum" that one can visit.

Friday offered some "local colour" experiences for me: Ivo took me to the Women's Market where I was able to see the range of goods on offer, from pottery to live animals. I bought some of the former and was photographed by Ivo with some of the latter, a lively rabbit, as I recall. We took a coffee and drank in the colours and noise; then went to meet our lunch companions, Tzvetan and Antoineta Tzvetanov, at the Writers' Club. Such a nice, albeit exclusive, idea: to have a pleasant social environment to be enjoyed by people sharing the same interests. During our two-week stay we experienced this positive atmosphere – food, drink and talk... somewhat less of the first, great quantities of the second and third – in the Journalists' and Artists' Clubs as well. Later I went with Lina and Jeannie to the cathedral. These days one would no doubt make a visit to the national icon collection, housed in the crypt. At that time, however, the collection had not been brought together nor the crypt developed to accommodate these artistic and religious riches. Progressively, and under the strong, wise and far-sighted guidance of the then Minister of Culture, Ludmila Zhivkova, Bulgaria has achieved a serious position in the domain of culture, although it is very sad that the majority of people in the west who show any interest in the country come more for cheap, wine-fuelled holidays and cheap property acquisition. On the matter of culture and the seventies, let it only be said that it was due to Minister Zhivkova, ably assisted by Professor Alexander Fol, that the British Museum hosted the exceptional exhibition of Thracian treasures in 1976. It is of course a matter of some regret, at least to those who love culture – if not to those who place Mammon first – that the National Palace of Culture, built to commemorate 1,300 years of the Bulgarian state, should have now been largely turned into such a shoddy commercial venue. Enough of my views…

Saturday, a whole week since I arrived in Bulgaria, so many visits and impressions, places and people… and, after a relaxed morning, Ivo and Ivaila joined us to go for lunch at the Bulgaria Hotel where we met the actor Stefan Getzov (Bulgaria's Laurence Olivier, I was told) and so the talk at the meal was of theatre, plays, productions in London and Sofia and of actors.

We later went for tea – and there was always a cake! – with

Pierre's mother. My diary tells me that we "walked back to the hotel"; a good idea to have the chance to walk off some of the immense amounts of food we seem to have taken in! Vanyo brought over the photos which he had taken on Vitosha and at Rila and which he had developed; mounted in a tooled leather-covered album to which I am referring while recalling some of these events. He took us in his car to our next "social engagement": tea with the Miroslav Mindov and his wife, sweet people, another theatrical family later to visit us in London, in their pleasant apartment in a most unsightly block but with the advantage of a splendid view over the Mosque, the Market Halls and the Synagogue.

We went for dinner with Vanyo and his wife to the *'Russian Club' Krim* (now virtually my next door neighbour on Slavianska...how could I have ever imagined? But now rather

too "smart" and too expensive for the casual friendly meal…). It was the place for old-world charm, not a little threadbare, but with a good selection of food and wine. I have seen it go further downhill before being closed recently for some while, undergoing a thorough make-over and, no doubt, a sifting of the clientele. The evening could not, however, end without going back to the Rumenovs' cosy book-filled flat, in a house now completely overshadowed by the gigantic *Rodina* hotel, and joined by his sister "for coffee and cakes until 3a.m." How did we stand the pace?!

A little peace on Sunday for the wicked…whereas Vanyo came for Pierre at around 10a.m., I stayed in the hotel until we were due to go for lunch with the Hadjimishevs. A relaxed, friendly, "Sunday lunch" after which we all four wrote a postcard (one still did in those distant days…) to Jonathan and Kathie Griffin.

From the Hadjimishevs' flat on Graf Ignatiev with its view

out over Patriarch Evtimi (the statue and the street), we walked easily to our next appointment: Poli and Vena Spassov and their flat on Boulevard Bulgaria. They were a sweet and gentle couple, he a writer and a long-standing friend of Pierre's.

By then I was just beginning to unravel who was who among those friends of Pierre's from the old days. Generally they were not permitted to travel abroad unless attending a professional and approved conference or with an organised travel group, for they were seen as belonging to a different world from others, ministers, party members, "top brass"…However, it was not always easy to reconcile, for example, tea with the Spassovs and, later, a dinner at the *Ropotamo* restaurant and I know that I occasionally put a foot seriously wrong. Nowadays I wouldn't care: if people are decent, right-thinking and open-minded and, importantly, genuinely appreciative of Pierre and all that he always did to promote Bulgarian culture and to bring a knowledge of world culture to Bulgaria over the airwaves, then I will always speak positively of them, whatever the perceived "background".

At the very upper bracket *Ropotamo* on Tsarigradsko Shosse, now reduced to a rusty iron and concrete shell, we were dined by, among others, the "Minister of Trade". (I would need to check who it was who held the post at that moment.) Among the guests were Ludmila Zhivkova and Emi Damianova and we all moved on for drinks at Ludmila and Ivan's apartment, where we stayed until midnight.

Plovdiv scenes and people

Monday 29th was to be the day we went to Plovdiv, at the invitation of people in the arts. This gave Pierre a chance to meet up with friends from school days and even to visit his old school building situated not far from the big main square. We left Sofia in pouring rain and, on arrival, checked in to the huge, gloomy, Soviet-style *Trimontium* hotel. A suite, with huge armchairs in uncut moquette, brown carpets and beige wallpaper, an enormous television set, a large and completely tiled bathroom. The painters of the "Plovdiv group", Ionny Leviev and Christo Stefanov, came for lunch with us at the hotel, after which we visited their studios; a marvellous, Parisian ambiance. We looked at paintings, canvases, work in progress; Pierre talked, they listened and talked. A lovely atmosphere. It has been a great pleasure to keep in touch with the two painters, visiting Ionny's last exhibition at the Katy gallery in Sofia before his death some ten years ago, and with Christo and his charming actress wife Maria who have both attended some of the commemorative events we have organised for Pierre. After the studio visit we walked around the Old Town, admiring the houses on the cobbled streets, the museums and galleries, taking in the feeling of old Plovdiv. Pierre stayed on at the Ethnographic Museum while I returned to the hotel to write my postcards until 8 p.m. Pierre and I then went together to the Ethnographic Museum for a meeting with writers and poets, readings and dinner.

Next day the rain continued, but Pierre was up at 7a.m. to see a school friend on his way to work. I well remember the times, through to the mid-eighties when, if you wanted to contact someone you would phone at about 6h15. Those were the days of "disciplined", extended working hours... now the rot of the West has set in and phoning at 8h45 is considered possibly too early. I did our packing and then went down to take breakfast in what was then an "oriental-style" cafe: old men sitting talking, smoking and playing chess or backgammon. Strong coffee, sweet cakes, ham and cheese constituted the breakfast. The *Trimontium*, nowadays "Under New Management", is luxuriously renovated, the top floor coffee lounge enjoying a fabulous view on all sides; the breakfast room offering a full spread, though still of course serving strong Turkish coffee.

Pierre went later to visit the studios again and I stayed in the hotel room, reminiscent of a set from an Anouilh play and, with the rain outside, listened to the direct broadcast of the

Proceedings of the XXIV Congress of the Communist Party of the Soviet Union. Not a wide choice of listening or viewing was at that time available... At noon we left to return to Sofia, Christo and Ionny accompanying us. We had lunch on the way at one of those small roadside pull-ins where one took pot luck with whatever food was being prepared that day, but which was always extremely tasty. Most of those have now of course disappeared (except for the lorry drivers' pull-ins near Ihtiman), to be replaced by the ubiquitous, and anything but tasty, Happy Eater. For me Plovdiv long remained something of a mystery. Subsequently, however, and especially since the excavation of the Roman theatre and with my academic links and many very good friends, Plovdiv has become for me a true City of Culture.

Back in Sofia we went for dinner, meeting up with two of Pierre's school friends, to the Balkan Hotel – now the Sheraton – where, I imagine, it was then as unlikely for "ordinary" people to be able to afford the prices in the restaurant as it is now. Only the type of customer has changed: a different type of elite with money and privileges. We were then, of course, one of the 'elite', the minority, in that we were Westerners and able to pay in hard currency. A particular kind of luxury denied to many of our "ordinary" friends, though not to others, it has to be said.

The following day saw us meeting old friends, Ivo escorting Ivaila Vulkova to the hotel. I, as a "second wife" – and indeed Pierre – was seeing rather a lot of "the first wife"... We had coffee and then went and lunched with Vanyo Rumenov and the Spassovs at the Russian Club, relaxing after the days spent in Plovdiv. The evening was a very pleasant one, spent with Jenny and Nikolai Haitov, both very close friends of Pierre's and, increasingly mine too. They had a lovely apartment in a newish block on Latinka Street. Jenny, a warm approachable person with a perfect command of English, I knew from her translation of Robert Graves' *I, Claudius*; Nikolai, probably because we could not really communicate, I always remained in awe of, but with Pierre there was such a warmth and closeness, both personal and in relation to their writings, that any and all potential awkwardnesses, caused by the then regime of close control and censorship, were overcome and the two men remained in close contact, by letter and publication and, more recently, literary award until their death.

Our penultimate day in Bulgaria brought me a new experience: with Jeannie Rumenova I went to have my hair done. Jeannie took me to her hairdresser and, of course, was there to ensure I made myself understood and didn't come out shaved, permed or coloured... What I do remember is that this was the first time I had ever had beer used as a setting lotion but, upon later examination, I learned that it is the sugar content of beer that ensures a good, holding hair set. Anyhow, I am sure I came out looking good for our first engagement of the day: lunch with minister Goshkin. He was an absolutely charming, well-travelled and amusing man who, I have been told, as a matter of modesty and discretion, changed his real name from Georgi Dimitrov to Goshkin. We went by car to his office on Dondukov (these distances now seem so short to me as I like to walk almost everywhere in the centre of Sofia, such a human-scale city). The building was previously that of a German bank, all black marble interiors. There was the usual serving of the "the 3 Cs": coffee, cognac and cola; much talk and greetings from different members of his staff before we set off to pick up his wife whom I noted as "smiley and nice". We went for lunch to *Vodenitzata* restaurant on Vitosha where the spring sunshine made it a delight with much vegetation now in bud or bloom. After lunch I went shopping for some presents for friends in England. The State craftshops had a surprising range of ceramic brooches, pendants and other items, often with a historical theme. These would prove unusual and very typical.

A literary evening

In the evening we were invited to the home of the playwright Georgi Jagarov, whose play *The Public Prosecutor* was presented at the Hampstead Theatre in London. Jagarov was one of the top ranked literary figures and a person whom Pierre had known well, whose work he had kept abreast of over the years and with whom, it was natural, he would wish to talk and exchange ideas and news of the London theatre and literary scene. These were always fascinating encounters: a warm intimacy in a home and the deep and wide-ranging conversations on so many subjects and, except by his aunts, I do not believe that any political comments or judgments were ever made. We ate in some 'm*ehana*' and afterwards, another first, went to a nightclub, the '*Astoria*' (located, I think, in what is now the '*Tabu*' club 21h – 04h, with many enticing photos of young ladies and an imposing 'bouncer', opposite the Austrian Embassy Residence. At least from there we would not have had more than a couple of minutes' walk back to the hotel!).

It seems the night did not take too much of a toll as Pierre was ready for early meetings with Donchev of the Puppet Theatre, about which he had broadcast in 1969 during their appearance at the Edinburgh Festival, and others who wished to see him. It was my birthday and many kind friends brought presents for me to the hotel, but we were to save up festivities for the evening. Pierre went with his mother to the cemetery to visit his father's grave (the family one in which, now, both he and his mother are buried). We both went to have a final tea-time visit to his mother's apartment. Being able to visit her at last in her own home had been such a moving experience for Pierre. The evening was split, although not deliberately, into two parts: at 8 p.m we were invited for dinner with Ludmila and Ivan at their apartment where the Traikovs were also guests. This was a dinner on one level: political, yet personal, with many subjects of conversation especially on the matter of cultural policy. At 11 p.m., back at the hotel, our friends Vanyo and Jeannie Rumenov together with Karl and Lina Ognyanov, other professionals and friends from childhood, came to wish us the warmest of farewells. These were people who, despite certain setbacks, due in part to family background and political non-allegiances, had made successful advances in their careers and always remained good and dignified people.

We had to be up early on Saturday for last-minute packing. Pierre met with his very good friend Bigor, the cinematographer who, to my great pleasure, still attends the events that we organise in Pierre's memory in Sofia, a lovely man. My diary tells me that Pierre "changed money". I am puzzled as to which currency may have been changed into which and why, on the last day. Was it to pay the hotel? Did we have to pay in hard currency? Ironic, really, now that all prices are quoted in euros, having displaced the dollar.

Pierre and I were now on our way, we in one car and the suitcases in another, quite the regal train! I took a last look at Vitosha (the view that always gives pleasure when driving to the centre on arriving in Sofia!). All our friends made the special effort to come and give us a magnificent VIP send off. Karl, Vanyo, Jeannie, Vladi, Tzvetan and Antoineta, Poli Spassov and Goshkin, with presents and flowers, in the VIP lounge – no customs, no passport formalities – coffee, cognac and cola and many toasts, to friendship and to more meetings, wherever that may be. Take off was about 9h15, the plane very crowded, no stopover in Brussels.

Back at home in Chelsea we re-created Bulgaria. What an extraordinary two weeks in another world!

* * * *

An English interlude

It is almost impossible to believe (but my diary says so and therefore it must be true!) but the following day, and a Sunday at that, I was up at 6h15 to drive down to Eastbourne to attend the Easter School of Philosophy, leaving Pierre to relax, reflect and talk to friends about his quite extraordinary three-week stay in Bulgaria. About a week later, having settled back into a

"London life", we were ready to invite our friends Jonathan and Kathie to come across for dinner and for tales of Bulgaria, friends, activities, painters and poets.

It may have been the idea of possibly making a film in Bulgaria, or perhaps just on-going film plans, that induced Pierre to leave for Paris and meet Carlo Ponti. That was on July 16th, and I, juggling teaching days, followed on Saturday morning. Apart from this, of course, the weekend offered the perfect opportunity to tell Dora, Luben and their son Pierre-Christian all about our stay in Bulgaria. For Dora the best must have been hearing from Pierre about their mother; from me they were probably interested to hear an "outsider's" view. We showed masses of photos and talked and talked. It was also a great pleasure to be back in Paris, such a beautiful, civilised city, and I walked along the Quais and in the Latin Quarter while Pierre and Ponti "talked cinema". The weekend was over all too quickly and on Sunday evening we flew back from Orly. A moment of professional reckoning came up for me towards the end of April. Encouraged by the work I had been doing with the Art Teachers Diploma course at the Institute of Education together with the philosophy course, I had applied for a senior post in the department of Art Education at Goldsmiths' College. This, of course, would have been a complete change from the Languages work (although I had been following the two paths for several years), but I felt ready for this and it would also have been a move nearer to Pierre's work in reviewing art exhibitions for the Arts Review and teaching courses at Chelsea and Croydon Schools of Art. The interview appeared to go well but there was strong competition for this post and, some days later, I learned that I had not been appointed. I would have to continue the art studies in a more "amateur" capacity!

May, June and July offered a rich tapestry of visits, lectures, friends, opera. Several Bulgarians now coming over to visit us! Marin Goleminov was in London (he gave Pierre records of all his compositions, recordings which I have now returned to

Sofia as part of Pierre's collection and '*memorabilia*') and went with Pierre to the opera at Glyndebourne; two days later we gave a dinner party for him, inviting our musical and operatic friends. Aldo Ceccato was also in London to conduct *Otello* at Covent Garden. It was at this time that Pierre was to hear from Gerald Savory, Head of Plays and Drama at BBCtv, that their joint project with the Bulgarian authorities and Christo Santov, for a production of *As You Like It* was, for financial and other reasons, not to go ahead. As Savory wrote: "I am sorry...I know you have been to a great deal of trouble..." and this must have been a disappointment for all concerned.

To add to all Pierre's interests and activities, one most unusual event took place in May: he was asked to "model" for an advertisement for Martell brandy. The advertising agency obviously knew a man of taste and distinction! The enormous hoardings were on show all over London for at least six weeks.

Operatic events

On 13th May (and I sit with the programme in front of me!), together with Grigor, we attended the first of five performances of *Boris Godunov* which were to be the last in which Boris Christoff was to take the principal role (to be replaced, in the 1974 series at Covent Garden, by Nikolai Ghiaurov). With Edward (Ted) Downes conducting, this was a star performance with a star cast: Joseph (Joe) Rouleau as Pimen, Josephine Veasey as Princess Marina and Kiri Te Kanawa, singing for the first time in 1971 at Covent Garden, as Xenia among many other well known singers. After congratulating the cast, we dined afterwards with Boris Christoff and Ted Downes (still conducting in his eighties!). Talk was of opera!

At the weekend we went down to stay with Eliana and Aldo Ceccato and their two boys at the house they had taken at Barcombe in Sussex while he was conducting at Glyndebourne with Misho Hadjimishev producing. What glorious countryside, everywhere covered with bluebells, and we sat in their garden enjoying the sunshine and, later, with other Bulgarians, went over to the theatre for drinks, to see "work in progress". How quickly a lovely weekend passes! During the next week I had a problem with my back and stayed off work and also our usual social engagements, one of which was an invitation to dine at the house of Pashanko Dimitroff. Pierre went with (I note in my diary) Ivaila Vulkova. Truly, the Bulgarians were now coming over to us! What had we set in motion?! The next day I was still unable to move, but Pierre, with Jonathan and Kathie, and Jeremy Noble (the early music specialist) in my place, went down in the afternoon to Glyndebourne for the dress rehearsal of *Queen of Spades*. I was very sorry to miss that as I had so much enjoyed the performance we saw a few years previously in Frankfurt on our return from Salzburg.

A few days later it would appear that we arranged a dinner at home to which Misho was invited, together with Chavdar

Damianov (in both his friendly and his "cultural attaché" capacity) and Ivaila. The accepted British habit of current wives behaving impeccably to previous ones would seem to have been tested to extreme limits (I must say that I am pleased and proud to be British for I am told that open animosity is the more frequent reaction in Bulgaria...). A couple of days later Pierre went to see her off at Victoria Station. With regard to visits from Bulgarians, it was an enormous pleasure to greet dear Jeannie Rumenova who had managed to get herself included in a group travelling to England for a week. These were highly organised affairs, carefully supervised and usually for members of a professional body. Fortunately, as well as seeing her at the hotel where the group was staying, in Queen's Gate near the Bulgarian Embassy, we were able to "free" her to come over and spend time with us on a couple of occasions. Her group had several excursions arranged and normally stayed together as a group ('*sus grupata*'; it was the only way to travel abroad in those days).

Enough of Bulgarians... our London life continued: work, visits, friends, theatre, end of term parties. It was also the time of year when Pierre was invited to take part in a *Brains Trust* at the 'Q' theatre where he so enjoyed working with the students, several of whom were later to achieve prominence on stage, screen or television. I, meanwhile, had applied for another new job: as Modern Languages programmes producer at the BBC which, of course, would have secured me firmly in the languages area of my activities. Despite my own view of my interview performance and encouragement from Pierre and colleagues, I was to prove unsuccessful in this. Never mind, their loss... and I could continue with the range of things that I enjoyed doing.

A family visit

Summer, and the holidays, brought us other visitors and, in particular, our nephew Pierre-Christian for whom I had arranged an exchange stay with the brother of one of my students. They were to spend two weeks in each other's home. We picked him up at Heathrow (no convenient Eurostar in those days!) and spent a day in London before driving up to Coventry for the weekend as Pierre was to attend the opening of an exhibition of sculptures by his friend Witold Kavalec. (Visitors to Markham Street will know the lovely, tactile piece of cream coloured alabaster on the table in the sitting room.) The exhibition, for whose catalogue introduction Pierre wrote:

"Kawalec becomes Coventry: the dignity of the setting is matched by the integrity of the artist"

was in conjunction with the re-dedication at Coventry cathedral, for which Graham Sutherland had designed the splendid tapestry. We had a marvellous couple of days, visiting Warwick Castle where the peacocks obediently opened their fan tails for us and going to a matinee performance of *Twelfth Night* at the theatre in Stratford-on-Avon. Some very 'English' experiences for a Bulgaro-French boy! Back in London he was also exercising his English, spending time with my friend Pamela's son Peter. Shopping was not forgotten either and a week later he went off by train to Bristol. Not much was heard about the stay with Gareth but we heard that, on the exchange leg in France, Gareth, no doubt a very typical young English boy, absolutely refused even to taste most French dishes...

To Russia with plans

In early August, and in a very literary context, we had the pleasure of an evening at the home of Baroness Moura Budberg, mistress of Tolstoy, H.G.Wells and others. What a recreation of a pre-revolutionary St. Petersburg apartment! As indeed was the other guest, John Gielgud, with his beautiful 'theatrical' voice and stories! There is a very Russian connection to this social occasion since, and these things were always a last-minute surprise, Carlo Ponti seemed suddenly, finally to have decided about the project for filming *Anna Karenina* in the Soviet Union. (The 'treatment', or '*sceneggiatura televisiva*', with Sophia Loren in the title role, as written in Italian by Pierre for Ponti is in front of me now.) And so it was that, on 3rd August, Pierre flew out of Heathrow for Moscow. Never a dull moment in our lives… One or two appointments kept me from joining him there until the 7th when he had arranged my ticket, teasing me and making me guess with which airline, telling me I would definitely be the tallest passenger by several heads, until I guessed correctly that it was with the delightful Japanese Airlines.

This was the first time I had flown from Terminus 3 "Intercontinental" as the flight was to Tokyo. We took off in torrential rain, glad not to be going on to typhoon-struck Japan and crossing fingers that Moscow would be fine. We were wished "a most pleasant flight", which indeed it was. In first class (the advantages of associating with film makers!) I chose the "Japanese lunch". The stewardess, sweet and smiling in kimono, offered fans, hot flannels and slippers (I may still have them… everyone knows that neither Pierre nor I ever threw anything away… thank heavens, I say, since I have access to so much '*memorabilia*'!). I had a window seat but it was mostly cloudy as we flew over the Baltic, the bottom of Sweden with the top of Denmark coming briefly into view. After a very short-seeming flight we were "arriving at Moscow Sheremetovo" airport. All was very straightforward at what was then a very small airport. I saw Pierre even before the baggage came up; everything was so informal that I could even hand over to him my coat and umbrella; hardly believable today! I was introduced to Paolo, Ponti's Russian-speaking film business negotiator, and Sandra, his wife. Paolo seemed to be able to come through and to help me with my – as ever – mountains of luggage. It looked as if the customs officer was not very civil, checking everyone for gold objects, money, fruit… but he did appear to believe me and didn't open my bags as he had for the American woman in front of me. A poor Indian behind me got pushed away to make room for "a group"!

I had arrived at 19h35 Moscow time but Pierre, Paolo and Sandra had only just about finished lunch followed by a "Dostoevsky-inspired" walk in the country.

A room with a view

When I think about it, the amount of walking we did in Russia never ceases to astonish me, especially as Pierre became increasingly anti-long walks and pro-car drives. Paolo had an *Intourist* hire car and with all my luggage and us finally inside, we drove the twenty or so kilometres to the centre of Moscow and the hotel along *ulitsa Gorkovo*. On our arrival at the hotel there were the passport and visa check-in formalities. This was in the enormous, palatial-style entrance hall, all grey-black marble and wood. We took the lift up to what Pierre was told, and which, with its view, most definitely was, "the best room in Moscow". Number 2022 on the 20th floor with two large double windows on two sides, penthouse style. From the sitting room side right out directly over the Kremlin, all the churches, the three towers of one wall, the Lenin mausoleum in direct line, the Historical Museum, over Revolution Square to Red Square, St. Basil's church at the end (and the hateful new *Gostinitsa Rossiya*, for which three old churches were demolished) and GUM, 1887 and glass-panelled, domed, arcades and roof, to the left. To the right the Moscow river, the University and skyscraper blocks. This is all really amazing! And this in a hotel that was then only and simply called *Gostinitsa Intourist*! I have no doubt that the film budget paid a good price even then for such a magnificent suite, but can hardly speculate on how much such accommodation would now cost in today's "rich Russia"!

After unpacking, we changed ready to go out and eat when, at

21h., the lights came on illuminating the Kremlin, the Lenin Mausoleum and St. Basil. What a fantastic sight! Leaving the key at the "floor desk", we saw women intently watching television; it was *The Forsyte Saga*, good to know there was some cultural crossover. It was not dubbed or even sub-titled but with a Russian male voice overlay, the English still audible. We went around the corner of Revolution Square to eat in the National Hotel restaurant, in the "foreign currency" room. This was the privilege accorded then to foreigners with hard currency; now, of course, both nationals and foreigners can eat or stay at the National but only if they are millionaires in any currency! We later went to the studio of a painter friend of Paolo's. This was in the inner courtyard of a big old building. The studio, semi-basement, with large pieces of antique furniture, was crammed with interesting paintings, some illustrations of Sholom Aleichem and some stage sets. Everyone was speaking Russian and, although I was introduced to the painter, I paid little attention at the time but, since those days, Yuri Kuperman has made his way first to Israel and later to the West, become Yuri Kuper, exhibited in England and now lives in France. We followed his travels and development with interest as we bought a beautiful ink sketch of Pushkin which still hangs in our Chelsea house. All of this activity, until past midnight, and it was only my day of arrival!

Discovering Moscow

The next day, Sunday, we had intended to spend the day driving out into the country to visit a monastery and see the icons but, at 11h30, we saw Paolo downstairs at the rent-a-car desk and learned that the car had been stolen during the night. So, instead, we walked around Red Square, looking at the second-hand bookstalls and flower sellers and joined the queue to visit the Lenin Mausoleum. Interestingly, the police put the taller of any two people to the right and so there was some hesitation because, although I am the woman, Pierre was shorter; what to do? Inside was the reverential silence, Lenin under a huge glass case, black marble walls with red, flamelike, insets. All was quickly over as they moved you on, kept you in line and quiet, and out again, to the living and the heat! Back around the square and St. Basil's cathedral and then lunch. We decided on the *Metropol*, first looking at the incredible nineteenth-century décor before sneaking a table on the terrace. The waitress told us certain things were "only for breakfast", others "not on" and so we ended up with a mixture of mixed cold fish and kefir. Shortages in supply and availability, combined with the need to pay in hard currency, began to make for interesting meals. After the walk, the meal, Lenin and the heat, it was time for an extended siesta. Later, when it was cooler, we all went for a long walk along *Gorkovo* and exploring interesting-looking side streets with low, decorated nineteenth century houses, of which, I noted at the time, "fewer and fewer remain". How many more may sadly have been destroyed during the "new capitalism" rebuilding of Moscow! Back to the *Metropol*, the only place still open at about 10p.m., to the '*Tchainaya*' (Tea Room) for, as well as lemon tea, blini with caviar. People of all nationalities were eating here, since you must pay in '*valuta*', and we spoke to a charming Moroccan doctor.

Monday, and we were supposed to be here to work ... but as there was still no replacement car, we decided to benefit from being in this extraordinary city. We went to the Kremlin and visited the magnificent churches, now museums; past the old University, across to the *Manege*. We were lucky to find a taxi, and Paolo took us to a Georgian restaurant where he successfully queue-jumped, no doubt telling the others waiting that we were important foreign magnates – which, of course, we were! In a basement painted with murals of Soviet life, we consumed an enormous and delicious lunch: fish and chicken in strange nutty sauces, hot and cold cheese, strange and delicious salads, pork *shashlik*, ice cream and Turkish coffee, leaving at 3p.m. and walking back to the hotel. In the late afternoon Carlo Ponti phoned, no doubt to see if we were actually doing anything or seeing anybody related to the *Anna Karenina* project. In the evening we went to visit another painter friend of Paolo's, Groman, whose studio was similar to the one we visited the first evening of my stay. Here we met a fascinating group of painters, poets and teachers and Pierre was well able to join in the lively intellectual conversation.

Some work to be done

On Tuesday Pierre and Paolo made their phone call to Ponti about contacts, writers, a studio, the accounts...so at least something seemed to be starting. I went out to visit St. Basil's and to enjoy Moscow generally and then to GUM, down one of the transversal passages under the splendid nineteenth-century 'Crystal Palace' type glass domed roof. I had a delicious ice cream, the first and only, I think, that I have had with gooseberries. At least there was no need to speak during the transaction! Then back to the hotel. Here, late in the afternoon, we met a scriptwriter (of *Ballad of a Soldier*) and Pierre and Paolo spent time discussing the Ponti project. Valentin came with his girlfriend Vika, an actress, and this time we went to eat at an Armenian restaurant. Another amazing meal, plus music and dances. Pierre got on marvellously well with Valentin, knowing all his films and of course having his own highly placed Bulgarian film contacts. The meal in the restaurant went on until 11h30 p.m. when we went by car to where *Mosfilm* were filming in a motel outside Moscow. Pierre spent about half an hour on the set talking and, after midnight, we drove back to Moscow with the director. This was another long, full, fascinating and exciting day in a world that felt outside the world.

On the night train

The next day was to be our last in Moscow until after our trip to Leningrad and it was a chance to visit the Tretyakov Gallery.

Not quite as large as the Hermitage which we were to visit later but still quite daunting! After lunch we had to pack and be ready to take the night train. Later, we met up with Paolo and Sandra who were with Valentin, a musician who had composed the music for 'War and Peace' and a French-speaking director. They all played poker until it was time to leave. We took taxis from the hotel to the '*Leningradski Vokzal*' for the '*Krasnaya Strela*' night train. There were trains, on other platforms, going to '*Arktika*' and to Turkey, very romantic and exotic, I thought. We found a most helpful porter for all our baggage but, since our Georgian contact, Teneshvili, had not yet turned up, we did not know into which carriage to load them. With minutes to spare he arrived and we went to our carriage, right at the end of the train! There is something about travelling by train, especially at night, and when it is in Russia...! The compartments were for four people but Pierre and I had the only one for two. We woke to a "northern" landscape of pines, birch trees and wooden houses at around 7 a.m. Pierre shaved, on a rolling train, in what can't have been hot water and without a towel in a malodorous railway toilet. We then had tea from a Russian-rail type samovar, secured in a wooden-fronted corridor cupboard, before arriving in Leningrad at 8h25a.m. There was military music playing over the loudspeakers at the station (to welcome us? to hearten us?) all very morale boosting!

Our companion Teneshvili, a chubby, large, laughing Georgian, was the director of *Sovexfilm* and it was with him that connections with Ponti had been made for the film project. He was to be our guide and had organised a *Tchaika* to pick us all up at '*Moskovski Vokzal*'. We drove through an already-better-than-Moscow Leningrad to '*Gostinitza Evropeiskaya*' ("restored 1834"!), all marble columns and bronze, nothing comparable in London; Paris yes. Yet another hotel we had the pleasure and privilege of enjoying in 1971 (with rooms on the '*bel étage*') and which, today, would cost a fortune for just one night! We had a huge breakfast on the 5th floor in the "Hall for Individual Tourists" and met Teneshvili at 10 a.m. for a tour of Leningrad by car. The beauty of the city simply takes your breath away: the enormous eighteenth-century baroque palaces in seaweed green and white, chrome yellow and white, aquamarine and white, pink and white...the Neva, canals and ironwork bridges everywhere. This, of course, was where the filming was to take place and we were being taken to and shown some of the possible scenes and interiors. We went to the Winter Palace and, leaving the Tchaika, walked, looked, admired...all in the rain.

Lenfilm

In the afternoon we went visiting palaces and, especially, the interiors with a view to finding appropriate places for filming. We were accompanied by a splendid white haired, seventy-year-old artist with a great sense of humour, Igor Nikolaevitch, who was the head of set painting at *Lenfilm*, and whose responsibility it was to advise about interiors. One particularly interesting visit for Pierre was to the Shuvalov palace, ancestral home of his good friend Paul (now Sheriff), the film designer. Back at the hotel we rested until going out for a long walk, the rain having finally stopped, as far as the Winter Palace, marvellously illuminated. Back down charming, quiet side-streets and canals and via Pushkin's last abode to the hotel. Another day full of new, marvellous and unexpected experiences.

Friday, and I had been in Russia nearly a week; it seemed longer, so full had the days been of interest, activity and novelty. Pierre had placed a call to Ponti and he and Paolo were downstairs with people from *Sovexfilm* discussing business and so Sandra and I decided to go shopping. A universal activity but something of a novelty, at least for me, in the Soviet Union. We went to '*Univermag*', then one of the only possibilities, and bought a few small things. Somewhat to our surprise, the salesgirls were, on the whole, very pleasant, smiling and pretty. I was fascinated to see the army exercising and could have got a good photo had a woman and then two civilian men not verbally (and almost physically!) attacked me, telling me it was "*Verboten*" (why is a tall blond automatically German?) and that my camera would be thrown to the ground. At least I had an opportunity to attempt some Russian, in the most bizarre of situations. '*Univermag*' became too Kafka-esque in its repetition of stands and stalls and we went back to the hotel, having been addressed in a variety of languages by a variety of men.

The car was at the hotel to take us to the *Lenfilm* studios, which were quite far outside the city, in a vast wild type of park. We were accompanied by Igor Nikolaevitch, and a twenty-four-year-old English-speaking producer, the youngest in the Soviet Union, whose name my diary notes tell me only was 'Zhen'. A historical film was being made, complete with a whole '*Kursaal*' set and a station with a nineteenth-century train. Girls, extras no doubt, were sitting around, freezing cold. Again the director was splendid-looking with white hair and a stick. After the business talk we left the set and drove to visit Petrodvoretz. There was too long a queue to go in, so Pierre and I walked in the amazing park: the fountains, the cascades, the sculptures, the canal and down to the sea. I filmed Pierre against the sea at '*Monplaisir*', it seemed very appropriate! We visited the "Marine Study" of Peter the Great with the sextant, telescope and books on his desk. Outside, children were playing in the trick fountains and we walked in the park until it was time to return to the hotel for lunch at 4h45 p.m.! Pierre then went with Paolo and some others to basketball matches (my diary tells me: Czechoslovakia v. Yugoslavia and USSR v. Finland – of these only one remains an intact country!). They had to walk all the way back and at 11 p.m. we went with Teneshvili to Sadko for dinner.

Sightseeing

Saturday was again a delightful, indulgent mix of sightseeing (lovely for Pierre and me) and of genuinely searching for sets for the film project. We went to Pushkin, all blue and white beneath a bright blue sky. The palace was undergoing reconstruction, so we walked in the park and to the lake. By a canal we came upon two soldiers playing a strange, apparently very old and very popular, Russian game: with staffs or poles which they hurl horizontally from the shoulder to dislodge batons placed in certain patterns.

We went on to the '*Kameron*' pavilion with its beautiful parquet floors and also to the famous 'Agate Room' used, I believe, by the Nazis to store their motorcycles... The pavilion containing the coaches is surrounded by bronze busts of philosophers. Pierre photographed me with Plato! Ice creams (gooseberry again) were in order and then lunch in a small snack place before going on to Pavlovsk, yellow and white, but we did not go inside because of the weekend queues. We wandered along meandering paths and through fields of long grass until we came to a lake, where Teneshvili, Paolo and Sandra went rowing, while Pierre (not one for activity on water...) and I sat watching their occasional comings-into-view. All the walking we did must have been very good exercise but, in such heat, hard on the feet.

An extraordinary concert

In the evening there were more basketball matches and Paolo went on his own to watch Italy play. For us, however, the great joy and excitement was that Dean Reed, staying in the same hotel, had left us four tickets for his concert. The driver took us to the concert hall and, somewhat to my surprise, started removing things from the car, both inside and out: the battery, the windscreen wipers... and locked them in the boot. Not a thing I had ever seen in England. He then came in with us, using Paolo's ticket. We had very good seats and the house was absolutely packed with people standing in the aisles. At 8p.m. the show started. Dean Reed spoke a little Russian but had an interpreter and the show was perfectly designed for the audience, tugging at heartstrings and playing on all the emotions. He sang Russian and Cuban "revolutionary" songs: *Solidarnost, Mir i Druzhba*, anti-class and colour distinctions. The audience was in raptures, the applause deafening; it was the most perfectly composed programme of songs, together with slogans and all "Big Band" type although with a small scale orchestra of jazz and violins. This was a tailor-made show (OK, *schmaltz*...) presented by a consummate showman. For me, the crowning touch was – as regards audience reaction – the girls who, after every number, came up on stage with flowers and other gifts (I confess I thought it was a 'plant', part of the act, but no, it was entirely genuine). Some also asked him to autograph their programme. Dean kissed each girl and made some jokes. It was very well handled and incorporated into the act. At 9p.m. there was an interval and after the second part Sandra and I went backstage (concert "groupies" as well!) but, even after this proclamation of non-discrimination, our driver was not allowed by security to come with us. So unfair... Back to the hotel and Dean joined us all for dinner, together with Marina, his interpreter. She was a very interesting person who had worked with and for the London Symphony Orchestra when John Lill had performed and had been to Leeds as Russian interpreter for the piano competition. It was a pleasure, finally, to be able to introduce our driver to Dean! He spent some time signing autographs in the hotel and then six of us went up for a very pleasant dinner. The seating at table divided along linguistic lines with Dean speaking English, Paolo (back from the match), Pierre and Marina Russian. Dean Reed made a very strong impression on me with his strongly and genuinely held (albeit maybe misguided) views. Almost unknown in the West, such was his fame in the communist bloc that he was known as the "*Red Elvis*". It was with sadness that we learned, some years later, of his mysterious death in East Germany.

Sunday means church – worship or just visit – but under any circumstances, wearing trousers turned out to have been a mistake... But first we had to go to the post office for Teneshvili to send a telegram to Ponti, no doubt explaining how much (or possibly how little...) work had been done in the search for suitable sets, actors, directors. We then went to the 'Dostoevsky' church where, somewhat to our surprise, there were masses of people, but it seemed that of those who were there to worship, most were old or crippled, and mainly women. A funeral was taking place and others waiting. Many people seemed scandalized by my wearing trousers, pale-coloured to make matters even worse. What a change in 35 years when, now, "anything goes", even in church! In the necropolis we paid our homage to Dostoevsky, Tchaikovsky and others and then went on – every day a sightseeing day – to the *Petropavlovskaya Krepost* where the church reminded us of our German tour in 1965 with its south German baroque, gilded to the very roof! We did not visit the fortress as there were far too many people and, after his experiences of internment during the war, Pierre had always had a phobia about fortresses. We spent Teneshvili's last evening in Leningrad in a Caucasian restaurant of his choosing and then, on leaving, he was accosted by a drunk and, with my heart in my mouth, I watched as Pierre intervened in what might well have turned very nasty, but it seemed that his diplomatic training paid off and we were able to accompany Teneshvili to the station for his return on the night train to Moscow.

Monday began to feel like a real work day although, since there was no car for us in the morning, Pierre and I went shopping; so much more interesting than in Moscow. In second hand shops there was furniture, porcelain and rugs to die for but I restricted myself to the transportable: in a little shop on *Nevski Prospekt* a set of 6 plates with views of St. Petersburg (which hang in my house until today) and a Meissen dish which adorns my desk. Pierre, on the other hand, bought as many books as he was able to carry at an antiquarian bookshop near to the Winter Palace. We have always set great store by these "souvenirs" but I do wonder if the little shops where we found such treasures are not now expensive boutiques... After lunch at the hotel we went by car to visit "interiors": the Teachers' House on the canal but it was closed (even for us!) on account of an international conference on climatology (a word which, at the time I note, I found an incomprehensible neologism!); the Composers' House, the Marriage Palace (where we did actually witness one), the Writers' House ("closed for reconstruction") and the Pioneers' Palace. In a "totally" ordered world, what ordered luxury for each profession to have a special place to meet, talk, relax.

Some working meetings

In a world where time, appointments, arrangements... began to appear flexible, to say the least, we were collected at 8 p.m. to go to the studios of *Lenfilm* for the projection of two films, each featuring the same excellent actress. At last, something resembling the aim of the visit? Pierre was able to discuss the Ponti project with the film crew and, I think, began to see things take shape. After two films and dinner at the studio, it was well after midnight by the time we got back to the hotel. Several years before, Pierre had already nicknamed me *Otetz Paissi* for the long and late hours that I took in keeping a journal. Despite the teasing, I am always happy to be able to look back and read through my notes, descriptions and sketches of such interesting and enjoyable times; such a privilege to have been able to share them with Pierre.

Tuesday and the visit became more focused: the technical director of *Lenfilm*, Josef Alexander, was to take Pierre to the studios and, of course, I wanted to go with them. An enormous and fascinating site: cranes, lights, cameras, dubbing and re-recording rooms, various sets. After the technical visit and discussions, we went to a projection room for a showing of a Russian *Anna Karenina*, a massively cut and not very convincing version. Hopefully there will be an audience for the Ponti version! In an interval we went to see the animal enclosure and

Pierre stroked a peaceable two-year-old lion and the keeper brought me a four month old bear who sucked at each of my fingers! Back into the screening room and it was a showing of *Uncle Vanya* with Innokenti Smoktunovski and Sergei Bondartchyuk. After this real film work, we went for dinner to the *Astoria* which, I noted, was "nicer than the *Evropeiskaya*". Would that, these days, I could afford even a coffee at either!

Mixing work with pleasure, we spent Wednesday morning at the Hermitage: what a cultural feast; but where to start and how to proceed? We saw Russian, English and, particularly, French Impressionists, Monet, Degas and some marvellous Sisleys. A complicated process to find the post-Impressionists: down one flight, back through a million galleries, down again and...hidden away were Derain, Marquet, Vlaminck and, in a sunburst of colour, Matisse. Finally, two rooms, but badly lit, of very interesting Picassos of various periods. And to think: I would have been allowed to take photos, but did not have the camera with me! This was a real treat at the end of a mentally and physically exhausting morning. I should imagine, or at least hope, that the collections and galleries have since undergone some radical re-ordering. It is, anyhow, a great joy to know that, given the enormous size of the holdings, parts of the Hermitage collection are now regularly exhibited in London.

In the early evening we went again to *Lenfilm* where we stayed for three and a half hours watching (or, in my case, mostly sleeping through) *The Brothers Karamazov* in three parts. The Hermitage and Dostoevsky take their toll and culture must be compensated for by sleep. Later, refreshed, we all went to eat at what was to become a favourite restaurant, *Sadko*.

The next day Pierre went to *Lenfilm* to take his leave and to thank all those who had been so friendly, positive and helpful. Certainly everything about Leningrad seems graceful, open, appreciative; almost the exact opposite of Moscow where all seems hustle and bustle, much surliness and dour faces. The people whom we met in Leningrad were all interested in foreign culture, books and music, spoke excellent English and had read a wide range of, particularly, modern English literature. A real thirst for knowledge on the part of intelligent people confined within a restrictive environment.

With my cinecamera repaired by the technicians, Pierre and I went wandering along N*evski Prospekt* filming like mad in the sunshine. Not for long though, as we were off to the studios for a showing of *Crime and Punishment*; another three and a half hours but a very good interpretation. We had high tea at the studio and met the actor Alexei Batalov; so good looking… from *Lady with a Little Dog*. He stayed and spoke about films with Pierre. Looking back I realize what an unusual privilege it was for an English woman to meet all these people, talk with them, watch them at work… and all this linked to such an interesting life with Pierre, to whom I owe so many things.

It was time to do the packing as we were to return to Moscow that evening. During dinner at the hotel all eyes (including of course Pierre's!) were glued to the television as there was football, Spartak versus Dynamo. At 11 p.m. it was off to *Moskovskii Vokzal* for the night train and farewell to magnificent Leningrad. We must have had good compartments as it seems I wrote my journal until 1h30 a.m.

Return to Moscow

Having experienced the tea routine on the way north, I made sure that we got our tea well before arrival and, what luxury, with a lemon brought from Leningrad in my washbag! Back to the *Intourist* and the same magnificent "Moscow view" again on a clear, bright, sunny morning. After the night train, and before going off to meet Teneshvili, Pierre luxuriated in a long hot bath. We had lunch together in the hotel, in the company of the members of the "XXIV International Congress of Surgeons", carving only their meat. We then went to book our return flight for the following Wednesday with Aeroflot this time, so no Japanese slippers, sushi and hot towels... In the evening we went out for a long walk. As with sailing, Pierre had never really shown much enthusiasm for walking, and the walks we both did in Russia during these weeks must surely have used up all his credit! This time it was the shops (again not a passion of his...), finding nothing very much to buy except in *Gastronom*, where I realised my mistake: do not go out to the shops in Moscow without a shopping bag – you just might find something and then how can you carry it? Balancing my meagre purchases of cheese and juice, we went back to the hotel and enjoyed our "student-type" cheap supper in the room while Pierre watched a spy story on television and then went to bed at the unusually early hour of 10 p.m. Sandra rang asking us to go out with them but we were "too tired".

Exploring the metro

Saturday, again a leisure day, and the plan was to go on a boat trip. First, though, Pierre had a message from the travel bureau to say that Aeroflot was full in first class on Wednesday (film-related trips were my only ever experiences of first class!) and would we go by BOAC. We had to meet Paolo and a friend at 13h30 and so Pierre and I set out to see how long it would take to get to the boat terminus with a view to taking the trip after lunch. To do this we decided on the "metro experience"! I wanted to see the famous chandeliers. We started out from *Prospekt Marksa* (no chandeliers here!) and found it a very complicated system and must have missed the "illuminated plan" which helps you to work out which way to travel and where to change. Wrong train, wrong direction... back to the start, like a game of "snakes and ladders" or Kafka. Pierre bravely asked a station guard who did explain to us: "three stops and one change". The hanging lamps, if not actual chandeliers, began at *Park Kultura* station, where we had a very complicated change, via several escalators. We persevered, both

Pierre and I trying (he more easily with the Cyrillic!) to decipher the signs for the different connecting lines in each direction written up on panels, above head height and while on an escalator! This kind of thing could well constitute a language test, in my opinion.

After only about thirty-five minutes altogether, we arrived at the metro station of legend: *Kievskiya Stantziya*. Mosaic panels celebrating "victories" and "solidarity", Lenin "our leader"; oh, to have had a flash on my camera! Out onto the square and crossed to the river. A longish queue for tickets and then for the boat. What to do? Trip? There wouldn't be time for it. So, while Pierre filmed the boats, I went and queued to get tickets, calculating that they would be un-dated and we could use them later. A horde of people was wanting taxis. Better the metro, now that we had mastered the system; we were back to the hotel, arriving in unexpectedly perfect time for Pierre's meeting with Paolo and his friend Sergei. Paolo must really count as one of the world's best negotiators, as well as having – from his time as a student in Moscow – a collection of the most interesting and cultured friends and unimpeded entry to the haunts and studios of painters and poets. We went for lunch to *Slavianska Bazar* where tablets commemorated the fact that Chaliapin, Repin and Chekhov used to eat here ("founded over a 100 years ago"). BOAC confirmed our seats in first class for Wednesday afternoon. Later, fearing we had overdone the eating, I went again to the *Gastronom* for our "bread and cheese" supper; Pierre watched television and I, in an attempt at some culture, went to bed with *Soviet Short Stories!*

Not having been able to use the tickets for the boat the previous day, we decided, in theory, to do it on Sunday but, with torrential rain, it did not seem such a good idea. It must be said, however, that the downpour did nothing to discourage people from queuing for the Lenin Mausoleum! Paolo and Sandra came back, soaked to the skin, from their short boat trip. We, making the most of a bit of sun, went by metro and, after only a short wait, took the first boat, with good seats on deck; past the Lenin hills, the university, to the pre-Kremlin stop where we got off and walked. Pierre stood with others to read the newspapers posted up in glass cases.

After the boat and the walk I was exhausted and we were supposed to go and visit two painters, Yuri Kuperman, from whom Pierre had bought a lithograph on my first evening, and another, Glazunov, whom we were yet meet. Pleading fatigue, I went to bed and later learned that both visits had been cancelled.

Monday, in theory a "working day" and Pierre was to meet Teneshvili, but by 11h30 there was no news and so he had to wait at the hotel while I went out for some "last minute" visits and, quite by chance, caught the "changing of the guard" at 13h at the Lenin Mausoleum. I have long been known as the *Queen of Postcards* for my devotion to sending them to friends, but Moscow defeated me: not a single card of the Kremlin, not even at the cash desk. (It might be mentioned that, over the years, Pierre put together a marvellous collection of old postcards showing different views of Bulgarian towns and historic sites.) He was still waiting in the hotel when I got back and so we allowed ourselves a siesta.

An unexpected visit

At about 5 p.m. the meeting seemed to materialize and after dinner I went to bed while Pierre was to go with Paolo to visit the painter Glazunov. He phoned up to say that, really, the evening was in my honour... and so, with heavy limbs and heart, I got up, dressed again, and we were driven to this strange 1930s style "tower" block of only eight storeys. We went up in the lift to the seventh floor and then walked up to the eighth "studio" floor; "*sous les toits de Moscou*". Here was an enormous door, with locks and bolts, a corridor stacked with working materials and... into a huge, high studio (with stairs to a gallery and terrace) absolutely crammed with an incredible collection (the "best private collection in the USSR") of icons; really too much to take in... and distaffs, samovars, "*objets*" of all kinds... a real Aladdin's cave! Pierre and I could hardly believe our eyes. But this was not to be only an "artistic" visit, for the Glazunovs had kindly invited us for a social evening. There were friends of theirs from the arts and the ballet and, while reflecting on what an extraordinary "out of this world" experience this was for us, I am sure that the chance to meet, talk and simply be with cultivated and interested people from the west, must also have been a valuable breath of air for them at that time. Pierre spoke to everyone, the conversation was of films, music and painting. Sandra and I spoke with those who had either English or French, but were just as happy taking in the atmosphere.

After a while we all went down to the apartment on the seventh floor, to the Glazunovs' flat, another surprise of "out-of-this-worldness". It was hardly spacious, except for the sitting-room, which was chock-a-block with Empire or Directoire French and Russian furniture... table, sofa, chairs, cupboards, buffet; the walls and furniture draped and decorated with "*d'époque*" rugs, prints, paintings, porcelain. Beautiful pieces and in an incredible ensemble of a flat. And am I glad that Pierre said that I "really ought to come"! Although I wouldn't have known what I would have missed, I certainly would not have not gone! What a country, and what a city, of contrasts! Beautiful Leningrad, dour Moscow but with secret surprises for those lucky enough (as we were!) to have an "*entrée*" into these "other worlds".

The following day Pierre became officially a "free man": free from *Sovexfilm* and Teneshvili although, in truth, the demands of the former had not weighed over heavily on him; and the company of the latter had, on the whole, been extremely convivial. I must say I wonder if, in the "new Russia", the Georgian and other ethnic restaurants to which he introduced us still exist, or are they all replaced by the dreaded McDonalds? And is the quality of the Georgian wine still as good? Memory, admittedly, gives a rosy glow to the past, but we did have a quite extraordinary and very privileged experience.

With the "freed" Pierre, I went, determinedly, in search of some postcards, he in search of yet more interesting books (our customs declaration on departure listed his purchases as "books on Marxist philosophy, art and theatre". If the officials paid any attention it would certainly have earned him good points!). In a big bookshop I did find some packets of not very exciting cards and was thus able to keep up my reputation for sending impressions of travels to a wide range of friends; a habit now, sadly, in decline except for myself and a very few friends. How can an e-mail or a text, admittedly bearing much the same message, replace the visual excitement of the card depicting, for example, the mud brick walls and blue tiled domes of Khiva, the swirling movement of Djema-el-Fna? After lunch I settled down to make sure that the cards got written and Pierre went with Paolo to where Valentin was filming with Vika in room 2013, "because it's supposed to be abroad"; though how the panoramic view of Moscow could represent "abroad", I am not sure.

Pierre and Paolo had one last, but very important, thing to conclude: the financial accounts for Carlo Ponti. I had already shown my total and truly shameful non-numeracy when asked by Pierre to make myself useful and calculate expenditures in *roubles* and change the sums into Swiss francs (film accounts) and U.S. dollars (the "hard currency" we had had to use when only *valuta* would do!). This completed, Pierre and I went for one last "Russian romantic" dinner in the hotel before going upstairs for a last look out from our room over the astonishing panorama.

Leaving the hotel fairly early next morning we made our way, no *Tchaika* this time, to the airport and, having neither *roubles* nor anything of great interest to declare (although I personally valued that part of Russian history and some person's treasured possessions that I had bought: the six plates with views of St. Petersburg), we checked in easily and took our first class seats on the BOAC flight to London, where we landed mid-afternoon and made our way home, used to luxurious treatment, by taxi!

Thus ended the second of our two visits in this one year to countries of Eastern Europe.

While, in many material and practical ways, Bulgaria and the Soviet Union could be compared, as indeed could the type of VIP treatment we received on both visits (cars, drivers, restaurants, invitations, "top people"...), it is obviously the case that, on an emotional level, Pierre's return to his native land in March, had been of a different order of importance.

Down to earth!

We spent the following days "winding down", Pierre lunching with his friend and film company director Harry Moore, me inviting various friends to meals with us at home in order to "talk Russia". One of them, Peter Montagnon, a director of Sir Kenneth Clarke's monumental television series *Civilisation*, was especially interested in all that we had done and seen. At the weekend I went down to Folkestone and had tea with my beloved and inspirational teacher, Miss Maggs, to recount my impressions and see how they might match some of her own "travels across Europe from west to east in a small black Ford car". A truly indomitable lady!

There was of course follow-up work for Pierre: the next week he was off to Rome for several days for meetings with Ponti about the viability of the *Anna Karenina* project.

September, and the conference season, was upon us. I was also to start a new research project, based at the University of Sussex, assessing pupils' performance in modern foreign languages. This involved many meetings on the lovely campus set among the Sussex downs. In late September at a conference organized by the British Society of Aesthetics, Pierre read a paper on the *Aesthetics of Cinema* which, I noted at the time, was a *"grand succès"*.

October saw the opening of the opera season at Covent Garden and we attended a performance of *Falstaff* with Aldo Ceccato conducting. There was a post-performance party attended also by Peter Glossop ("discovered" we always heard, at the international opera competition in Varna). At the Vanbrugh Theatre, training base for students of the Royal Academy of Dramatic Art (RADA), there was a production of Lorca's *Blood Wedding*, at which the role of the 'Mother' was taken by a young Bulgarian, Madlena Nedeva. This was an unusual pleasure for Pierre, bringing together a Bulgarian student and his interest in 20th century drama. November took us to Paris for a weekend (Friday evening to Sunday evening, how easy to skip off after classes!) and to visit Dora and Luben for the first time since our return from Russia. There was also the chance to take in the Francis Bacon and Fernand Léger exhibitions at the Grand Palais. Just before going to Yugoslavia for an art jury commitment at the end of the month, Pierre and

I dined at Baroness Budberg's apartment and among the guests that evening were the Knittels, and the dancer and choreographer Frederick Ashton. It was a pleasure to be able to speak knowledgeably about things Russian!

December brought an event that touched upon Bulgaria: a reception at the Embassy to say farewell to Ambassador Mitko Grigorov and his wife. He was to be replaced by the delightful and urbane Alexander Yankov, but that is a story for the following year.

* * * * *

1972

A major theatre production

Each new year seemed to bring exciting events, fresh challenges; where 1971 saw Pierre's return to his beloved native land and our discovery of Russia through the good offices of 'Bridge Films' (directors Carlo Ponti and Pierre Rouve), 1972 offered the thrilling possibility of presenting a major work by the French playwright Paul Claudel, *Partage de Midi*, in a translation by Jonathan Griffin, poet, translator and himself a playwright. *Break of Noon* was to be staged at the Ipswich Arts Theatre.

At the beginning of January Pierre went to Paris for a few days for discussions with agents regarding the performance rights of the English translation and, once back in London, he spent several days in discussion with Jonathan and the director of the Ipswich theatre, John Southworth. The whole thing began to take off! A key factor for Pierre and Jonathan was, of course, the casting of this intense emotional drama. Eventually it was decided to engage Ann Firbank for the one female role, Yse. But who was to play opposite her in the role of Mesa? Would it be Bernard Horsfall, an actor I had known when I was at Nottingham University? No, the choice was Ben Kingsley, then an associate artist with the Royal Shakespeare Company, later known for his portrayal of Mahatma Ghandi in the film of that name.

On the 2nd of February Jonathan and Kathie invited us to dinner, together with Ann Firbank and Ben Kingsley. I remember thinking: "Why do they both seem so young?" (This was thirty five years ago!) But I was thinking "young for the parts of Mesa and Yse", comparing them, I suppose, with Jean-Louis Barrault and Edwige Feuillère who played the roles in the classic Theatre de France production. This was directed by Barrault, who had brought it to the World Theatre season at the Aldwych Theatre in 1968, where happily Pierre and I had seen it. Pierre and Jonathan were able to get a feel for both actors in the social setting, but Kathie and I, more "star struck", just enjoyed being with them. Ann Firbank we found very sweet, and, unsurprisingly, this is a feeling that has grown over the years; we have kept in touch and see each other when we can. She has been to visit me and several of my friends in Bulgaria, and agreed to take part in the film which Bulgarian National Television made in 2004 about Pierre's life and activities: *A Bulgarian Voice in Europe*, remarkably conceived and directed by Stanislava Kalcheva. Ben Kingsley we found very intelligent and interesting and, as is of course well known, he has gone on to achieve fame in film roles, although his magnetic personality, and what Kathie and I described as his "devouring eyes"(!) were so well suited to the stage.

After many days working on the script with Jonathan, making adjustments to suit a contemporary audience ("trying to remain faithful to Claudel – to what he says and to his unique style") and the Ipswich stage, Pierre put the plans to John Southworth and, at last, on the 21st of February, rehearsals began. These were supposed to take place in Ipswich over long weekends so that the production could be set within the stage. This, however, proved impossible for some technical reasons and so all the rehearsals took place in a church hall in Hackney in London. Ann remembers the additional disadvantage of power cuts: all rehearsals had to take place in the eery atmosphere of candlelight!

That same week Jonathan and Kathie invited Marie-Sygne Claudel-James, the playwright's grand-daughter and her husband the Honourable Christopher James to dinner but, in view of the power cuts throughout north London, they were all to come to us at Markham Street. Kathie, an excellent cook, offered to prepare the whole meal in my kitchen, so I had only to act as hostess! We found the Jameses absolutely charming although she, with her intimate knowledge of the play, was a little bit intimidating. They had planned to arrange a "publicity – P.R." party for the 2nd of March at their house and we were asked to spread the word and invite anyone whom we felt might promote the production. I went to this after one of my usual busy days: lunch with my professor at King's College (where I was later to apply for a post), tea with colleagues after an exam board meeting and home to change... Pierre arrived much later, after rehearsals; the actors, probably totally exhausted, did not come, but friends from the French Cultural Institute were there, no doubt impressed that the first production in an English translation of *Partage de Midi* was to be staged in Great Britain.

On the 11th of March, with only four days left before the opening on the 15th, Pierre travelled to Ipswich. In the pouring rain, I drove him to Liverpool Street Station, pleased that a conference I should have been attending in Oxford had been cancelled. Later in the evening he phoned – disaster! – to say he had left his all-important briefcase, with script, notes etc., behind at the house. The problem was: how to get it to him for the next day's work? It involved finding someone who would be going down to Ipswich. Whom to contact? Luckily I thought of Ben Kingsley who, very conveniently, was at the Aldwych Theatre in Central London for the last night of *A Midsummer Night's Dream* in which he was playing Demetrius. So, briefcase in hand, I dashed round to the theatre, double parking the car near the stage door and had him paged... What a relief, he was there (of course!), free for a few minutes and agreed to take charge of the precious briefcase. We only had time for a few intense words about the Claudel, with which I felt so unfamiliar!

The 15th of March, opening night, was a mad day for me (no

doubt for Pierre as well, but he was in Ipswich!). There was teaching in the morning at college, a visit to see a student on teaching practice … and only at about twelve noon did I get to the centre of London where I wanted to buy presents for Pierre, Jonathan, the cast and others. I had decided on a *"chinoiserie"* theme, in keeping with the play; next, I needed gift-wrap paper (in the end the presents had to be wrapped on the train, with scissors and sellotape from home!). After that, it was the hairdresser, home to pack and a taxi to Liverpool Street, where many friends were to gather, for the 16h30 train. I travelled with Aldo and Eliana Ceccato (he being in London for *Simon Boccanegra*), Brigitte Marger, the French Cultural Attachée, my colleague Anne Lyne, straight from college, and other friends. Finally installed in our first-class, non-smoking carriage, we could relax before arriving in Ipswich and getting taxis to our hotels. Pierre was nervous and tense – naturally – and we nearly had a row about the presents!

The excitement was palpable: the publicity department had done an excellent job; the house was completely full and among those present for the first night were Benjamin Britten with Peter Pears, the Mayor of Ipswich and the Bishop. During the first interval the theatre manager arranged drinks in his office; this was a chance for all to talk: Brigitte and the Mayor discussing French culture, Britten and Aldo music … It was indeed a marvellous performance and, in my case, I felt it better not to have read the play or been to rehearsals, as it made such an impression with its strange and moving end. Jonathan Griffin wrote of this "spiritual thriller":

> "Our guiding principle is Jean-Louis Barrault's: to try to be faithful to the young Claudel and yet not leave out the essence of Claudel's final sense of the meaning … For the last scene, Pierre Rouve and I ended by taking the 1905 version, cutting it and adding one key passage from the 1949 text."

Success!

The applause and the curtain calls showed what a big success the performance was! A big congratulatory party was held afterwards, with actors on stage and in the stalls, until quite late. I made a note that the stain on my programme was made by a quantity of red wine! The following days the press reviews were to confirm the success of the whole production.

Those of us who had travelled from London took the train back the following day and were able to buy the *East Anglian Daily Times* at Liverpool Street Station:

> "Last night's world premiere of Jonathan Griffin's English translation was not only a moment of glory for Ipswich, but an evening of some national importance.
>
> It was a majestic and magnificent interpretation of a poetic masterpiece and, I would think, well worth the attention of, say, the Royal Shakespeare Company."

The next day Irving Wardle's review in *The Times* gave the opportunity for a second "opening" party!

> "Ipswich has overcome Anglo-Saxon resistance... with an eloquent new translation by Jonathan Griffin, a cast including Ben Kingsley and Ann Firbank and a cosmopolitan director, Pierre Rouve, with firm intentions of releasing Claudel from the Gallic hothouse."

For the Saturday performance, Kathie and I had arranged for a coach to take our friends and a great number of my students (after all, it was a French play!) to Ipswich. This was, in fact, a lovely opportunity for a "weekend in the country" and proved to be a very jolly occasion. The following week, the professional journal, *The Stage and Television Today*, wrote:

"Pierre Rouve's direction is masterly, allowing Claudel's poetry to flow like music – poetry not only of words but of gesture and grouping... fulfilled in a highly dramatic final act of almost Wagnerian intensity."

After such reviews there was discussion by the management regarding the possibility of a transfer to a theatre in the West End of London.

The following week Pierre was back in London and giving a lecture on aesthetics at the University. In another intensely cultural atmosphere we had the privilege of seeing the whole, reconstructed, nine-hour version, of Abel Gance's *Napoléon*, at the Institut Français. Almost all activity was centred on the production in Ipswich and, when we could, we would take time to see it, as we did the following weekend, together with Professor of Aesthetics Louis Arnaud Reid and his wife. For Pierre it was a chance to see how the production was shaping, to make some adjustments and to enjoy the fruits of so many people's efforts. On the Saturday we made a trip to "Constable country", visiting some of the still existing sites of the paintings. On the Monday Pierre and Jonathan and the company had arranged an "open discussion" where all were invited to put their questions and views. This was well attended by local theatregoers who showed a great interest in the play, the author, the translation and the interpretation.

Topolski sketches

All good things come – only too quickly! – to an end and Saturday April 1st was the final performance of *Break of Noon*. In the morning I collected Feliks Topolski, the famous graphic artist, and we drove to Ipswich, stopping for lunch in the beautiful Suffolk village of Lavenham and arriving at about 16h. Topolski knew, and had drawn, almost everybody one can think of. His 'Memoir of the Century' is now preserved in a museum-gallery in two of the railway arches which served him as a studio, near Waterloo Station. Pierre went to the theatre, making sure to reserve a front-row seat for Topolski so that he could sketch. Jonathan and Kathie joined us at the hotel and we had dinner early, going with several friends to the theatre for 20h curtain up. The house was completely packed and, in our opinion, the production had worked up to this, and the final performance was the best of all! Needless to say the party in the bar afterwards was both cause and opportunity for great celebrations!

Relaxing and winding down was the order of the day for Sunday although, as it was my birthday, we allowed ourselves a slow drive back to London, calling in for a tea party at a lovely country house belonging to some friends of Feliks Topolski. Lots of talk, cake and gentle enjoyment. This was, in fact, the perfect bridge between activities: Pierre had to resume his broadcasts and lectures on the Monday and I was due to fly to Germany to attend a language conference with my research director, Vaughan James. It amazes me now not only how much energy I had in those days (and at that age!) but also, quite specifically, how I managed to choose, launder, pack, unpack and repack... so many changes of clothes – for me and for Pierre – for so many different types of activity and potential audience. Pierre and I were noted for our elegance as, I hope, may be observed from some of the photos accompanying this text.

Getting to the conference tested my virtually non-existent German to the limits since we had to get from the airport into Cologne and catch a train to Saarbrucken. It was certainly what is known as "survival kit – situational language"! This was the conference of the 'Fédération Internationale de Professeurs de Langues Vivantes' with internationally known speakers such as Rebecca Valette and Wilga Rivers. Vaughan and I needed to attend as part of the assessment project on which we were working for the Schools' Council. As well as the talks there was, as always, the social side and it was a pleasure to sit, talk, eat and drink with such luminaries as Rene Richterich, John Trim, Peter Newmark and others.

When I returned to London, Pierre and I continued to enjoy the social and cultural life with friends: Pierre visiting and writing about the exhibition of works by Paul Feiler, one of my very favourite artists, whose "white collage" is hanging on the wall in the sitting room. Paul Feiler wrote to me only recently saying:

> "I have very strong recollections of Pierre's writing. It was, as good criticism should be, timeless and concerned with looking. There were never many critics of his ilk – and sadly none today".

There was a *Falstaff* at Covent Garden with Eliana – Aldo was conducting; dinner at Jonathan and Kathie's house with the Ceccatos and the Ipswich actors, to whom I was able to show all the photos I had taken. Another day I went to Feliks Topolski's studio for him to start the four metre high portrait he was to paint of me! (The problem has always been finding a wall high enough for it to hang; once I had a study at King's with high ceilings, now at home it still waits to be placed in the upper stairway.) The end of the month saw the second of the London concerts that Stoika Milanova gave in 1972 (first at St. John's, Smith Square, then the Royal Festival Hall and, later, at the Royal Albert Hall). The one at the RFH was a programme of Bach, followed by dinner that lasted until 2h in the morning! Alongside all these treats, I continued the research for the Schools' Council Project and there was a committee meeting at the University of Sussex on the 18th of April. What a lovely location for work: it was sunny and warm for the drive down and the 11h meeting allowed us to report back on our findings and future direction, all to the satisfaction of the committee. The same evening, back in London, Pierre and I went to a production of Garcia Lorca's *Yerma* with Nuria Espert in the title role; what a superb interpretation.

To end the month Vaughan and I, together with other colleagues in the Modern Languages field, attended yet another conference, this time first in Malmö, flying via Copenhagen where we exchanged and read each others' papers in the transit lounge – never a wasted moment! We then moved to Stockholm, where we would hear presentations by the Canadian expert Merrill Swain of the Ontario Institute, regarding the "French immersion" system, and Stephen Krashen (of *Monitor Theory* fame) from the States. Vaughan and I made our report and it was received with interest and questions. As usual at these conferences there was much socialising, useful when one remembers that for the "Eastern Bloc" members it was a much-valued opportunity to exchange ideas. I also seem to recall that there was a lot of singing of soulful Russian songs… Stockholm was also a beautiful discovery and, as well as attending lectures, we visited the National Museum to see the collection of icons and took a boat trip among the thousands of little islands.

London University events

In May Pierre was much involved in the conference arranged at the Senate House by the School of Slavonic and East European Studies of the University of London and where, this time, Jana Molhova and Vera Despotova from Sofia University were also to present papers. On this same day, 5th of May, I was to attend the "conferment ceremony" for my Master's degree and, to my delight, my marvellous and much admired teacher Miss Maggs had agreed to come up from Folkestone to be with me. She came by train and we all convened at the Senate House at 17h30. The impressive ceremony lasted for a couple of hours, after which Pierre and I took Miss Maggs to dinner so that she could share in my academic success which, since school-days, she had always predicted for me. To have Pierre, who had always so encouraged me, and her with me, was a truly moving time.

Somewhat later the same month it fell to me to present our Languages Project in Scotland, and Vaughan, a Welshman, was very happy to do the same in Cardiff but, in those years, nobody would have undertaken a visit to Northern Ireland... I took the night sleeper "The Flying Scotsman", of historic fame, from King's Cross Station and awoke to the crossing of the Firth of Forth, recalling McGonagle's (in)famous poem. We drew into Dundee and I made my way to a hotel where I could freshen up, do my face and hair and have some breakfast before going to the University. During the day I presented the "work in progress" – our United Kingdom-wide research – to the meeting of the Scottish Modern Languages Association. I have notes in my diary to tell me that I phoned Pierre two or three times during the morning; would this have been to reassure myself or to check on how some project of his was going? Most likely the former!

Music in Suffolk

June was the month of much musical activity at the Aldeburgh Festival and we seem to have attended it whenever we could free ourselves from other commitments! In my case, this meant teaching and research. But not only that: after ten years of marriage, it was certainly important to be thinking about enlarging the family. So a series of check-ups, investigations and discussions followed, each with a different specialist in his or her field.

Our first weekend visit to Suffolk was a beautiful one: we set out on Saturday with J.C.Trewin, the famous critic, and his wife. I managed to mis-navigate us (a common event and I was never allowed to forget about the quarry in Germany...). and so we were late for lunch, but we had a splendid drive, with Trewin and Pierre talking about Shakespeare productions. We were also, unfortunately, late for the performance of *Saul* which started at 15h. Kathie (the Griffins spent every festival in

Aldeburgh) was waiting for the Trewins who were not going to *Saul* and Pierre and I managed to slip into the Maltings concert hall after a "Hallelujah". James Bowman, perhaps one of the earliest and best of twentieth century counter tenors, was magnificent. Kathie and Jonathan were dining with the theatrical agent Laurier Lister and then going on to hear Max Adrian at 20h30. Pierre and I settled into the Brudenell Hotel where we were to stay for the weekend and then went to the show of that marvellous mimic, Joyce Grenfell. On Sunday we had a late breakfast at the hotel and then went along to Regent Cottage, rented by the Griffins for the season. In the afternoon we all drove over to Blythburgh, where John Williams gave a guitar recital in the impressive church. The splendid churches are often almost all that remains of these East Anglian villages, whose mediaeval wealth was built on the wool trade.

In the evening there was a concert at the Maltings given by Peter Pears and Benjamin Britten; was there ever such a perfect composer/performer pair? In life as in music they had a charmed existence, many of Britten's works having been composed for Peter Pears' remarkable tenor voice. It was a privilege to have had them attend the production of *Break of Noon* in Ipswich and to hear them perform. The next day (this was to be a long weekend!) breakfast in the hotel brought a great surprise: hearing Bulgarian spoken! We listened carefully (one did in those days…) before joining in! At that time, Bulgarian musicians were rarely heard outside the London venues. What a delight to be in the presence of the members of the Dimov Quartet who were to perform that evening at the Maltings. Breakfast for Pierre lasted an extra hour at least! The following weekend it was the same excursion: Snape on Sunday for an afternoon performance of *Faust* – we stayed overnight – and on the Monday a concert of international dimensions: Mstislav Rostropovitch and Benjamin Britten; glorious!

The month ended with some more social events: a visit to Glyndebourne with Chavdar Damianov and his then partner Stefi for the dress rehearsal of Misho Hadjimishev's production of *Macbeth* and, on the 29th, a celebration of Pierre's name day with, first, a reception at the Great Britain-East Europe Centre (no, not in Pierre's honour, although he deserved such recognition!) for minister Goshkin and attended by Ambassador Alexander Yankov and Professor Dramaliev, who was on a visit to the British Museum, and afterwards we went on to dine at a famous restaurant in Chelsea, the *Aretusa*.

A lovely summer continued and on July 1st Pierre and I attended the wedding of one of my students at the college, Jane Theodorović, at the Serbian Orthodox Church in London. Happily Pierre and I found a parking space without difficulty, but Jane's father, who was to give her away, found himself stuck on the motorway down from Yorkshire, and, as this was well before the days of mobile phones, everyone sat waiting, not quite knowing what to do. The priest made a suggestion: since baptized members of the Orthodox Church were in short supply...would Pierre please take Mr. Theodorović's place! Although not known for regular church attendance, he did so with elegance and grace!

The wedding lunch was held at one of the restaurants where Jane's then husband Jacques worked as a chef and the party continued later in our garden in Chelsea, where Pierre, in his new 'witness' role, was generous with the champagne!

A Month in the Country

Later the same month one of the specialists I had been consulting recommended an operation with a view to putting my reproductive capacities into good working order. This meant being in hospital for about ten days where, while recovering, I was spoilt with flowers and cards and visits from Pierre and others. On my release, I first went to convalesce at a home in Sussex, and then we took over the country house of our friends Rosemary Gordon and Peter Montagnon in Coolham. During all this time Pierre was, of course, on the move: a "Brains Trust" appearance at the 'Q' theatre, spending some time with Ivo Hadjimishev who was in London to pursue a photographic specialism and, very importantly, an evening's discussion and dinner at the Savoy Hotel with Marcel Marceau, then performing his wonderful mime show in London.

While convalescing, I continued to work on the assessment project, dictating my notes for the secretary at the university. On one of his regular visits, Pierre very helpfully brought me a typewriter. No escape, therefore, from work! Staying in Sussex also meant that I was not far from the university, and so Vaughan would come over for discussions and lunch. It seems to have been a very warm sunny summer in 1972 as my diary notes that much time was spent in the garden! There was also the usual inspection of villages, deciding whether we wanted to buy a "country cottage" and looking in antique shops (all enduring interests of mine!).

By 17th August I was declared well enough to give up this rural existence... and return to life in London, where, in relation to house buying, I note in my diary for that week that a house in Markham Street had "sold for £46,000". As we had bought ours ten years previously for less than one third of that sum, it was certainly surprising, although, of course, nothing compared to the totally ridiculous house prices quoted now! For some reason, possibly related to the increase in value, we decided to have the house painted and, to general astonishment, purple! For me there were more visits to specialists; would we be having a baby? What were the other options? Adoption was, of course, another possibility and we were given application forms from different local authorities. (IVF had not then been invented.) I still spent days down in Sussex at meetings and even managed to catch the first night of a play *Fallen Angels* in which Annie Firbank was acting and to have a drink and a pizza with her after.

At the end of the month Pierre was to fly to Bucharest to attend the Seventh International Congress of Aesthetics and to present his very well received paper on street and community theatre, *Face and Place of the Theatre*, later to be published in the Proceedings.

> "...imagine our inborn theatrical potential bursting out of industrially-conditioned buildings and flooding the whole city of the future, and...above all there would be new patterns of urban configurations...the future belongs to brave dreamers. Let us dream".

However, the evening before leaving, he managed to close the heavy door of the Daimler car on his thumb and that meant our urgent visits to the Accident and Emergency department at the local hospital where, as he said, "I asked them to give me a dose that would be more appropriate for a horse", but it seemed to do the trick as the blood blister and the bruising diminished, not to mention the pain! My calls to him in Bucharest were not the easiest to put through in those days! While he was away I made some time to visit Topolski's studio for him to continue work on the portrait.

September brought a new and very interesting challenge for me after the submission of the final version of the assessment project on the 1st. John Gainsborough, the son of Pierre's great friend Dr. Richard Gainsborough, founder of *Art News and Review*, had received a proposal to re-launch a monthly magazine *The Linguist* as one of the Gainsborough Publications list. *The Linguist,* house journal of The Linguists' Club, had long been edited by a remarkable Pole, Tade Pilley, but now needed wider circulation. The proposal was to launch *The New Linguist* and I was asked to edit it! This was really the most wonderful professional opportunity and, of course, after discussing the conditions, I jumped at it! It was to be a monthly, in five languages (English, French, German, Italian and Spanish) with pages from the press to illustrate a different theme each time, together with pages for practice, book reviews and competitions. Producing the magazine meant very strict times, dates and editorial supervision of the copy. But I was fortunate to inherit the specialist editors for each language from the previous publication. In fact, Pierre and I made a long-term friendship with the Spanish editor, Mariano Garcia Landa, who had worked, and still does, as a conference interpreter in the United States and in Europe. A man of immense charm and intelligence, with whom we had many long and interesting meetings. He began to record conversations with Pierre which, had they not always veered off in so many directions, would have served as the basis for a fascinating memoir.

All these activities meant a busy time, not only for Pierre and me, but also for friends whom we saw and invited, and colleagues with whom we had meetings. There were performances and concerts to attend: Annie Firbank in *Twelfth Night* in Sussex,

Stoika Milanova at the Royal Albert Hall, Pierre's regular lectures at the 'Q' theatre as well as his weekly broadcasts for the BBC Bulgarian Service (some of which, notably his "radio play" on the life of James Bourchier, have recently been re-broadcast on Bulgarian National Radio). Following the completion of the project, Vaughan had invited me to do some teaching at the University of Sussex, so a weekly drive down from London became part of the programme. With the Master's level completed, I found little time for the necessary research and reading, let alone writing, for the Doctorate level but, luckily, I was able to incorporate material from academic projects on which I had worked as a researcher. I feel sure that both Pierre and I found the range and intensity of all these activities very stimulating. Certainly neither of us would have wanted to give anything up!

Bulgaria comes to London

Autumn brought a host of Bulgarian visits and activities: the Great Britain-East Europe Society hosted a reception for Professor Petar Dinekov, here to work at the British Museum and the School of Slavonic Studies; Pierre gave a lecture entitled *The Other Europe* (recently reprinted in Bulgaria) at the Sussex conference of Slavonic Studies of which Vaughan James, President of the International Association of Teachers of Russian, was director. Pierre presented a broad perspective on European chronology and cultural developments which was very well received. The 27th of November saw the Sofia Philharmonic Orchestra at the Royal Festival Hall and the 29th the opening of the first United Kingdom exhibition in the gallery at *Balkantourist* in Regent Street of paintings by Georgi Baev, still one of my favourite Bulgarian artists. What a pity we did not buy a painting then! Death not only brings sadness but an increase in prices... although I still live in hopes of acquiring a Baev and, indeed, a Genkov! The following day a reception was held at the Embassy, no doubt for all these august visitors. In retrospect, somewhat paradoxically, it seems to have been a "golden age". Where, now, are the Roussev, Pamoukchiev, Assa exhibitions in London, where the Bulgarian base and soprano voices, where the instrumentalists? However, I must pay tribute to Ivo Varbanov, director of Bulgarian Creative Arts, who has put tremendous effort into bringing Bulgarian films, as well as other cultural events, to London year by year.

Another reason for the reception was that it was our sad duty to bid farewell to the Cultural Attaché, our good friend Chavdar Damianov. We matched this with a party at our house and Baroness Moura Budberg also arranged a party for Chavdar.

Christmas took on a new turn this year as Pierre and I accepted an invitation to spend a few days in the country at 'The Grove', the house of Rosemary Gordon's parents. We drove down on the 24th with the presents and a stock of wine. Christmas day saw us opening presents, talking, taking photos and going on a long walk in the country with the dogs. Back for a late lunch and watching the Queen's speech at 3p.m. on television – an unbreakable tradition! We then prepared for the Christmas evening meal: turkey with trimmings, the pudding with brandy flames and lucky charms inside. Boxing Day was fresh and cold, just the thing for long walks (without Pierre...) and then a drive over to Long Melford for lunch (with Pierre!). What a lovely way to spend the festive season, with good friends, good conversation and good food... ideal!

10 years married!

The year is quickly coming to a close and, with its end, or at least on the 29th of December, our tenth wedding anniversary. We had arranged a big party for friends for the evening but, already in the morning, presents, cards, telegrams and flowers were arriving every moment. Topolski's present was the finished portrait. I went to the hairdresser, collected the food from the caterer and Pierre brought the champagne. The party started at 8p.m. and Jane, a student of mine, and Jacques, the pastry cook brought a magnificent cake, all decorated with sugar roses. It was a most wonderful party (although I have a note that reads "Kevin and Harry, drinks, quarrel"...) and went on till very late. Hence the "Up VERY late" entries for the next two days, while gathering strength for seeing in the New Year with friends at another party! 1972 was certainly another busy and exciting year and, as we enter 1973, we shall see the outcomes of many of those plans and activities.

1973

Such a year, so full of changes: the arrival of Mila-Gina in June, moving home (albeit only temporarily), taking on a nanny, Pierre's attendance at the World Congress of Philosophy in Varna, the launch of *New Linguist*, my taking up a lectureship at King's College... But all these events are still in the future when, as usual, the first days of the year show the effects of previous evenings' celebrations!

That marvellous tenth wedding party and then New Year's Eve should have meant that we slept in late on January 1st but no, it was "up at 8h30" to do last minute shopping (yes, that was before New Year's Day had been declared a holiday in England!). So, yawning all the way, I went off to Peter Jones at Sloane Square and other favourite shops, buying presents (to be taken the following day to Sofia by Chavdar Damianov) for Pierre's mother and aunts, and for several friends. The result of the present buying spree was the need to buy another suitcase just to transport them!

Culture followed commerce and, in the evening, we went to Covent Garden with Greg and Romayne for a performance of *Nabucco*, going afterwards to congratulate Ted (now 'Sir Edward') Downes and on to dinner. Fog meant that we were late home. What energy we all had!

The next day was the planned departure (with "excess baggage"!) for Sofia. Pierre and I left for a fog-bound Heathrow where we discovered that the flight had been cancelled and so Zhivko and Chavdar, otherwise condemned to hang around, came back – plus all cases! – with us to Chelsea. I could not stay for long as I had to drive to the annual Languages Conference in the north. This proved to be the usual excellent meeting place for the exchange of ideas and contacts – and for socialising! As usual, the Russianists put on a very good show: a dinner, followed by much vodka and singing, until at least 3 a.m.!

Back in London I was busy with the editing of *New Linguist*, and doctor's appointments, and was alerted by my friend and tutor Professor Perry to the imminent publication of an advertisement for a post as Modern Languages Tutor at King's College. My application for this required a lot of preparation and it was a while before I heard that I was to have an interview.

The launch of *New Linguist* (Volume 1 No. 1 was to appear in February) was keeping me very busy: selecting material, conferring with the individual language editors, deciding on themes, checking copy and going to the printers. Appropriately for early 1973, the theme was *Europe* and, as I wrote in my editorial to the first issue:

> "We shall have a theme for each issue and this month it is the Common Market, to mark the administratively official step of UK entry. Another new feature will be the foreign press articles with commentary".

The magazine, my first "baby" of 1973, went on to achieve good sales and, even then, at 20p per issue, was excellent value!

Yugoslav arts

Pierre had been invited to give a presentation in the Gallery of the University of Bradford, known for its excellent department of Yugoslav Studies, where one of his protegées, the young painter Lilya Pavlović (now a longstanding friend but then doing post-graduate work at Chelsea College of Art) had an exhibition. He wrote of her in *Arts Review*:

"She bears witness to the span and spirit of visual creativity in a *sui generis* Socialist country...the cloying cliché of 'Socialist Realism' sticks in our minds, allegedly accounting for everything "artistic" produced East of Vienna. Now this young Yugoslav artist comes to prove how wrong we can be".

Here in England Pierre was further able to cement his positive attitude to the Balkans as he was closely involved in artistic activities, often as a member of the jury, in Ljubljana, Rijeka, Zagreb, Tuzla and Belgrade over many years and we are fortunate to have many examples of the work of these artists in the house in Chelsea. As well as work by Lilya Pavlović, I particularly value a tapestry by Jagoda Buić, a painting by Nives K-K and several pieces of sculpture.

Back in London, Pierre had the usual personal and professional commitments, writing regular reviews of exhibitions for *Arts Review* and his cultural broadcasts for the BBC Bulgarian Service. London was also full of good and interesting Bulgarian friends: in late January we hosted a dinner for our excellent friends, Professor Alexander Yankov, the Ambassador, and his wife. I can truly say that the period of his mandate in London was one of the most fruitful, positive and enjoyable that we experienced: urbane, intelligent, open and friendly, Alexander and Elsa showed what a diplomatic mission should be.

But there was theatre as well: the famous actor Apostol Karamitev was in London on a visit, no doubt organised through the "Mixed Commission" (yes, probably a "George Smiley-type" body...) and it was a joy to take him, as both Pierre and I did, to a range of theatrical performances: Ustinov, Moliere, Shakespeare and, bizarrely, a performance in Esperanto. Esperanto, I believe, used to be very popular in Bulgaria. His presence in London was the occasion for a "get together" at home with, among others, teachers and actors Elisabeth Sotirova, Dora Glindjeva and Bondo Sertchadjiev.

A new building to represent Bulgaria

This was also the time during which Ludmila Zhivkova was doing her post-graduate research at St. Anthony's College in Oxford and she and her husband Ivan Slavkov would often be in London. It was then that she, together with Ambassador Yankov, was able to negotiate, via Mr. and Mrs. Siefert, the purchase of the magnificent "island site" building at 186–188

Queen's Gate to be the Embassy of the People's Republic of Bulgaria, then presided over by Ludmila's father, Todor Zhivkov.

In early February, prior to her coming with Ivan to us in Chelsea for dinner, I had a most interesting lunch with Ludmila, during which we discussed many things of mutual interest and concern; both academic and personal. I have to say that not only have I always maintained that she did excellent work in promoting Bulgarian culture and artists (it was then still three years to the magnificent Thracian exhibition at the British Museum in 1976), but that I remain personally in her debt for her kindness, intervention and support. Pierre was also impressed by the seriousness of her research, on which she would often consult him, and which resulted in a book on relations with Turkey.

On Friday the 9th, Pierre set me off on a very busy day: not only did I have a doctor appointment and meetings about my research project, but he had invited Ludmila and Ivan for dinner together with our friends Rosemary Gordon and Peter Montagnon and the Yankovs. This demanded serious menu and entertainment planning… as well as cleaning up the house a bit! In addition, as it was winter, it meant making sure that all the possible heating was on in the house. This was before we had gas central heating installed, and I have vivid memories of Ludmila, on more than one occasion, not wanting to take off her fur coat! A lively evening and, the next day, Pierre had to attend the wedding of a Bulgarian friend, leaving me enough time to deal with the washing up!

Pierre had, increasingly, been taking over from me some of the teaching of the graduate students at the Institute of Education with, as can well be imagined, great success! He was now thinking of making formal applications for academic posts, in the field of either the visual or theatre arts. It would soon be time for filling in all those application forms, citing experience, publications, objectives… and casting them upon the waters, hoping for positive results…

To assist in the process, he had asked Peter Montagnon, in his capacity as Head of Open University Productions, to write a reference for a post at the University of Manchester. His high opinion of Pierre can be seen from the following extract:

> "I consider Pierre Rouve to be a man of the highest intellectual calibre. His knowledge of literature, the visual arts and the theatre is, in my opinion, profound... He also has, to a remarkable degree, the ability to express himself with great clarity and precision. I have always considered him to be a man who epitomized what is best in the European savants.
>
> With regard to his major work as a producer and director of feature films, he has a very special contribution to make to the professorship for which he is applying... It is rare to find an individual who combines high professional standing in the film industry with the intellectual and scholastic capacity to relate techniques to content."

In March, always thinking about the possibility of moving to a larger house (thank heavens we never actually did get round to moving from this beautiful home in Chelsea!), we took to visiting some really very large houses but, in the end, always found something not quite to our liking (being in Clapham, for example). The other alternative was a "country cottage" and we often went on drives out to Kent or Sussex, once even entering an auction, but found ourselves outbid (luckily!). The purchase of a "second" home in the country was to take place only a decade or so later when we bought a cliff-top house in Normandy, very near the village where Dora and Luben had bought. Here we spent many summer holidays.

March also brought a letter for me from Pierre's mother with a *"martenitza"*. This, of course, was later to become a very familiar annual tradition, even though, by now, the very notion of sending anything by the postal service has become outmoded.

On Sundays we always tried to attend the "open house" gatherings held by Jean and Catherine Gimpel, owners of the well-known Gimpel Fils Gallery. There would always be interesting people and conversation in a relaxed and homely atmosphere. This was the kind of salon that someone should revive. Intellectual exchange, which Pierre greatly enjoyed, was also on offer at the Institute of Contemporary Arts later in the month with two intellectual giants, Tzvetan Todorov and George Steiner, in discussion. At the ICA that month Miron Grindea had a retrospective of his literary review *Adam*, for which Picasso had contributed the palindromic cartoon and caption "Madam, I'm Adam". Music was supplied by Stoika Milanova, who gave a Mozart concert at the Royal Festival Hall, which we very much enjoyed.

A "regal" appointment

April brought me, on my birthday, the news that I had an interview for the post at King's, something which Pierre had always encouraged me to pursue: a permanent post at a prestigious university. The interview panel was daunting: the Principal, a priest (King's has always been linked to the Church of England), a senior member of the French department and my tutor Professor Perry. I passed the test and was offered the appointment, to start in October, although Professor Perry did tell me afterwards that it was considered that I was "wearing too much make up"! I wonder what, if any, comments might have been made about a male candidate... In fact my research colleague Vaughan James had an interview the same month for the Deputy Directorship of the Centre for Information on Language Teaching. He was also appointed, but I am sure there were no questions about his personal habits!

It soon became obvious to me that Pierre and I were going to be juggling even more activities: his lectures, visiting and reviewing exhibitions for *Arts Review*, broadcasts for the BBC, film and theatre plans, as well as keeping a look out for interesting university posts being advertised (The University of Manchester had not shown the good sense to appoint him!). I would have to complete my tenure at the College, prepare a postgraduate level programme for my new post at King's, keep up to date with each monthly issue of *New Linguist* and continue with the research into language teaching as well as our personal and social engagements with friends and visitors. All this on top of my regular medical checks undertaken with a view to our enlarging the family.

May was particularly busy in every respect: one Sunday we were invited to visit the artist Bernard Stern, at his lovely old house in the country, which was full of his paintings (one of which has pride of place in the house in Chelsea). Another day Felix Topolski came with the film director Andrei Wajda for dinner and lots of talk. The 24th offered a big party at the Bulgarian Embassy with, as appropriate, representatives of the press, education and culture. In the 1970s, of course, Bulgaria and Embassy invitations were treated in different ways, both by those invited and those who accepted. The days of the blustering Robert Maxwell were still to come, but members of the British-Bulgarian Friendship Society were usually in attendance, Mercia MacDermott and those representing Collett's Bookshop and Progressive Tours. On the 28th Pierre was to fly to Sofia; he had become increasingly sought after by intellectuals and academics and was invited to lecture, especially by his good friend Professor Lubomir Tenev of the National Academy of Theatre and Television Arts (NATFIZ). He was also becoming involved in projects at the Boyana film studios and had already begun discussions of treatments of certain works with Bulgarian TV, in collaboration with the BBC. I drove him to Heathrow for the Balkanair flight, as usual with many kilos overweight, but their representative was able to organize clearance!

He was to stay a couple of weeks and meanwhile I organised my ticket to Sofia for the 22nd of June, by which time I would have finished all the end-of-year marking for different groups of students; attended leaving parties held for me at the College and the Institute – I was giving up both posts in order to go full-time to King's – and, most important of all, checking at the Bulgarian Embassy that all the documentation was in order for that all-important event: the addition to our family.

And so, suddenly, on the 22nd, two years after my first visit to Bulgaria, I went to Heathrow for the flight to Sofia. Among the passengers, looking so much like the "Don", was Peter Glossop; this was confirmed when we heard that he was to be singing in *Tosca* at the opera on Monday. After the "special" coach to the "special" entrance, I saw a little face behind a drawn-back curtain in the VIP entry lounge: it was Vanyo Rumenov, and inside were Pierre and Zhivko Popov. It was a good feeling, seeing them all again. My passport was soon dealt with and on our way to Grand Hotel Sofia I noticed several new buildings (*Mladost* was growing even then …); all seemed green and there were roses planted along the roadside. We were to meet with Vanyo and Jeannie that evening. Their son Vladi was doing his military service. The following day Zhivko was to come and collect us to go to the Mother and Baby home. Our room in the hotel was 201, just two along from the one we had had on our first visit and with the same incredible view, the same clear light, the beautiful soft yellow ochre buildings and the golden domes of Alexander Nevski. Time for a bit of unpacking and then Goshkin was sending a car for us to visit him in his office on Dondukov, in the building with the marble entrance and stairs. His wife came to join us and we laughed over the photos taken in London during his visit last year.

Later we walked, slowly, enjoying all the sights, sounds and people, towards Pierre's mother's home on 6th September Street. On the way we sat for half an hour to take a coffee at the Budapest restaurant café, and were joined by an ex-diplomat colleague of Pierre's (London 1938–1941) who spoke the most fluent and idiomatic English and, to my delight, was also a philatelist! Zhivko walked past; Sofia was then so small and human-scale that you always saw someone that you knew! I still do, perhaps because I know so many people, but certainly Sofia has changed enormously in the past 35 years! We walked on to the house and it was lovely to see his mother, to talk and show photos; then the "aunties", first Vena with cakes; next came Pashanko's mother bringing presents for her grandsons in London and, just as we were about to leave, Aunt Bogdanka. We made no mention of Vanyo, whom we were to meet later as there seemed to have been some disagreement or other. Always be diplomatic...! Walking back to the hotel we met Isaac Passy (the "Blue Jeans Professor"), so young looking, such excellent English and wearing, of course, blue jeans! By this time Alexander Nevski was illuminated, we waited for Jeannie (a pediatrician, how useful!) and went to what was then known only as "The Russian Club" where tables were laid out in the summer garden. We certainly consumed a lot of food and, although I was getting very tired, we phoned Lina and Karl Ognyanov to say that we would come on to them for coffee. Tomorrow was to be a busy day...

"Lorsque l'enfant paraît"

Saturday, up at 7h. to sort out some of the masses of presents, for the baby and for Professor Shterkalev. After a quick breakfast we went with Zhivko, in an official car, to the Mother and Baby home for 9h. It turned out to be the wrong one – after we had sent the car away! Zhivko did try to phone the Central Committee, but a taxi came and finally we were there: a big, dark, cool, old building. We were shown to Professor Shterkalev's room and talked. Well Pierre did; I was not very *compos mentis*. There was a knock at the door. The baby? No, false alarm... but then: lots of very dark hair, grey eyes... What else can one discern at two weeks? I took a photo of her with the nurse, Pierre took a photo of me with the baby, who was yawning and looking very sweet. I had forgotten to bring the presents and was so overcome with emotion that I failed to ask any of the necessary questions. We left and took a taxi back to the hotel before going on to have lunch at Pierre's mother's home. All his favourites: stuffed peppers, chicken and rice, cherries from the garden.

There was much talk of the baby, plans, returning to London... Later a great-nephew, Vesko, came with his mother Meglena. This was, of course, well before post-1989 property claims and the duplicitous dealings into which Pierre and his sister, and later I, were dragged by these two members of the family. One somehow feels that, if once, only once, they had had the common decency to say "thank you", and to acknowledge that it was only through generosity on Pierre's and Dora's part that they were able to take over the whole family inheritance...

After this copious lunch and emotional talk, it was time for a siesta before getting ready to have dinner with Ludmila, Ivan and Zhivko at 20h30 in the hotel. On the way down to the lobby, Pierre met Kiril Krustev, author of *Atlantida*. He also said to me something like, "It's A.J. Ayer". I rushed over to the lift and, amazingly, it was! Pierre saw Professor Spassov who told him that Ayer was in Bulgaria for the organisation of the International Philosophy Conference in Varna in September. You certainly do see a lot of interesting and important people in Sofia! For our dinner we went up to the Panorama restaurant, passing the "professorial" table and greeting Ayer. Our table – the best in the house for the best people! – was out on the balcony with a breathtaking view of Alexander Nevski. At 21h it was still warm and Sofia by night was very beautiful. We had an excellent meal, with lots and lots of *Exinovgrad* wine, talking of "*bebeto*" who, as Ivan said, would be a good age for their son. Things have subsequently, of course, taken very different paths...

On Sunday Pierre had to get up early as someone was coming to see him. I had been thinking since waking that I would so like to visit "*bebeto*" again and what a shame not to have asked, but Pierre said we really couldn't bother the Professor on a Sunday. Besides, with no common language nor means of identifying myself, it hardly seemed feasible. Pierre decided (I think to take my mind off "*bebeto*"), that we would go for lunch to the *Vodenitsata* restaurant in the foothills of Mount Vitosha. Before that, however, we went to see the icon collection, Pierre telling me so much more than I had known before. We walked, took photos, saw the Synod, Ivan Vazov sculpture, St. Sofia; how marvellous it was to have the very best guide to Sofia, even if, for him, some of the changes he saw around him needed explaining! What a pleasure it was for him, while strolling, to meet a fellow pupil of the French College, not seen since 1947! There had been a reunion recently and they talked of their Plovdiv days. They were all full of admiration for Pierre!

When we came out of the Ethnographic Museum it was raining and so we crossed to have a drink at the coffee shop in the Grand Hotel Bulgaria, at the same time thinking that there was little point in going to eat outside Sofia. Rather we should invite the Hadjimishevs for lunch. That was our plan but, in fact, they were expecting us for lunch and so we enjoyed an "English-style" Sunday lunch! Ivo also gave me copies of the photos he had taken at Jane and Jacques' wedding in London the previous year. I wrote several postcards to our friends . We stayed, talking music, London, friends etc. till mid-afternoon when we went on to visit Isaac Passy. He and Pierre talked and talked: of philosophy, the Varna conference, Ayer. There were raspberries and *"torta"* as well! Passy is a very nice, relaxed and friendly person. Nor, since Pierre's death, have I lost contact with him, seeing him at the University and when he spoke on the occasion of the donation of Pierre's books to the University library. These visits and talks certainly cheered Pierre who had been somewhat depressed at not having had much news from Bulgarian TV about their joint projects. Our last visit, before leaving for London the following day, was to his mother; such a warm, loving and welcoming person – the perfect balance with the argumentative "aunties"!

An early flight to Heathrow, full of impressions, emotions… the change to our life, the addition to our family, was to bring enormous joy, responsibilities, but for the moment this was only represented by a pile of documents, all requiring signatures, in both London and Sofia. We had also thought long and hard as to whether we would need to have more space. How could we achieve this? Buy a larger house? Extend the Chelsea house? These were very real questions and we decided to enlist the professional advice of our neighbour, an architect, as to the possibilities of extension; those who have visited us here will know Pierre's remark about our living in a "furnished chimney": the only way, in these small Victorian houses, is to go upwards and outwards, and so we did, thereby creating what Pierre would jokingly refer to as our "seven storey" house. Not, in fact "storeys", but "levels", full of interesting corners. We agreed that the extension building should start in the autumn and so it was that, when we did return to London with *"bebeto"*, we lived temporarily at another address.

Back in London in June, however, our friends came over to

hear the news and look at the photos: "What a gorgeous tiny baby!" In addition there was the usual round of work, students, classes and, for Pierre, an article on the exhibition of a good friend, about whose work he wrote:

> "Milein Cosman is a master in evoking the incontrovertible presence of... visual absences... the reason is evident: she does not aim at satisfying the eye but at stirring the imagination".

I quote this as I myself now find that to be so true since, when *"bebeto"* was about six months old, Milein made a sketch of her which not only "satisfied the eye" but "stirred the imagination" as to how she would grow and develop into the charming and beautiful young woman that she now is, full of love and thoughtfulness, interest in and a proper concern for Bulgaria.

I was due to return to Sofia in late July. Meantime the summer term had to be completed, and the architect and builders briefed as to the changes in the house. Zhivko was now back at his Embassy post in London and he and his "eccentric scientist" wife, Julia Vassilieva, were our frequent guests. Zhivko proved such a reliable and good friend and organiser of all our affairs between London and Sofia. I was not to escape the "present-buying" spree: our dear friend, oncologist Vanyo Rumenov, had given me his orders: various medical tomes, obtainable only at Lewis', the specialist bookshop next to University College Hospital. This is how the kilos in the luggage begin to mount up!

20th July saw me off again, this time on my own, to Sofia. It is true that we had such good, kind and reliable friends there that I had absolutely no need to be concerned about how I would manage. Pierre, meanwhile, was of course perfectly well able to manage without me in London, even if cooking or preparing food had never been his forte! The very same day that I left, he went down to Glyndebourne with Jonathan

Griffin for the dress rehearsal of *Capriccio*. They will have had a marvellous time, listening to and talking music with all their professional and other friends!

This, my third visit to Sofia, began at Heathrow where I was able to supplement the packed presents by visiting the Duty Free area. This time I was flying with BEA (as it then was) and what a blessing to realise that they had instituted a "non smokers" section (well, in those days, you had to be grateful for small mercies…). One certainly noticed the difference when, cutting through the fog, one went, to the toilet at the back of the plane. The flight was completely full and among the passengers were at least twelve delegates on an agricultural visit, led by Sir William Harpham, previous Ambassador to Bulgaria. On our greeting each other he expressed surprise seeing me on the way to Sofia. I must say that, typical English gentleman, he was wearing a heavy three-piece suit, carrying a hat and a coat and, as one might imagine since it was the middle of July, perspiring, mopping his brow and complaining of the heat! We were, however, told to expect showers in Sofia, and this after Pierre had convinced me to leave my Burberry behind!

It was in fact lovely and warm in Sofia, with the view of Vitosha as one came down the aircraft steps. No VIP coach for me this time… but whom should I see in the terminal building, waiting for Sir William, but Ambassador Alexander Yankov whom I had thought was in Geneva. Great greetings all round. My effusiveness, however, may not have been entirely appropriate to Sofia airport and his status. He then introduced me to Emil Alexandrov who speaks excellent French and who took me, my passport and my luggage in hand as we went for the traditional welcome coffee (and cognac and coca cola…) to the VIP lounge, where Sir William and the delegation were being entertained. Emil drove me to Hotel Sofia where I had a very nice room on the third floor, with the same splendid view of the cathedral. First things first: unpacking the tons of presents to take round to Mama and the aunties, make some phone calls and then walk round to 6th September. Then my Bulgarian language ordeal began: "Basic Bulgarian for Beginners" and I am all on my own this time... Not too badly, I managed a couple of hours. It appears that "the whole of Sofia" knows about "*bebeto*". Who, I ask the aunties, is "the whole of Sofia"? But I have become quite used to the expression "*Tzyala Sofia znae...*" ("All Sofia knows...") and know it is a group of ladies... Back at the hotel there are great crowds and police, tricolours flying. I have competition in the shape of Monsieur Messmer on an official visit and am no doubt very lucky to get a room at all.

Breakfast the following day proved a problem as, on arrival, I had not been given my "vouchers" (such was then the system, now incomprehensible...). I found myself becoming very adept on the phone in Bulgarian: my "*Molya, moga li da govorya sus...*" ("Please may I speak to...") had got me into some complicated conversation with Maya's grandmother, Passy's daughter and Annie's housekeeper. However, Emil Alexandrov was there to save me and drive us both to the Mother and Baby Home; a roundabout way as the road was up for a new tram route. We had to go with the pediatrician, Professor Koeva, to the hospital for infectious diseases as "*bebeto*" had colitis. There we met the director, Professor Kirov. "*Bebeto*" Mila Gina was alone in a large white room, looking very sweet and very angry at being woken up! She was very sleepy, still had lots of black-brown hair and greyish eyes. I was able to hold her and talk to her (memory does not serve to tell me if this was in English or Bulgarian...) and take some photos. Professor Koeva confirmed that three months was the maximum age to take her into the family in London and so plans, travel, documents etc. must be on time. Later, back at the hotel, Isaac Passy came to have a drink on the terrace and we talked of books, articles, philosophy and how A.J. Ayer, who was here in June, had played chess with him. Many university colleagues were greeted as they passed by. In the afternoon I went strolling and watched the children playing in the gardens in front of the Mausoleum (not the Battenberg one, but Dimitrov, for those who remember …), walked up towards the Balkan (now Sheraton) hotel past a useful shop: *Detmag*, whose sad, remaining sign still hangs on the building, but which, as a prime site for development, will no doubt soon become, if not a 'Toys R Us', then a Hugo Boss or Zara… Then I was able to stave off hunger by venturing into a self-service "workman's cafe" (now a bank) on the corner of the square and had a full meal for 78 *stotinki*! It is true that now one can still eat well and at reasonable cost at places like *Trops Kushta*, although it is sad to see how many of the poor and elderly queue at 20h. to take advantage of the reduction in the price of all the remaining food. Then, in the '70s, I was able to afford to eat at the Russian Club and now I am in the fortunate position of still being able, should I wish, to eat there, although I do prefer *La Capannina* or *Egur Egur*, if only the latter would implement the (non-) smoking policy.

An elegant evening garden party

After a rest at the hotel I had a call from Ivan Slavkov, asking me if I could be ready in twenty minutes… as he and Ludmila were going for the evening to Detchko Ouzunov's. We went by car, the house accessible again, across the completed tramway. Olga, whom I had probably last seen in Paris, was very surprised to see me; no doubt also to see me on my own. I was certainly feted as the honoured guest and after a couple of Yeastvite tablets and two quick glasses of white wine I was being immensely sociable and speaking very fluently in my pretty atrocious but efficacious Bulgarian! We were all sitting out in the cool, delightful, lamp-lit garden (on a recent visit to the House-Gallery I was puzzled because the long garden seemed no longer to exist. And indeed it did not, for blocks of flats had been built on it). I see from my notes that "Dora's 'Kitaika' arrived"; this, of course, was Soon, Chinese wife of the artist Marin Varbanov. Soon was to become a very good friend and, from Paris, she and the children, Boryana and Feni, would come and visit us in Normandy in the 1980s. At that point, however, we ladies, together with Ludmila and Jenny Bozhilova-Haitova, would often meet at the Varbanovs' flat on Oborishte Street. More painters, more actors; the two Manev brothers; delicious food laid outside and "Bai" Detchko wearing a recently acquired Algerian habit. Later on, the politician Venelin Kotzev and his wife Yonka arrived; everyone, absolutely everyone was so nice, friendly and welcoming. I moved from one end of the table to the other to join Ludmila and a man who, I later discovered, was Svetlin Roussev. What a pleasure it was to be able to tell him how very much I liked our painting by him!

I did an anti "at John Mortimer's and on the staircase". It could have been one of two possibilities: " sit on my own, hiding on the staircase" because I didn't really understand what people were talking about, and just be the silent English "wife of Petar Ouvaliev"; or, plunge in – and survive – casting all linguistic etc. (and particularly "English") inhibitions to the winds. I chose the latter and had a marvellous evening! There was talking, laughing, dancing... with Detchko commissioned on the spot for a portrait of *"bebeto"*. Ludmila, who had been in Kazanluk all day, and Ivan left early and I was driven back to the hotel in the early hours.

Sunday morning and Pierre phoned at about 9h. Our conversation was drowned by the cathedral bells! Despite that, we spoke for at least half an hour: of Sofia, people, *"bebeto"*, his mother... I did the Sunday thing: went to Alexander Nevski to attend a part of the service and, especially, to light a candle for *"bebeto"* and her future, for us, for friends and family. I noted at the time, obviously somewhat shocked, that "some tourists were in shorts... one tends to think that they are German". Sadly, now that respect for church has declined, I would no longer identify by nationality... I then continued the Sunday tradition: family lunch, explaining, in every detail, my phone conversation with Pierre; listening to a friend whose daughter lived in Paris, trying to make appropriate comments. It was always something of a sad irony that the difficulties and cost of obtaining food, combined with the overwhelming kindness and generosity shown, meant that one was confronted with a loaded table and that not to eat everything, rather than just taste it, was to offend. To enquiries as to where "*bebeto*" was, I replied that she was in the infectious diseases hospital, whereupon Mama was told by the aunties that she could not visit with me. As if adults could possibly contract baby colitis! Aunt Vena was in a particularly argumentative mood: nobody, but nobody, who was a communist could possibly be any good (giving as an example the present Ambassador to London!). I have to say that, although I always tried hard to weigh things in the balance, I could certainly understand and appreciate their situation and point of view. Members of the family had certainly suffered greatly from "the system".

An "English Nanny"

Mama and I later spoke for a while about "English nannies" and, taking my leave – or so I thought – with a few nice words about Pierre, I unleashed a near-incomprehensible forty minutes of memories (oh, that I had understood and could remember, it would so add to this picture...). At least I feel I was then able to be somewhat more tolerant and patient than I used to be with my father (oh, that I had listened, it would have so added to another picture...). I returned to the hotel, vowing not to eat again for at least a week!

Monday morning (skipping breakfast!), I took a taxi to Mama's house. She, lovely lady, was in her best: a suit with matching bag and shoes. After all, this was a very special visit: she already had a grandson, now she would have a granddaughter. And so, despite Aunt Vena's objections, we went to the hospital and were met on the steps (of the "diphtheria" section!) by the nice blonde nurse. Mama asked about the director:

"Which Kirov?"
"Professor Ivan Kirov".
"Oh, my ex-pupil!"

So the nurse went to announce this fact to Professor Kirov who, I must say, was very moved and pleased to see her. (Everywhere I go, even to this 21st century day, when I mention "Gospozha Ouvalieva", there will be somebody who, or whose parent, has been a pupil of hers. I have heard nothing but the highest praise for this kind, supportive and forward-looking Headteacher at the Denkoglu School.) Professor Kirov was also surprised to learn that one "Sonia Rouve" was the daughter-in-law of "Gospozha Ouvalieva". We all went to see "*bebeto*", henceforward to be known as "Midzhi", and to take photos although Mama would not agree to hold her, following Aunt Vena's orders... With the family visit over and Midzhi swept away for feeding, Mama and I went back home by taxi, she all the while singing the praises of "English nannies"... I left them before lunch, much to Aunt Bogdanka's dismay, but not before hearing a long story about money, Paris, *leva*, Pierre... and will he please phone them. On my way back to the hotel, I took some photos of buildings and signs in the old orthography, snacked at the self-service café and then walked around TZUM with its displays of one or other item. What a contrast to the present altars of consumerism: Wolford, Timberland, Swatch... In the evening I was to dine with Emi and Chavdar Damianov; she, a ballerina, so sweet and friendly, he such a very good and reliable friend from London. (A remarkable coincidence kept us slightly in touch, even after his second marriage, as he and his wife Zhivka visited a researcher colleague in Normandy – small world.) It was such a pleasure to see him again in Sofia, to reminisce, laugh and talk about London. We tried the Russian Club, but it was full and so we ate at the Panorama. A lovely evening where the toasts were "To friendship!"

Pierre had said that he would phone on Tuesday morning but I had no call, only one from Aunt Bogdanka! I tried ringing

London but got "your number doesn't answer". Ensued a saga on the phone with Aunt Bogdanka and Mama. If only they would learn some discretion... In those days one did not speak openly about things on the phone! Hard to remember now, but the telling off I got from Pierre for having mentioned, in the hotel room, the name of a certain English friend...

In the afternoon Emi Damianova came to take me to visit what I still remember as an extraordinary exhibition, by both size and kind. Not only Bulgarian painters but those from "friendly" countries: Georgia, Vietnam and Cuba. The Vietnamese pictures were all lacquered, the Cubans were in very fierce colours, the Georgian's was a huge and impressive "Lenin". In the exhibition, at what is called "Shipka 6" (and possibly was even then), the display space of the Union of Bulgarian artists, we were able to see works by all our friends and those whose work we knew: Detchko Ouzunov's *Levski*, Tzanko Lavrenov's *Night Music*, Svetlin Roussev's *Last Day*, Lilyana Rousseva's *Mother*, Christo Stefanov's *Portrait of the artist Panov,* Dimiter Kirov's *19th November 1919*. The weather was cool, cloudy and rainy but, as there was no air conditioning in the gallery, a new building, this was not so good for the canvases or, indeed, for us while we were viewing. Afterwards, in the pouring rain, there being no taxis available, Emi and I, with very effective rain-hats made of the 'Rabotnitchesko Delo' newspaper, made our way to her flat. Drying out, we sat down, phoned Jenny Bozhilova and drank Nescafe with condensed milk; a treat, "*moloko*" imported "from USSR". The Damianovs' apartment (on what was then 'Tolbukhin') was absolutely huge, a "mansion flat" indeed: rooms and halls opening off in every direction. The solidly built building is one I nowadays pass whenever I turn the corner from Slavianska and walk along Levski.

I left Emi to go and visit Jenny. The taxi driver, even though he had a friend with him, was defeated by 'Latinka'. As I so often feel in London, my sketchy knowledge of Sofia proved to be the most useful in that we had to go up past Ouzunov's house and then into Latinka. They still (two years later...)

hadn't completed the Haitovs' building at No. 15, pleading shortages of building materials etc. Jenny and I had, as we always do, a relaxed tea on the balcony admiring, what was then, the splendid view. She is such a lovely, warm, friendly person, intelligent and an excellent translator from English. This had certainly been a full and social day.

On Wednesday I was to be ready by 8h45 to go and sign various official documents. Pierre rang at 8h and we spoke for a few minutes and were then cut off; probably a natural phenomenon (international calls were not easy to make in those days), but I was ready to blame Mama and the aunties and their interminable questions...I set off with Emil Alexandrov to a typical government office building; I remember there being 'BKP' in stained glass windows on the stairway. In the office I met the woman jurist who had already signed all the necessary papers, if Mila Gina (later to be known for a while as Midzhi) was to be well and truly ours! I was obviously feeling extremely nervous at being on my own, that is to say without Pierre, and having to sign papers for such a hugely important event. Everyone was very helpful and informative and, with my passport details given and all papers officially stamped, I was given a set for the hospital. Midzhi has a very smart birth certificate in a cover like a passport. Which it was to be: passport to us, to her new life. Emil and I drove to the hospital where I then had to find my own way, geographically and linguistically, to the director's office to hand over the papers. A lot of nice things were said about Pierre and me and I can only hope that we have always lived up to their expectations that we would be good, caring parents.

I was taken along corridors to Midzhi's ward. While looking for her, a nurse went past carrying a baby. Not recognising her, I thought: "That's a nice baby". Of course it was Midzhi...! A good story against myself! I went to see her after her feed and cuddled her so much that, as soon as I put her down she cried and was miserable! When the blonde nurse came along we all played with Midzhi. I was then shown which trolley to take to the centre. My adventures on Sofia municipal transport could equal those of *Zazie dans le Métro*. Where does one get the tickets which one then punches? Take out one's purse, look innocent, hope that a ticket inspector does not get on. How to travel for free: ask one's neighbour in broken Bulgarian where, how... tickets... She indicated to me that one could buy one from the driver but he said: "*Nyamam, nyamam!*" ("I haven't any!") and indicated to me to get off and, since it was the stop I wanted and he wasn't going to make me pay... I did just that. I then walked to Mama's house and told the aunties off severely for all this talk of money (needing it, paying too much for things...) and saying that this was no doubt getting Pierre into trouble since "everybody talks...". My next call was to the British Embassy to make an appointment to see the Consul about an entry into my passport; this was arranged for the following day and I went on to join Maya, daughter of Zhivko and Julia, to buy some food and go back to their flat on Gurko Street (a place I remember with affection, having been received there with great warmth). That evening there were lots of young people there, the Sofia gilded youth of the time, often London-bred, a fascinating cultural mix. Now, of course, this group would be the members of the London City Club and students at the London School of Economics. Then, the opportunities for visiting a country in Western Europe were severely limited.

The next day the ever-reliable Emil Alexandrov phoned early to arrange our visit to the Embassy. Pierre phoned at 8h30 and we were able to have a long talk – about everything except the controversial subjects! I updated him on the paperwork, the chances of everything being done in time, my visiting Midzhi whom he had not seen for quite some time, her progress, our friends, his mother and the dreaded aunties. It was good to feel I was putting him in the picture and to hear something of his activities in London. At the Embassy all was not entirely clear; a certain amount of humming and ha-ing since Volume 25, paragraph ... seemed to say no entry could be made onto a passport. Well, that had to be looked into and so Emil and I went to the hospital, in time for Midzhi's feed, and we also assembled the cot mobile (another product of Mothercare). Lunch was with the Hadjimishevs. We talked of music, Tcham Kuriya (as that generation still referred to Borovetz) and a possible visit to Koprivshtitsa. Afterwards, proudly equipped with tickets, I could take a trolley back to the hotel!

On Friday Mama and I were going to see Midzhi together with Jeannie Rumenova who, as a pediatrician, would be able to give lots of good advice. The Rumenovs were just back from one of their travels, so it was lovely to see Jeannie again, such a dear and supportive friend, such a complement to her kind but outspoken husband Vanyo. An argumentative but devoted couple, both of them friends since childhood with Pierre. We collected Mama, very elegant in her dark grey French raincoat and grey dress and jacket, and went in a taxi to the hospital. There Jeannie greeted her professor and Mama was welcomed. We discussed the question of Midzhi going back to the Pediatric Institute and took lots of photos. She was dressed in red, not the most flattering colour for a baby, but we had her pink shawl. This time Mama did take her on her lap.

Jeannie had to leave and Mama had quite an audience as she regaled the nursing sisters with stories of Pierre (the well known *émigré* intellectual, when a little boy…). "Our" blonde nurse, Penka Georgieva, came downstairs. She would not accept even a little gift for all her kindness, but wanted to invite me to her home. Mama and I were due to have lunch with Goshkin and his wife and so returned to my hotel to wait for them. We were driven to Hemus hotel and up to the 18th floor to the Terrace Restaurant with a magnificent view of Vitosha and Sofia from the balcony. This was a very nice event as I could see how they admired and respected my mother-in-law, had so many things to talk about, and were interested to hear about all the things that Pierre had achieved in the West. As Goshkin had an official meeting at 15h, Mama and I returned home and I went on to the hotel as I was due to have tea with the ladies – Jenny,

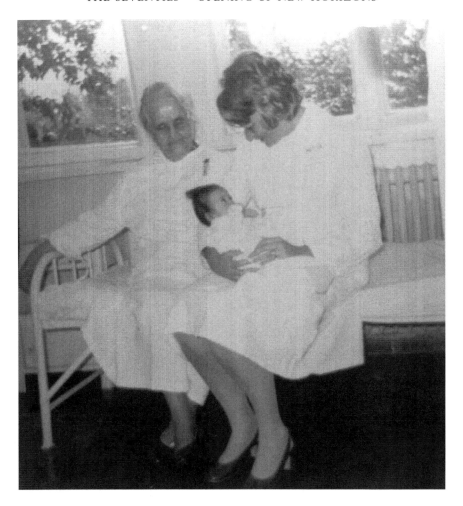

Ludmila and Olga – at Soon's flat. For the evening I was invited to the home of Ancheto Fadenhecht, doyenne of the famous Sertchadjiev theatre family, and I was fetched by Bogdan ('Bondo'), whose son Stefcho was to be exactly the same age as Midzhi.

Live longer with yoghurt!

A lovely weekend outing was the trip that Misho and Annie Hadjimishev arranged for the following day to Koprivshtitsa.

First, however, I had a long call from Pierre updating me on London, friends and his many activities, so I was able to pass on his news to all our friends. The drive – Misho had hired a taxi for the day – was very interesting, taking us past fields full of sunflowers, to places I had not previously visited. For me, Koprivshtitsa was a real discovery: the historic houses, the church, the "Bridge of the First Shot"... a real "museum town". The present, however, showed itself in the strangest way: on the hill on the way up to the 'Balkantourist' hotel, was a Japanese film crew, making a film to publicise Bulgarian yoghurt with Bulgarian characters in national dress looking as if they had lived to 100... on yoghurt! We walked, admired and talked, and saw a man of 90 with flowing white hair sitting in front of his house, who remembered Pierre. He was a well-known citizen of Koprivshtitsa, Dontcho Palaveev (I seem to recall some connection with tobacco growing). What a wonderful day!

Sunday was equally dedicated to my discovery of Bulgaria, but first I went with Jenny and Soon to visit Miss Midzhi – quite the little princess with such attention and care. The excursion was with Vanyo and Jeannie.

Vanyo was to drive the trusty Moskvitch (a "Moscow agent" as he called himself) in a way that only a determined (=pigheaded...) Bulgarian man could... Never mind that, we had the most lovely day exploring the countryside, villages, stopping for a picnic (thanks to Jeannie). Idyllic was the only word for it: forests as one dreams of them, streams, rocks, moss, pine trees... We drove up incredibly bad roads; at one point the car stalled and it was necessary to put big stones under the back wheels, but the Moskvitch was magnificent! The route was to Malyovitza and then back via Borovetz; mountains, mountains all the way and a small village with a delightful church with two towers. What a beautiful country! Back at the hotel I had to pack for the following day's departure: strange, quite a routine, visiting Midzhi, watching her, learning all about her... and now back to London to

prepare for the family return, more paperwork, and to plan the next visit. But that evening there were phone calls, visits of friends with presents; kind, kind people. Early on the Monday morning Emi and Chavdar came to the hotel and drove me to the airport for the flight to London. Pierre was at Heathrow to meet me and to hear all the news (this became a regular thing since each time I went to Bulgaria I would be able to tell him things which he might be able to work into his BBC broadcasts). I certainly had a lot of news this time, plus the emotions. We went home to relax – and check on the building work.

Bulgaria soon began to seem another world; and so it was, since work and meetings in London had a quite different rhythm. It was vacation time and, in August, it was unusual not to go somewhere on holiday but I had to prepare for the new job and to oversee *New Linguist*. Zhivko and Julia were quite often with us and, of course, there was the signing of documents at the Embassy and also placing an advertisement for an "English nanny". Yes, Mama would get her way! We also had the great pleasure of meeting up again (after Moscow!) with Yuri Kuperman and showing him that we had hung his two drawings at home. Now shortened to Kuper (rather like Pierre's Ouvaliev to Rouve...), Yuri has had exhibitions of his work in Cambridge, London and Paris. Our ink drawing of Pushkin, purchased directly from him in Moscow will always be special.

Having interviewed and appointed a nanny, Miss Sauvage, she and I went together to do lots of shopping! The best that Boots, Peter Jones and Mothercare had to offer for the best, and specially chosen, baby in the world! It was agreed that, although Pierre and I would be going out to Sofia at the end of August, she would join us there in the first week of September. The BEA flight on August 31st was very full and we, of course, were loaded with parcels. Going to a conference on the Black Sea coast was Bert Pockney of the Association of Teachers of Russian, while the Sieferts were attending a wedding, and Mercia MacDermott was going to take up a post at Sofia University. Our arrival at Sofia was smooth, Emil Alexandrov seeing to everything, including my return ticket for the 11th, and we were whisked off to Hotel Sofia, another marvellous "room with a view".

In the afternoon Pierre and I went to the hospital. Would she have changed, would she be the same, would she recognise me? Of course, when we got there and saw her, she just looked gorgeous. We had clothes, toys, all sorts of things for her.

This visit was an occasion for Pierre to spend more time getting to know her, but also to continue with his work plans, meeting people from film and television as well as seeing so many of his friends and, of course, his mother. That same first evening Jeannie and Vanyo came to the hotel and we enjoyed a lovely evening and dinner at the Russian Club. The following day we had lunch with Jenny and Nikolai Haitov. Conversations with him were always a great pleasure for Pierre

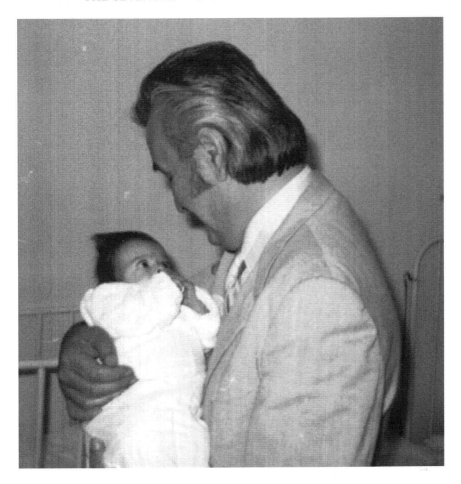

and, as usual, they must have discussed the whole field of literature, writers and periodicals. Sunday was a very special day for our friends the Yankovs: their daughter Svetlana was getting married, to Nikolai Lazarov, and the reception and luncheon were held in the restaurant of Hotel Sofia. This was a very grand yet warm family occasion and Pierre and I were seated very near to the high table, opposite the Sieferts. Quite an international gathering! There were toasts – and even I put together a few words for the happy couple – delicious food, fun and laughter until quite late.

On Monday, a working day, I went to the Embassy to get the entries made and documents stamped. The procedure, now that

I look back on it, strikes me as having been pretty straightforward when compared with the length of time now required by United Kingdom local authorities: visits, checks... as well as the overseas official bodies. Or, perhaps, we were given a degree of special treatment... Pierre, meanwhile, spent the morning with another longstanding friend, the writer Poli Spassov, and the routine of visits included lunch with his mother and going to the hospital to play with Midzhi – I think Pierre surprised himself at how well he could get on with a baby! We invited Professor Kirov and his wife to dine with us at the hotel. The next day too, with his mother, we went for our daily visit, and in the evening we attended a big family gathering at Jeannie and Vanyo's delightful small house past the Russian Memorial. There were so many friends, singing and photos!

On Wednesday, while Pierre met with his friends in town, Vanyo organised another glorious Bulgaria-discovering day together with Christo Alexiev and his daughter Juliana, the well-known musicologist. The men sang songs, the one considerably better than the other... and Juliana and I enjoyed the scenery as we made our way to Tcherepiishki Monastery, tucked away down by the Iskar river among the limestone rocks, a tiny, calm, quiet jewel. A cloister, vines, hens and Father Romil, an acquaintance of Vanyo's. We lit candles in the church, a big one for Midzhi, and for us all. Christo began to sing, in his beautiful bass voice, and then he and Vanyo and Father Romil sang a three-part *"Mnogaya leta"* for *"bebeto"*. Naturally, I was weeping buckets. It was lovely, so moving. Such good friends! We lunched by the waterfall before returning to Sofia where Christo came with us to the hospital and took a lot of photos. His are some of the most treasured that we have; not only of Midzhi but of events and friends. Later that evening Pierre and I were invited by his great friend Lubomir Tenev, Professor of the Theory and History of Theatre at the National Academy, and his wife the actress Beba Kabaivanova, to dine with them. Every meeting, with each and every friend, gave Pierre such pleasure and the opportunity to discuss his passions: theatre, literature, art. Although I cannot recall, and for the most part could not understand the discussions he had with his friends, I know that they gave immense pleasure to each and every one. The next day I took Lina to see Midzhi while Pierre spent the day with film colleagues, and on the Friday Nanny Sauvage arrived in Sofia. We took her first to the hotel and then, of course, to the hospital to meet her new charge. She was to spend quite a lot of time there until we flew to London on the 11th of September. Pierre was to return the following day and so we all spent the evening together as Nanny had to become accustomed to Bulgaria. Her most daunting task was to come the following day: lunch with Mama and the aunties.

Pierre had business in London with Carlo Ponti and left on the early flight and I went with nanny to the hospital where she spent time checking on professional matters: weight, feed, sleep etc. I took yet more photos, now gracing my many albums, together with those taken by our photographer friends.

9th September in Sofia

This was to be the schedule for the next few days except that Sunday was the 9th of September. It had been suggested that I might like to attend the "manifestation" marking "The 29th year since the Triumph of the Socialist Revolution in Bulgaria". This was such an unusual opportunity that I was obviously interested. Glorious weather and cathedral bells at 8h. Downstairs in the hotel I met Emil Alexandrov, he who had been able to fix so many things, brought me a personalised ticket for which I needed to show my passport. It was for *"Dr(ugarka) Sonia Ruv – Anglichanka"*.

All roads to *"Ploshtad 9th September"* were closed, so we had to take a special route to get near to the Mausoleum. The pass was for a specific location: *"Tribuna B"* and I selected my

> ДР. Соня Рув — англичанка
>
> ТРИБУНА ЗАПАД **В**
>
> ПРОПУСК № 005742
>
> за наблюдаване манифестацията на софийските трудещи се по случай
> 29-ТА ГОДИШНИНА ОТ ПОБЕДАТА НА СОЦИАЛИСТИЧЕСКАТА РЕВОЛЮЦИЯ В БЪЛГАРИЯ
> **ДЕВЕТИ СЕПТЕМВРИ 1973 г.**
> ВХОД ЗА ПЛОЩАД „9 СЕПТЕМВРИ" — БУЛ. „АЛ. СТАМБОЛИЙСКИ"
> И УЛ. „СОФИЙСКА КОМУНА"
>
> Пропускът е валиден при представяне на документ за самоличност
> Местата на трибуната се заемат до 9.45 часа

place for the best view of the processions. There was loud loudspeaker music, military bands, floats, parades, flowers, gymnastics. I must say that it was a most impressive display of the power of the party.

I certainly had occasion to mull over the political aspects of the day's events and it was obviously not without great significance that I went later for "Sunday lunch" to Mama. This was to be nanny's introduction to Bulgarian hospitality and home cooking, not to mention third degree questioning... After a copious lunch, plus, for me, the task of interpreting for nanny and the aunts and, at the same time, judiciously "editing out" certain questions and comments, we were all tired, and the last thing I felt like doing was to go with the lovely, kind nurse, Penka Georgieva, to her country place in the foothills of Mount Vitosha. But there was absolutely no question of cancelling, so I went to the hotel for a short rest and then to meet her at the hospital after work. The visit was one of the most friendly, warm evenings I can remember. We took a bus, then walked, way up and up... (I can no longer identify the exact location amidst all the destruction and concrete horrors of the current "building boom".) She and her husband, a colonel, had a garden with vegetables and chickens. It was Penka who introduced me to an unknown fruit, medlar, and her son to an unknown pop singer Suzi Quatro. These are some of the heartwarming yet unexpected pleasures that I still occasionally experience in Bulgaria. Life was tough then and it is still tough now, though in a rather different way...

The next day was the last before going back to London. Yuri Kuperman

"a welcome newcomer... arrived from Moscow where his name is rated high in the list of gifted young artists",

was to open his first show at Kettle's Yard Gallery, Cambridge, which Pierre was to attend. Nanny, Mama and I went to the hospital, mainly to arrange for the pick up the following day; then followed a round of last visits. One thing it seemed I was able to effect was a peace treaty between Mama and Vena Spassova (who knows what might have come between them?) and we went there for tea where the talk is always of "the baby".

Off to London!

Tuesday, departure day, was tightly programmed: check out of the hotel; Vanyo came to collect us and all the luggage; at 11h to the hospital to take our leave, thank the staff for all their kindness and care, sweep Midzhi off to a new life, new language, new home... This was to be possible on account of the next stop: at the British Embassy where all was efficiency personified: papers stamped and delivered, copies for all parties concerned. At 13h a last call on Mama; difficult to leave her, she is so much a part of everything – everything that Pierre left behind in 1948 and which he found again more recently. And at 14h, with Midzhi in her smart carrycot, we set off to the airport to be met by my ladies: Soon, Jenny, Julia and Ko-Ko the photographer.

The airport director Nachev saw us on to the BEA flight and so, via Bucharest, we were off to London.

In London everything was different: Pierre had arranged with Carlo Ponti that, while the alterations were being done to the house in Chelsea, we could live in an apartment he owned in Davies Street, in the heart of Mayfair. This was ideal, with a lift and three bedrooms, each with bathroom: for Pierre and me, nanny and Midzhi. Also we were very close to Hyde Park for walks, to Oxford Street and Bond Street for shopping and to several of the best galleries for visits. So family life in London was off to a very good start! Now it was the time for our London-based friends to visit. Midzhi was, of course, invited to lots of "baby parties".

While the extension and alterations to the Chelsea house

were to give us rooms and another bathroom for Midzhi and a nanny, the downside was that Pierre was giving up the huge open space which had always been his domain on the top floor and where he received all his Bulgarian and other friends, consulted his library of books and journals and typed out his articles and broadcasts. His library, even then, was enormous, and we pondered over what arrangements could be made. For storage he received a very sound suggestion from a close friend of the time, Donna Marinova-Ireland: she and her then husband Kevin had a large house in Clapham and often let rooms; what better than to let to the books... and to Pierre. They occupied a large room on the first floor and Pierre was able to go over, consult, collect any material he might need. It was only later that he discovered that, unfortunately, another tenant must have had access to the room and several precious items disappeared, including copies of articles later published under another name...

Philosophy in Varna

Pierre was juggling, as ever, with several plans: film projects with Carlo Ponti and articles for *Arts Review*. Moreover, he was invited to attend a philosophical gathering in Varna, the "XVth World Congress", at which he was to make a presentation. In those days, however, getting there was not so straightforward. We were up early on the 15th of September to go first to the house in Chelsea to collect some more clothes for him, then to Victoria for the train to Gatwick and the plane to Bourgas – yes, Bourgas – from where he was transported to Varna. On the 16th I received a cable (yes, cables still existed) from Pierre telling me of the splendid "Reception Committee"! The proceedings ran from the 17th to the 22nd, attracting top speakers, including, of course, Professor A.J.Ayer! Pierre was staying in Varna at the Ambassador Hotel, from which the delegates went each day to the large, new conference centre situated in the Sea Garden. It was marvellous for Pierre to be doing what he really enjoyed: engaging in philosophical debate, with some of the world's great thinkers and writers, in the company of his own fellow-countrymen and in such a pleasant location.

Meanwhile, nanny and I were looking after Midzhi, going out for walks, receiving friends. On the 16th, to my surprise and seen from the balcony, we observed red banners and marches along Davies Street. Not the BKP this time but solidarity for Allende in Chile!

Misho Hadjimishev was in London and his son Ivo was due to arrive as he was to follow a postgraduate course in photography at Bournemouth. He always remembers that he was able to stay in our Chelsea house, despite the building work. It was then that he took some of the best photos ever of Midzhi and me in Berkeley Square. I remember something technical about soft focus, the trying out of different lenses or exposures. At any rate, the results were outstanding.

Pierre was due back on the 22nd, full of news and stories of Varna, the talks and the interesting people he had spent time with. We went to Chelsea to see progress and to introduce

Midzhi to Chelsea life. Hardly back, and on a Sunday, Pierre had to fly to Switzerand to meet with Ponti as they were deep in negotiations concerning a new film contract, plus there was the matter of appropriate thanks for letting us all stay in his flat! While in the Montreux area, Pierre had the unusual opportunity of getting together with that "true friend of Bulgaria", Marcel Aier who, as he wrote in the visitors' book:

> "had, in two acres of land, created Bulgaria in the heart of Europe".

And this is true: the family's Swiss chalet, high in the mountains above Vevey, even flies the Bulgarian flag!

Back from all of this travelling, Pierre was able to review the exhibition of a colleague of mine, Carole Hodgson, a most interesting sculptor, about whose work at the Angela Flowers gallery, he wrote:

> "Carole Hodgson excels in what the Germans call 'eine kleine Plastik'... yet sculpture cannot be measured, it must be lived... and Hodgson shows that minute forms can be endowed with monumental authority".

And so, art, film, philosophy and languages soon came together in the first week of term for me at King's and for Pierre in his ongoing projects. In October the script for the Ponti project, *Ghosts,* was completed and a week or so later Pierre was to discuss the details of this production. On Monday 1st October, I met the new postgraduate students and some of the staff; for Pierre I had devised a plan to involve him with my students: as graduates having studied a foreign language and planning to teach French or Spanish, it was important that they realise what hurdles they would be placing in front of their young charges and so they were to be put into the situation of having to learn, and to respond in, a new foreign language: Bulgarian. Pierre and I planned this together, I the methodology and he the language. This proved a great success: the students were fascinated, terrified (as young learners might well be...), and entering into the game, afterwards asking lots of questions. Pierre, I think, was strengthened in his desire to take on more adult teaching; at any rate, we all had great fun! Straight after the session he flew off to Switzerland where he was to meet up with Ponti at his villa above Vevey. Talking on the phone would doubtless have been less effective, and much less pleasant. Once back, he was immediately invited to review a prestigious exhibition held at King's; we were becoming a "regal" pair. The exhibition, conceived by my colleague Professor Leslie Perry, was devoted to the work of Hermann Nonnenmacher, about which Pierre wrote:

"King's College has remembered that universities were once islands of universality and has staged a remarkable exhibition of this dramatic painter".

King's figured in our life later in October when, together, we attended the Principal's reception for new staff. This was a grand event, attended by many of the senior staff; Pierre talked with Professor Perry and the Dean, I with Professor Hywel Lewis (Philosophy of Religion) who had attended the Varna conference, and with Professor Taylor, of "black space" renown, and with Professor Harvey, who joined me in developing a project for future teachers of Spanish. At a certain point Pierre, claiming he had to check on the builders, slipped away and went back to Chelsea and watched football on television...

All the while, the newest addition to the Rouve family was being taken good care of during the day by nanny Sauvage and, although she had a routine for feeding and bath time, both Pierre and I were able to spend "quality time" with Midzhi (increasingly known by our English friends as 'Mila Gina' or just 'Mila'): reading books, playing, telling stories. This was something that Pierre was to develop an unexpected (by him) talent for and to this day Mila speaks of the stories he used to invent for her. Some days, too, if I didn't have classes, I would take Mila for a walk in the pram around the nearby art galleries and we became quite an item at the Estoricks' Grosvenor Gallery and at Gimpel's. An early, never too early, start to her aesthetic education. Pierre, meanwhile, was covering the "outstanding exhibition" of twentieth-century Russian art at the sadly demised Fischer Fine Art Gallery. It was a convenience at that time that he could combine taking his own text to Gainsborough Publications for the *Arts Review*, and mine for *New Linguist*, and bring back proof copies, or I would do the same thing for him! A little later in the year there was a special celebration to mark the 25th anniversary of the *Arts Review* and Pierre brought together tributes from the foremost critics and gallery owners of the time. One quote, from Dr. Fischer:

"I would like to stress how much the *Arts Review* means to me personally as an art historian and a writer and how much I appreciated it as an art dealer"

This covers its broad appeal.

Bulgarian news

Some "local" Bulgarian events were on the calendar: a reception at the Embassy for Patriarch Maxim; a "Bulgarian" *Simon Boccanegra* at Covent Garden and dinner after; Julia Vassilieva and Yonka Kotzeva (wife of the politician Venelin Kotzev) leaving London. It seems there was chaos – no doubt with the amount of luggage upon departing – at Heathrow, but it was Pierre who went to see them off, not me! The worst, the most unbelievable news was what Pierre heard a few days later when he visited the Embassy: Apostol ("Cho Cho") Karamitev had died! It was not said from what, but this was a great shock, as it must, of course, have been for the Bulgarian theatrical world.

Georgi Markov, who had, with Pierre's support, obtained work with the BBC Bulgarian service, often spent time at Davies Street as he had started a relationship with the film project secretary, Penny. He was later to marry Annabel Dilke, whose scathingly witty depiction of the Bulgarian community residing at 11 Shipka Avenue in Clapham, *The Party Wall*, published in 1989, had a knowingly appreciative readership.

As nanny Sauvage would have completed her three-month contract at Christmas, there was a vacancy to be advertised and interviews to be held. In addition, there was a limit to how long we could inflict ourselves on Carlo Ponti's generosity and it was necessary to think of renting another property. The building work in Chelsea was taking the traditional amount of extra time and so we looked for somewhere we could take for six months. We were very fortunate in that Pierre's friend Harry Moore knew of a house in Putney near the Heath, which, as it turned out, was ideal for us. We could move sometime in the New Year. Early in December, I interviewed and appointed probably the best nanny one could wish for: a delightful young Scotswoman, May Campbell, who was to stay with us for a considerable time and whose family we were later to get to know. May joined us before Christmas, as Mila turned six months and produced her first tooth!

In the run up to Christmas, Julia and Zhivko, the latter due to leave his London posting, came to visit us with their younger daughter Jultche, bearing gifts. They enquired what plans we might have for the festive season. Dora, Luben and Pierre Christian were due to come over from Paris, and so we organised a "get together". The family arrived on 23rd and we settled them in to Chelsea (habitable if not completed) and took them over for dinner at Davies Street. Mila slept through this and so was not to be admired until the following day when, among other things, there was the turkey to be collected; a 16 lb bird. Who weighs more, the turkey or Mila? Mila, by a short lb. I took everything and everybody over to Davies Street and we all set about preparing the Christmas meal for the next day. Meanwhile Mila charmed everyone and Pierre Christian was appointed "playmate". After lunch, while Pierre took Luben in the car for a tour of London, Dora and I wheeled Mila in the pram to Oxford Street (envisaging Oxford Street now, I can hardly imagine how one would have wanted to go there in the Christmas crowds…).

On the 25th we had our Christmas lunch and, by sheer "beginner's luck", the turkey, the stuffing, and sausages – the latter all seized by Pierre – were all a great success. This was followed by the traditional pudding, all very English!

Afterwards, we exchanged presents, and Mila had all sorts of lovely toys and sat in her chair all afternoon, smiling and laughing, until bath time. We tried to phone Mama in Sofia but it was impossible to get through, not even so much as an operator. We finally did manage to speak the next day and the days passed lazily with talk, food and television. On the 28th, Zhivko and family came to us for what was to be their "farewell dinner"; they were leaving for Sofia the following day. The great surprise of the very nice evening was Luben and Zhivko's deep, long and passionate conversation about the Bulgarian scene when Luben played his important political role

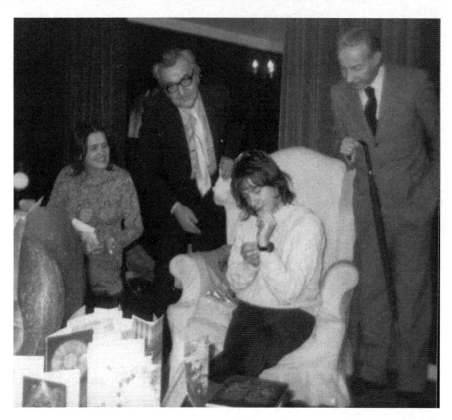

in the 1940s. From two members of extreme opposite sides, views and political allegiances, this was surely a win for friendship! The year was drawing to a close and, on the 29th, our eleventh wedding anniversary, Stanislas and Anna Frenkiel came over for tea (he, Head of the Art Department at the Institute of Education, she a child psychologist) and the talk was of art and of Mila's progress. She was deemed to be very advanced for her age (in "locomotor" terms) and... beautiful! Well, we couldn't but agree.

The family was then due to return to Paris and we relaxed, thinking over what an amazing year it had been and looking forward to 1974.

* * * * *

1974

From W1 to SW15

January 1st, even though a holiday in Scotland, brought May back to us and I was able to go off to the annual Languages Association conference held this year at the University of Warwick. Otherwise, it was a good month for exhibitions: we attended, and Pierre covered, Camargo at Gimpel, Paul Wright at Grabowski and a major show of Edvard Munch at the Hayward Gallery. February, too, was art-oriented, and the delightful Ulrico Schettini (now Montefiore, in honour of his village) came to us for dinner. His two "20th century icons" still enjoy pride of place in the dining room. We also had to "register" Mila Gina with the local authority and her papers were duly put in to the Magistrates' Court. In all of this, we were greatly assisted by another Anglo-Bulgarian couple who had, one year previously, been through the same procedures when registering the adoption of their daughter in the Public Index.

March saw the first appearance of Nikolai Ghiaurov as Boris Godunov. He was to take over the role that we had associated with Boris Christoff for so many years. Of course he was not new to Covent Garden, having sung King Philip in *Don Carlos* in 1963. It was a strong cast: John Lanigan as Shuiski, Josephine Veasey as Marina, with Edward Downes conducting. In the intervals we were with Zlatina, Nikolai's first wife, and later went to talk and congratulate Nikolai in his dressing room. As usual, we all went for an excellent dinner at *L'Opéra* afterwards. We also got tickets for the production of *A Streetcar named Desire* in which Claire Bloom was starring and we went to the first night party afterwards. Having known Claire for so many years, Pierre was always happy to follow her theatrical successes.

As well as being involved with the stage, Pierre made a significant contribution to art criticism with his coverage of Roger Hilton's exhibition at the lesser-known Serpentine Gallery:

> "Roger Hilton lifts the Serpentine Gallery to an artistic position akin to its urban location: he puts it at the very heart of London."

In 1961 Pierre had published a major article in the European art journal *Quadrum* on the work of Roger Hilton. Now he wrote of the neglect previously suffered by this remarkable artist, in whose subsequent recognition he had a role:

> "the only true Existentialist painter this country has ever had, went on for years unsung and unhailed. The time has come to atone for our blindness".

Later in the month Pierre and I both attended a reception given by the Oxford University Press on the occasion of the publication of one of their dictionaries. We talked a lot to the renowned A.S.Hornby, author of, amongst many publications, *Guide to Patterns and Usage in English*.

The 24th was Mothers' Day and I had the great privilege of a special card from Mila Gina... via the creative intervention of Pierre! April 2nd and I was again treated, as only Pierre knew how, to a fantastic array of fantasy birthday presents! Bebche Mila and I had great fun unwrapping them on the bed and scrumpling up the paper! In the afternoon we went to the Gimpel Gallery and then out to dinner.

On Good Friday we were all invited to Bernard Stern's

country house. The carrycot in the car was a new experience for Mila. She slept for most of the way. On arrival, however, she yelled no less than the Sterns' dog barked! Subsequently, she got on very well with Bernard's mother, as I did too, and Pierre was free to talk art with the painters there. We had an absolutely lovely family day, leaving at 4p.m. to drive back home. Mila was extremely sociable. Bernard promised to paint us both. (As with Detchko, this did not materialise... just think what a collection we might have had...) Another day, when we had to go and check on the building work, saw Mila's first ride in a taxi. While in Chelsea we stayed for dinner with Jonathan and Kathie, who were missing our presence, and also the actor Robert Eddison. Later in the month there was a new and unusual event held at the Bulgarian Embassy: a reception for "Bulgarian residents in London" (then probably about thirty, now thirty thousand, and certainly would not fit into the Embassy building!). There was music and dancing. A rather delightful event.

In early May, rather later than planned, we moved from Mayfair to the house in Putney. Quite a different kind of environment: near the heath, houses with big "country type" gardens. We had had a child seat put into the car and so, once the removal van with all our accumulated possessions had set off, we drove over. It was a pretty hectic, back-and-forth, day. We had a nice courtyard, Pierre had a place to work and there were the three bedrooms we needed. It was strange, after being in the centre of London, to be woken the next morning by birdsong! For receiving visitors it was rather more out of the way than before and so, with Stefan Popov over from Germany for a few days, Pierre went to meet him and entertain him in central London. These were to be times when I would come home to Putney and stay put or else occasionally invite people over. It was particularly nice to be able to walk with Mila to the Heath where there were always a lot of children with parents or nannies to mix with. The sculptor Carole Hodgson lived in Putney and we would call on her; she and her husband had decided to call their new baby 'Mila'! Another Bulgarian friend who visited us was David Peretz; he and Pierre had long conversations not only about art in general but about exhibition possibilities. I still have a copy of his painting 'Portrait d'enfant' which he signed "A Sonia". (Not the painting that he gave us, but that is another story, and I shall come to that.) Another art event was the opening at the Gimpel Gallery of an exhibition of the work of the sculptor Robert Adams. Pierre acquired a striking piece by him in pierced metal which is now somewhat rusted, due to Pierre's determination always to create a "sculpture garden"...Other art works in our courtyard are a huge purple "hanged man" (sculptor to me unknown), a triptych enamel by Stefan Knapp and, until she disintegrated, a decorative piece from the set of the film *Monsieur Topaze*.

At the end of the month Pierre was to meet with film financiers to discuss locations and casting. It should have taken place in Paris but got moved to Venice, so what was to have been a flight became a train journey; the boat train from Victoria to Paris and then on, via Milan, to Venice. A lovely journey but hardly the best way to travel on business. The stopover in Paris did, however, enable Pierre to visit the impressive exhibition *Découverte de l'Art Thrace* at the Petit Palais. With its support from Michel Joubert, French Minister for Foreign Affairs, Alain Peyrefitte, Minister of Culture, and Ivan Boudinov, Bulgarian Ambassador, and members of the Organising Committee, Ludmila Zhivkova, First Vice President Arts and Culture and Professor Alexander Fol, Director of the Institute of Thracology, this was indeed a major international event; a real "discovery" and precursor of the British Museum's exhibition which was to take place in 1976. On another note, the very day after Pierre left London the England-Bulgaria football match from Sofia was shown on BBC television. How he would have loved to watch that!

June 9th was Mila's first birthday, and nanny May and I organised a very traditional "birthday party": a cake with one candle, games and songs. There must have been about ten infants with their mothers and I must say that it was probably a good thing that Pierre was away since, marvellous father that he was, the noise and the mess might just have been too much. His return was well judged for the following day: he arrived at Victoria in the evening so that we could have supper and hear each other's news. His sense of style was admired, as he had brought two very pretty Italian dresses for Mila.

Also in June a "Bulgarian Film Week" was held at the National Film Theatre on the South Bank. On that occasion we saw *The Last Summer* and afterwards ate with Feliks Topolski at his nearby studio. Rangel Vulchanov was in London for the festival and that afforded much pleasure and enjoyment for Pierre. At this time of the year we were both involved in end-of-year exams and Pierre was invited to write about the shows put on by art students: *Diploma Shows – a Tribute to Art Education.* As he wrote:

> "It is not everyday that a grey haired critic forsakes his parochial Mayfair beat to wander from New Cross to Oxford and from Brighton to Ravensbourne… Why scurry about…? Is it only to bring back… lists of names…? Certainly not. These professional travels are also sentimental journeys, pilgrimages of atonement for a sin common to all art critics: their irresponsible disregard of art education."

Pierre was at this time writing a book about the Polish artist Karolina Borchardt. One day, he went to visit her in Wimbledon. Having driven him there, May and I decided on an excursion: we went for a pizza lunch, and were somewhat surprised that Mila had developed an early taste and ate everything! We then went for walks on the Common until it was time to collect Pierre. A lovely family-and-work day!

A week in Scotland

July brought us Pierre Christian from Paris for the beginning of what was to be an extended "family summer holiday": London,

Scotland (briefly) and Normandy. For some reason I had had the idea that, instead of heading as usual towards Europe, we should really explore more of this country and so, on the strength of an interesting-sounding advertisement, I booked a week in a cottage on an island on the west coast of Scotland. To a Londoner this sounded perfect: sea, unspoilt country... yet May was somewhat less enthusiastic. On the 16th Pierre Christian and I set out by car to drive to Glasgow. This in itself was an experience: Birmingham from the M6 motorway looked nightmarish, the rain, solid grey, pelting down. Then came amazingly beautiful Cumbria, a stone-grey sky over stone grey walls and velvety faraway hills – very Bulgarian. At Penrith it was time to eat, phone Pierre (who, sensible man, was to join us by train, a day or two later). We went on, via Stainton, a charming village with its chunky 18th century stone houses, each with a date, rose gardens, bright green lawns... and on to Ullswater where, lured by the description in an old 'Good Food Guide', we had an excellent dinner and gave Pierre news of our progress. The sunset was magnificent, and night had fallen by the time we reached the Central Hotel in Glasgow. It has all the grandeur and opulence of railway hotels, *à la Anouilh*. Checking that May and Mila were on the night train, we were able to relax until 5h30 when, beneath bright blue sky, they alighted from the train in good early-morning form. We all piled into the car and made our way via impressive scenery, bridge and ferry crossings, to this rather delightful outpost: Cullipool on Seil Island. When the cloud and mist lifted, there was an impressive view westwards. However, the more general experience wass that of vertically falling, slate-grey rain. Never mind, it was cosy indoors and one could walk even in the rain ...among ferns and foxgloves with sheep perched improbably on rocky outcrops... and more rain. Cullipool had a small village community centre and shop, and was charming in its own way. However, after a few days (we had arrived on the Wednesday), I was inclining more to May's view... and Pierre did not plan to arrive to join us until the Saturday... Pierre

Christian and I drove to Oban to meet him off the train, to have lunch and spend time in this highspot of civilisation, the weather briefly fine for once. Pierre's introduction to Cullipool was soon effected and his inherent dislike of walking confirmed us, after some discussion, that we would not prolong this "Scottish adventure" for much longer. On the Monday we dropped May off at her parents' home in Glasgow, where we were very well received, and then made our way back by road to London, arriving in Putney ready to collapse into our own beds. But for some reason Pashanko came over in the evening and kept Pierre talking. Never mind, staying up late in an urban environment and talking with Bulgarian friends was always a pleasure for him. As was his next engagement, a lecture to be given in Richmond for his great friends the de Leons at the 'Q' Theatre. Pierre was always a great success with their students and he loved their youthful exuberance, and his productions were very well reviewed.

... and a month in France

Whereas, in 1973, we had foregone the typical "summer holiday", 1974 was to see it come back in force: we were to spend the month of August in France with the whole family (and they say Christmas brings about family stress...!). Before departing, however, we moved back to Chelsea and, on the 1st the removal firm came to Putney to pack up everything we had accumulated during our stay there. At Chelsea I checked that spaces were cleared for the awaited furniture and saw to the installation of a new fridge and cooker. The next day was busy as we had the car serviced prior to leaving for France, the removal van came and, in the afternoon, no doubt for granny's admiring eyes, Mila had her first official haircut, nowhere else but in Harrods!

Were we ready for departure on the 3rd? No doubt as ready as it was possible to be... Packing luggage and supplies into the car, with Mila in her child seat and Pierre Christian in front with me, I drove down to Southampton to take the night ferry to Le Havre (a crossing we must have made nigh on a hundred times since) on what was then the Townsend-Thoresen line. Pierre was to stay behind in London for a few days (his last few days of solitary peace for a month...). Eating, exploring the ship, sleeping in a cabin... we passed the time on what was a hot and stormy-rough night and, at 7h on Sunday morning, we disembarked and drove north-east towards Etretat, Fécamp – places that were to become so familiar to us – to the Château de Fiquainville. The roads were completely deserted so early on a Sunday; we passed Normandy towns, hamlets and countryside, but I was to discover that Dora was not a gifted map maker and we took several wrong turns. She had booked a whole floor for family accommodation at this delightful manor house with its large grounds and farm nearby. We had spacious rooms and Luben declared himself the cook; granny was looked after; Pierre and Dora were able to engage in professional talk; I was happy to be in France; Mila was unable to distinguish this from home, but Pierre Christian, being a teenager, felt the absence of friends, nor could he find much to do.

Pierre phoned to check that we had arrived, to say that everything had been moved to Markham Street and to confirm that he would be coming on the night ferry. At the very crack of dawn – 6h15 – I set off with Pierre Christian, who was desperate by now for something/anything to do, for Le Havre. It meant fog lights as the morning sea mist was thick along the country roads. The rendezvous point, Bar Spi, turned out to be the only one to be closed, but we picked Pierre up and made our way to another cafe for warming coffee and croissants. I tried to hire a television set as the apartment did not have one. The concept of the extended family holiday was something quite new, and adjustments had to be made.

There were lovely moments: Pierre pushing Mila on the swing in the garden, my walking with granny and Mila in the garden, going to nearby towns and to beaches for picnics... but

the weather was inclement: rain, rain, rain... making things somewhat claustrophobic. There were family discussions, well... occasionally "arguments". I had active, often rebellious, youth with me and Pierre, as ever the perfect diplomat, after spending time with his mother, sister and brother-in-law, would often come on outings away from the house and it became a tradition to go down almost every morning to Valmont for a coffee and for him to play "Babyfoot" with Pierre Christian, at the same time collecting references to 'Berger', a type of drink but, by association, Rene Berger, a writer and very good friend of Pierre's.

Pierre did his filial duty each afternoon: conversations in Bulgarian with his mother. Pierre Christian, after his time in England, seemed very anglophile (at the same time francophobe, as well as Fiquain-phobe!). Dora was quite set on our all buying property in the region and we made a point of visiting various *notaires* about houses for sale; another idea was to take on a French *au pair* at a later stage. And still it rained...I found it quite difficult, sometimes, to tell where I was: France, yes, but besides French we spoke English and Bulgarian, and I listened to Radio 4, received quite clearly on long-wave. This was a mixture of persons, languages and countryside...The 8th of August took us into yet another dimension as we wondered what President Nixon would do. Knowing perfectly well, we nevertheless stayed up, or got up again, until 2a.m. to hear quite how awful and shameless he could be.

The days followed one another and soon we needed to re-book our return ferry. This was an opportunity for Pierre, Mila and me to go to Le Havre for the day and also for me to send off my *magnum opus* text for the October issue of *New Linguist* at the central Post Office. We had lunch and went shopping; very nice French children's clothes! Another day we went off early with Dora to Sassetot and visited the castle and grounds, bought a picnic and went to the beach. A lovely, family-type, unpretentious, Normandy beach. Mila seemed quite determined to eat the sand, not to wear her sun hat and to scream at the water. The weather had by now turned hot and on the "15 août" Pierre, Pierre Christian and I went to the annual antiques fair in Cany Barville, coveted some items but knew that we could not really find room for large items! We bought our picnic for the beach but, feeling hungry, set off along the "vallée de la Durdent" and, near to the chateau de Cany, discovered a shady, non-waspy field for a lovely relaxed time. At the beach in the afternoon, Mila walked in and on the sand, anything not to have to sit on it! One would not perhaps have expected it – of a teenage boy – but Pierre Christian was to prove a very good companion for Mila, playing hide and seek, reading and talking. This, I can imagine, set him up well for the fatherly responsibilities he later took on with his own four children!

On the 20th Pierre was to travel to Lausanne, to visit an

exhibition and to meet Rene Berger (or, possibly, to have a break from "the family"...). In the morning we drove him to Yvetot for the train and afterwards enjoyed a drive around a new area. I was later to be subjected to endless discussions concerning the "best way" to bring up a child, including, mostly, views on diet. Perhaps if given this, she'd turn out to be a genius, if not given that, she'd never develop... Are all families like that, I still wonder? Maybe only Bulgarians. A few days later, with thick early morning mist presaging heat and, outside in the garden the same nine "groupie" cows, we set off to collect Pierre at the station, to be enchanted by all his news and stories and set off to indulge ourselves with lunch in a restaurant we had discovered along the valley. Now that Pierre was back, we – that is Pierre Christian and I – felt able to spoil ourselves by going out for meals, coffees and drinks. Mila certainly also picked up the "high life" habit pretty quickly as well! I had the greatest difficulty in persuading Luben once or twice (maybe only once) to join us for a coffee in Fécamp or Valmont. One day we were invited to visit Jeanine Warnod, friend of Dora and a fellow art critic, at her family's holiday house in Pourville while Pierre stayed behind to spend time with Luben. It was suggested that we might like to look over the next door house: a large, very "turn-of-the-century" villa. Should we become boarding house owners? Lovely idea, but no. Other days we went to view cottages, villas, all sorts of potential properties; we also did the visit of the amazing Benedictine building, abbey, art gallery and, most importantly, producer of the famous liqueur, tasting it on '*crêpes*' at the end of the tour. One morning we went early to the farm attached to the chateau to collect our own supply of milk, seeing calves and hens. Again something of a novelty for us town dwellers.

...and to SW3

Towards the end of the month and, to quote a title of John Mortimer, the *Summer's Lease*, the weather began to turn autumnal, with cold nights and early mornings. It was time to pack up, close up and depart, leaving the family to return to Paris, hoping against hope that granny would be able to visit us soon in London. Nobody would believe now what difficulties there were in those days in obtaining a visa for England, with a return to France, for someone who had had such difficulty in obtaining an exit permit from Bulgaria. We took the midday ferry at Le Havre and were home – really home, in Chelsea! – by nightfall. This, of course, was quite a big change for each of us: for Pierre and me just being back in our own house; he with his study "downsized" to be in the "garden room", nice but small; for Mila complete novelty: upstairs in the front part of the top floor, so recently vacated by books and the big desk; only her cot must have seemed vaguely familiar to her.

Pierre was generous-spirited in the extreme, as ever, not complaining about the reduced space he had for sitting, thinking, writing. In addition, if he wanted or needed to consult one or other of his books, he had to make the journey to Clapham. While it can honestly be said that I was initially the keener to have a child, Pierre turned out to be the most marvellous, thoughtful, fun, generous father anyone could wish for.

September was marked by the very grand reception at midday in the Bulgarian Embassy on the 9th to celebrate exactly 30 years from that date: *"Deveti Septemvri"* 1944, the significance of which, while well understood by us as we tried to arrange granny's travel permit, may have had other resonances for the mostly left-leaning deputies, academics and "Friends of Bulgaria" who attended. On the 17th Pierre decided to go to Paris and try to resolve the situation as regards his mother's permit. It was thanks in no small measure to the husband of my colleague Annie, Robin (now Lord) Renwick at the British Embassy, that the visa and travel permit were issued. Tremendous! Soon mother and son were both back with us in Chelsea. A granny, at least for a while, with us for Mila. Bathtime and bedtime were high points, and even though I

always regretted being out late at work or in the evening, the two of them had great times!

The time for term and other work activities was approaching and Pierre and I attended an excellent leaving party hosted by Jean and Catherine Gimpel for the dynamic French cultural attaché Jean-Marie Benoist who had done so much to bring interesting speakers to London. Pierre wrote a review of an exhibition of Ben Nicholson drawings at Fischer Fine Art, in which he challenges the very notion of "drawing":

> "His last works show that, in his case, the conventional term 'drawing' is quite inappropriate since '-ing' denotes a continuous action. He traps harmonious essences in his line, trace of calm concentration and unrelenting purification... Nicholson mirrors the serenity of Being".

I was to begin the year with another group of graduate linguists and, again, I organised the session where Pierre introduced them to that unfamiliar language: Bulgarian. This would become a feature of the first week of term for several years to come. I also had text for each issue of *New Linguist* to take care of. Weekends we spent very pleasantly, visiting friends, going to the local church playground for Mila to meet her new friends on the swings or roundabout. Granny seemed quite taken by life in London: playgroups, health centres, tea parties with nannies...and she was much valued by us all. A truly lovely lady, at last able to enjoy a bit of freedom, in Paris and in London, to do as she wanted, shop, eat, walk about without the constrictions imposed by life in Bulgaria at the time.

At the end of October Pierre travelled to Warsaw for a meeting of the International Association of Art Critics of whose United Kingdom branch he was a committee member. This organisation, and particularly the added chance to meet his friends and colleagues from eastern European countries, was a great joy for him. I can, of course, only speculate on the discussions (and drinking...) that must have gone on.

He was back at the beginning of November and, meanwhile, Dora had been in Bulgaria. She too was now recognised as an intellectual, a writer whom one could invite on a certain level, and it was with enormous interest that Pierre spent hours on the phone with her the day after her return, hearing about her meetings, lectures to various audiences, their friends. Gradually, members of the Ouvaliev family were to become *persona grata*, having for so long been *non*. On the 10th of November, Remembrance Sunday, I took Mama to the Russian Church in Ennismore Gardens for the special service (now, of course, there is the chapel in the mews behind the Bulgarian Embassy but at that time the division between Church and State was absolute...). She was so pleased to attend an Orthodox service and to have the opportunity to "remember" the dead. Pierre spent time visiting King's College, where he enjoyed the range of interesting people and artistic and musical activities. We attended the inaugural lecture given by my colleague, Pat Harvey, Professor of Spanish and another day, we both had lunch with Professor Hywel Lewis whom Pierre knew from Varna the previous year. That same day there was a meeting at the Great Britain-East Europe Centre, so admirably run by Sir William Harpham. Here Pierre came across Alexander Yankov who, after his years as a member of the International Maritime Organisation (as a lawyer he dealt with matters concerning the *Law of the Sea*), was to lead the commission for the establishment of the Bulgarian Constitution. I had the pleasure, some years later, of seeing him again in London at a meeting held at King's. Another inaugural lecture was soon to take place, again at King's: Professor Leslie Perry, my guide and mentor, who had previously been on the staff of the Institute of Education, had taken up his Chair at King's and gave a fascinating talk on the philosophy of education.

More space needed!

We were still thinking how we might resolve the "space problem": books, work... and in early December we went to view a studio in Chelsea. Chelsea's days as an artists' colony were reflected in this, so, besides being separate but close, it would have chimed happily with the work Pierre was doing in the field of the arts. But it did not quite fit our requirements. Others were progressively lined up, till a few years later we found the "ideal" place: 46 Markham Square, known to so many friends and visitors.

By mid-December things were getting into Christmas holiday mode: Ivo Hadjimishev had an exhibition at the National Photographic Society. This was marvellous for him: here were the results of all his efforts and his studies the previous year. The Bulgarian Embassy held a reception for the signing of the Cultural Agreement which gave us the opportunity to see Chavdar and, on subsequent days, to get together with him and with Ivo. They both returned to Bulgaria a few days afterwards to be replaced by Julia Vassilieva, who was visiting London and her college. May was away for Christmas, which meant babysitting duties for granny. Christmas Day that year we spent with Pashanko and Margaret Dimitroff at their lovely large house in Willesden, and this was to develop into quite a tradition. Here there was an ever-changing cast of visitors: "Bobby" Daskaloff and his wife Nadine; musicians, both Bulgarian instrumentalists and members of the London Symphony Orchestra; opera singers and even, once, a bellydancer from a Turkish restaurant. Lovely, exotic parties. Mama was introduced to crackers, paper hats, turkey and Christmas pudding. Both she and Mila seemed to love it!

To usher in the New Year Dora, Luben and Pierre Christian came to London, braving force 9 gales in the Channel! And so it was that, back in Chelsea, the whole family, together with friends, saw out 1974.

* * * * *

1975

"Is it warm enough?"

Settled back into the house in Chelsea, Mila thriving, and Pierre was more and more in demand for lectures, broadcasts and reviews. 1975 and the following years proved extremely rewarding and pleasant. But films took a back seat as, in general, the British film industry went into a period of inactivity.

The early days of the year were taken up with something very much "closer to home": Pierre's mother was to return to Bulgaria after her lengthy stay in France and in London. Dora, who was still with us after Christmas, went with me to see Pierre and their mother off at Heathrow. This was a strange combination: Pierre, a London resident, flying to Sofia with his mother, a Sofia resident. It was comforting for her to have him with her, what with the emotion of returning after her stay and the formalities which, as an older person, she would perhaps have found difficult. It was also pleasant for him to accompany her and also, while spending a week in Bulgaria, to try and advance some of his projects. The mother-son relationship must have been at its most relaxed, positive and normal since the day he left Bulgaria, almost thirty years before.

After seeing them off, I took Dora to Victoria Station where she was to catch the train back to Paris (no tunnel then and at the mercy of the winter winds and waves…). Luben and Pierre Christian had returned earlier to resume work and school.

At teatime the following day I enjoyed a pleasant surprise

visit from the Zhivkova-Slavkov family: Ludmila and Ivan brought young (then I think about nine) Evgenia (Jenny) with them, and she and Mila got on very well, playing and eating cakes, while we all talked.

I remember how impressed Ludmila was with Mila's progress, and that she refused to take off her coat, very politely indicating that the room was not warm enough. Didn't Pierre always tell me to increase the heating, calling me a "Nordic monster"? Eventually, however, individual gas central heating having been installed, I was able to keep even "tropical beasts" warm!

Dora phoned me from Paris to let me know that she had spoken with Sofia and all was well. I sent off a greetings telegram on the 11th of January as Pierre was to be 60 the next day. When he returned on the 14th I heard all about his activities, friends he had seen, visits and birthday celebrations.

It was not long before he was off again to Sofia but before that he had to meet with Harry Moore regarding their "joint venture" film project, and there was also a symposium at the School of Slavonic and East European Studies (SSEES) where Michael Holman, one of the very few British academics to take a deep interest in Bulgarian language and culture, was to give a talk on Nikolai Haitov's literary output. In Sofia for a couple of weeks Pierre was involved in attempting to get "the Eichenger film" off the ground. I can only imagine that this meant a lot of meetings, lunches and visits to the Boyana studios as well as relevant Ministries. When he got back he was immediately taken up with covering the Royal Academy's Turner exhibition (and later, in May, the 300 Turner drawings shown at the British Museum) – especially fascinating for him as he was already turning over his ideas for the remarkable book he would subsequently write on Turner and which, in 2006, would be so beautifully translated and published in Bulgarian.

Meanwhile, May told us that she would be leaving us to accompany her fiancé Jim to South Africa. That was certainly a blow as she had been so marvellous and it meant that I would have to go through the process once again of advertising, interviewing and appointing a new nanny.

Activities and visits continued and Pierre and I were invited down for the day to visit Professor Hywel Lewis and his wife at their country house: tea, a walk in the woods, dinner, philosophy... marvellous! Pierre and Hywel talked plans, conferences, colleagues, controversies... One thing that struck me was that Hywel and Megan, his wife, spoke to each other in Welsh (why not? they were both Welsh; I had just never encountered it before). Another day Mila and Bubi Kraus, with their daughter Ann-Marie and her family, came to tea. There was a reception at the Great Britain-East Europe Centre for Professor Alexander Fol who, in both his ministerial and his academic capacity, was to be a key figure in the organising of the major exhbition of Thracian Treasures the following year at the British Museum. A close friend of Pierre, he has been a valuable member, until his recent death, of the Ouvaliev Foundation which Mila and I set up in 1999. Pierre, on being asked by Professor Louis Arnaud Reid if he would take some of his lectures for him at the Institute of Education, jumped at the chance and, on several Tuesdays, spoke on such favourite topics of his as "Taste" and "The Critic"; absolutely spot on!

Pierre and I also went to visit other prospective properties: houses in Putney, where we had enjoyed living in 1974, and Richmond but, although it was fun to visit, we always came back to the idea of Chelsea!

More Turners were on display that summer at Marble Hill House and so Pierre and I went over and had a picnic in the grounds with Mila. It was soon to be her second birthday and preparations were in hand for a party in the garden in Chelsea. Nannies and children soon filled up the space with their toys, presents and games! It was about this time that a plan was put forward for spending a part of the summer with one of the families in England, not repeating the French experience and hoping for better weather!

An "Honoured Artist"

This was also the time that Pierre started to teach on a regular basis at Croydon School of Art, working for and with his good friend the artist and critic Eddie Wolfram. This was to prove a most productive and enjoyable commitment. Bulgaria was also in our diaries as Misho Hadjimishev and his choreographer came to dinner. We were able to celebrate Misho's elevation to "Honoured Artist" of the Peoples' Republic of Bulgaria.

I was also considering an academic visit to Bulgaria with a view to studying their language teaching and learning policies and practice. To this end Pierre and I invited the consular official Nikolai Trunkov to lunch at King's College where he could meet groups of students and get an idea of my plans, as well as checking whether I was to be given a visa…! Another good Bulgarian friend who visited us was the late Kiril Milushev, the serious and committed teacher of English at the department at the Bulgarian Academy of Sciences (BAN), where Julia Vassilieva headed a research group. It was a pleasure for me to accompany Kiril to Dillon's and other bookshops where he could check on the most recent publications and research in the field of English language teaching.

August was the time for children, games, tea parties and a short holiday on the Suffolk coast where, with our new nanny Gill, her friend Carole with her charge Freddie Burt, Mila and I had a most enjoyable time: beach picnics, games, meals outdoors, lazing in the sun… while Pierre was spared all this by staying in London. In early September we were again invited to the Lewises and we were much congratulated on "such a lovely and well behaved little girl". Mila was obviously on her best behaviour!

The following day I was up early to take Pierre to Heathrow, not bound for Bulgaria this time but Poland, where the annual AICA conference was to take place in Warsaw, with Pierre making a presentation.

I replaced him at the opening of the Diploma Show of students at Chelsea School of Art and would have done so at the reception at the Bulgarian Embassy on September 9th except that it was "Men only", as I was given – oh, so politely – to understand! People nowadays do not believe that it could have been so, but then things have changed... Oh, well, "all dressed up and nowhere to go", I decided to take myself out to lunch! On the 19th Pierre was back from Poland, but the very next day he was off to attend the annual conference of the British Society of Aesthetics with his friends the journal editor Terence Dilley, the critic Paul Hodin and others. A few days later it was to Fischer Fine Art for the Klee and Bissier exhibitions, and, *Arts Review* published Pierre's review of R.F. Hoddinott's *Bulgaria in Antiquity – an archaeological introduction.*

> "...the exceptional importance of R.F. Hoddinott's accurate and exhaustive portrayal of 'Bulgaria in Antiquity'... both scholars of Bulgaria and Bulgarian scholars should be greatly indebted to R.F.Hoddinott: the former because he will widen their horizon; the latter because he makes their achievements known to a wide readership for which Bulgaria is 'almost an empty space on the archaeological map of Europe' . Or rather – was".

The appearance of this book, and of Pierre's review, were well timed since, a few weeks later, the British Museum held a press conference to promote the forthcoming exhibition of Thracian treasures. Pierre was of course delighted and contributed to the planning.

Languages, languages...

Later in October, having deposited my passport at the Embassy, I was able to collect the visa and, after trying to juggle with various things: students, classes, nanny... on the 26th I flew to Sofia with plans for an intensive programme of visits. This was an official visit under the terms of the Cultural Agreement and I had asked for and was given a very full programme. Nevertheless, I found time to see friends and family.

Paying the usual amount of money for "excess baggage" (!) on my three suitcases... I was seen off at Heathrow by Kolyo Trunkov and, after a smooth flight, welcomed in Sofia by Emil Alexandrov and Zhivko Popov. The funds evidently stretched to my being able to stay at my favourite hotel: the Grand! After unpacking I went round to see Pierre's mother, with copies for her of all the photos we had taken at Christmas and New Year in London. Looking at photos was, for me, always a lovely way of talking, remembering... the happy times and events we had all shared – particularly so in that she could not always be near us. Later I went back to the hotel and had dinner with Emil and his wife, Svetlana, and Zhivko, while Julia joined us later from her Institute.

Monday, and work starts: my "programme maker" Malvina Naltchadjian, senior English teacher with the Ministry of Foreign Affairs, came with a driver to the hotel and our first visit was one that I had specially requested: to the Lozanov Institute. Much had been published in professional journals about Lozanov's theories of *Suggestology* and *Suggestopedia* and I was keen to experience this for myself. In retrospect, I must say that I had the most incredible luck as Dr. Lozanov did not always permit visitors to his Institute, let alone to attend the classes. He received me graciously and talked about his methods, on which I made notes, and I then attended a French lesson, acting as a participant observer. Afterwards I went with Malvina to sit in on one of her classes for diplomats destined to be posted to English-speaking countries. A late lunch and a long talk with Malvina were followed by a siesta and then a walk through Sofia – all our old haunts! The next day I was again at the Lozanov Institute, this time to attend an English lesson given by the charismatic teacher Marlise Dimcheva (about whom Fanny Séféris writes in her book *Un nouvel art d'apprendre*). While I could say that the basics of a "Lozanov lesson" (relaxed atmosphere, classical music, comfortable seating, student interaction...) should, and are, the prerequisites for any "good teaching situation", I was particularly impressed by the student-student and student-teacher interaction and friendly support given in this lesson. It has been a pleasure for me to keep in touch, albeit infrequently, with Marlise over the many years since I first observed her in class! (We were to meet up soon after, together with other Lozanov staff members, at a British Council summer course on which I taught in Sofia in 1978.)

Work over for the day... I was invited by Jenny Bozhilova to her home and other friends came to join us: Soon, Ivo, on his way to meet his father back from London, and, later, Nikolai. A good mixture of tea, talk, laughter, memories. I later went round to Mama but got no answer since, I found out later, they were all watching television. Back in the hotel I met the daughter of an old friend of Pierre's, Venera Naslednikova, costume designer for the Philip Koutev Ensemble. Maria and I talked over a drink. (It was a great pleasure to be invited, with a group of my friends visiting Bulgaria for the first time in 2000, to an evening at their house where Venera showed us her portfolio of sketches and paintings of regional costumes.)

On Wednesday I spent a morning at the Institute for Foreign Students (IChS), which catered for those who needed to learn Bulgarian prior to taking up a post in the country. This Institute has undergone many changes of name, status, purpose... but has always been a model of teaching excellence; whatever the current ideology – structural, situational, communicative – the Institute has produced excellent results. In no small measure this was due to the outstanding contribution of Professor Andrei Danchev. Moved from the University under shameful circumstances, he nevertheless proved to be an absolute godsend to the Institute. With what pleasure I remember Andrei taking out a slip of paper over coffee – concerned though I might have been that a word or phrase I had just uttered would land up in textbooks! That day I was with a group of Palestinian doctors, learning to ask if it was raining. The fact that the phrase has stuck must mean the teacher was good! The evening was spent with friends: Vanyo came to collect me and, together with Karl and Lina, we all went and dined at the family home of Naiden Gerov.

And so the days of this exceptionally interesting ten-day stay in Sofia continued: another visit to the IChS discussing their current research with the Director; taking Mama and the aunties for a "family dinner" at the Russian Club – a much commented event; visiting Julia Vassilieva's Institute and making "native speaker" recordings for her, and for Malvina; invited by Julia to go with her and colleagues at the weekend to her villa at Metchka near Samokov where we talked, drank, laughed, walked in the forest and took photos; attended classes at the French language school where I was bowled over by the fluency, grammatical correctness and proficiency of these young learners. I have always subsequently held the system of Foreign Language Medium schools in the highest regard. On the day that I was there Professor Patev, the French language methodologist at the University, was visiting his students on teaching practice (shades of King's College for me…!) and told me how very much he admired Christo Ouvaliev, Pierre's father, the first academic in Bulgaria to develop a theory of teaching French. It was my great privilege to be given a copy by Mama of the original edition, dated 1915, which Sofia University has recently republished in the *University Classics* series. In the afternoon, very nervous, I was to give a lecture in French at the University, but it did seem to go well and there were quite a lot of questions about the teaching of French in England. Later that day I went with Soon and Yancho Takov to Detchko Ouzunov's home for drinks. Many of our friends were there and we went on afterwards to dine at Park Hotel Moskva, just opposite. I recall a terrifying ride back into the centre with

Soon in Yancho's sports car and going to a nightclub until 2 a.m.!

As well as professional meetings and seeing friends, there was also the very important question of catching up with and reporting to all those concerned with "*bebeto*": nurse Penka, Professor Kirov and others. Penka, with whom I have sadly lost touch, brought presents for Mila. My last day was a very full one: with Vanyo, Jeannie, Christo and Juliana we drove to Belogradchik; an amazing drive and place: such strange rock formations, especially in the fog! It is to Vanyo and the Moskvitch that I owe so many of my early discoveries in Bulgaria. Jeannie's knowledge of history and literature was enormous and Vanyo's love for his country matched hers. But, on this occasion, it meant a late return to Sofia where some people were waiting for me in the hotel, and others had phoned. So many friends came to say goodbye, but I just had to get changed as we were due for drinks at Ludmila and Ivan's apartment on Tolbukhin. We were about ten in the party, with the Gerasimovs and Zhivko, and went after to dine in the '*Panorama*' restaurant which then, as no doubt now, was the place to be seen at... Those also present that evening, to my great joy, were Nikolai Ghiaurov, Lubomir Levchev and Sasha Beshkov. Luckily I only had to go upstairs to do the packing, in preparation for leaving the next morning after what had truly been "out of this world"!

An early flight, the usual overweight luggage, seen to in the VIP lounge, and I was back at Heathrow by midday, where Pierre met me and took me out to lunch, over which we talked about everything to do with Bulgaria! This was to become something of a tradition when either of us went to Sofia: go for lunch and "de-brief". Often his pleas would be for interesting items he could use for his BBC broadcasts. At home, Mila welcomed me back, shyly and with a card: "Mummy back!". Some of my excess kilos were in the shape of green and red peppers, kindly donated by Julia for me to use in attempting Bulgarian cuisine in London. So, for days after, we had peppers, even taking some over to Pashanko when we went for lunch. To this day I usually bring a couple of kilos of peppers home from Sofia, given the ridiculous price they fetch in Waitrose!

My visit to Bulgaria had coincided with Pierre being busy in London, but in early December he went for a few days to Paris (I do not recall why but I hope that it was simply to relax and see his sister and maybe some exhibitions). He was back in time to attend the cocktail party given on the 17th at the Bulgarian Embassy for the group who would be in charge of the Thracian exhibition, together with British archaeologists, notably from the University of Nottingham, which had been linked with Bulgaria.

After Christmas, again spent with Pashanko and Margaret, I was to drive to a conference and, with nanny Gill, we had agreed that I would drop Mila off at her parents' house in the Midlands. Mila had a wonderful, fun three days there with Gill and her brother Karl, and I collected her on my way back home in time to see in 1976 on 31st December.

* * * * *

1976

The year of the Thracians

The year's activities started early: the 'Thracian team' were to arrive on January 5th and, that morning, Pierre and I took flowers round to the Residence to welcome Ludmila and, while he talked with Alexander Yankov, his wife Elsa showed me around the house. How women always like to do the "guided tour" of someone else's home! The delegation was met on arrival by representatives of the British Museum and, no doubt, had talks about publicity, presentation. The following day Pierre was involved in organising an exhibition at the Camden Arts Centre, and in the evening Alexander (Sasha) Beshkov came for dinner.

Wednesday, traditionally the first day of term at King's, meant work for me, including interviews with students and classes, before getting ready for the 17h30 opening of the exhibition at the British Museum. It was lucky we had special passes as there must have been at least two thousand visitors. There were excellent speeches by the Director, Ludmila Zhivkova, and Alexander Fol and, after a chance to see the exhibition, Pierre and I went for dinner with some of the friends who had attended the opening.

To mark the opening of the exhibition of the *Thracian Treasures from Bulgaria*, on January 7th The Times newspaper published a special four-page feature, written and sponsored by the Committee of Recreation and Tourism. This publicised not only the exhibition but all aspects of Bulgarian history and culture. This was certainly the first and major promotion of Bulgaria in the British press. Pierre was to write of the exhibition:

> "By the hundred, by the thousand, Londoners line up the stern stone stairs of the British Museum to stare and marvel at Thracian treasures that go back to the fifth millennium B.C.... If this admirable collection had not been gathered in Bulgaria, the Thracian trail would have ended in some small lecture room. We must pay a well earned tribute to Dr. Ludmila Zhivkova, Minister for Art and Culture... an uncommon personality... with an exceptional academic background... The Thracian exhibition offers scientific cognition... but also... the rare rewards of immediate aesthetic experience... direct communion with the glory that was Thrace."

It is heartening to reflect that research and excavations have continued and that, some thirty years later, Bulgaria has allowed similar collections to travel, but the 1976 exhibition was a "first" in every sense. When not out of the country, it is to the National History Museum and to the Archaeological Museum in Sofia that any visitor should go to experience "the glory that was Thrace".

The opening was followed the next day by a grand reception at the Bulgarian Embassy when, and in the next few days, we saw quite a lot of our friends: Alexander Fol and Ludmila Zhivkova (at home I made sure that all the heating appliances were switched to "high" well before her arrival... after all, this was January), and Sasha Beshkov. Our social life continued: dinner with Greg and Romayne, an LSO concert in which Pashanko was playing, and dinner at his house another day, when Claudio Abbado, their '*maestro*', was the guest of honour. Pierre was involved in setting up the festival at the Camden Arts Centre and, on March 3rd, there was an academic seminar at the British Museum which he attended together with several specialists. Another day, R.F. Hoddinott addressed a group at the Great Britain-East Europe Centre. On the 8th at the Arts Club there was the launch of the book he had written to accompany the paintings of the Polish artist Karolina Borchardt; this was well attended by the very active members of the Polish artistic community in London (of which one might consider Halima Nalecz, owner of the Drian Gallery, to be among the most influential). At about this time Pierre also covered the exhibition of his great friend Marek Zulawski.

Paris doubtless had the support of the Bulgarian Ministry for Art and Culture to thank for a splendid exhibition of icons, which opened on the 17th. Pierre and I were to visit this only later as he was covering several exhibitions in London: Russian works at Fischer Fine Art and also Stefan Knapp's *Polish Tapestries*.

At the end of the month our previous nanny May returned from South Africa with Jim and they both came and saw us, to Mila's enormous joy. We all went to the local playground and heard stories of their life over there. There was also a meeting of the AICA and the critics all met at our dear friend Nigel Foxell's home in London. Nigel has been a continuing source of support, ideas and friendship to me (since Pierre's death) as he always was to Pierre. This quintessential English gentleman, a fount of European culture and knowledge which he shares most discreetly, put Pierre up for membership of his club, the Savile, where they must have enjoyed many interesting times with fellow members.

In April we attended a ceremony at the Polish Embassy to confer an honour for artistic achievement on Marek Zulawski. He then left for a week in Paris, staying with Dora in their lovely flat in the Rue de Babylone. I took the opportunity, taking Mila along with me, to visit a schoolfriend and her family in the Sussex countryside where we all enjoyed a lovely, country, family treat time, staying overnight and going for a long walk the next day over the South Downs. Ivo Hadjimischev, who was later to have another exhibition, was with us in Chelsea at the end of the month and we had a "photographic session" in the beautiful Ranelagh Gardens, next to the Royal Hospital in Chelsea. We were lucky in that Ivo "photo-documented" Mila's early years. We all visited the Constable exhibition at the Tate Gallery with my cousin, a regular attender and "Friend of the Tate", Joan Hamilton Martin. An elderly lady then, she had an amazing range of acquaintances and a real love of art.

As well as new beginnings, there were also departures: on 10th June a farewell party for the Yankovs, probably the most dedicated, cultured, urbane ambassadorial couple one could wish for. The Andre Zavriews were also leaving the French Cultural posting. Pierre and I viewed more houses, one particularly beautiful one situated a few metres from where we had rented in Putney and near the Heath. Probably we decided that we couldn't afford it... though who could have guessed how cheap such sums would appear now! Mila was to start in the Nursery Class at Park Walk School at the end of the month: she went running in on her first day but started to scream as I turned to leave, only to start again to scream, not wanting to leave, when Pierre and I went to collect her at the end of the session! Before we could leave for the holiday in France, Pierre had his "summer school" with the drama students at the 'Q' theatre in Richmond. Another extremely successful course with a well reviewed production.

A French summer idyll

Well, yes, we had decided that we would give France and the idea of a family holiday another go...Dora and Luben were again to rent the apartment in the château at Fiquainville and she had, via the local Syndicat d'Initiative, found and rented for us a part of a large villa which was to become a part of "family history", thanks to the owners, the large Bigo family. Indeed, we maintained contact for thirty years with the seaside hamlet of Vaucottes, renting for a few years from the Bigo family and, in 1984, buying our own, large, white, clifftop house in Vaucottes. Pierre had gone over to France ahead of Mila, nanny and me, quite possibly to check that his sister's choice of rental accommodation would meet with (my) approval...he would perhaps not have any particular expectations of a "holiday rental". On August 2nd we drove down to Newhaven for the ferry crossing to Dieppe, making sure to book our return passage as everyone would need to be back at the end of the month for the beginning of term. The drive along the coastal road was smooth and, recalling our visits to Cany and Fécamp in 1974, we made good time to Yport and up to Vaucottes. And there, on the balcony, was Pierre. If the house was neither well-appointed nor aesthetic, it nonetheless had a garden, proximity to coves and the beach, and could, therefore, if the fine weather continued, be relaxing. We spent the following days exploring: Etretat, shopping and some beach games and, later, a concert by the 'Salzburg Trio' in the lovely Romanesque church.

Another day to Goderville (whence some of the guests at the wedding of *Madame Bovary*). On sale at the market, to Mila's delight, were baby chicks and ducks in baskets. After coffee (always an absolute must for Pierre...) and ice creams, we went to Fécamp and to the beach with a picnic, then back to Vaucottes where, after a siesta, Pierre and I left Mila while we went for a walk around the extraordinary "turn of the century" villas in the hamlet. Meanwhile Dora and Luben, whom we had tried to contact, turned up and were entertained by nanny before we all had dinner. One day we drove over to Pourville but the Warnod villa was all closed up (the next door house still for sale...). We tended to follow the market days round about: Saturday meant Fécamp where Pierre and I stocked up on provisions, and managed to persuade Luben and Dora to join us in a café. For lunch we went off to Yport and then took Mila to the "children's beach". What a good idea: a mini-pool, swings, seesaws, sand. By this time we had more or less established a routine: games, cows etc. in the morning, lunch, rest in the afternoon, then beach (in view of the uninterruptedly marvellous weather!). Sunday found us lunching at Fiquainville – a Luben-lunch to which we all did justice. We then repeated the rituals of 1974: visit to the farm, time on the swing. So much was the same, so much had changed since that previous summer: Mama not with us, no cows or crops because of the drought ("the hottest summer"). We go to the same beaches, to the same cafe in Valmont. Mila has accumulated two very rich years of life, language, experience… On a beautiful warm sunny day, in green countryside, Pierre pushing our besottedly beloved Mila, to the accompaniment of her delighted laughter … joy and marvel indeed. Moments of captured and considered bliss.

Days followed days: the '*Corso Fleuri*' in Yport, market days, family visits, Mila with the Bigo children. It is not easy to penetrate "Vaucottes society" but our being French-speaking, being forthcoming, sociable and willing to mix and make the first approach… all helped us to take a few steps! Indeed, we have remained long-term friends with several of the '*Vaucottois*'. The weather continued exceptionally hot and sunny; blue sky and sea, a soft light on the green, green valley, made up for the fact that the accommodation was not "4 star" and would definitely not have done for a wet August… We had an almost "secret garden", glimpses of the sea from the windows and the terrace, tall trees opposite with glimpses of the other villas, a sort of Swiss mountain valley by the sea. We did not miss having television, for Pierre was using this perfect environment to plan and begin to start work that was to become his major study of JMW Turner. Mila played, was read to and invented games, the ideal student for Pierre! She was utterly delightful: amusing, inventive, lively, observant, talkative, affectionate ("Tell you a secret… 'Love my Daddy'"!).

A final day, and a final Sunday lunch at Fiquainville, on the 29th and, appropriately for the end of the holidays, it rained! Monday the 30th, Bank Holiday in England, after packing up and saying fond farewells to the Bigo family, Mila, nanny and I took the ferry to Newhaven while Pierre stayed to return to Paris with Dora and Luben. It was certainly an ideal family arrangement: so easy for us to visit, London or Paris, by train or plane. Pierre of course often needed to visit Paris and, indeed, wanted to as he was always so very close to his sister, with whom he had shared the experience of exile and emigration and of missing the family whom they had left behind in Bulgaria.

However, it was to Lisbon that Pierre was to go in early September, to the annual conference of AICA. I was still on vacation from the university but Mila was due back, with all the friends she now had, at Park Walk nursery. Back from Portugal, Pierre and I attended the "9th September" reception at the Embassy. My diary makes no note of it being anything special, nor even the name of the new Ambassador (although it was Vladimir Velchev, who had presented his Letters in early July), only that, afterwards, we ordered an "Indian take-away" to eat with friends at home (perhaps there had been a cutback in the Embassy catering…). Pierre again went off to Paris soon afterwards. As far as art was concerned, towards the end of the month there were two Bulgarian events: Luben Dimanov had an exhibition (after which he kindly gave Pierre a collection of his graphic work) and Ivo exhibited his work at the Royal Geographic Society.

Art and music for autumn

October saw term begin for me and Pierre give my students his traditional "First lesson in Bulgarian". He had meetings with Andre Boucoureshliev, who was over in London to lead an advanced musical workshop at the Institute for Contemporary Arts (ICA). Andre and his wife were our guests during his stay. It was also a time for theatre as our friend Jonathan had a production of his translation of Heinrich von Kleist's *Prince of*

Homburg in Manchester, to which they both went for the opening performances. Art also had its place as Ulrico Montefiore had the launch of his book – a beautiful artistic album, a copy of which he inscribed to Pierre – at the Royal Academy – and another day it was a meal with Berenice Sydney, about whom Pierre had promised to write but, as her ironic drawing ("Pierre not writing article"...) reminds one, which he appears to have delayed doing.

On November 9th, and in his capacity of Vice President of AICA, Pierre presented the work 'Art and Plastics', prepared by his friend and fellow art critic Franco Passoni, at a ceremony at the Royal Academy:

"A youthful book is welcomed in the oldest British artistic institution".

Both Pierre and his sister Dora had been invited to contribute to a series of talks: *Approaches to Contemporary Art* at the Musée d'Art Moderne in Paris. The series was to cover the period from November 1976 through to February of 1977 and Dora gave her talk, *A new language: Abstraction* in mid-December. Pierre went over to attend and to spend a few days with her.

The year was coming to a close with the, by now traditional, Christmas Day (friends, lunch, presents, Queen's Speech...) at Pashanko's house, but with a most unusual celebration of New Year's Eve in the sense that, on December 31st, Pierre flew to Casablanca from where he was to go on to Rabat at the invitation of members of the Moroccan artistic circle whom he had come to know at the AICA meeting there and during our subsequent visits to the country.

And so we all moved into another year of activities, travels...

* * * * *

1977

Bulgaria and Morocco – Bulgarians and Moroccans

A taste of 'Taste'

What marks 1977 is our visiting Morocco, where Pierre began the New Year, and Bulgaria.

In itself, writing up activities and events of 1977 proves a little different from almost all other years: this is a year for which I found an "engagement diary" of Pierre's to help me identify and recall the different things which we did then. Friends of mine ask me, and readers of this book no doubt will too, "What did you base yourself on?" "How could you possibly remember what you did more than 35 years ago?" Well, the answer is 1) several things of course made too strong an impression to be forgotten, and 2) I have always kept an "engagement diary" (and sometimes a "journal"). An "engagement diary" tells, and reminds, you simply what you did, needed to do, where you went, with whom, on what train or plane. This is of course an excellent "memory jogger", except that notes saying "lunch with R. & P." tend to mean little or nothing 35 years later ... Who on earth were "R. & P."? The occasional "journals" (usually an account of some very special or unusual event) are a different matter and allow for a much fuller picture of the past: places visited, interesting people met.

The fascinating thing for me is that, putting Pierre's and my "engagement diaries" for 1977 side by side, there are different (naturally) yet equally skeletal entries; in his: "BBC 9h30" but no title of the particular broadcast; "Gimpel" but no reference to whose exhibition; "Milan" but no reason for the visit... In mine: "Ashford School" but no reference to student or lesson; "Interviews" but in what context? Pierre may not normally have kept such a diary: his starts in January, but by mid-March he has given up entering engagements, taking it up again only at the beginning of October. And although he was obviously keeping a note of his own commitments, there are dates on which we both note the same event: Wednesday 5th January "Fly to Paris" (Pierre) and "P. to Paris" (me). Sometimes with a greater or lesser amount of detail: Sunday, February 20th, "Greg Raina" (Pierre) and "7.15 p.m. *chez* Greg and Romayne for dinner" (me).

Now that I have revealed a part of my "working practice", I'll revert to the events of 1977.

And so... the year started with Pierre being in Morocco and, on January 5th "Fly to Paris". He arrived in London on the 6th and, on the 7th, he went to the Bulgarian Embassy for a visa (yes, he needed a visa to visit his own country...). On the 8th Pierre notes that he had a meeting with our friend the semiotician Dino Sandulesco but, since it is in my diary too, I must have attended as well! This would have been to discuss Dino's paper on the *Semiotics of James Joyce*. He also notes a lunch with the art critic and writer Terence Mullaley at the Arts Club. From 10th to 15th he was in Sofia but no reason is given. Whatever it was, he would have had his birthday there. If I study the diary entries, however cryptic they may often be, I can discern a rhythm to his weekly activities: regularly on Mondays (17th, 24th, 31st...) he went to teach at Brentwood College; on Wednesdays (19th, 26th...) he recorded at the BBC; on Fridays (21st, 28th...) he taught at Croydon College of Art. One could say the same of mine: there were meetings, students, lectures... on regular days. The picture of Mila's activities is not dissimilar: swimming, dancing classes, piano lessons, gym, tea parties, visits to the Hurlingham Club (for Alex Walford – grandson of "Tolly" de Grunwald – and his fifth birthday party). What an extraordinarily energetic life one led!

As proof of this, after his BBC broadcast on Wednesday 2nd February, Pierre flew to Paris, staying until the 10th. My diary makes very little mention of this or the reasons for the visit, except "P. lecture Paris" on the 7th. No mention, though, of topic, the audience or the location! His own diary is no better: "Paris 6 p.m. Lecture". Would that one had kept fuller notes, had a better memory, could find any programme or invitation…

Well, quite some time after writing this, among the piles of documents, I found the programme for the 1976-1977 series of talks at the Musée d'Art Moderne, so all is revealed: Pierre was to give his talk: *Conflict of Taste(s)* on February 7th. I even have the text: 16 typewritten pages in immaculate and elegant French. Always a great admirer of David Hume, Pierre uses the great Scottish philosopher's *Treatise on Taste* as his springboard:

"Today, in our aesthetic explorations, only 'taste' is banished... Taste is, more than ever, the Cinderella of the noble family of art."

He illustrated this "conflict" with slides.

The following day, at 9 a.m., he had a meeting with Pierre Descargues, the presenter of *Les Après-midi de France Culture* to which Pierre contributed regularly from London (in some ways similar to his BBC broadcasts in that they presented aspects of British cultural life but to the French listener). On the 9th he was at Radio France at 10 a.m. and it is unclear from the diary entry whether he was to speak about Romain Gary or to meet him later in the day. The pages reproduced give a flavour of Pierre's engagements. On the 28th we would appear (from my diary only) to have attended a performance at Covent Garden of *Otello*; this would probably connect with the dinner the week before with Raina Kabaivanska at Greg's. There follow visits to galleries, a series of lectures and seminars on Thursdays (getting to be a completely full week!) at the Institute of Education, which he undertook at the invitation of Professor Louis Arnaud Reid; a dinner with the Polish artist Zdzislaw Ruszkowski... but here the diary notekeeping ends.

Meanwhile, however, in our regular search for different, larger accommodation, we went to view an enormous house near the Royal Hospital in Chelsea. Ideal in every way: masses of rooms on several floors, access to a large garden, views over to the river Thames... except the price! Also the fact that the lease was only for about 19 years. In those days banks were not throwing money, loans and mortgages at people, even those with decent incomes. However, we did use the excuse of wanting to view the house again to watch the Queen's Silver Jubilee procession from the garden.

At the end of March we had the great pleasure of receiving the Serbian art critic and writer, Professor Katarina (Katya) Ambrozić. Pierre, who much admired her work, made sure she had the chance visiting many exhibitions. We had all been together on a previous occasion at an AICA congress in Scandinavia, and it was Katya whom I had invited in 2003 to give the fourth Memorial Lecture in Pierre's name at the University of Sofia. Sadly, her terminal illness was already quite advanced, so she was unable to make the journey from Belgrade to Sofia.

In April I was preparing a series of lectures that I had been invited to give in Morocco at the University of Rabat and for the British Council, but I note that on 28th we attended a performance of

> "'Tosca' with Raina (and Pavarotti), a superb interpretation and Covent Garden reception!"

Morocco for me

Morocco was to be a different kind of "theatrical" experience for me: the atmosphere, the lifestyle, the academic context. I flew to Casablanca for a two week stay, meeting up with Claude Castelli and going on to Rabat where my host, Professor Mohammed Abu Talib, had arranged a series of interesting meetings with his own students of English and visits to schools to observe language teaching, besides the lectures I was to give. I was also able to catch up with some of the Moroccan friends that Pierre and I had made on previous visits. There were also poetry readings and a visit, on 1st May holiday, with Claude and friends to his beach apartment at Cabo Negro; a day of sun, sand and sea followed by a barbecue. It was not even too difficult to place an international call to Pierre and let him know how everything was going. This visit to Morocco offered me everything I could have expected in the way of talks, discussions with fellow professionals, an insight into the education of young people, social and cultural visits...truly a rich experience. Professor Bill Murray, from Lancaster University in England, was also visiting and, one Sunday, Mohammed arranged to drive us all to the small town of Chaouen where he had a house. Bill had decided to wear his Scottish kilt! All day, walking in and through Chaouen, we heard shouts of "*falda*" from giggling and pointing groups of youngsters! Mohammed greeted his many friends and introduced us to local customs and artisans. A lovely day!

On the10th, after breakfast on the terrace, I packed and prepared for the flight home. So many memories to savour.

A dedication, dated 2nd May, 1977, on a leaflet containing "Notes on the work of the actress and poetess Nevena Milosheva", reads "For Gospodin Ouvaliev...from my mother and me". Who mother, who daughter? To me unknown. Her (their) visit was made while I was in Morocco.

During this time, and later in the year, Pierre was writing for

Arts Review about the exhibitions of Ian Stephenson at the Hayward Gallery:

"In Stephenson's work all that soothes the sight spurs the mind";

on Fischer's Contribution to the British at Basel :

"Wolfgang Fischer's... serious art historical upbringing... initiated us into the hard art of being truly European";

Ovidiu Maitec at the Alwin Gallery :

"Maitec is such a miracle maker... carving is for him manual meditation";

Bernard Stern at Aberbach Fine Art:

"... for Stern, forms are much more than paint masks of things seen... enriches them with the possibility of harbouring an infinity of meanings".

The Silver Jubilee

The month of June was when the Queen's Silver Jubilee was celebrated: by ordinary people with "street parties", by schools with "Jubilee parties" and fancy dress and, on 7th I took Mila and a friend to King's College where, by special invitation, we could watch the Queen's carriage processing along the Strand. We had to be in our places by 9h30. After the excited viewing and loud cheering, we all went to have our lunch picnic in the courtyard. A short while later, we were at Somerset House, next door to King's, where, taking Mila with us, Pierre and I saw the exhibition "London and the River". This was to be one of the first of those occasions which have subsequently always given such pleasure: going to exhibitions with Mila. There was also to be theatre when we went with her friend Emma and her mother to see a puppet show at the Royal Court Theatre.

August is strangely blank in my diary too... At Vaucottes, renting again from the Bigos, but without Pierre this year as he was working hard on the Turner book in London. I myself was preparing a Spanish textbook, but this could be done in Vaucottes. Dora and Luben were again in the area. She encouraged me not only to view properties but to see about recruiting a French au pair. The weather being less hot and sunny, I cut short our month's stay, arranging that Claudie Brouillard, a new French au pair, should join us soon in London.

Pierre's diary takes up again in October and he seems to have been busy on two Fridays with "Bauhaus Painters" although I can find no review of this, so perhaps it was a couple of Friday lectures at one of his teaching venues. On two Tuesdays there is a somewhat comparable note of "Greek Drama". There was the Bulgarian lesson at King's and regular broadcasts, though no titles given, for France Culture. A first visit to Richmond, as later entries show, was to culminate in a performance at the theatre. On October 21st, for no reasons that I can recall, Pierre goes to Paris, on the 23rd to Milan for several days and then on to Lausanne and from there to Munich. Mysterious travelling and visiting...

Such is the complexity of putting together the activities of this many-faceted personality. Much later I came across a letter from the 'Secretary General' of the *Comitato Nazionale Premio Umberto Biancamano*, dated 'Milan, 30th October 1977', expressing great pleasure at having made Pierre's acquaintance and thanking him for his contribution to a jury. Another nice touch is the reference to meeting

> "a person of Anglo-Saxon culture possessing such fine European feelings".

Pierre must have liked that touch. Well, at least I now know what he was doing in one of these places!

Richmond picks up speed with two or three visits each week until the "Show R." on 24th November. Meanwhile, on 15th, there is an exhibition of Christo and preparation for "25 years" – but of what?

Family activities and outings included lunch with the Pastirov family and Pierre taking Mila to see *Pinocchio* at the Wimbledon Theatre. On Saturday 10th December his diary simply notes "Richmond", but mine tells of how he took Mila to see *Hansel and Gretel* at the 'Q' theatre : "M. and P. to Richmond and backstage after. M. enchanted!". Art exhibitions and theatre performances, what better early introduction could a child have had than with "Daddy Pierre"!

And Christmas was – where else? – with Pashanko and Margaret.

* * * * *

1978

A spot of family history

The year began, as so often, with my attending a Languages Association conference. Meeting colleagues and exchanging ideas was always a very rewarding way to start the year but, once back in London, there was art to interest both of us; two very different major exhibitions opened in January: 'Dada' at the Hayward Gallery and Gustave Courbet at the Royal Academy and I had the pleasure of accompanying Pierre to the Press or Private view of both.

For a short "winter break" I had been organising a visit to Istanbul, partly as a secret, as I knew that Pierre had always wanted to try and trace the footsteps of his "grandmother from Constantinople" (the one renowned for her marvellous soups!). It was an arranged trip: flights and hotel pre-booked, but then our time was our own for exploring and discovering this intriguing city, a strange mixture of Europe and the Muslim world. We flew out on January 26th, leaving Mila in the charge of the *au pair* (a different one by then, a delightful Austrian called Bea; the French never did last very long …); both, no doubt, happy to have their own freedom for a week! We were staying at the Pera Palas (nothing but the best for the Rouves!), haunt of aristocrats and Agatha Christie and certainly a somewhat faded glory, but glorious nevertheless! In search of yet more authenticity, we walked until we found a small, cheerful, friendly, workingmen's restaurant. The next day we walked and walked…over Ataturk Bridge to the Old Town and, dodging unbelievably uncontrolled driving, down to the Bosphorous, on the track of the ancestors in the Balat district. We didn't have papers, documents, photos or precise addresses but it was fun to wander and to wonder. We lunched at a fish restaurant on Galata Bridge; the fish all in bowls outside for one to choose. We had planned, read up and set ourselves the target of visiting the Blue Mosque the next day. This we did by bus and, in teeming rain, we found a "grey" mosque under a strangely leaden grey sky. Nor was the interior "blue" at all and mostly being restored. On then to Aya Sofia whose exterior could easily be mistaken. We walked right around, convinced that there must be another "main" facade. Anyhow, the interior was splendid, unbelievably spacious. After the sightseeing I was quite sure that Burberrys do not resist rain… A hot bath and a siesta later, we took the bus to Taksim Square, searching for a theatre, and dined on "*meze*", served by a Bulgarian-speaking waiter!

Sunday was sun-day, and clear too; one could see right across to the Vieille Ville. With our confidence in local transport we went by bus to a concert on Taksim Square: strange modern presentation of Turkish music. We lunched and watched young Istanbul meet, drink, sit, eat and talk. One of our most impressive visits was that afternoon to Topkapi: reposeful paths and gardens and interesting small museum sections: fabulous jewels, clocks, tiles, miniatures… they eventually closed around us! Planning a trip on the Bosphorous, we went and checked the ferries and piers and sat in the sun and had coffee and sticky cakes. Placing a call to London took forever and so we ate in the hotel.

Monday the weather did not look promising and so, instead of Bosphorizing, we bazaar-ized; buying lots and lots of gifts and souvenirs and being propositioned re leather and carpets. There were some strange and beautiful antique objects among the modern copies: that was the fun of the bazaar. Laden with all our purchases, Pierre insisted on a taxi back to the hotel where, between us, we must have written about twenty postcards.

Tuesday dawned reasonably clear for a ferry trip. Bright and light, the water blue and calm, a perfect day for calling in at small towns up to the last point: Rumeli Kavagi, a one-horse village (with several restaurants...), with enough time between boats to have an excellent meal and then walk and have coffee and baklava. The return sailing took us to the Anatolian side; extraordinary riparian residences and palaces, wooden, Venetian, shuttered, dilapidated, deserted (no longer, of course!). The sun set before our eyes over the Golden Horn. What perfection! Back at the hotel Pierre found *Programa Horizont* on the radio, after which we had dinner. Our life (the hotel, restaurants, shopping...) we found to be expensive; but "everyday" things – buses, a three hour ferry trip, coffees and fruit – were very reasonable. In the same hotel we had noticed an actor whom we knew (Edwin Richfield) and after breakfast the next day Pierre got talking to him about theatre. We arranged to go that evening to a performance of *Mother Courage*. That left us the day for more discoveries: the Mosaics Museum with marvellous Byzantine floors, swirling stripes on a pouncing tiger, a deer, a griffin, a hunter... and we had the place entirely to ourselves! Totally neglected and with the rain pouring in. On to the Tiles Museum (it is a well known fact that Pierre, given the chance, would have had tiles on virtually every surface...), then lunch at the Topkapi restaurant with a stunning view and the "Orient non-Express" running below, before visiting the Harem with its really splendid tiles. Back to the hotel in time to change for the theatre; a striking production, "in the – right – round", with swivel chairs in the centre. Dinner and talk of theatre with Edwin Richfield and his wife afterwards.

That was our last, and very full, day visiting and "discovering" Istanbul; the kind of perfect, semi-planned, exciting trip that we so enjoyed taking. It was always fun to be with Pierre, to experience new things, new places, share jokes and stories. A lovely life with a lovely man. Our final morning before flying home to London was to be the most expensive last-minute shopping time on Istiklal: I recall a soft and luxurious grey suede coat plus a need to change money...

Back in London Pierre resumed his routine of College and Art School lectures, gallery viewings and, in February, attending a particularly fascinating lecture given by the polymath George Steiner, *La Maison du Langage*, a topic of special interest of course to me. Both to thank Bea for looking after Mila while we were in Istanbul and to celebrate her 18th birthday, we took her for dinner to an Austrian restaurant. She and Mila both enjoyed the food and the music! I applied for Mila to have her own passport as Bea was going to take her with her to visit her family and spend about three weeks with them over Easter. This was great excitement: we drove them to Heathrow and they flew to Zurich to go on to the Gesson family's home just outside Feldkirch. No time or opportunity to miss Pierre or me... much too exciting to be going on a plane with Bea! And so it turned out: Bea phoned in the evening to report on the journey (bumpy) and the arrival (Mila ecstatic) and "doesn't want to come back to London". She was said to be "very good" and already asleep, sharing a room with Bea's younger sister. About a week later we phoned but "Mila was too busy to speak much", still loving it in Austria and celebrating the young brother's fourth birthday. And she was right: when we all visited a few years later, we were welcomed into their lovely house and taken for walks.

In a way it could be said that Pierre and I could profit from the "child free" time we had at our disposal but, on the one hand, we certainly did miss her bubbly, chatty and loving personality and, on the other, I had a a Hispanists' conference to attend in Cambridge, and Pierre was very busy preparing for the presentation he was to make in Helsinki, where he was attending the AICA conference. This paper, *Visual Grammar* which incorporated children's drawings and a lot of his experiences gleaned from his work with students in the Art Schools and Colleges, was very well received at the conference and was not only reprinted by the committee but was, much later, translated into Bulgarian and published as a booklet at the initiative of his great friend Svetlin Roussev. I, meanwhile, stood in for Pierre at the opening of Stanislaw Frenkiel's exhibition at the Institute of Education. As could be imagined, there was a plethora of Poles, of whom so many filled the London art scene.

In May, and with Pierre back from northern climes, there were meetings and openings, notably William Scott, a great favourite, at Gimpel and *Romanian Art 1870-1970* at Somerset House. This was the occasion for many Romanians to gather and for us to attend the reception and a dinner after, and for Pierre to write:

"The road to Romania cuts across a philosophical ante-chamber where we must pause and ponder... it is not every day that London art lovers are summoned for a pilgrimage to one of the springs of modern art".

A library for Pierre

We were still on the lookout for some variation of more space: the smaller room in which Pierre worked was certainly unsatisfactory and, all the while, a great number of his books were still in the rented room in Clapham. By happy coincidence, we had a notification from one of the many estate agents with whom we were registered that there was a ground floor flat for sale on a long lease at a reasonable price in... Markham Square. This could not have been more convenient. Luckily Pierre was, quite literally, "first in the queue" for this extremely desirable property!

We paid the deposit, had the necessary checks made and, after quite some weeks, were able to exchange contracts. It was some while before the team of Bulgarian (of course!) workmen could come in and fix the kitchen, the lights and paint the walls.

A 'Summer Course' in Sofia

1978 was to be the first of three years during which I would work for the British Council, teaching on the Summer In-service Course on the Teaching of English as a Foreign Language in Bulgaria, and then directing it. One can only imagine that Council staff, when seeking staff for a particular course in any particular location, go through the CVs of their contributors and, in this case, came up with a person – me – who had registered some familiarity with, some knowledge of, some contact with, Bulgaria and/or Bulgarian. Hence, I was to spend the month of July "refreshing" the knowledge of English, and introducing new ideas and techniques for teaching, to a group of about sixty practising teachers from all kinds of establishments, from all over Bulgaria, and with all levels of English. A month before setting off, I had a planning meeting with my colleague, Roger Flavell, at which we reviewed the likely needs of the participants, ordered textbooks and audiotapes and, generally, decided who would do what during the four weeks. We were to be joined by an American colleague, provided by USAid, whom we would meet once in Sofia.

Meanwhile there was Mila's fifth birthday party to organise; again the same entertainer and, the following day, with her friend Tammy, a visit to London Zoo where, I seem to recall, the goats ate their little straw bags... probably the picnic as well. Pierre, Mila and Bea would remain in London while I was in Bulgaria and then we would go to Normandy, while Bea went home for August. Friday 30th June was the last day of the graduate course at King's and the day that I was to fly to Sofia; to settle in and prepare for the start of the July course. We were all to be accommodated at Park Hotel Moskva ("all" was not only English teachers but also the French and German). This was on a par with, and possibly even better than, other accommodation we might have had. However, in terms of location, the choice was hardly ideal: the course was held at the Teachers' Institute in Knyazhevo! Those teaching the first hour of the day would need to be up and away (on what was then the 19 tram route, along '9th September Boulevard', changing onto a 5 for the 'Spirka Ohrid' stop) by just after 6h30! To be accommodated at the Park Hotel did, however, mean that I was but a short stroll from Detchko Ouzunov's house and the Haitovs' apartment on Latinka, as well as the opportunity for pleasant walks in the forest.

The participants were, without exception, delightful, and I have maintained – albeit irregular – contact with many of them from that first year. I was to meet up again with Marlise from the Lozanov Institute and some of her colleagues, with Malvina, my guide from the 1975 study visit, with Radka Strahilova who had visited my school in England many years before and with Pavla Tsonkova from the Varna English Language Medium School. We of course had our "*otgovornitchka*" ("reporter" would be too mild a word…), ready to report back to "the authorities" on all our activities, even (in our eyes) the most innocent. I have to say that I felt that, compared with Roger, I had a more developed sense of what one could and couldn't – should or shouldn't – do and say!

Our American colleague was Richard Wanderer, whose ponytail was not much appreciated by various officials. More ironic, however, for the English, was the fact that, despite the glorious sunny weather, Richard felt the absolute need to purchase an umbrella. In retrospect, one might have thought it not quite the thing to be asking for that summer… although the event on Waterloo Bridge was still to come.

For me the course was a marvellous opportunity not only to be engaged in an interesting and challenging professional venture but also, naturally, to be able to visit friends in the – few – hours that we had free. As three lecturers, we formed the participants into three groups which we rotated according to our personal interests and specialisms: language and linguistics,

THE SEVENTIES – OPENING UP NEW HORIZONS

literature, current events, American Studies. We received a very adequate *per diem* allowance to cover our monthly transport pass, copious meals either in the Institute canteen or at the nearby *'Biraria Ohrid'*. This is a course which, together with the two subsequent ones for which I was Director of Studies, I recall with the greatest pleasure: enthusiastic and hospitable students, warm sunny weather, excursions organised for us to places of interest... and we didn't even find the bureaucracy too, too burdensome!

After a first "hard day" on Monday 3rd July, I went later for dinner with friends to the Panorama restaurant at Grand Hotel Sofia (old habits die hard...!). Another evening it was a drive up to Boyana with Karl and Lina in their new Lada. They were to leave Sofia a little later for their summer break, renting rooms at Nos Galata (visiting them on the coast was a pleasure I was to have during the second British Council course in 1980). One Sunday a drive with Vanyo and Jeannie Rumenov to Panagyurishte and Oborishte, hearing about Bulgarian history, stopping for a delicious picnic and going later to Christo Alexiev's country place in Pancharevo. Another day I was invited by the Rumenovs and I saw their son Vladi for the

first time in seven years! A huge, smiling, charming, gentle, bearded young man of 22. The painter Elsa Goeva, a friend of the family, was there, and we saw the reproduction of her painting of Vanyo in *Rabotnitchesko Delo*.

One day I was able to introduce Richard to Karl and Lina, two graduates of the 'American College', and another evening I went into town with Ivo and Jenny Bozhilova-Haitova to meet Nikolai at the new and very swish Cinema Union Club; there we also met a director, Popyordanov, who knew Pierre well. Nikolai was charming. quiet and calm as always; everyone wanting to claim his time and attention. At that time they were casting a new historical series which he was to write. There was also discussion of a joint project with Ivo, text and photos, a book on the Rhodopes. On the 15th July (having seen the French team at breakfast very much the worse for Embassy and '14 *Juillet*' celebrations!) I went with Jenny to spend the weekend at their beautiful house in Yavorovo, stopping in Plovdiv to buy vegetables at the market. Much seemed to have changed, but still to come were the excavations which would reveal the huge amphitheatre so splendidly used subsequently for the 'Verdi festival' and other performances. On to Asenovgrad and up into the Rhodopes, hundreds of bends and curves, past 'Bulgarian Hollywood' (Lyaskovo) where Nikolai's films were shot. He was there most of the time in the summer. For me it provided perfect relaxation: lunch on the terrace, Jenny's friend Violeta with her crazy poodle Aho (after Scott's *Ivanhoe*; Bulgarians are extremely well read in foreign literature) coming over for tea, a barbecue in the evening. Jenny proposed a "house swap" for the following year and I was sure that Pierre would love being up in the mountains, talking literature with Nikolai. Sunday up latish and going down to buy the fresh bread, drinking coffee *chez* Violeta, who read the grounds and told me: "You are not relaxed." But I was! All too soon we had to leave and drive back to Sofia.

The morning shift over, I would sometimes go and lunch with the aunties, always taking flowers as a little tribute for

Mama's room; they managed fairly well, just the two of them left, always wanting news of London. Sometimes, too, we spent time with the French lecturers although not much with the Germans since, coming from East Germany, they had many of their own friends and contacts. One day Malvina organised an outing for Roger, his wife, Richard and me to Koprivshtitsa in her car. Although we left in good time after classes, Malvina, enthusiastic but not a great map reader, took a wrong road but, although this did not prevent us from having a marvellous picnic in a field, it did mean arriving too late to visit any of the museum houses. Trying door handles, on the principle that people might be living behind some of them, Malvina the invincible was proved right and we even came upon a lady who spoke English. Her father had been Ambassador to the Court of St. James and she told us about Koprivshtitsa and her house and asked us about ourselves. Given her age and the circle of references, I mentioned the Ouvaliev connection. "But then you must know there's a Petar Ouvaliev living in London"! I revealed the connection and she told me how he used to write in her door balcony for the theatrical productions that they

organised. Only at that point did I learn that she was Anna Kamenova!

A couple of the course participants invited us to their homes (after putting in the necessary request in triplicate... after all, this was social, as opposed to professional, mixing with foreigners, Westerners, an American even!). I kept in touch with nurse Penka, updating her with photos of Mila. Detchko and Olga Ouzunov gave their "summer party" (exactly five years since I had last been), attended by the then Mayor of Sofia; Christo Stefanov, by then living in Sofia, Zlatka Dubova and... Chavdar Damianov, what a lovely surprise; he was on leave from his post in Stockholm. Detchko was to be 80 in August, so there was much jollity. The "diplomatic service" butler who had recognised Pierre seven years before was on duty. Young Stefan, latest in the theatrical dynasty and grandson of Ancheto Fadenhecht, was about to celebrate his fifth birthday and his parents, Bondo Sertchadjiev and Dora Glindjeva, invited me for tea.

More theatre news was that Beba Kabaivanova and Maria Stefanova were to visit London in September, so many plans were made.

Yes, it was indeed a golden summer. As it drew to its end, we returned some materials to the Embassy, held a "farewell party" on the last evening at the Boyana Hanche and, on the very last morning, organised a much appreciated "lottery" of the textbooks.

I took my leave of friends; many came to the hotel with cards, flowers and presents; dinner lasted for hours and packing had to be done for the early Balkan flight on 29th. I was in London by midday and, collected by Pierre – eager of course to have news – and at home, there she was, my lovely, welcoming, smiling, running ("Mummy!") Mila, her hair in plaits. We sat down to open everything... lots of presents for her, and to take photos for the givers.

A *Summer's Lease*

We had booked 'Les Mouettes' in Vaucottes again for the month of August but it seemed far too soon to be going off again and, indeed, with the purchase of – and renovations needed to – 46 Markham Square, we spent a shorter time in France. Dora and Luben had decided to join us in Vaucottes and had rented the top part of another of the extraordinary "turn of the century" villas: 'Le Chalet', further down the hill, and, when we did go across on the 11th, we went almost straightaway to join them for a "family reunion" dinner, ending in our having to carry Mila home up the hill! The days went past in the usual activities: beach, swimming, market, down to Yport, fireworks up at the "big house" with the Hareng family on the 15th August. By this time we felt slightly more "accepted" into Vaucottes society and several Vaucottois friends were telling us about the possibilities of property for sale in the village.

September brought the annual conference of the British Society of Aesthetics and Pierre had prepared a paper on 'Bulgarian Aesthetics' with Isaac Passy. I, meanwhile, was putting together my report on the British Council course with recommendations for the future. At Covent Garden there was to be a full *Ring* cycle and I begged Pierre to get tickets. At no doubt enormous expense he was able to get tickets for all four performances, and we were lucky enough to attend the opening night of *Das Rheingold* on the 11th, followed the next day by *Die Walkure* and, ten days later (one needed a break…), *Siegfried* and *Gotterdämmerung*. It was perfect to see the *Ring* in its entirety and in order. This was the production, cosmic, black and white, a mirror fantasy, of Götz Friedrich, conducted by Colin Davis with a stunning cast, amongst whom were Gwyneth Jones, Zoltan Kelemen, Josephine Veasey and others whose names are now so well known.

Icons at the Courtauld

Aged 5, Mila had started the new academic year at the French School in South Kensington, the ideal way to learn the language: immersion. There were new friends and new excitements. For the new session at King's we had to appoint a German specialist and I was involved in interviews while, next door at the Courtauld Institute, Pierre and I both attended the opening of the exhibition of Bulgarian Icons, followed a couple of days later by a symposium on the theme of 'Icons' and a reception held at the GB-EE Centre. This was a fine follow-on from the Thracian exhibition held two years previously at the British Museum. The Honorary Committee of the Cultural Committee of the People's Republic of Bulgaria included Petar Mladenov, Minister of Foreign Affairs, and Ludmila Zhivkova, President of the Committee for Culture. Among the organisers was Emil Alexandrov, Deputy Director of the Board for "International Cultural Activities". Assistance was given in all of this by Rumen Spassov, then Cultural Attaché at the Bulgarian Embassy.

On October 20th at lunchtime, at the church opposite King's, St. Mary-le-Strand, a memorial service was held for Georgi Markov who had died in mysterious circumstances in September. This was attended by many of the BBC Bulgarian Service staff together, no doubt, with members of the "Special Services".

November and December followed their usual course: lectures and seminars for Pierre, including a presentation to the French Department at King's; reviewing an exhibition of 'Pictures at the Savile', masterminded by his dear friend, writer and cultural historian, Nigel Foxell; receptions for a Bulgarian 'Cultural Delegation' and... Christmas, at our house in Chelsea this year, together with my dear cousin Joan Hamilton Martin and, on another day, Julia Vassilieva (would she have been a member of the 'cultural delegation'? Probably not). And so on into the final year of the '70s.

* * * * *

1979

Bookshelves for No. 46

My diary has few entries of interest (only meetings, students, interviews...) and is therefore of little use in reviewing the year. However, correspondence, articles and other documents enable me to recall the major events. (The "archive" to which I have access is enormous and cross-referencing is essential: files with dated articles written for *Arts Review*, letters from artists about whom he wrote, letters from friends, copies of BBC and France Culture broadcasts, letters from listeners to his *Five Minutes with Petar Ouvaliev*, interviews in newspapers, articles published in journals, lectures given in Bulgaria, papers given at a whole range of Yugoslav art gatherings, film scripts and playbills, invitations, photos from almost every event... The whole of the Chelsea house is just bursting...)

Early in January, and continuing an excellent family tradition, Pierre (in many senses the boy who never grew up, ever youthful, ever enthusiastic), took Mila to see *Peter Pan* at the theatre. And as she was now attending the French school, we had even more reason to be around in South Kensington, attending a lecture on *Poetics*, or going to the cine-club or the excellent library.

In February, our new Principal at King's, Professor of Philosophy and Religion Stewart Sutherland, gave his inaugural lecture on the subject of *Goodness*. Pierre, who attended with me, was so impressed that he used the event as the subject of one of his BBC broadcasts

THE SEVENTIES – OPENING UP NEW HORIZONS

All this time and, slowly but surely, Pierre was establishing himself at 46 Markham Square. He had several rows of shelves erected along all the available 3 metre high walls. These, as many friends and visitors will recall, were soon filled and the books and papers overflowed onto the floor, tables and almost every available space! The books were brought back over from Clapham, the big desk was set in the front part of the through reception room in this ground floor apartment and, at the back, a comfortable sofa from which he was able to watch … football, what else? … on television. In the early days he did not have a separate telephone and Mila would, for example, run round to "tell Daddy supper's ready". Increasingly, also, this became the "smoking den" and, as witness thereto, the colour of the walls when the books were taken down to "go home" to Sofia University, had become a striped yellowish-brown! But nothing could have pleased him more than his "personal space" where so many of his lectures, articles and broadcasts were composed on his trusty manual 'Olympia' typewriters; surrounded by his beloved collection of books – on all subjects and in many languages – and able to entertain his Bulgarian friends, offering whisky or rakia, give interviews and, later on, talk for hours on the phone…

There were to be more theatre visits for Mila with Pierre: to see *Rumplestiltskin* at the Old Vic and, on Mother's Day, for the three of us, *Gulliver's Travels* at the Unicorn Theatre. Slightly theatrical and extremely well attended was the launch of Sophia Loren's autobiography *Sophia – My Story*, held at Claridge's Hotel towards the end of March. Pierre and I had the chance to spend time with her and Carlo Ponti while they were in London. A most dedicated actress, she spoke impeccable English. It was time, however, for me to go off, with Mila, for two weeks to Palma de Majorca to teach on the Easter Spanish course organised each year by our colleague John Galleymore. Leaving Pierre in London, I had recruited some of my graduate students to teach on the course and, of course, they were also available to me as occasional child minders! These travels, I am sure, planted in Mila the seeds of what was to become her dedication to travel and discovery: Australia, Singapore, the USA...!

Back in London, we rounded off the Easter holiday with excursions to Richmond Park to see the deer, and to Hyde Park, followed by tea in a five-star hotel. With Pierre everything was fun and as luxurious as we could make it! Also I think that he astonished himself at what an exceptional father, this man who had previously declared no interest in children, he had turned out to be!

The weeks and months to follow were, however, to be dedicated more to adults: Andre Boucoureshliev was back in London for concerts and he and Jeanne came to us for dinner; I attended the Bloomsbury Bookfair with Pierre; we were both invited for lunch by my colleague Professor of French Brian Juden at his country house near Royal Holloway College. On May 26th – for no reason I can fathom, except perhaps the convenience of its being a Saturday – there was a reception at the Bulgarian Embassy. Culture arriving two days late?

A month in the sun with sociolinguistics

I had been very fortunate in being selected to attend a course for French language lecturers in the south of France for the whole of July. Pierre had wanted me to take an *au pair* with me as Mila was accompanying me but I judged that it would be informal enough for her to be around with me; and so it proved. While he was left entirely in peace for a month... I drove Mila and myself part of the way, then putting the car on the *"motorail"*, to arrive at Nice in glorious sunshine and drive to the university campus at Luminy. There we met a fascinating range of teachers of French from almost every imaginable country, from Afghanistan to the United Kingdom. I partook in a challenging series of mini-courses: sociolinguistics, semiotics, functions... and made many new friends. It turned out that I was not the only one to have "smuggled in" in six-year old... Jean-Pierre Paquet, then teaching in Tangier, was accompanied by his wife and their daughter Styliane. These two children joined in everything and Mila was even used as an example of "early foreign language acquisition"! The French she was learning and using at the French school in London took on a quite distinct fluency. There was also the Paquets' dog "Monsieur Zodi" to keep the girls amused.

The only notes that I have in my "engagement diary" for this month relate to missing a final examinations meeting, attending a retirement party and, for Pierre, a reception at the GB-EE Centre for Nikolai Haitov. The two of them must have had a splendid time together. Such good friends, they so enjoyed each other's company until what was to be one of Pierre's last commitments before he died, the writers' award to Nikolai in Dobrich in 1995. I can well imagine that they spent hours together that summer in the new "writing space" at 46 Markham Square!

At the end of this unusual but blissful month, I drove back with Sabine Ernst, a course member from Belgium, to Vaucottes for the relaxed and lazy days of summer. She stayed with us for a week and later in the month the Paquets came to visit. I recall that "Mami Bigo", our landlady, was not too impressed with the amount of jumping on beds that Mila and Styliane got up to, accompanied by Monsieur Zodi, to the strains of their singing: *On saute sur le lit, on saute sur le lit, avec Monsieur Zodi*"! Others who came to visit were my colleague from King's, John Jeffrey, with his family: they had followed my good advice and had rented a place near us. Another day it was the French art critic Jeanine Warnod-Sonkin with her husband Roland and their daughter Nicole. Pierre and Dora had long discussions, regarding his *Turner* and other matters art-historical, with Jeanine while the girls played tennis and Roland and Luben talked. On account of the size of their lodging at 'Le Chalet', lunch had been voted at 'Les Mouettes'. Thank heavens for good French prepared produce! Daniel and

Jacqueline Boutry, later to become some of our closest friends in Vaucottes, often came up to sit and talk. All too soon the August holiday was over for another year.

Our close friends Genee and Bill Fadiman (a "film family" from California) were in London in early September; seven years since we had seen them but it was "but an evening gone". Sadly, although I have tried by every means to contact them more recently, I have drawn a complete blank. Such good friends do not usually "disappear": they may well have died. There were gallery openings: Gimpel gave a one-man show to Alan Davie, about whom Pierre had written on many occasions, and there was a "Sunday lunch" at the Bernard Sterns. But soon it was a week in Milan, and meetings with Pittaluga to discuss the proofs for the *Turner*. The book was really on its way!

Later in the year our colleague at the Institute of Education, Alfred Harris, held an exhibition and we attended the private view of Carole Hodgson's exhibition at Flowers. We heard the good news from Bulgaria that Jeannie and Vanyo's son Vladi and his wife Nadya had had a little girl, Annie, and Mila and I went to Mothercare to buy some baby clothes and other things ready to send off to Sofia. In October we heard the news that Zhivko Popov had been appointed Ambassador to Prague and he and his wife Julia Vassilieva invited us to spend Christmas there with them. Pierre would have loved to revisit Prague but, as it turned out, we were to accept another invitation.

Luxury festivities in Marrakech

After the intellectual challenge of attending the lecture by Jacques Derrida at the Institut Français and the end of term in all our establishments, Pierre, Mila and I set off for Gatwick to take our plane to Casablanca, for we had been invited to spend Christmas and New Year with Claude Castelli in his magnificent villa in Marrakech! We were met by his chauffeur and taken to the *El Mansour* hotel where Claude had made a reservation for us, a lovely room on the seventh floor. Francette Delage, one of the friends Mila and I had made during the Luminy course, came to visit us and later we had dinner with Claude at his apartment. Claude, of course, was very taken up with his beautiful antiques business in the run up to the festive season, but nevertheless found time to take us out to see his aeroplane. This was the first of many things to impress Mila, but Claude was so generous, inviting us, giving Mila lovely dolls, always sending presents…a tragedy that he was killed some years later in Morocco. On the Monday we drove to Marrakech, stopping on the way for coffee and for lunch. In Marrakech we had to follow one of Claude's colleagues into the Medina – how else would one ever find the way…? Once at Claude's amazing villa (later requisitioned by the royal family …one can see why…), we unpacked and had a delicious *tagine* for dinner. The following morning we saw the extent of this mini-palace and sat sunbathing in the huge garden. We were, of course, invited by the many friends, contacts, artists, teachers… whom Pierre and I both knew from our different worlds. They also came to us at the villa: Boualam, Aherdan, El Wahdi, Mahfoud. Aherdan became one of Pierre's longest-standing artist friends, about whose work he wrote, and it was a joy to know his family in Marrakech. We walked, we explored, the souk, shopping, Djema el Fnaa, Mila enchanted by the snake charmers. Our friends the Paquets were also down for Christmas from Tangier and came over to visit us. Mila was delighted see Styliane again. It was only on the 24th, Christmas Eve, that Claude was able to get away from work and come down to Marrakech, together with a couple of his friends from France and his antique dealer colleague, Dominique Gagnon, who came over from Agadir. This, I realise in retrospect, was truly a golden age for ex-patriates…the French colony enjoying a very good standard of living.

We put up the traditional Christmas tree, decorated and with lots of presents and had smoked salmon with our dinner. On

Christmas Day we slept late and then drove up into the Lourika valley (at 140 kph, as always with Claude!); snow on the mountains for a truly "White Christmas"! The days passed in lazy luxury, with invitations and excursions here and there, although Claude had to return to Casablanca. But he was back on the 29th when, with champagne, he toasted the seventeen years that Pierre and I had spent together! More friends arrived on the 30th for the New Year celebrations and, on the 31st, with a whole house party to look after, Dominique prepared a magnificent meal with which, together with appropriate wines, we welcomed not only the New Year but the new decade!

What a wonderful way to end one year and to see in another! Prague was going to have to wait!

Our own story now continues into and through the 1980s.

* * * * *

The Eighties – Eastern Approaches

1980

Turner is ready!

The start of the new year, and this new decade, saw us still enjoying a dreamlike holiday at Claude's villa in Marrakech. Just a few days and then we left for Casabanca, with so many extraordinary memories. After a final lunch with dear Claude, and promises to see each other soon in London, maybe on one of his buying trips, we boarded the plane for Gatwick, but not before he had made a last present to Mila of the doll who came to be called 'Claudie' and who lies, to this day, in antique cot here in the house.

On January 12th we made it a big day for Pierre's 65th birthday: a card, lunch, a birthday cake and a visit to the theatre. What better celebration could there be, family style! In February he went to Italy for a week; all the copies of the *Turner* were ready, beautifully printed with a wealth of full-colour illustrations, the text appearing for the first edition in French. Together with Dora, he had worked on his original text to produce a superb French version.

Friends and theatre

In March we had the great pleasure of meeting up with our dear, dear Lina and Karl Ognyanov. He was in England to attend a medical conference on some aspect of his work as a gynaecologist. It was marvellous that Lina was able to accompany him. We saw them at the reception at the GB-EE Centre and again the following day after their "official dinner" (a bit like me going on to them after a dinner in Sofia!). Another day we were able to get them away from official business and took them to the National Theatre to see Eugene O'Neill's *The Iceman Cometh*. They returned to Sofia and I was pleased to think that I would most probably see them in the summer if the Council were to ask me to run the Summer Course again. For Pierre, of course, every meeting with friends from his "earlier years" was a bonus, a real gift to be treasured. Who could tell when he might – or might not – be able to visit Bulgaria, or friends come on a trip to London? Despite our academic and social "respectability", who could tell what changes (of committee membership, allegiance...) might not take place?

My birthday, at the beginning of April, was a lovely one: Pierre and Mila decorated the big room at 46 Markham Square and there were cards and gifts. I was summoned round when all was prepared and had such a surprise! There was to be a birthday lunch and, in the evening tickets for the three of us to see *The Bartered Bride* at Sadlers Wells (opera, circus and a girl getting married.,, what better and more romantic a story for a six year old!). Pierre had this creative genius for making an "occasion"!

On the 15th of April there was a reception at the Great Britain East Europe Centre to mark the retirement of Sir William Harpham as Director. He had previously been British Ambassador to Bulgaria and was a dynamic force in setting up the Centre. There was a great turn out to wish him well.

A 'Ruby' celebration

Later in the month we were invited for the weekend by my cousin and his family and set off early on Saturday, stopping for lunch at Salisbury where we had a chance to look around the glorious cathedral. We arrived at about 6p.m. and, when we saw so many of the family assembled, realised that in fact it was a fortieth wedding celebration! We were invited to "change for dinner" but Pierre had not brought a suit with him! Nor had we thought to bring a present but, very kindly, we were invited to join the others in contributing to a complete set of "ruby red" glasses, chosen specially for the "Ruby Wedding". Dinner was completed with toasts and photos and then we went off to sleep at the nearby Convent which, being the house of a religious order, proved somewhat spartan! We gathered, except for Pierre who slept in, for Sunday breakfast with the family. Later on, more neighbours arrived for a drinks party. All the generations had a marvellous time and we drove back to London with Pierre feeling very much included in my family. This was important for me too, as I knew how much he missed the contact with his own family, scattered about Europe.

Early in May Pierre went off to Milan where he was to take part in a Colloquium organised by the art historian and critic Lea Vergine whom he so admired. The theme was women artists, *L'Altra Metà dell'Avanguardia*. This was an ideal opportunity to catch up with his other close friend Carlo Argan. Italy always proved to be an intellectual stimulus for Pierre; it was the country where he had spent many of his formative years and, of course, he was completely fluent in the language. He was later to write a review of the exhibition for *Arts Review*. During this time I was to meet up with the person who would become a great friend as well as colleague, Alison Piper, at what was then Ealing College of Higher Education, later Thames Valley University. Alison had been recommended to me as a member of my team for the second British Council EFL summer school which I had been invited to direct in Sofia in the summer. In this connection, she and I both attended a presentation of materials by Oxford University Press at International House. This proved to be one of those rather crowded days since there was also the opening of a splendid exhibition of William Scott, one of my (many!) favourite artists at the Gimpel Gallery to which Pierre and I both went. Another lovely evening was one we spent at the apartment of George Buchanan, whose poetry was published by Carcanet. He was hosting a meeting of the *Société Européenne de Culture*, which always brought together a truly fascinating group of likeminded intellectuals, writers and artists.

Pierre got news that the Italian publishers of his book on Turner were ready for the launch. The French version was extensively promoted in France and received excellent reviews. Claude Lévi-Strauss, to whom Pierre had asked that a copy be sent, acknowledged it in a very complimentary letter. Roman Jakobson wrote that the book was "a unique approach to the work of a great artist" and the whole of his review was included in the book jacket.

The end of the month was the time when, in line with the very rigorous demands of the French education system, parents were informed if their child was to go up to the next class or to be held down for a year. Luckily, Mila had little problem in going up in the following September to the next class.

June 1st was 'Mothers' Day' and Pierre and Mila had prepared a beautiful present in the shape of a collage of "portraits" which they brought to me with breakfast in bed! After lunch, Pierre was to meet up with Rangel Vulchanov, over in England for a film festival, who was always eager to meet and talk with Pierre about film business and, no doubt, other plans. The following day it was the turn of George Ganchev to call round; he, too, was by then starting out in the film business, subsequently spending more time in Los Angeles. For Pierre and me, however, travel was to be in the opposite direction, to Eastern Europe, and as Mila would be remaining in London for the early part of the summer, we had asked Eliana and Aldo Ceccato to recommend a young *au pair* who could, at the same time, improve her English. Anna arrived mid-June, Pierre meeting her at Heathrow. She soon settled into the routine and on the 24th Pierre flew to Yugoslavia to participate in the Rijeka Biennale. This was something he always enjoyed: the chance to be with artists and friends, to be in a position to judge and award prizes, to be valued for his knowledge, judgment and experience. This year he had been particularly impressed by one of the students, Stephen Foster, whom he had taught at the Institute of Education, and he planned to invite him to attend the next gathering in Rijeka. This was, indeed, to come about a few years later.

An early arrival

I, meanwhile, was due to go to Sofia on the 30th but, for some reason never to be satisfactorily explained, I was informed by the British Council that the Ministry in Sofia had requested that the Director arrive on the 28th, a Saturday and at least two days before the course was due to begin. The effect of this was that my plans, ticket etc. all had to be changed but, as ever, Rosa Georgieva managed to arrange everything for the best.

A few words here: what I am writing is the biography – life and times, activities, adventures – of Pierre Rouve; this is for him and about him, but I allow myself my own reflections on Bulgaria as I "met" it: via Pierre's contacts, family and friends since I feel that many of the experiences I had were reflections of things that we might well have done together, and indeed often did, especially when we were in Bulgaria together.

Well, on that Saturday there was nobody to meet me from the Ministry. However, there was a charming young (my goodness, it's like policemen…) Cultural Attaché who assisted me through customs, none other than Richard Stagg, later to be appointed Ambassador to Bulgaria. He drove me to the Park Hotel where I had imagined we would be staying. No reservations had been made so I booked myself in, sent my cases to the room and then went with Richard to the British Embassy to phone to the *dezhourna* at the Ministry. What do you expect on a Saturday? Finally we got hold of a French lecturer colleague and I exploded in French, only to be told that we were not expected until 2nd July and that we were all to be accommodated at Hotel Bulgaria. At this point I threatened to return to London and to report everything to Alexander Fol... Richard and I went back to the Park Hotel and transferred to the Bulgaria, hardly luxurious to my way of thinking but at least nearer the tram! This was not what I had given up my weekend for! However, I felt that Pierre would have been proud of me and of my firmness! Richard Stagg was indeed astonished: French and anger!

It was hopeless to imagine that people would just be around waiting for me on a summer Sunday so I made the best of a lovely sunny day, tried Karl and Lina's apartment but there was no reply, went on to the aunties, whose only criticism was that I refused a second portion of cherry cake! Since they had managed to get rid of the "lodgers", the flat had become enormous but they had become megalomaniac and were trying to take over the first floor as well. Would that they had succeeded as it might have meant that Pierre and Dora could have enjoyed some inheritance. Instead the whole of the family property was taken over by stealth and morally dubious dealings ("Sign this or else..."). Well, on with my travels: I was going to visit Jenny on Latinka when, at the tram stop, I quite literally bumped into Karl and Lina with their rucksacks. They were sorry to have missed the chance of having me for the day.

Monday and everything should have been in order: after all, Alison was to arrive. By 10 a.m. nobody had phoned. I knew that I had the advantage and could make virtually any demands... The Ministry of Education course director, Rumiana Todorova, would not agree to come to the British Embassy (she would have needed to ask for all sorts of permissions...) so Richard and I went to the Foreign Ministry. Everything was very amicable, especially when I asked to see Goshkin... We then went back to the Embassy from where I reported this chaos by phone to London. Life then got a bit better as, Sofia being what it is, I bumped into George Ganchev and then Isaak Passy. Alison arrived perfectly on time but, as we later discovered, some of the books that we had ordered had not arrived and this meant a visit to the Embassy the next week to collect them (I have a wonderful memory of penetrating darkened and alarmed rooms and, with Richard – at that time also in charge of EFL materials – climbing over goodness how many boxes).

The summer school 1980 was much the same as in 1978 and, in itself, is of no interest to report. I shall thus limit myself to writing about meetings with friends and family where there is a link to Pierre.

Alison and I were invited to Julia Vassilieva's Institute but got hopelessly, nightmarishly, lost among the "blocks"; we later went to eat at '*Kristal*' in the centre of Sofia and near our hotel, then the centre of importuning, no doubt for sex and currency! At the Ministry of Education we met Lili Litkova and our American colleague Diana Bartley, who had driven down from Warsaw in her Mercedes, with which she continued to terrify Sofia citizens. I went to the opera with Karl and Lina and saw a delightful and witty production of *An Italian Girl in Algiers*; got told off for jay-walking outside the Party HQ building; letters home to Pierre got written in time to go off in the diplomatic bag.

In the 1299th year...

In response to my letters, detailing all aspects of my activities, Pierre would write in his usual witty style. To give something of the flavour of his wordplay, covert references to history, personalities and current events etc., I quote from his letter of July 9th in which he picks up on all that I have told him:

"My Majesty

In this 1299th year of the creation of your State, life in your angliska kolonia is more than satisfactory. Your letters have arrived safely and have been handed to me in the splendour of the Bulgarian Embassy. Which is something of a miracle as, in our late night telephone call, you had announced to all who cared to listen that you were sending me mysterious messages via Goshkin's personnel – herself very much one of those who listen. Still, the lady in question has been rewarded with an Escort-ed tour of London in the pouring rain and a King's Road Italian supper.

I was truly sorry to learn that you have had a taste of what it means to be an ordinary mortal in certain parts of the world and, as you have rightly guessed, I am very proud of your frightening the natives and startling the Brits. But such is the local existence, with its unpredictable follies such as Ielite's expansion plans and the Palace Builders' (you know who) even bigger megalomania. But things out there have a way of coming right in the end, so I hope that Your Majesty will, when all is said and done, enjoy Her adventure."

The letter continues with more amusing stories about life in London.

Other activities included visiting the City Art Gallery, seeing the Petrovs from Lina's father's collection; lunched with Radka Strahilova and her husband and son. On my way to Vanyo and Jeannie Rumenov's house, I saw that the hotel Rodina, which had been a building site in 1978, had risen to about 28 storeys, completely overshadowing their house.

Visits: Sofia and beyond

One Sunday Alison and I were invited by Vanyo and Jeannie, together with Karl and Lina, for a drive (Vanyo's clutch and acceleration were, if anything, worse than in 1978!). We visited the collection of international bells ("gifts from friendly countries") and then went on to Borovetz and picnicked in flower-filled fields, returning via Samokov and an abandoned church in a country field.

The aunties were back on form the next time I went round: "Pierre never wrote to his mother", "Vanyo is favoured by the regime (because he still works at 66)". We were joined by sad Detchka Dimitrova, asking endlessly about another son (Pashanko) who never seemed to write...Inspired, I wrote letters to both Pierre and Mila and dropped them off at the Embassy. Lina and I went to visit Vena Spassova, so distressed, Poli having died a few days before. Margo Hadjimishev also came to visit; an amazing lady! Another day I had a meeting with Alexander Fol and, while waiting, an interesting-faced but very crippled man asked me about the British Council. A painter, he had studied aesthetics with Isaak Passy and wanted to go on to Oxford. Fol was harassed, busy, late and strange; formal yet bantering: "What are you doing in Bulgaria, and for the British Council, 'that famous spying centre'?" An unsatisfactory visit, maybe just "protocol".

Another day it was Emil Alexandrov and Pavel Matev, both with many messages for Pierre. Then it was a whole gang of Julia Vassilieva's friends and we drove to Samokov to her villa and talked and talked. Those who learnt English with Eckersley (acknowledged master of English language teaching methodology) are indeed competent. After supper we climbed up to the plateau and were rewarded by a star-filled sky, stayed the night and were back at the Institute early the following morning. I had a brief meeting with Ivo Hadjimishev, who was to leave on a photo mission to the USSR; he was, by then, married to Boyana, daughter of the famous writer and acknowledged translator of Shakespeare into Bulgarian, Valeri Petrov. We talk of Pierre, "the situation" (what "situation"? Nobody would say...).

Sandanski, Melnik and Rozhen Monastery were the focus of the next weekend I spent with Vanyo and Jeannie; lovely to be with such good friends. At the Embassy one day the PA came through and said "I've just realised who you are". "Yes, I'm

Sonia Rouve, so...?" "No, you're Pierre Rouve's wife" "So? You knew that." It transpired that she had known Pierre 20 years previously on the London art scene with Eddie Wolfram. "Pierre was the bright new star in the ascendant". I told her about the Turner book. Small worlds within small worlds... Another evening there was an invitation to Julia Vassilieva's, a huge mansion flat, the whole top floor of a 1930s block on Gavril Genov which they had bought for themselves but given to the "young generation". Maya and her husband Luchezar seemed very happy. One day a serious, intelligent man, Georgi Vassiliev, came bringing several books for Pierre, very kind and thoughtful.

An appointment at the Committee for Culture was interesting: I was on time for the meeting but all seemed locked up, very disconcerting! I sat down to wait and a charming English-speaking girl from the Indian desk came over to speak to me. We graduated to Emil Alexandrov's office, he arrived, I had my notes ready. Then it was the "hand over" of the copy of the Turner book; it was duly wrapped and locked away, to be further handed over... The pleasant girl (Anna Sendova, as she later became by marriage) gave me the "protocol gifts": copies of Ludmila's speeches, books and records, and I went away with more weight than I had arrived with!

Alison and I were invited for an evening to Andrei Danchev. It was a fascinating time with linguistics shop-talk! Alison had got used to his habit of drawing out a slip of paper to note down an unusual utterance. We made our way to a minute, two-room, flat in a shabby, impersonal building on a shabby, impersonal estate – *Druzhba*, as it turned out, but indistinguishable from *Mladost* or any other... It was his study-bedsit and his widowed mother's lounge-bedsit. And this was not "transit camp", but what a member of the bourgeoisie had been reduced to.

Staying out late, as this intensive social life required, meant that I was at the hotel for the late phone calls that Pierre put in, when we would catch up on his return from Rijeka, London and all activities, and he would listen to all the talk (ever indiscreet...) of my meetings with his friends and family.

A diplomatic party

Richard Stagg hosted a cocktail party for us one evening at his beautiful apartment, later to become the library of the British Council, on Todor Strashmirov (Tulovo), where we met several foreign diplomats. Alison and I were extremely fortunate in that, this year, the Council had approved a weekend in Varna for us. We flew out early on Friday with one of the course participants, Pavla Tsonkova, and were taken to meet the French group at their hotel. We were staying at the Teachers' Institute but, as Karl and Lina were by then on holiday at the Joliot-Curie Institute, we arranged to meet up. Another day we went for breakfast to the new-ish Grand Hotel (the "Swedish"), took a boat trip to Baltchik, the palace then abandoned and sad; visited Pavla at her in-laws' mansion flat in Varna and watched the Moscow Olympics on television. Slogans everywhere: *'Moskva – po uspeshno ot* (more successful than) *Monreal'*, which could be considered ambiguous...

Back in the real world of Sofia and teaching, washing the Black Sea sand out of my hair. A visit to the aunties who were proud to show me that their "disposal of Pierre's mother's estate" consisted of large glass-framed family photos, packages and albums and some truly amazing historic photos (some of which are used in this publication). These were to form the basis of a very pleasant and informative evening during August with Dora and Luben when I distributed the family "photographic record" as seemed appropriate.

The month was drawing to a close but still there was the plan for Sasha Beshkov to do a television interview with me; this, had it taken place, would no doubt have caused a certain astonishment. Somehow other things intervened, notably a visit to the Bulgarian Academy of Sciences ("Block 6a", are these places findable...?) for a discussion of curriculum innovation with Blagovest Sendov and his team. This was to develop, in later years, into a very interesting project on educational reform with which I was to be involved.

The last evening was one of last visits: a dinner in the Panorama restaurant at Grand Hotel Sofia where we were joined by Nikolai Ghiaurov; a visit to Detchko Ouzunov's house; so many messages and gifts for Pierre and Mila; late night packing and, on the 31st, off by Balkan Airways to Zurich. Back in London with Pierre and Mila the talk was of friends, meetings, events... things which he was best placed to interpret.

Before setting off for a summer holiday in Normandy, Pierre had undertaken to review a major exhibition of the work of our great friend, the Polish graphic artist, Feliks Topolski. His *Chronicles*, covering all important events of the twentieth century, were on show at the ICA and in the two railway arches which served as both studio and exhibition space. Once in Vaucottes, we quickly settled into the holiday routine: visiting Dora and Luben, seeing our friends in all the other houses in the village. It was also pleasant to be able to meet up, by arrangement, in Rouen with Hervé, one of the 'French team' from the Varna course. Pierre was, of course, interested to get another perspective on time spent in Bulgaria.

The 'library' takes shape

While we were away in France, work was being done on Pierre's studio in Markham Square: ever more bookcases were needed! The work was successfully carried out by a Bulgarian handyman (this was long before the days of "the Polish builder"!) and, on our return, some of the piles of books were put on their shelves. It was always a joy and an intellectual challenge to take down a book, whether on art, philosophy, theatre, or poetry from one of the many shelves.

September saw a gentle return to the routine of term time; for Pierre it was to be Chelsea and the Institute of Education for his art and philosophy classes, a theatre production to plan for the theatre in Richmond. The annual AICA meeting was held at the Savile Club and we both attended two gallery openings: work by Patrick Hughes, famous at that period for his rainbows and once a student of mine at the Institute of Education, and by Kenneth Armitage. Pierre felt particularly honoured in that Professor Arnaud Reid had asked him to take over his lecture schedule at the Institute, which meant a regular presentation each Tuesday; this was the kind of continuity which he really enjoyed and was to lead, the following year, to classes with the Master's degree students. In November, he was also asked to make a major contribution to the symposium on *Teaching Art History*, one of his passions. I, meanwhile, had my report to compile for the British Council, recommending yet again that there be a branch set up in Bulgaria. November also saw the arrival of Kiril Shterev as the new Bulgarian ambassador.

Work, visits and social gatherings saw the three of us through to the vacation and the traditional Christmas Day festivities, with lunch, presents and watching the Queen's speech on television at Pashanko's house. A calm, London-based time after the excitement of Morocco the previous year, although again there was an invitation, and the possibility, of spending Christmas in Prague, where Zhivko Popov was still Ambassador.

* * * * *

1981

For Pierre, Zagreb, Rome, Salzburg and even Mexico! For Bulgaria, 1300 years For Roman Jakobson, the Encaenia at Oxford University

¡Que Viva Mexico!

The year began well: we had the visit of our delightful Austrian au pair Bea and her sister Bibi for a week and, much to his surprise, Pierre found himself taking them with Mila to the circus! Despite his initial concerns and misgivings as to how he might be able to act as a father, Pierre was in fact the ideal one: kind, amusing, generous, always ready for fun activities, a theatre visit... and this is exactly how Mila recalls him: "the best Dad in the world". Another aspect of this was the fact that he agreed to our having a dog. This was a "rescue dog", from the Battersea Dogs' Home, where we went, together with a friend of Mila's. I can only describe their reaction to seeing all the dogs in need of a new home as a Greek chorus: the weeping and the wailing that went on as they wanted to take all of them home! We finally settled on a charming mongrel that Mila christened 'Patapouf', after the dog in one of her story books. He was very hairy and it was only when, one day in the park with Pierre, Patapouf jumped into the pond, that we realised how skinny he was!

In February, Professor Elisa Barragán of the National University of Mexico, whose acquaintance Pierre had made at an international conference, was in London and took the opportunity to put a very interesting proposal to Pierre: to undertake a lecture series at her university towards the end of the year. This was an idea that excited him greatly: he could put forward his ideas to a very different group of graduate students and explore a completely different culture and civilisation. During her stay in London, Elisa came several times to discuss the programme and declared herself very satisfied with his ideas: a course of ten lectures on *Retórica de los Hechos de Vista*. His programme – and the titles of the ten lectures were all in Spanish – was something that he worked on during the course of the whole year. Here, however, was a potential problem: having written his texts in English, should he arrange to have them translated into Spanish? Would he speak in Spanish? (Did he know Spanish?) We came to some interesting decisions, helping to answer the two questions. I can still see, on his original texts, the additions that I made, in red ink, putting certain phrases into Spanish (it transpired that it would have been excessively expensive to have the texts professionally translated). Not only this, however, but, as a long-term proponent of the importance of learning Spanish, I prepared for him a three-page set of *Notes towards an intensive Spanish course for adult beginners, based on a contrastive analysis of Spanish with English/French and Italian*. A mini grammatical guide!

Many other activities were, however, to take up his time and energies during this exceptionally busy year. There was a review to write in a March issue of *Arts Review* of the exhibition of paintings by his friend and colleague at the Institute, Stanislaw Frenkiel, held at the Drian Gallery – a Polish venue for a Polish painter. And Halima Nalecz, the Director, was such a dynamic woman. Not only painting but theatre also took up Pierre's time: working with students at the De Leon Drama School in Richmond, he fashioned a play around Shakespeare's *Othello: All About Othello*. I wrote "fashioned", for indeed he would always both write and direct and, ever happy as he was to play on words, he came up with

"By Mark Millar" for the poster (Markham Mila). He was brilliant at creating theatre, and students much appreciated working with him. As one might imagine, Mila and I both enjoyed the performance.

My own diary contains a few notes that seem to indicate that Pierre travelled to Zagreb at the end of March. He was certainly at a symposium in Cergy-Pontoise, organised by his friend Fred Forest in April. After that he was in Rome for ten days.

In May we had the pleasure of a visit from two of the 'Plovdiv group', who dined with us: Christo Stefanov and Ionny Leviev. This was a wonderful reunion, about ten years since we first visited their studios in Plovdiv! This was added to, a few days later, when Ionny's brother Milcho the jazz pianist, who was over from Los Angeles, gave us the excuse for a marvellous "Bulgarian evening", and private concert, at home!

These fun activities were balanced by the seriousness of a reception and viewing at the Royal Academy for the *1300 years Bulgaria* exhibition. Diplomats, ministers, historians… all were present and, in retrospect, one can say that this was to be one of the very last major events that Ludmila Zhivkova was to live to see.

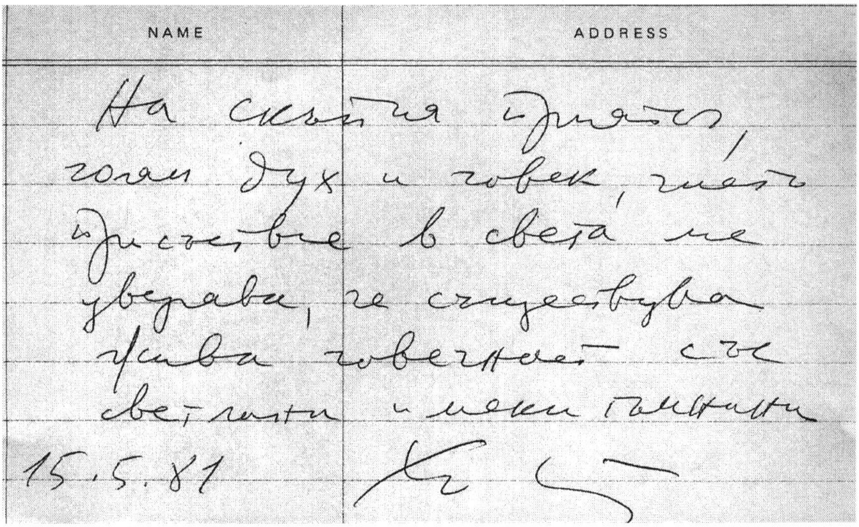

[Handwritten note in Cyrillic, dated 15.5.81]

Honouring Roman Jakobson

June brought the inestimable pleasure of hosting the great linguist Roman Osipovich Jakobson and his wife Krystyna Pomorska, friends of Dora who had been invited several times to work with Jakobson in the United States on her theory of colours and language. Jakobson was to be honoured by Oxford University, at Encaenia in the Sheldonian Theatre. They arrived in London on 20th (the same day that Pierre went to hospital with tonsillitis and a very high temperature), but went straight on up to Oxford where the ceremony was to take place on the 24th at midday. We drove up to Oxford, reserving a hotel room at the charming Bear Hotel in Woodstock (where Pierre had stayed while filming *Diamonds for Breakfast* many years before). The academic gathering was immensely impressive with almost everyone in robes. Later in the day we had an invitation from the Vice-Chancellor and Lady Richards to a Garden Party in Merton College, again in "Academical full dress". We had invited the Jakobsons to stay with us from the 25th as they were the University's guests on the 24th. Throughout the days that followed we relaxed, talked, dined, exploring the beautiful countryside. Jakobson, such a great man, was intimidating but lovely and natural also. What a privilege to be able to talk, listen, hear his views... On the Sunday he and his wife were to fly back to the States and so, on Saturday afternoon, Pierre and I drove them to East Grinstead, where we had reserved a hotel that was conveniently close to Gatwick. I must say it was difficult to drive while also trying to eavesdrop on the fascinating conversations that the three passengers were having! After an early breakfast we took them to the airport. Once again, upon reflection, I can say that not only was this an incredible experience in itself, but that it was one of the last great events in which Roman Jakobson was involved: he died the following year.

Krystyna later wrote to us:

"After Oxford, and especially Blenheim, we both felt splendid... Both of us remember and talk much about our

England sojourn. It was my very best English trip. I feel now that I know England. Needless to say, it was entirely your doing: your sweet hospitality, knowledge and organisational talent of both of you!"

Earlier in the year I had had a call from the British Council to see if I would direct a 'Summer School' course in northern Poland for the month of July but, having done the course in Sofia the previous year, I decided to have a year off. This year July was to be a bit different: we had, all three, been invited to visit and stay with Bea's family in Austria. Very conveniently, my friend and colleague Dominique Gantelme, the French lawyer, was very happy to stay in our house for the month. We had the security of knowing that the house was being looked after and she was able to explore London at leisure. However, before leaving, we had to take Patapouf to the farm where he was to spend the summer. In retrospect, I think he probably preferred the long country runs to being in London with its hard pavements!

Travelling with a puppy

There was, however, one more thing to do before setting out: Bea had expressed an interest in having a puppy and had asked us if we could get them one from the Dogs' Home and take it out to them. Imagine! Driving through Europe: Belgium, Germany, along the Rhine, into Austria, staying in lovely hotels, always having to take the puppy out for a walk, making sure it did not create chaos in the hotels! We made sure to visit some of the lovely places we had been to when we drove to Salzburg in 1965: Aachen, Bacharach, Lindau on Lake Constance, arriving in Feldkirch where Mila was enchanted to see Bea and the family again. Having handed the puppy over, Pierre and I stayed a few days in a hotel, joining in excursions in the surrounding countryside. He decided to go and visit his dear friends Christo and Inge Ognyanov in Salzburg; poetry, art and history this time and not music. On the 20th of July we heard the awful news that Ludmila Zhivkova had died: an accident, an illness...No details were available (conspiracy theory would claim that details are still, to this day, unclear...).

Driving back to England after this delightful holiday, we stopped in Switzerland and made a point of staying in Fribourg where, some eighty or so years previously, Pierre's father had studied! This was a kind of pilgrimage for Pierre who could relive in his imagination the things and places his father had told him about. We stayed two nights at the *Hotel de la Rose*, 28th and 29th of July. The dates are significant in another way: sitting in the hotel room watching television, we saw the whole of the wedding ceremony for Prince Charles and Princess Diana *en direct* from St. Paul's Cathedral in London! (I was personally to learn news of her death by, again, watching the early morning television news in my hotel bedroom while attending a conference in August 1997 in Macerata in Italy.)

We were hardly back in London when, on the 1st of August, we set off for the month-long summer holiday in Normandy. This was the usual relaxing, family-type holiday: seeing Dora and Luben, trips to the beach, seeing friends, Pierre ensconced in his "working – and smoking – room" (the one with the view over the valley) preparing his series of lectures for the month he was to spend in Mexico at the end of the year.

September brought us back to London and back to school and, towards the end of the month brought Alexander Fol and colleagues for the closing of the *1300 years* exhibition and a reception organised at the Great Britain-East Europe centre. October brought very different news from Bulgaria: we heard that Zhivko Popov, still Ambassador in Prague, had been arrested "for gross financial irregularities", later to be condemned to 20 years' imprisonment. Another situation which was not entirely clear.

Things were becoming more urgent as regards Pierre's trip to Mexico. He had already written in September, saying:

"You make no reference to the language in which I may be expected to speak...I had previously been given to understand...that it would be preferable...in Spanish".

Pierre then goes on to ask about the possibility of his texts being translated, but received no satisfactory answer. I continued, meanwhile, applying the red ink to his manuscripts.

Flying westwards

Early in November he collected his ticket, flying to Mexico via Miami and, on the 12th, taking all our best wishes with him, he flew off from Heathrow with Pan Am. We were only later to have news of the flight, the stopover, the arrival, such things as e-mail and mobile phones having not then been invented...Some days later we received a card bearing the message:

"Here I am in Miami...The Air Mexico plane is one hour late. Some Fidel Castrian porters grabbed my luggage and the impassive *'caballero'* at the AM desk said "OK". If I ever get it back it will be a *'milagro'*!"

Meanwhile, however, a telegram arrived – from Mexico – bearing the mysterious and slightly worrying message:
"*Vsitchko* OK *Nishto* OK Love Pierre"

To this I replied, by letter:

"A beautifully binary statement, but the formal balance leaves a substantive emptiness to be filled in: what is the *'vsitchko'* that is OK, and what is the *'nishto'* that is (seemingly equally) OK?"

Detailed descriptions were to follow, in the marvellous letters for which Pierre was always so justifiably admired. I shall quote at some length as his letters give a real flavour of his experiences.

> "Mexicans...not that I have seen much of them. On Thursday midnight I flew in by the champagne flight of Air Mexico and was met by the largest American car I have ever been in, belonging, not to Elisa but to her Institute. The car took me to an Anouilh-type *pension de famille* infested by old ladies and poor American tourists. It is, funnily enough, opposite a macabre British Embassy and over an hour's bus ride to the University. But Elisa will take it as a deep personal insult if give the slightest sign that I don't like it. So here I stay and eat, *table commune* with the other inmates".

He goes on to write about his first session, Monday the 16th, when the Director was due to introduce him but, having waited an hour, Elisa

> "introduced me, in the lamest possible way, to the ten or so students, and I started on the wrongest possible foot".

A week later, "having signed all over every possible document", he had still "not received a single peso".

Things, we hoped, could only get better... And they did!

> "I manage to talk for more than an hour to my seven students who are admirable, not at all like our Elisa. They have read Wittgenstein, Husserl, Gombrich, Panofsky, Jakobson, even John Berger. It is rewarding to see that they all find me not only comprehensible, but "erudite" and even witty – *en castellano*!
> The *Casa Gonzalez* – once one has come to terms with the resident drug-addicts, American expatriates, dying old

ladies on social security and passing luminaries from Texas and Arizona – has proved pleasantly conducive to work. Up at 7h, one hour to the university, back at 2p.m. and work on the lectures until 1a.m.

The weather is beautifully sunny and I have never felt better. The altitude seems to be exactly what I need."

The ten lectures which he had prepared and whose titles he had submitted together with his choice of slides, became, at the insistence of the students, sixteen. The whole series represents a remarkable exploration of *The Rhetoric of Sight Facts, Semiological Analyses of Looking and of Seeing*, presented in his inimitable style, and add to the body of his work which, if not retained in published form, is in the archive, where I am privileged to keep it.

At the end of the month's course, Pierre expressed himself extremely impressed by the *"alto nivel académico"* of this group of postgraduate students. They too expressed "delight at having been introduced to so many fascinating, novel and challenging ideas".

Back in London, we waited for each letter with the descriptions of his life and activities, the Graham Greene-like *pension*, his attempts to have the ticket reimbursed... And, at the same time, I had the pleasure of spending a weekend with Stoika Milanova, in London for a concert at the Queen Elizabeth Hall and to have her violin checked over. We went together to visit the Portobello Road antiques market, and sent a postcard to Pierre at 'Casa Gonzalez'. Mila was allowed to "play" Stoika's daughter's violin; the most one could say is that she did get some sound out of it!

One Sunday we had a surprise visit from Gill, one of Mila's earlier nannies. She came for lunch and we were able to catch up on her visits to America. In the afternoon we went to the traditional 'Bach Choir' Christmas family concert at the Royal Albert Hall, where children were encouraged to go up on stage and join in. My student Andy Godfrey was a member of the choir and so Mila immediately had someone to go up and sit next to. It was good to meet Andy's father after the concert.

Pierre's course ended on the 16th of December but, despite trying to change his ticket, he stayed on in Mexico until the 23rd. At least he finally had the chance to explore and to see some of the fabulous museums. The Pan Am flight came in on time – 7h50 – at Terminus 3 and it was an early Christmas as regards presents! What talk, what stories, what catching up! It was, of course, also the subject of conversation on Christmas Day, spent at Pashanko and Margaret's house. Where else?

What an incredibly full, busy and fascinating year!

* * * *

1982

House "For Sale"

And, indeed, in my 1982 diary (or 'Memorandum', one of the many presents brought back from Mexico), there are no entries at all for January. I can only assume that Pierre was enjoying a well-earned rest although, of course, he would have had the usual teaching commitments.

Working as I am from my diaries, it is clear that my own commitments and activities are noted in some detail, and such is the case for two weeks in late February, when I was invited as a "specialist adviser" to join the *'Problemna Grupa za Obrazovanie'* (Education Research), working in Sofia. As on previous occasions, I shall use notes of my activities to illustrate some of the interesting events which involved Pierre's own friends and colleagues.

22nd February and an early flight from Heathrow. In the light of the recent chaotic situation at the new Terminus 5, my notes sound an eerie echo: "It's the baggage handlers – or lack of same – that take time. No baggage check-in, no food, only plastic containers to take onboard. BA gets more like Balkanair (with its kettles!) all the time". Apologies to Bulgarian Airlines!

As I was part of a *'delegazia'*, I was accommodated at the Balkan Hotel (now the Sheraton and I doubt if an educational research group – for that is what it was – would be able to run to its current prices!). My guide, Yavor, accompanied me to the group's offices where I met Boyan Penkov who, I noted, "speaks English as well as he writes it". This was to be my first meeting with the person who was to become and to remain one of Pierre's and my closest friends, and since Pierre's death he has been a great support, not only to me in what I have attempted to do personally, but also to the '*Ouvaliev Family Foundation*', which was set up in 1999. I met him through our work on education and he represents for me the very best of old-fashioned values. All I wrote then was "Penkov is a 'good chap'"; but how right I was! A programme of visits was organised so that I could observe the new curriculum materials in operation and we then went for lunch.

In the evening Vanyo and Jeannie Rumenov, together with Karl and Lina Ognyanov, went to a superb concert at the Bulgaria Hall, where the Bulgarian Radio Symphony Orchestra was playing Rachmaninov's second concerto for piano and orchestra. The soloist was Ivan Drenikov, and this was yet another 'first experience' of a person whose talent I was later to become more familiar with. On another note, I particularly recall being amazed by the organ flaps in the second half with the third symphony of Saint-Saëns. An extraordinary concert hall: retaining its original 1930's woodwork. And to think that there has recently been talk of demolishing it or, just as bad in a way, building a 'trade centre' around it! Philistinism partners Mammon...

Weighed down by at least 20 kilos of documents and '*Bukvar*', I drank strong coffee in the hotel room before going to the Bulgarian Academy of Sciences HQ (Pierre's ex-domain) with my offerings of documents from the UK Schools' Council. There I was to meet the project director, Blagovest Sendov, of whom I noted: "Sendov is young, organised, efficient, English-speaking, amusing".

Yavor later took me on a 'guided tour', during which we visited the Mausoleum, Moscow-style. I got the distinct impression that he was encouraging me to utter indiscretions but, having learned a hard lesson from Pierre...I was at my most diplomatic. It was, however, interesting to hear his views of cultural policy and I also nearly thought that I was going to hear the details of 'the' scandal ("Two weeks ago…in the Committee for Culture…"). What 'scandal', what 'situation', what truths? How truly a 'situation' of distorting mirrors!

My interest in language teaching took me to visit Malvina Nalchadjian and her class of diplomats on Moskovska, working from the audio-visual course *The Blacks*, and, in the evening, to a lovely relaxed evening at Richard Stagg's apartment, followed by a dinner in the *Panorama* restaurant at Grand Hotel Sofia where, the previous time, I had dined with those around whom a 'scandal' was now being woven, and whom I was not to see again. "How are the mighty fallen…"

School visits

The following day it was a visit to the English Language School for an observation. It was at that point that I first met the, then, Inspector for English, Todor Shopov. What marvellous contacts and what especially excellent friends I have had the good fortune to make through my academic connections, but most of all through the network of wonderful people who were either childhood friends of Pierre's or whom I have met over the years on account of their admiration for him. With Todor Shopov I have shared almost every possible language teaching experience over the years: research, conferences, materials, students. The list is endless and the encounters have been international.

Yavor was delegated to take me to the National Palace of Culture (NDK). The park, the sculpture, the building, all was completely overwhelming. I could never have imagined it could have sprung from the rubble of 1980! But what are two years when commemorating '1300 years'? In the evening I went, as Maria Stefanova's guest, to a performance at the National Theatre where, with many friends, we ate and talked in what was then 'the Club' on the top floor, now a beautiful restaurant but way beyond the means of the average actor.

On what was Karl's 66th birthday, February 28th, "the usual five" set off for Borovetz. All covered in snow, it was a complete change from the July excursion during the British Council course of 1980. We crunched in the snow across the meadows to the Musicians' House, where we drank champagne for Karl and with such love for these dear, dear friends. Vanyo perforce left quite early as he had to take the train back to his hospital in Yambol.

After the weekend I was to make a presentation at the University of various Council of Europe documents. Later, having checked about flowers – even number for the dead – I bought 6 white lilies and went on a strange pilgrimage on a tram into the unknown parts of Sofia, to the huge central cemetery. I asked for directions and was surprised, not being too familiar with rituals, to find that Ludmila's grave still had the red pyramid. I placed the lilies and sat in the warm spring sunshine, remembering times and places. Back in the centre I noticed many official cars outside Hotel Bulgaria and (oh so odd, for it was eleven years since her husband had been Ambassador in London), I saw Nina Velcheva, who gave me her *martenitsa*!

My own evening invitation was to dinner with Blagovest Sendov in another less known district: the diplomatic quarter. It was a pleasure to meet again his lady companion whom I had seen at the Committee for Culture when delivering the copy of Pierre's book on *Turner* for Ludmila in 1980. They were extremely hospitable and we spent a most agreeable evening, the talk roving over many subjects.

My visit to different schools was to take in the observation of some lessons in Varna and, one morning early, together with the British Ambassador who was also to make some visits to schools, we flew into a warm and sunny Varna and were taken to the English Language School where we had a splendid "official" welcome, accompanied by the usual Schweppes and chocolates. My friend Pavla was astonished to see me. Lessons over, we went for a leisurely, sea-view lunch by the 'Sea

Garden'. The view of Varna and the harbour from my 9th floor room at the *Cherno More* hotel was fantastic. In the evening we went to a club – loud music and smoke – until late. Perhaps not such a good idea as Pavla had an early lesson the following day! All went well, I thanked the Headteacher and the Inspector and spent the rest of the day in the delightful old part of Varna.

Back in Sofia I paid a visit to school No. 119 accompanied by Georgi Angushev, the project's educational psychologist, and joined by Lili Litkova. In the afternoon we went to see the *Maistora* exhibition: Bulgarian women, centrally placed on the canvas and surrounded by bright flora, are not really my taste. Outside, I met Lubomir Tenev, what a pleasant surprise. He had, of course, many spontaneous messages for Pierre! Meeting later with Mila Setchenska, a scientist colleague of Julia Vassilieva, I heard what (little) she knew about Zhivko, and she showed me the previous day's newspaper giving the decision of the Plenum, and told me that the case against him was to open that very day. In the evening Julia left me a letter, incomprehensible as always but from the heart. What must they both have been going through? The following morning the phone rang in my room: no names but a hurried, hectic Julia, with greetings from "all the family". What, I wondered, would be the outcome, and how would I be able to make sense of and explain all the strangeness to Pierre on my return to London? He, of course, would be able to make his way through the Byzantine intrigues... At one level, it really did seem that Bulgaria was in a state of paranoia, intrigue and suspicion.

On my last full day I had an interesting meeting with the co-director of the project, Dr. Novachkova. We were not entirely on "the same wavelength" as regards all educational aims but the team did appear to want me to return for the next stage. I was then treated to a truly "personalised" guided tour of the mural art of the National Palace of Culture by the artist himself, Christo Stefanov. This was certainly some project and I still have occasion, when attending a presentation in the Zala, to recall the descriptions given to me that day. We went up to admire the view of Sofia from the 7th floor balcony since Christo, of course, "opens all doors"!

Three hours' flying time to re-adjust to London after such a full and interesting fortnight: work to think about, reports to start to compile, friends, visits, scandals... The true letdown came at Heathrow: the only time and place for a long while where there was nobody to take me in hand! Home to Markham Street with presents for Mila and a quiet evening with Pierre telling him all my tales, and hoping that he could make some sense of Bulgarian events.

But what had Pierre been doing while I was setting the world to rights? Quietly enjoying the peace and tranquillity of his workspace at 46 Markham Square, giving his lectures at the Institute and at Chelsea, lunching with friends and keeping a distant eye on Mila, her schoolwork and the *au pair*. In March we both did social things like attending exhibition openings, and going to Pashanko's for Sunday lunch. On the 22nd we had the pleasure of a visit from Boyan Penkov who was on his way to a conference in Lancaster. I was so happy that Pierre had time to get to know Boyan properly: "a most excellent and civilised Bulgarian". In the media context, he knew his brother Jonny better. As Evelyne, the Swiss au pair, was to go back home, Pierre assumed duties as dogwalker. Well, this was good exercise at least! Meantime, his work with students had led to another appointment of which he was particularly proud: Examiner in Drama for the different Colleges of the University of London. On three dates between the middle of March and the end of April he was examining Bachelor degree students, both for *vivas* and for production, at West London and Roehampton Colleges.

April in Paris...

In April, Mila and I accepted an invitation to go and stay in Claude's flat in Paris and to meet up again with friends we had made in 1979. It was the Easter holidays and so we drove over to France and spent several days in Paris, the children playing at the Champ de Mars, going up the Tour Eiffel and doing several other touristy things. We also visited Dora and Luben with whom we were later to stay in Criquebeuf as the Bigos did not let 'Les Mouettes' except in the summer. Pierre travelled over to join us, once he had negotiated the kennels for Patapouf during our absence from London, and we went to collect him at Dieppe. At this time he was doing a series of broadcasts for his friend Pierre Descargues on *France Culture* and this was an excellent opportunity to collect ideas and materials, rather as he did for the Bulgarian broadcasts.

Another Summer School

In May I had a first meeting with the person I had chosen to work with me on the third of the British Council summer courses that I was to be involved with. Carolyn Walker and I complemented each other in terms of our interests and experience and were able to compose a good programme for the forthcoming July. There were also several exhibitions to visit and, on 15th, an invitation to meet Pavel Matev at the Embassy. As the person responsible for overseeing the activities of "Bulgarians Abroad", he was able to talk to a good number of people.

For 2nd July, just before my departure, Pierre had one of the many invitations which involved exhibitions of the work of JMW Turner. This was at the art gallery in Burnley, a town where, in 1799, Turner had made a painting. Pierre, however, was still teaching and could not make the journey up north. Instead, we enjoyed a "farewell supper", over which I received my briefing as to what to ask about, try to find out about, whom to see...while in Sofia. He himself was due to go to Rijeka for the Biennale, and Mila would be in London with Evelyne until the end of term at the *lycée*.

The summer course

As this was the third course of its kind, and the second time I had been in Bulgaria that year, I shall limit myself as severely as possible in my narration.

All started well as Rosa, director at the time of Balkan Air's London office, seated us in first class but... the problems were not long in coming... Another "hotel saga". We were told that we would be living in the hotel in Gorna Banya. Now I know that this is the area where the diplomats play tennis and is now no doubt covered in kitsch "gated communities" of "villas", but, believe me, nobody would have wished to spend a month at the Gorna Banya hotel in the '80s. My well-known methods got us transferred to Hotel Bulgaria. By that year it had become my hotel of choice...

By then it had become possible to listen to Pierre's broadcasts on shortwave without too much interference and this was a pleasant link with home. Bringing papers and books from Pierre, I was to see Dimiter Avramov, the cultural historian. It is such a shame that, through ill health, I have not, since Pierre died, been able to enjoy a visit to this charming and intelligent man. I met up again with Georgi Angushev whom I described as "a dream of a modern Bulgarian, quietly spoken and cultured". ("Quietly spoken" is, I think, something that not only I appreciate among the many "loudly spoken"...) Todor Shopov and Lili Litkova were in evidence, professionally and socially speaking. I invited several of my colleagues out to talk to the teachers at the Institute, who thereby gained, I think, a very good idea of all that was going on in educational research. One day I met Ivo Hadjimishev for a coffee and "a good, long, real talk about things, him, the world..." Another time we were joined by his wife Boyana and Jenny and Nikolai Haitov for a lovely "talky" evening, followed by coffee (and spaniel) in the Hadjimishevs' apartment on Joliot Curie in the Iztok district. Andrei Danchev was also happy to meet another "genuine"

English teacher and we talked of linguistics, conferences and gossip...

When Mila finished school on 16th, she went with Evelyne to Switzerland, leaving Pierre in relative peace in London!

One weekend we had an excursion to Plovdiv which I found much changed, not entirely for the worse. Marvellous excavations: amphitheatre, arena; a pedestrian precinct, as in Varna, very well done. The central Post Office and the Party HQ building... better left unmentioned. Up into the Old Town and I was amazed that our American colleague Charles had not heard of Lamartine. We had a meal in the excellent *Puldin* restaurant. I later learned from Pierre by phone that Roman Jakobson had died on 18th. Blaga Dimitrova came to see me one day to collect a letter I had brought her from Pierre and I saw, in person, her pleasure and how touched she was on reading it. She was to remain a very good and true friend.

There were diplomatic drinks parties, film shows for ex-pats in the club, visitors to the Institute, all wanting to claim a part of the book collection. I renewed my recommendations with Richard Stagg who "is one of the best". People brought books, articles and papers for Pierre and I knew he must have spoken on the radio about David Peretz as I had a message saying how thrilled his daughter had been to listen. I had a very interesting talk one day with one of the participants, Nadejda Berova, about the school where she was then teaching: the National Experimental School of the Committee for Culture in Gorna Banya. I was, of course, interested in another "experimental" curriculum, but also to have news of Jhenia and young Toshko, pupils at the school set up by their mother, Ludmila Zhivkova. Nadya (as I think she is more commonly known) went on to become an excellent Director of Studies at the BBC Centre in Sofia.

I learned that Boyana and Ivo had a baby girl, Annie, for whom I later had the pleasure of finding a Victorian lace christening gown. Carolyn and I were invited to Andrei Danchev one evening. Even though I had visited him before, I made the classic error: following all instructions, seemingly to the letter, we arrived at Block 82, entry G, apartment 39, only to discover an unknown family...we were in *Mladost* instead of *Druzhba*! Find a phone, find a *jeton*, phone Andrei to explain, go back for the trolley, re-trace one's steps...A nightmare! The end-of-course dinner demanded many speeches, an art I had by then perfected...There was the closing concert, and films to be taken back to the Embassy...On our last morning, the phone rang very early. It was Julia, the day after her birthday. But she made no mention of anything; their situation was difficult. I had heard it said that she had divorced Zhivko, but we never knew for sure if this was so, or indeed if it would have been simply to "distance" herself from a "situation".

But, after transiting in Zurich, I was back in London with many more tales to tell. Not much travel respite for me, however: on August 1st, Pierre and I set off by car for Switzerland where we were to collect Mila before all heading for Vaucottes for the whole month. I think she was torn between wanting to stay in the lovely village of Evionnaz and going to Normandy with us. Pierre, meanwhile, found himself beguiled by the '*St. Augustiniens*' of St. Maurice and by the strange proliferation of Yugoslav newspapers. We negotiated for a possible Swiss *au pair* to replace Evelyne and were lucky to find Nicole who joined us in the autumn. We then left for the drive back via the delightful mediaeval town of Troyes, stayed the night and watched television in bed!

House 'For Sale'

Vaucottes – we again rented part of 'Les Mouettes' – was the usual social whirl: beach, drinks, visits, dinners, tea on the terrace...when, one day, Louis Bigo told us that the "white house" high, high, high up on the cliff-top, was for sale. Pierre and I walked up and "broke in" to the grounds to investigate. It was a perfectly splendid location, with a huge garden, a terrace and an extraordinary view, but it was in such a sad, dilapidated state that even the *A Vendre* sale board had fallen down! The following day we rang the notary; the house had not been sold. We went to see Dora and told her about it. All excited, she came over and, when she saw which house it was, she could not have been more enthusiastic. Another friend told us that there were other houses for sale in Vaucottes but, by now, we had become interested in the "white house" and went with Dora to see the notary and put a series of questions. We had to leave the matter for the time being as it was the end of the month and we had to return to London, seriously interested, however, in acquiring our own piece of France.

At the beginning of September, on the very first day of term, Nicole arrived from Switzerland to join our household. Pierre resumed his teaching and, of course, his Bulgarian broadcasts, and there were exhibitions, including a fun one, especially for children, of Tinguely at the Tate. On the 11th Jenny Haitova-Bozhilova arrived in London for two weeks. She was to stay at 46 Markham Square with as much reading matter as she could possibly want! This may well have encouraged her as she also combed the second-hand bookshops and the excellent one in the courtyard of St. Paul's Cathedral.

In October it was a pleasure to attend the song recital given by Anna Steiger, Claire Bloom and Rod Steiger's daughter and later, Lili Litkova was in London with colleagues for talks. They were to stay at the Penta hotel but, as their plane was late, there was no record of the group when I went to leave flowers. I was told that some "had cancelled". What to do? I left the flowers and went home.

In December, at MIT, a memorial service was held for Roman Jakobson. A good man, well remembered and honoured. On the 29th, Pierre and I celebrated 20 years of being married. Thus ended the "Mexican diary" year.

* * * * *

1983

A wedding in the family

In a year when, for whatever reason, I kept no diary and, hence, have no record of "day to day" activities, the irony is that so much should have gone on. But what, and how do I know? How can I recall?

Well, the "archive" documents (dated letters, publications, pay slips, photos, invitations, visits...) reveals a treasure of major events: Pierre travelling to Finland, Rijeka and the USA; negotiations to purchase the "white house" in Normandy and so much more. I feel myself like a veritable *'Otets Paiisi'* or *'Pimen the Chronicler'* as I attempt to unravel the marvellous multitude of *realia* that, between us, Pierre and I have amassed over our many years together and which now assist me in the telling of his rich and varied life.

In January Pierre was invited to attend the opening of the *Homage to Giacomo Balla* exhibition in Padua. He would have really enjoyed what must have been a remarkable display of the work of the famous Italian Futurist. It is worth noting that, when in Italy as a young man, he had a print dedicated to him by another famous Futurist, Marinetti.

In March he writes from Paris to his good friend the Yugoslav artist, Radovan Kraguly, following up on

> "scribbled notes on a Hotel Bonavia, Rijeka notepad ...dating from when you triumphed at the International Biennale: R.K. calligrapher of enigmas".

At this time, Kraguly was perhaps best known for his "series of packing cases which are also rabbit cages", several examples of which remain in our collection.

But why was he – were we – in Paris? Well, Dora and Luben's son Pierre-Christian (now usually known simply as Pierre) was to marry his *fiancée* from student days, Letizia. The wedding was a simply marvellous "family affair".

Pierre, Mila and I booked our flights, Luben booked us in to a hotel not far from their apartment in the Rue de Babylone and, on the 18th, at the Prefecture, they were joined in marriage, with Pierre signing as a witness.

A reception followed. We spent a splendid few days with the whole family, and Pierre and I had the opportunity of visiting the Beaubourg Centre and introduce Mila to the Paris art scene, not only the exhibition spaces but also to the teaching areas where young people were having great fun with paints!

Towards a Visual Grammar

A week at the end of May sees Pierre attending the 16th Congress and 35th General Assembly of the International Association of Art Critics (AICA) in Helsinki and Tampere. At the Congress he presented a paper *From Opteme to Sight-Sentence –Towards a Visual Grammar*, a truly groundbreaking approach and a work which was later selected by Svetlin Roussev to be one of the first of Pierre's works to be translated and published in Bulgaria. The paper

> "intends to outline the structure of a new visual grammar... It is, in fact, an act of reverence... above all a tribute to the memory of Roman Jakobson, one of the

founding fathers of modern linguistics…But what of the yet unborn visual grammar and visual semantics?"

Such an exploration was to be the basis of this seminal article, a true homage to Jakobson.

1983 marked the 12th Young Artists Biennale in Rijeka and, as usual, Pierre was invited to attend. The opening was on June 30th, running through to September, and the organisation was in the capable hands of Boris Vizintin, Director of the Moderna Gallery and Aleksander Bassin from Ljubljana. A pan-Yugoslav approach can be detected in the foreword to the catalogue, in that Novi Sad and Pula are involved and "so, too, sporadically, is Subotica". I mention this since it was there, in 1983, that Professor Katarina Ambrozić's book about the artist Ana Beslić was published and, in July, both Katya and Ana inscribed a copy of the work to Pierre.

Back from Yugoslavia, it was time to take our summer holiday in Normandy and to pursue the idea of buying the house on the cliff. All went well, we had several meetings with the notary, agreed a purchase price (taking account of the fact that the house had been fairly neglected for a considerable time) and Pierre went over to visit Madame Natin, a retired dentist, in Lillebonne. He declared himself convinced of her worth and seriousness in that her dental surgery was in the *Place du Général de Gaulle!* Dora was behind us in all these discussions and decisions as it would be so nice and convenient for us to have our "holiday home" so near to theirs. Ours by the seaside and theirs in a village. Perfect combination!

Back in London after the summer, we found a postcard from Lina and Karl – "our vacation comes to an end" – and thanking me for a present I had given her: "You will see me with it next time you come". This would have been either a length of material for a dress or a handbag, but in either case it would have been blue, her very favourite colour!

A shock, however, awaited us in the shape of another letter, this time from the notary in France, telling us that our vendor,

Madame Natin, had died. It was, of course, necessary for all the inheritance papers to be dealt with before the sale could proceed, on the assumption that the son and daughter would agree. The notary wrote that he "hoped to be able to confirm the sale, on the same terms, by the end of the year" and asked if we would agree to wait. Pierre wrote on 10th September to confirm that we were happy to do so but that, if more damage were to occur during the winter months, this should be reflected in the price. At a later stage we were to meet and discuss the sale with Madame Natin's son, who seemed surprised that we should wish to buy the house and asked us why we didn't buy something in Kent…! Yes, Kent is lovely, but that was hardly the point. The English like to have something a little bit different and, in this case, in France.

Back in England at the beginning of the academic year I can see, from an "Engagement Form for Teaching Staff", that Pierre started a weekly course in *History of Art and Complementary Studies* for BA degree students at Chelsea School of Art at the, for the time, reasonable rate of £13 per hour.

Chicago!

A most unusual and interesting engagement was about to take place: Pierre had, together with his longstanding and close friend and colleague, Professor of Art and Technologies at the University of Lausanne, René Berger, been invited to present a paper at the 12th International Conference on the Unity of Science. This was to take place at the end of November in Chicago, Illinois. Following on from his AICA paper on *Visual Grammar*, Pierre worked on a presentation: *Reel to Real – the Cinema as Technological Co-reality*, later published in the book *Art and Technology* , a book edited by René Berger. In the Introduction one can read:

"Some of the most fertile minds of our time discuss the

critical questions concerning the relationship between the arts...and modern science; Pierre Rouve on the cinema as a creative force in his paper 'Reel to Real'".

Pierre had requested that, at the Conference, a colleague of his, the artist Eddie Wolfram, be invited as 'respondent'. Eddie wrote:

"Once again, Pierre Rouve does not hesitate to swim against the current and convincingly bares the inconsistencies of fashionable film theories...His paper is yet another 'structural scrutiny' bearing all the particular distinctive marks of his personal investigative method... Already praised by the late Roman Jakobson for his fruitful recourse to 'sign theory, philosophy and cultural history', Rouve is 'full of creative stimuli'. Professor Gillo Dorfles...declares Rouve's views to be 'epoch making'".

This was certainly a most successful conference and exchange of views among the eminent lecturers as well as being, for Pierre, a new cultural horizon. Indeed, he had often been concerned with films and film making in the USA, but then it was more Hollywood than Academe.

Back in England it was time to make the necessary arrangements to transfer money for the purchase of the house in Vaucottes, scheduled to take place at the end of December, and so it was that, with a letter dated 20th December in hand, we made our way over to spend Christmas with Dora and Luben, something we anticipated doing in our own house the following year. In fact, with the holiday period upon us, it was clear that the documents were unlikely to be ready in time.

And so it was that, over a French turkey and an English Christmas pudding, we drank to our new property and to the health of the whole family. The end of an extraordinarily busy year for Pierre.

* * * * *

1984

It's *1984*

This year represents, for me, a change in writing style and in recollections, being one year for which I have found an "engagement diary" that Pierre kept and, albeit with brief entries, it gives me the possibility of reconstructing the year's activities, especially since my own is not complete for 1984.

In January he started his series of regular Tuesday evening lectures at the Institute of Education, and on Fridays he was teaching at Chelsea School of Art. He noted several gallery openings: at Canada House, the Savile Club and the Tate Gallery. I have, in the "archive", a ticket stub for a performance of *Peter Pan* at the Barbican Theatre for January 20th. This would have been a family treat, combining Pierre's fatherly kindness and his theatrical interests.

In a letter dated 25th January his old friend Gerald Dorset (Ilko Iliev) wrote, following their meeting in the States in November of the previous year:

"Our brief encounter, after two decades of *razluka*, was a rare event. I enjoyed very much seeing you and spending a whole day with you after your hectic November itinerary in our United States. Our talk of 'aesthetic grammar' and of Wittgenstein was fascinating."

February saw Pierre busy writing an article for Lea Vergine. I have no record of the exhibition in question but recall that he was always enormously supportive of her artistic ventures in Milan. On the 16th he noted a "meeting with Stephen Foster", the former student whom he had invited to join him in Rijeka for the judging of the Biennale in the summer. Stephen recalls this invitation and the whole event with the greatest pleasure and it is wonderful that he has gone on to direct, first, the Cheltenham City Art Gallery and, more recently, the John Hansard Gallery at the University of Southampton.

A house in the country

22nd to 24th February simply says: "France". What, who, why … might have remained unclear were it not for the fact that, in another file, I have the copy of the sale document for the house in Normandy. We travelled across, just for the couple of days necessary to meet up with the vendors, son and daughter of the late Madame Natin, in the office of Maître Darras in Goderville and for all four of us to sign and countersign the 'Acte de Vente' on the 23rd. Staying in a charming small hotel in Yport, we celebrated our new acquisition in appropriate style before braving the stormy weather for the crossing back to England.

In March, and until the end of the spring term, Pierre continued his lectures but, in addition, he was involved in putting together a production of Shaw's *Arms and the Man* with students at the Richmond Adult College concerning which, on April 3rd, Beattie de Leon (widow of the founder) wrote:

"Dear Pierre
  First of all I would like to say how very much I appreciate the help you have given to Jean and me over the years and to thank you for the wonderful training the students have had from you, particularly this term."

Two days later Jean (daughter of Beattie) wrote:

"Dear Pierre

I cannot express adequately in words my extreme gratitude to you, not only for your valiant work on the production *Arms and the Man*, but also for the kind and inspiring words you said on the retirement of my mother. Only those who have known her a long time know of the immense amount of work she has put into all the ventures she has undertaken."

Pierre had, indeed, been involved with this theatrical family and their students over many years and this production, in a way, also marked the conclusion of an era for him.

Adapting Orwell

As if teaching art history and appreciation, producing plays and reviewing exhibitions were not a sufficient exercise of his time, Pierre had undertaken an enormous project: the arrangement, in the form of a 'radio play' in 15 episodes, of George Orwell's *1984*. This project, for the BBC Bulgarian service, involved not only his translating the work but also dividing it up into episodes of even length for weekly transmissions, and finding a cast among the regular staff and other contributors. This, it is clear, was not only a time-consuming task but one that was both necessary and appropriate in that particular year and in circumstances that could be so easily seen, understood and appreciated by his listeners, still within a tightly controlled system. This was confirmed by the letter, written at some stage during the total production, by 'Sammy' Samuel, Bulgarian Programme Organiser, on 20th June:

"My dear Pierre

Just to let you know that I am still listening and timing the episodes of Orwell's *1984*, and the more I hear of them, the more I like them. In fact I will be sorry when this is all over. In my opinion this is one of the best programmes to be broadcast in Bulgarian by the BBC and I would like to thank you once more for the excellent production and translation of the text… The members of the section who took part in the recordings thoroughly enjoyed working with you."

We were now going, at every opportunity, to deal with repairing and painting "our" house: a week over Easter, weekends, staying in the small hotel and having friends and family over to help. Mila helped me strip the 1950s style wallpaper from the sitting room, Pierre started an onslaught on the huge garden. Only slowly did we realise which instruments and tools were needed for these tasks which we had never before undertaken! Pierre allocated himself the north-facing second floor room which was to become his writing (and, of course, smoking) room, Mila was happy with the south-facing room with its view down into the valley, and I had a room on the ground floor next to the sitting room with its spectacular

view over the English Channel. Here, at dinner in the evening, we could watch the sun set in true Turner fashion!

May and June were busy with lectures, the regular recordings at the BBC and also a festival of Bulgarian films at the National Film Theatre, including *White Magic* and *Asparukh*. There is a note of an 'AICA' meeting and on June 25th Pierre travelled with Stephen Foster to Rijeka where he was to judge the Biennale, giving Stephen the promised opportunity to engage in an international event. On July 2nd they travelled back by train, the 'Kvarner Express', from Rijeka to Zagreb, paying 438 dinars. (His ticket proves it! Didn't I say that Pierre never threw anything away!)

Enjoying the "White House"

July and August are blank in Pierre's diary but it is obvious that we would have spent those months, at least from the end of term, in Vaucottes, enjoying having our own place, seeing friends and relaxing on the terrace when not working hard on the various improvements! My incomplete notes tell me that on July 23rd the holidays began: "Mila to Gatwick to fly to Genoa" (she was to stay with a school friend); "Penkov, meanwhile, to Heathrow" (so, he must have been visiting us or over for a conference).

The next day, the 24th, it was my turn to pack and go, the car crammed with items for the house. Pierre was already there and, as the boat was late, I tried phoning but got no reply. When I arrived at about 02h30, he was still up – to show me how he and Dora had painted the whole of the interior white. It looked beautiful. We took flowers over to Dora the following day to thank her for all the hard work! The days passed, gardening, shopping... We bought a fridge, a washing machine and a second-hand black and white television set. The sunsets always different... a paradise.

On Sunday 29th Pierre got ready to leave early the following day to attend the funeral of his dear actor friend James Mason in Vevey. It was train to Paris and then on to Geneva and Vevey. Sadly, we heard of two deaths and funerals within the same two days: Luben's sister died and so he and Dora took the train to Paris for the funeral. His niece Julia (now Boulle) was in a very depressed state. On the 31st Pierre phoned from Lausanne (where he must have spent some time with René Berger), but told me not to announce his whereabouts as he "wanted to escape". I went to pick him up from the station on August 1st and allowed him to "hide" in the house.

Two days later Mila was to join us on her return from Italy, so Pierre and I set off, in the worst possible rainstorm, along the *autoroute* to Roissy. We had a hurried lunch as Pierre was nervous lest Mila arrive before us, but Alitalia and all flights were delayed and the cases were in the wrong place! Back through the rain, we all convened at Dora and Luben's house for everyone to exchange news: funerals and holidays. We decided we really had to take on a gardener, so that meant more machines to be bought. Even among all this social activity, Pierre and I occasionally managed to "escape" and go to market or lunch out.

The great event of the summer in the hamlet of Vaucottes was the 100th birthday party for "Tante Loulou"; this could, indeed, have taken place a 100 years previously and been the subject of a painting: the period costumes, games and songs, delicious spread on the lawn of the old house. A fantastic, memorable day!

We received the title deeds and notary act in August and completed the payment at what was then a rather favourable rate of exchange of the pound to the French *franc*. Karl and Lina wrote to us from Golden Sands where they were spending their usual break by the sea, thanking us for having sent a "wonderful new dictionary" (I wonder if this was a specialist medical one for Karl?) and for

> "the photo of Milche who is probably as tall as I was at her age. This is a sure sign that she will be a splendid person".

September saw us all back in London for work called, but of a quite different kind: for Pierre, as I can see, meetings with Sammy, following the broadcasts of *1984*; with Stephen Foster, after Rijeka; and exhibitions – of Vermeer at the Royal Academy and of Japanese Art at the Victoria and Albert Museum. October, too, offered Matisse, and later Stubbs, at the Tate Gallery, and New Contemporaries at the ICA.

At the end of October, after a totally exhausting half term – for everyone – we set off for a week in Vaucottes. We took both cars and all the furniture we could pile into them. We had deconstructed Mila's bunkbed and most of the pieces were in Pierre's car. In my car went a sofa unit we had bought specially for our new house, a beautiful shade of blue to reflect the sky and the sea, which we made the dominant colour in the sitting room. Our two cars, loaded as they were, were put on the boat together with the caravans! There were, of course, questions at the Customs as to the value of the different items. Arriving late at the house, we nevertheless unloaded immediately for fear of rain though in fact the weather proved to be gloriously sunny for the week. We saw our friends Guy and Françoise Watine, walked down to the beach, collected chestnuts, went shopping, gardened...

November and December offer few entries in Pierre's diary but this was a time when we went at every possible opportunity to stay at the house: the crossing from Portsmouth to Le Havre made it quite possible to go over for a "long weekend". We enjoyed the peace of the French countryside and indulged in delicious meals. We could not, of course, miss the Christmas festivities at the Dimitroffs but, on 27th, we set off to spend the New Year in Vaucottes. Many of our French friends who had "holiday homes" in the village were there, and Mila's great friend Tatiana must have intuited that we had arrived as she phoned almost the moment we stepped inside the door! The 29th was our wedding anniversary; this was a truly unforgettable one: there were cards and presents, Pierre and I went to Fécamp for lunch together, friends later came up to the house for champagne, Dora and Luben for a family dinner, Pierre driving them back to their house in Criquebeuf along very icy roads. The following day it was our turn to go to them and to see the New Year in, together with Pierre-Christian and Letizia. A lovely evening, eating and talking until 2a.m., then back along those icy roads with a Force 7 gale rising. At least we could stay in bed on January 1st and reflect on our "New Year resolutions"!

* * * * *

1985

'Happy Birthday!'

This is a year for which Pierre did keep an "engagement" diary, but only between January and June, and so I shall weave together our entries and my recollections.

The year started with that Force 7 gale. Something to be quite scared of when the house is so near to the sea and so, after the New Year's festivities with Dora and Luben, we stayed quietly in our house until we took the ferry back to England. Pierre was to start term again quite soon but, meanwhile, there were the secret arrangements to be made for his 70th birthday on January 12th. This involved inviting a whole group of his close friends and notifying them of the special occasion so that they might prepare some appropriate speech or presentation. Luckily all his friends were able to come and Mila and I prepared the buffet and ordered a celebration cake on which the baker wrote the greeting in Cyrillic!

Everything and everybody were ready and waiting at the house at 7h30 p.m. and, as it was a normal time to have supper, I asked Mila to go round to 46 Markham Square and "bring Daddy round for supper"! She brought him, the house was quiet and the dining room in darkness when, all of a sudden, the lights were switched on and there was a joyful singing of 'Happy Birthday' to Pierre. I think I can truly say that he was completely astonished and, of course, overwhelmed! The champagne was uncorked, people read their tributes (which we later pasted into a special album together with the photos taken of the event).

Here it is certainly worthwhile reproducing a few, first a simple but heartfelt illustrated letter from Mila, then eleven:

> My Daddy
> He shows a lot of kindness
> Like taking me to museums
>
> He is really lovable
> He gives a lot of warm hugs
>
> He is gorgeous, sweet...
> He is the best daddy I could have!!

And from Suzanne King, lifetime partner of Dr. Gainsborough, founder and editor of *Arts Review*:

> "I simply can't believe it but I am told that my darling friend Pierre is 70 today!
> Exactly 16 years ago, in January 1969, to mark the occasion of *Arts Review*'s 21st birthday, he wrote in that Journal: 'We should be feeling old, all of us who for 21 years have used this paper to air our views, flatter our vanities or foster our fortunes. But we do not. And we owe this delusion of youthfulness to an undeniable reality: the vitality of the *Arts Review*'.
> 16 years later I reflect on these remarks and I think that our 70 year old dear Pierre owes his youthfulness to his remarkable vitality, and dazzles us with his brilliant mind, producing those electrifying salvos the "Rouve Fireworks".
> I feel honoured to be his friend."

And, from 'Sammy' Samuel of the BBC:

> "My dear Friend
> Only the blessed reach three score and ten. You have made it Maestro! I hope you will have many more happy years. For what you have done for our broadcasts and for

the listeners we owe a great debt of gratitude, and on their behalf, and mine, I thank you!

I know it has not always been a bed of roses (we Bulgarians know that roses also have thorns) and therefore this makes your achievements even more remarkable".

Dora and Luben could not be with us but sent tributes. What a memorable evening that was and so well merited!

Salute to the Southern Slavs

March produced another very interesting suggestion for Pierre: knowing of his close and longstanding contacts with Yugoslavia, its artists, critics and writers, Zdenka Krizman, Yugoslav Programme organiser at the BBC, wrote proposing a meeting at which they might discuss Pierre's "writing reviews for our arts magazine". An exciting new direction and one which, in a somewhat different way, materialised later that month: on the 21st he was invited to Edinburgh to speak at the opening of a major exhibition of Yugoslav art, organised by the Scottish Arts Council at the City Art Centre. In a 12-page speech, of which I am fortunate to have a copy in front of me, he writes of:

> "...a ghost...conjuring the spectre of a raven haired young man who, fifty years ago...first set eyes on Yugoslav masterpieces...wandering, restless but inquisitive, from Belgrade to Ljubljana; from Zagreb to Split and Dubrovnik The ghost of this young man is here with us tonight...with his reverence for Yugoslav art and the cultural openness of Yugoslavia as a whole. The flame of this reverence has been kept burning by the rare luck of the old man that I am now to preside the International Jury of the Biennale of Drawings in Rijeka, small Adriatic city but great artistic harbour..."

Now, in the 21st century, I am left wondering whether this "artistic pluralism" is still extant.

At the end of the month Boyan Penkov came to London, and managed to spend time with us, even though he was attending a meeting of his mathematics research group and going on to the States. May brought us visits from another Bulgarian friend: George Ganchev and from our American friends Bill and Genee Fadiman with whom, on this occasion, we went to a Pinter play. In June Mila turned 12 and I had a stay in hospital, after which I took over the "garden room" in the house to entertain my visitors, while Pierre was the most perfect "nurse"! Christo Stefanov was in London and he and Pierre spent lots of time talking at Markham Square and visiting exhibitions. Just before going over to Vaucottes at the end of the month, Pierre was involved in, and present at, a major exhibition of paintings by Ian Stephenson whose work he so admired and which he had persuaded Michelangelo Antonioni to feature in the film *Blow Up*. In France he had the great pleasure of welcoming Christo and Inge Ognyanov for their first visit to the house. By this time, we were "open for guests"!

It was time to buy a new car as our two had suffered from all that furniture removing from one house, one country, to another! I drove over in the new Ford 'Escort' at the beginning of August and the month's holiday pursued its usual relaxed, pleasant course: visits to and from friends, relaxation on the beach, time spent with Dora and Luben, Pierre-Christian and Letizia coming up from Paris. One day we drove over to Gisors to visit Mila and Bubi Kraus, friends of the family from "the old days". However, if one activity can be said to have taken precedence, it was Pierre's new devotion to gardening! Hoeing, cutting, mowing, weeding, planting... And the garden was huge!

Christmas was the traditional gathering, but New Year festivities were becoming more France-oriented and again we braved the winter weather and went across to Vaucottes, only returning in the first week of the New Year.

1986

More birthday celebrations

My own diary entry for January 5th is very terse: "6h up, 7h leave, 8h Le Havre, 9h boat; 15h30 Harris (my naval cousin and his family) for tea and talk, 19h home and discovered break-in". This was not a pleasant way to return home after the holidays and it meant we had to spend the next few days changing the locks and checking what had been stolen. Very little, fortunately.

On the 23rd Pierre undertook one of his most enjoyable engagements: he flew to Munich to attend the special celebrations arranged for his great friend Stefan Popov's 80th birthday. Pierre had been given some idea that, as one of the guests of honour, he would be called upon to make a speech and had, therefore, spent much time and thought in preparation.

Upon his return there were dinners: with Nigel Foxell at the Savile Club (that beautiful building which was later to feature in the Bulgarian TV film of Pierre's life), with my cousin Michael Harris, Captain of the *Ark Royal* onto which we were invited the following year. In February, Mila and I spent the week of her half term in Vaucottes, leaving Pierre to his many engagements in London. She and I attended classes at the school in nearby Fécamp where one of our local friends teaches English and Mila subsequently made several new friends and I was able to organise exchange visits for my students.

March saw the arrival of several Bulgarian friends: Vanyo

Rumenov came for a week and we arranged for him to stay with the Dimitroffs; later in the month Ivo and Boyana Hadjimishev came to London and stayed at 46 Markham Square and visited Cambridge and Stratford-on-Avon with Pierre. It was lovely to have Ivo back in London with us, this time with his wife! At the end of the month we were off to spend Easter in Vaucottes. This was a special time for, at the beginning of April, I achieved my half-century and so it was breakfast in bed, presents, dinner out at a beautiful fish restaurant in Fécamp. A few days later, we drove over to Gisors to celebrate Bubi Kraus' 70th birthday. What a year for decades! Bulgaria seemed indeed to be taking over Normandy as well as Chelsea as Ivo, Boyana and their son Ognyan drove all the way to visit us. This was another "first": the first time a Bulgarian car registration had been seen in the area! The holiday finished in a not so pleasant way as the ferry company was on strike and we had to drive all the way to Cherbourg to get a crossing!

On May 4th Pashanko Dimitroff had the launch party for his book on King Boris III. Thoroughly researched, this has an assured place among historical studies of Bulgaria in the 20th century.

In the same month, dear Jonathan Griffin – friend, neighbour, writer, colleague – also reached "four score", and a magnificent party was held for him at the Poetry Society's headquarters in London. Readings, speeches, champagne... it was excellent.

In June Mila became a "teenager", holding her party at a local swimming pool, a splendid idea which allowed her and all her friends not only to swim but to talk and eat cake!

Pierre went, as he did most years, to the festival in Rijeka. This was becoming a most welcoming "other home" as far as his expertise and interest in art was concerned. Here he met good friends from across the whole of Yugoslavia and took pleasure in seeing the work of a wide range of artists. Once back in England, he and Mila went to Vaucottes while I attended a conference in Salamanca, after which I joined them in Normandy. Towards the end of August our local friend Françoise Watine had a party for her 40th birthday. We were very pleased to be among their large family and local friends, feeling that we had really become "part of the scenery"!

Coming back to "real life" in England after the holidays was always something of a shock to the system but, of course, we were all kept busy. Pierre had his lectures and broadcasts. And there were visitors, a special one being Zaven Tchilian, whose daughter Elma was later to make her way in England and, in December, the greatest of pleasures was to receive Karl and Lina Ognyanov; Karl "on duty" at a conference of obstetricians but, around work, there was theatre-going: *Starlight Express*, performed entirely on roller skates; a Sunday afternoon concert at the Royal Festival Hall. Having these dear, dear friends with us in London was a delight.

They too enjoyed themselves, for they wrote in our 'Visitors' Book':

"Thanks to you, dear Sonia and Petyo, our London visit was made possible and thanks to you it has been a

delightful non-stop holiday from beginning to end. Thank you and we just want to say we love you".

Where did we spend Christmas and the New Year? I confess I have no recollection!

* * * * *

1987

Pierre marks another celebration

This is a year for which Pierre did keep brief, "engagements" notes in a diary, and they reach the period when, from September through until the end of December, I would appear to have given up keeping notes! He jots down his commitments: Chelsea School of Art every Tuesday, the opening of an exhibition of 'British Art' at the Royal Academy. In the middle of the month a strange and sad event took place: Andrei Yanev, Rosa Georgieva's son, who was studying for a Ph.D. at Birkbeck College, had something of a nervous breakdown. As Rosa was by now back living in Bulgaria, having retired from her post as Director of Balkanair in 1985, she had asked us to "keep an eye" on him. We had known him since he was quite young and followed his education in London. This final stage may have proved particularly stressful and he was taken to hospital from the College. As soon as we were alerted, Pierre went immediately to see what was needed, but it was a long time before Andrei was well enough to return home.

At the end of January Pierre flew to Munich for, yes, another celebration! Christo Ognyanov was 75. I have in front of me the German translation, the *Festvortrag über Dichtung und Sprache von Christo Ognjanoff*, that Pierre pronounced in the Preysing Palais Club on February 3rd. As one may imagine, this celebration was attended by both Bulgarian and German friends and colleagues. I shall quote in full the letter which Christo's wife Inge wrote to me from their home in Salzburg, describing their pleasure:

"Dear Sonia

It's really a pity that you didn't come with Pierre for the celebration of Christo's 75, here and in Munich, with Pierre as main and marvellous speaker. Of course, first, there was a lot of "Bulgarian talk", which we "Middle-European women" do not appreciate too much; but I had work to do, translating Pierre's speech into German because there were a lot of people who do not know Bulgarian, including dear Professor Kronsteiner, who teaches Bulgarian linguistics here. I had the impression that he never saw such a paradise-bird, not only speaking, but with all his theatrical talents delivering a scientific speech in Bulgarian of such a high intellectual level that they never thought existed. Pierre was really at his best and he left, of course, a deep impression on everybody here and in Munich. There was one Bulgarian lady who had tears in her eyes, not because he was saying sad things but because she was so deeply impressed by Pierre's Bulgarian language. The Germans regretted that, because they were reading his speech at the same time in German, they could not see his gestures and his whole performance, singing, jumping, accelerating and slowing his voice; a one man show par excellence!

Now we look forward to his 75th, not so far away.

We remember you and Mila always, the lively girl whom Pierre describes in all her activities and interests.

Love

Inge"

What could have been more rewarding for both of these lifelong friends!

Artistic activities

Once back in London there was the opening of the exhibition of work by a good friend Sergio de Castro at the Institut

Français. Sergio, Argentinian by birth, lives in Paris, and Pierre and he had a long-term project for a richly illustrated volume of his work for which Pierre was to write the text. Somehow or other, this never came to fruition.

March was also an "artistic" month: Alexander and Valeria Fol and Ivan Marazov came to London for a Thracian Symposium at the British Museum.

> 163. *St* Valeria and Alexander Fol Ivan Marazov | Thanks to you, dear Sonja and Petjo! Благодаря за искреприетието засега!पетко UM

We all spent a lot of time together: Pierre with them at the Museum and inviting Alexander on several occasions for talks at his studio in Markham Square, the three dining with us at the house. Bulgarian culture was the order of the moment as there was also an exhibition of Byzantine Icons at the end of the month. In a somewhat more contemporary mode, there was the opening of *The Turner Collection* in the magnificent and specially conceived Clore Gallery at the Tate. Pierre was, of course, very much considered the expert on Turner.

In April Mila and I went for a week to Tenerife where, among other activities, we had hoped to catch up with Mitko Grantcharov, the friend of Pierre's whom he and I had spent time with on our first visit to the island. We managed to contact him but he seemed to be suffering depression. Rather like Ilko Iliev, Mitko had not found his exact path in life outside Bulgaria.

Salute the Royal Navy

An unusual invitation in early June was to have lunch aboard HMS *Ark Royal*, of which my cousin Captain Michael Harris was then in command. This was at the mooring on the Thames and was a very grand affair. We were given a tour of the ship, hosted by the crew and entertained to lunch by the Captain!

The summer was spent relaxing and enjoying the house in Normandy together, this year, with a Spanish friend of Mila's who subsequently returned the hospitality, inviting her to stay for several weeks in Alicante. Pierre-Christian, Letizia and their growing family came to stay in Criquebeuf and... all was well with the world!

Back in London, Pierre caught up with an ex-student of his, Nick Danziger, now a famous war photographer, then – and still – a very interesting artist.

HMS *Ark Royal* was to come on the scene again in November as the ship was taking part in a NATO exercise, *Purple Warrior*, and was to be making an official visit to the French port of Cherbourg. On the 20th, Pierre, Mila and I crossed the Channel and drove up to Cherbourg where we were entertained by Michael and his crew.

His wife Tina was with him and, after the official business was completed, we all drove, quite late in the day, to spend the night in our house in Vaucottes. Unfortunately, as it was winter, Michael never got to see the beautiful view or surroundings as he had to go off very early the next morning to rejoin his ship! We four then made our way to Le Havre for the usual crossing. By chance, the captain on that particular crossing had also taken part in the NATO exercise and was very interested to hear of our visit to *Ark Royal*. We were allowed to spend some time up on the bridge, "steering" the cross channel ferry! Once back in England, we drove Tina home and carried on up to London. We all agreed that my own father would have thoroughly approved of our encounter with the Royal Navy and of our purchase of a house from which we could keep an eye on the shipping in the Channel!

The end of the month brought Bulgarian films to the National Film Theatre, together with Rangel Vulchanov, to whom Pierre dedicated quite a lot of time. It must be emphasised that, with his 'Bulgarian base' at 46 Markham Square, Pierre was the magnet for all visiting Bulgarian academics, artists and friends. There was always an ample supply of whisky, cigarettes and, much more importantly, fascinating talk on all sorts of subjects, usually until quite late!

A silver celebration

As the Christmas period came around, Pierre and Mila went to *The Wizard of Oz* at the Barbican Theatre. This, together with the film starring Judy Garland, has remained one of Mila's all-time favourites. This year we were to celebrate our 'Silver Wedding' anniversary and had booked to spend it and the New Year in a hotel in Tenerife. After Christmas with the Dimitroffs, we flew out on the 27th. Presents had been chosen, wrapped and taken with us for exchanging on December 29th. They were all silver in some way: a silver photo frame, a silver pen... What a lovely way to be celebrating 25 years of life together!

* * * *

1988

Change and Continuity

This is another of those years where the memory and documents have to take the place of diaries, for it seems that neither Pierre nor I kept notes of our activities.

It is, however, very possible to trace the usual rich seam of events which kept Pierre busy throughout the year. This I have done using letters, programmes, speeches and articles, and the photos and other family mementoes which I have always saved.

The year, as we know, started most agreeably in the warmth of the Canary Islands, in a hotel in Puerto de la Cruz. On our return to the chillier climes of London, I shall have to speculate that Pierre undertook his usual teaching commitments, and that all our holidays – half term, Easter, Whitsun … – were spent at our *Villa Horizon*, as the white house on the cliff with its uninterrupted view was now to be known.

At the end of January Pierre was invited to give a lecture at the symposium held at King's College on the subject of *Foucault and Education*. His ideas provoked great interest and he continued a correspondence with Professor Stephen Ball and with one of the participants.

In early March we had the pleasure of receiving the usual '*martenitsa*' from dear Lina, although this year the accompanying message was rather sad:

"Sending *martenitsi* was a pleasure for Karl and me, so I'm going on with this Bulgarian and family tradition...I am trying to adjust myself to life alone."

For Karl had died at the very end of the previous year but, as we were in Tenerife, we only learned of his death on our return. This was to be the first of the sad losses which Pierre was to experience in the coming years: so many of his friends from childhood were to predecease him. Lina did, indeed, "adjust...to life alone" in the years that followed, often telling me: "I'm waiting for Karl to call me, but it's not yet time". The time for reunion with her beloved husband of so many years, came in 2005.

March also brought Pierre information about a Scientific Colloquium dedicated to the work of Milan Konyovitch and an invitation to contribute to it. This was in honour of his 90th birthday ("and still going strong", as Pierre wrote on a postcard to Mila) and was to take place mid-June in Novi Sad. As Professor Ambrozić wrote in her letter:

"Knowing the interest you have in the work of Milan Konyovitch, we should be very grateful if you would contribute to the success of this gathering".

Pierre accepted immediately and set to work on his presentation.

11th to 15th April saw the 3rd Anglo-Bulgarian Symposium in the Humanities, held at the School of Slavonic and East European Studies. The Organising Committee of Michael Holman as Chair and Tomas Henninger, Secretary, put together a rich and varied programme on the theme of *Change and Continuity in the United Kingdom and Bulgaria since 1944*. With topics as wide-ranging as History, Tradition, Language, Literature and Geography, the speakers included Richard Crampton, Jana Molhova, Alexander Shurbanov and Pierre Rouve. His topic was *The Hidden Avant Garde: Bulgarian and British Poetry since 1944*.

In January Pierre had written to Michael (now Professor) Holman outlining his proposed topic:

"*The Hidden Avant Garde*. The paper will argue that the conventional assertion that Bulgaria (and for that matter Britain) have no authentic homegrown *avant garde* poetry is the result of an inappropriate methodological approach. Misguidedly, Bulgarian poetry has been expected to fall under certain established typological denominators... stemming from the subversion of language... but there has never been such a rejection of language in Bulgarian poetry ...embedded in the '*langue de la tribu*', Bulgarian *avant garde* is linguistically concealed while being poetically effective."

In a private letter to Michael Holman, Pierre gives the reasons for his choice of subject and the reasons for his rejection of a different subject:

"It would have been tempting to devote a paper to the sad lack of any up to date analytical instrumentarium in present day Bulgarian literary studies, still constricted by the straitjacket of obsolete Determinist studies... and enforced ignorance of even more advanced Marxist (Frankfurt School) views... But, however valid such a theme may be, it will inevitably hurt the ideological sensitivities or even the national pride of your Bulgarian guests...".

One must recall that Pierre is writing in 1988 (before change comes tightening up...). One can also see the enormous range of his own literary and critical knowledge and awareness and, last but by no means least, his thoughtfulness and sensitivity to the feelings and beliefs of other speakers.

In his paper, Pierre notes that:

"Mallarmé is a stranger in the Bulgarian literary paradise. Both P.U. Todorov and Yavorov spent time in France yet ignore Mallarmé. Geo Milev misjudges him... He is not mentioned in Miroslav Yanakiev's fundamental study of Bulgarian versification... But it would be wrong to assume that Futurism, Mallarmé, Dada... did not permeate the homegrown literary flora, witness: Geo Milev in *Septemvri*, Bagryana in *Seismograph* and Yavorov's syncopations and brusque juxtapositions of inconsequential sentences."

Pierre's presentation was judged, as Michael Holman had predicted, "quite fascinating".

Monday 18th April brought us the enormous pleasure of a visit from Pierre's cousin Metodi Tzvetanov. Pierre went to Heathrow to collect him and settled him into 46 Markham Square (mostly, as we know, a "talking, smoking and drinking" environment but also a most acceptable one-bedroom apartment!). Metodi (or 'Uncle Matyo' for Mila) was a joy to have as a guest: we took him on the traditional "tour of London", to visit Christo's exhibition at the Annely Juda Gallery, to our local church and it was also his pleasure simply to stroll around Chelsea.

He had brought with him, as gifts, some of the beautiful silverware that his late wife Penka had created. These looked sensational on formal wear! Matyo was the kindest and most positive of people and it is a great pleasure for Mila and me now to be so closely associated with the other members of his family and in particular with his grandson, also Metodi Tzvetanov, a most talented young musician. Uncle Matyo, shortly before his recent death, wrote and published *Da letim, da letim (Let's fly)*, his memoirs of being the personal pilot to King Boris III.

Salute the Southern Slavs!

June came around quickly and Pierre was off to Novi Sad for the Konyovitch symposium. The copy of his speech which I

have in front of me is in French with, of course, several phrases in Serbo-Croat, making me think that, at that time in Serbia, French would have been more readily acceptable to the international gathering than English. Konyovitch being relatively unknown in the West, Pierre thus begins his speech:

> "Milan Konyovitch has never been to London. But I do not need to remind you that, if the mountain would not come to Mohamed, it was Mohamed who had to go to the mountain. That is why London had to come to Konyovitch".

He goes on to say that the West's tendency to view Konyovitch as "a *Fauve* with Expressionist tendencies" denies his Yugoslav culture.

The very next day he travelled to Belgrade for the *Triennale of Yugoslav Art* where he was to spend time with his good friend, artist and Mayor of Belgrade at the time, Bogdan Bogdanovitch.

On his return to London he wrote to the President of the Academy of Arts and Sciences saying how proud and touched he was to have been invited to "that Athens of the Southern Slavs, Novi Sad".

It is worth noting, among the many expressions of gratitude and appreciation that Pierre received, a few lines from a letter from Professor Dusan Rnjak:

"Those several days which we passed together in Novi Sad, made it possible for me, thanks to your friendship and loyalty, to observe the world of art more widely and deeply".

This year saw Pierre extremely actively engaged and travelling. In July he was off again, this time to Tuzla where, an honoured position befitting his international and Yugoslav experience, he was International President of the Jury for the 5th International Biennial Festival of Portraiture. Also on the judging panel was Aleksander Bassin of Ljubljana, a friend and colleague of many years' standing.

At the very end of July, and at the end of term, Mila flew to Alicante with her friend Marina to spend three weeks in the family's seaside home at La Manga del Mar Menor. Mid-August brought the Rouves together again in Normandy and offered Pierre a little relaxation from his extraordinary range of activities. It was always pleasant to be in France, to see the family and all our local friends, and this year we made the most of it! It was also the year when, having noticed that one of the small cottages on the cliff path was for sale, the Rouve property gene went into action! More, really, Pierre's artistic and architectural tendencies, since he had clear ideas as to how the small structure should be enlarged and made more appealing. He had an architect come to visit, they discussed possibilities and the plans were put into action for what, eventually, was to become known as the "*Hija*", as in the Bulgarian for "hut", but also the Spanish for "daughter". It was to be Mila's own outpost!

As if he didn't have enough things to keep him busy, Pierre wrote during August to his friend and colleague at *France Culture*, Pierre Descargues. In his letter he describes what he has been doing "since we were last in touch":

> "I've travelled a lot, first Italy, then San Marino... visiting exhibitions. From there to Yugoslavia where, in Novi Sad, I took part in a colloquium dedicated to Milan Konyovitch, who enjoyed his hour of success in Paris in the Twenties... On to Belgrade, then Tuzla. You'll guess what I am going to say: would such a tour of a Europe not yet so well known sit well with plans for France Culture? Perhaps we could meet in Paris in September?"

I have a whole collection of his manuscripts of broadcasts for France Culture but, as they are undated, I cannot be sure if this particular project was taken up.

He did, however, also write to Pierre Descargues' partner, the artist Catherine Val, and she replied in September saying how flattered she was by his letter "and that what I do can be linked to your teaching in art studies". She goes on to write about her desire to find an appropriate location for an exhibition:

> "The house is so full of books, of paintings, of signs left by those who came... that it is not exactly the right place."

She ends by thanking him again for his long letter and saying that it will make an excellent preface to the exhibition catalogue.

Back in London at the end of the month, Pierre and I spent time with Rosa Georgieva and her son Andrei. Although she was by that time a very busy businesswoman in Bulgaria, she had been able to make time to come over to England to check on Andrei's mental state. He was gradually recovering from the stress he had suffered earlier.

September, of course, saw us all, very soon, back to study or teaching; Pierre to the Institute of Education and Chelsea School of Art, I to King's and Mila to school. However, Pierre was soon off again, this time to Italy where he was to review an exhibition held in the *Rotonda* in Milan. This was curated by Lea Vergine and entitled *Dionysiac Geometry*. In his *Letter from Milan*, published in *Arts Review*, Pierre writes:

> "A London look at a Milan exhibition is quite in order, all the more so because it is not only a forerunner of continental concerns that may become current practice much sooner than some think. It is also an honest endeavour to bridge the dreaded generation gap: undeterred by his ripe old age, this British critic strives to fathom the art of twenty four young Italians...Their credentials are established by the eagle eye of Lea Vergine, probably the most intriguing writer on art in Italy...In looking at this many-faced harmony of discords we grasp why Lea Vergine wants us to believe that there can be such a thing as a Dionysiac Geometry".

In mid-October, and also in December, we had the pleasure of visits from Vladimir Levchev, son of Lubomir Levchev and Dora Boneva, who was on his way to and from the United States. I can only imagine how much talking, and possibly drinking, must have taken place at 46 Markham Square!

¡ Que Viva España!

Christmas this year? Was it with the Dimitroffs? Of course! But with a difference! And what a difference!

Pashanko and Margaret had decided to sell their house in Willesden so that they might enjoy a somewhat better climate. Having done their research they bought a plot of building land just outside the lovely hillside town of Mijas on the southern coast of Spain. While the villa was being built to their specification, they had rented an apartment in Fuengirola. One could say that the social life of north London simply moved to southern Spain! We were invited to join them and their sons Andrew and Brian for the festive period, as were their very good friends Rita and 'Struki' Kalev.

I put my mind to renting a place for the three of us and found a delightful small house in the town of Mijas itself, and so we had the "best of both worlds": town and seaside, friends and family.

(The reason that I can write so confidently about these events is that, even without a diary to refer to, I have in front of me the receipt for the villa rental and even for the car hire plus several photos from the "family album". Yes, we never threw away a single sheet of paper!)

On December 23rd, laden with Christmas presents, we flew to Malaga where we picked up the hire car and made our way along the coast before turning inland for Mijas. The instructions we had been given were pretty good and we only had a few mishaps: hill roads, unexpected turnings... and found the house and let ourselves in, settling in for the three weeks we were to stay. The following day it was the great reunion and we also had a chance to go and see the progress with the building of the villa, where we all approved the idea of having a swimming pool!

Christmas day was the time for presents and, first of all, Mila and I gave Pierre something he was not only to treasure but also to find extremely useful: a Selena Vega radio on which he could tune in to the short wave frequencies and listen directly to Bulgarian radio broadcasts!

For the family it was a game of 'Monopoly', but the Spanish version. Later in the day we drove down to Fuengirola to enjoy

the "traditional" Christmas meal, accompanied by crackers and paper hats, in the Dimitroff flat. The days passed in beautiful weather with drives through the surrounding countryside.

It must be said that Pierre would not have been able to "sit and do nothing". He had already recorded his BBC broadcasts for the three weeks we were away but he had also brought with him everything he needed to work on the paper he was to present on the poet Elisaveta Bagryana at the February 1989 symposium at the School of Slavonic and East European Studies.

As we round off another year, we move into the one that will change so many things!

*　*　*　*　*

1989

All change!

The change was not, of course, immediate, nor did it come all at once. Indeed, one could rather say that, for us, 1989 began with a smooth continuation from 1988: after the New Year had been welcomed in with friends, we took a late lunch "Spanish time" at a countryside inn. Quite delightful, sitting out on the terrace in the sun with farm and domestic animals all around!

As Pierre and Mila had to return to London on the 9th, we had a special family birthday lunch a few days early for him at one of our favourite restaurants. The next day I took them to the airport in Málaga and then explored some more of the coastal area. A few more relaxing days with friends and then it was I who drove to the airport and handed over the hire car, returning to find a stack of paperwork awaiting me at King's! Pierre, meanwhile, had attended the opening of a major exhibition, *Italian Art in the 20th Century*, at the Royal Academy. Focussing on two of the major artistic movements, *Futurismo* and *Pittura Metafisica*, it lured several of his friends from the Italian art world to London. In a letter to one of the organisers, Senator Carlo Giulio Argan, describes Pierre thus:

> "…Professor Rouve, whom I consider to be the best English art critic…"

On Bagryana

A major reason for his needing to be back in London, however, was that he was committed to a major presentation at the Bulgarian Seminar series at SSEES. This series, spread over the academic year, consisted of one lecture by an eminent academic each month and, on February 6th, Pierre spoke on *Bagryana and the Prudes*. The following lines give a mere taste of his 14-page text:

> "Prudes and Prejudice appeared to have stifled forever senses and sensibility.
>
> But it was not to be. In the Twenties two tremors shook Bulgaria: an earthquake which measured 8 on the Richter Scale and a mindquake which shattered into smithereens the Prudes' scale.
>
> A true literary cataclysm was provoked by the appearance of the first volume of poems by a young, irresistibly attractive, schoolteacher... and the Prudes felt horror that a Scarlet Woman had burst in all her splendour amid their tame flock to sweep away their sterile taboos."

With his knowledge, references, juxtapositions, literary allusions, playing on words, he was a master of the vivid picture!

Later in February the three of us went over to Normandy to see what progress (not much!) had been made on the conversion of the small building on the cliff path. It was obvious that we would have to put up with a combination of builders and their delays, the weather and the fact that we were not always "on the spot"! On our return, London offered us a very interesting play: *Single Spies*, on the subject of the Cambridge spy ring and the part played by Sir Anthony Blunt, Surveyor of the Queen's Pictures.

As far as the weather was concerned, March was no better

for Channel crossing, but it was very pleasant to spend Easter with Dora and Luben. Mila was given the job, by 'Uncle Luben', of going to the Saturday market, choosing and then preparing the chicken for our 'Easter lunch'. Luben was the acknowledged "master chef" in the family, and these early lessons in food preparation and healthy eating have stood her in good stead!

Young people come to the fore in April as Mila was off with her school for an educational cruise in the Mediterranean and on the Nile and, meanwhile, Pierre had been asked by one of our good friends in Fécamp, Marie-Françoise Balesta, to guide pupils from her school round the Turner collection in the Tate Gallery. As Pierre loved being with young people, and was so good at enthusing them, this was guaranteed to be a great success. Talking, in French, about his favourite painter to a group of interested young people – ideal!

Lunches in London

It is worth noting that, as I look through the diaries and note the many events and activities in which Pierre was involved, there are nevertheless so many "friendly", "one off" meetings: coffee or lunch with London-based friends: Joe Grosz, the photographer; Branko Bokun, Serbian friend from Roman days; Valeri Tchukov, head of the Bulgarian Section; Jonathan Griffin, poet and playwright; Theo Lirkov, another BBC man (sad Theo who was "shortchanged" by the wife for whom he had advertised in the Bulgarian press). Pierre was also sought out, of course, by friends visiting from abroad: Genee and Bill Fadiman, from California; Sergio de Castro, Argentinian artist; Andrei Yanev, spending time in London. In May Nikolai Fadenhecht was over from Germany for ten days. At the end of July, Rangel Vulchanov was in London; he and Pierre spent a lot of time together, as well as attending the showing of four films at the Bulgarian festival, including *Ivan and Alexandra* and *Where do we go?*, Rangel's latest film.

A trip to Switzerland

I went off at the very beginning of August to France, leaving Pierre to complete some work before coming over with Mila on the 18th when I went to meet them off the night ferry for coffee and croissants in Le Havre. The very next day, however, we drove to Switzerland, where Pierre had some "Ponti business". I recall the drive being both hot and long. It did not help that we got lost in Paris, trying to find the exit from the "Périphérique" for Lyon. After that it was a boring but fast drive. Arriving in the charming historic town of Salins, we found a delightful hotel, had dinner and collapsed into bed! The next day we arrived in Switzerland. I dropped Pierre off for his meeting and some hours later we had the enormous pleasure of meeting up with dear Lina Ognyanova at her hotel in Geneva.

She had accepted an invitation from old friends to take a holiday in Switzerland, something that was greatly to cheer her after Karl's death. Having been with her in Sofia and in London, it was lovely to be with her in such a beautiful place by the lake. The talk and the laughter went on until late. The following day we went again to her hotel and Mila swam in the pool while we talked until, in mid-afternoon, we set off again for France, staying overnight in Charolles. This being the 200th anniversary of the French Revolution there were many celebrations throughout the country and, in Fécamp, our nearest town, there were to be re-enactments of the various events. Mila and her friends took part in the processions, dressed in period costume. Pierre, meanwhile, was firmly rooted in the 20th century as he had planned to use the time in France to prepare the presentation he was to make at the opening of a major exhibition of his friend the artist Denis Bowen's work later in the year. Indeed, the copy of his talk that I have in front of me bears the words: "Pierre Rouve, Vaucottes-sur-Mer, September 1989". Proof, if such were needed, that he was excused such tasks as shopping and gardening!

Back after the holidays I invited Julieta Savova, who had been studying for the International Education Diploma at the Institute of Education, to give two lectures at King's on the Bulgarian education system. I then went to Madrid for the administration of the new student placement ERASMUS scheme which I had set up at King's.

BBC Bulgarian reaches 50

To mark the half-century of the service, started in February 1940, BBC London organised a series of events starting in September and running through until April of 1990. A specially produced leaflet recalled many of the key broadcasts from earlier years and showed photos to illustrate the studios with their microphones and also outside broadcasts. Shown are the whole department in rehearsal for the broadcast of *The Life of James Bouchier by Petar Ouvaliev* in 1955 and *Grigor Grigorov at the Annual London City Parade in 1958*. The programme for the time also lists: *Sunday 19h after the News – Essay by Petar Ouvaliev.*

How much am I bid?

In late October, Pierre was able to attend a sale at the London

1955

Членове на българската редакция в репетиция за запис на "Животът на Джеймс Баучър" от Петър Увалиев.

1958

Г Григоров на годишния парад в Лондонското сити в подготовка за редовната си рубрика "Лондонски бележки".

auctioneers Sotheby's of *Post War and Contemporary Art* where, for the first time, a selection of works by Bulgarian artists was to be auctioned. This was an exciting new departure for, although Bulgarian artists such as Svetlin Roussev, David Peretz and Christo Yavashev had had individual exhibitions of their work in private galleries, this was an opportunity for the general art-buying public to acquaint themselves with paintings by Svetlin Roussev, Vassil Stoyev, and others.

At the end of the month we learned the sad news of the death, on October 20th in Munich, of Stefan Popov. Like Pierre in so many ways, Stefan Popov had made his personal, academic and intellectual life in another country, had maintained his contacts with Bulgaria, broadcasting on cultural subjects as well as writing on history and philosophy. Pierre wrote a very thoughtful obituary which was published in *Letopisi*.

> "Stefan Popov was unique amongst our thinkers in that he spoke about the world as a citizen of the world, but he spoke as a Bulgarian and to Bulgarians"

Change? What change?

On November 10th, as I was driving home from King's and listening to the car radio, the evening news announced the "deposition" of Todor Zhivkov. Although rumours had, of course, been flying around Eastern Europe over the course of the year, this announcement caused me to stop the car! The most important question, though, was would Pierre have heard the news? How could I get hold of him? Normally, it would have been a question of parking the car in Markham Square, going in and telling him to turn on the radio and the television. That very day, however, he had taken the train to go up to Huddersfield in Yorkshire to open that aforementioned exhibition of his artist friend and gallery owner, Denis Bowen. The news that was to change the face of a certain part of

Europe would have to wait... The cataclysmic date, "10th November", as much quoted now as "9th September" previously was, would have to take its place after Pierre returned from his, very successful, few days in the North.
About Denis Bowen, the first to champion Abstract Art at his New Vision Gallery in the 1950s, Pierre wrote:

> "For years, Denis Bowen has been the silent victim of a blatant miscarriage of aesthetic justice... an incapacity to assess the distilled depth of his pictorial vision and the wilful omission to stress the contribution of his New Vision Gallery to the reinvigoration of Post War British Art... This thoughtful show at Huddersfield both redeems and vindicates Denis Bowen".

November until mid-December saw me in Madrid for three weeks, teaching at the partner university in our ERASMUS programme, and it was in Madrid that, avid radio listener that I am, I heard the news of the downfall of the Ceaucescus.

A year of changes indeed!

* * * * *

The Nineties – Bulgaria rediviva

1990

A new decade, new departures

Very gradually the realisation dawns: there is a new spirit, there will be a new, a different Bulgaria. It is the year of the Union of Democratic Forces, of *Democrazia*, of student protests, of demonstrations, of President Zhelyu Zhelev and Vice President Blaga Dimitrova.

It is also to be, for the family, the year of "request for restitution". Restitution of family property and lands, expropriated by the former Communist regime. The story was told of how Dora made sure that her application for the restitution of her own apartment, the first floor of the house on Gotcho Gopin Street, now itself reincarnated Karnigradska, must have been entered in the legal annals as "No. 1", as she claimed to be definitely the very first to undertake the exercise. Many years of negotiations, changes of lawyers, outlay of money, issuing and signing of documents proved, however, to no avail since, somehow or other (do not expect the non-Byzantine brain of a British woman to understand how or why…), those to whom it had been allocated proved powerful enough not to have to part with the apartment. Why ever would they want to? 205 m2 right in the *"idealen centre"* of Sofia!

In January Pierre reached the three-quarter century mark but, as we had celebrated his 70th (more usual in England than 75) in 1985, this year was a quiet family affair. A dinner at home with a few old friends, good food, lots of wine and conversation! February and March saw us all travelling: Pierre to Hamburg for preliminary discussions regarding a production of *The Prisoners of Altona*; I to Madrid for planning our ERASMUS programme, where Mila joined me for a week, staying with the daughter of one of my colleagues. The experience of attending school in Spain was very useful for her. In late April she managed to persuade, or cajole, her father into taking her to a concert at the London Arena. This involved a somewhat long and complicated journey down to the London Docklands, all for the pleasure – for Mila – and a rather different emotion for Pierre… of a Kylie Minogue concert! Mila told me afterwards that she was not entirely surprised to see that Pierre had fallen asleep at a certain point and that, after the interval, or "smoking break", he had somehow got lost. We are both now fascinated to see how great a success Kylie Minogue has enjoyed in Sofia!

For some reason, never really explained, I was initially refused a visa for my official visit to Bulgaria for a symposium of the members of the "Problem Group on Education" with which I had been working as a foreign languages teaching methodology expert. The meeting itself had been scheduled to take place in the first week of June, but the imminent elections led to a change, and I flew to Sofia on the 21st prepared to meet the colleagues, present a paper and make several visits to schools where the new curriculum was in use. Naturally, I made sure to spend time with all our friends: the Rumenov family, Lina Ognyanova, "Uncle Matyo" and Sasha Beshkov, son of the artist Ilya Beshkov, many of whose graphic works we possess. However, these social and professional gatherings were to take their place amidst the excitement of political meetings, demonstrations and a state of fervour generated by the elections, with the promise offered by UDF party. How I recall a huge rally in front of the cathedral one late summer evening! Just one week later I was back in the calm of London, Pierre having picked me up at Heathrow. Over lunch at a restaurant, I went through the sheets of copious notes I had made to update him as best I could with the facts and my impressions of this exciting time in Bulgaria. July 6th saw Petar Mladenov resign and it was not, of course, until August 1st that Zhelyu Zhelev was to be installed as President of the Republic.

Given the alteration that there had been to my visit to Bulgaria, Pierre and I had been able to see Mila and her school friend Kate Roberts off to Australia where they had been selected to spend six weeks on an exchange that their school had with a school in Tamworth, New South Wales. Almost all English schools enjoy an exchange arrangement with another, usually in Western Europe, but this one was quite exceptional. We were to receive the girls with whom Mila had stayed when they came over during their "summer holiday" (our Christmas!). It certainly proved a fabulous opportunity to see the world, experience another culture and yet also be in school.

Meanwhile, from much nearer, Alexander Fol was over to visit, working with the research group at the University of Nottingham. He came to us one evening for dinner – at the last moment I learned that he was a vegetarian! – and we talked of old times and new, we had an extremely pleasant evening.

We had let the house in Vaucottes for the whole of August to a charming family who later not only became great friends but who also bought land and built themselves a large house in the same village. It seemed that we had made the right choice since others copied us! Pierre and I stayed in the recently refurbished "*cabanon*" on the cliff path, enjoying the same sensational view but fewer rooms and stairs. We had had a large terrace built and we could take our meals outside and could see all the activity on the beach below. Mila's many friends asked after her, surprised to learn that she had travelled so far! Pierre and I walked, went to markets, saw exhibitions at the Benedictine, visited friends, spent time with Dora and Luben and Mila and Bubi Krauss and, all in all, enjoyed a thoroughly relaxing summer holiday.

September 4th and it was time to be up at the crack of dawn to meet Mila at 6h30 at Heathrow on her return from Australia and, a week later, to see her off to school. Meanwhile, London Bulgarian cultural circles were in a state of preparedness for the visit of Blaga Dimitrova. She was to arrive on October 13th for a very full programme, invited by the Great Britain-East Europe Centre. Her first engagement, on the 16th, was a poetry reading at the Headquarters in Earls Court Square of the National Poetry Society. Pierre had been invited to introduce Blaga and, as reported in *Vsyaka Nedelya*: "Petar Ouvaliev was sparkling that evening". Indeed, reading through the copy of his text for that evening (yes, of course I have found a copy!), I see that he considered himself:

> "ill-suited to herald the presence in our midst of a poet who has restored the dignity of the Word, defiled and debased by sterile Stalinism – of Blaga Dimitrova, redeemer of Bulgarian poetry as a tool of truth.
>
> ...I am faced with the exorbitant task of pouring an ocean into a thimble, of describing in a few minutes and in the Third Person Singular – her, she, Blaga Dimitrova – the plurality of a most uncommon and truly awesome creative quintet... For indeed this profound poet is also a piercing critic who is also a trailblazing playwright and powerful novelist. And, God alone knows, with her courageous and relentless activity as a political dissident, how on earth does she manage to be so poised, so vigorous, so attractive and so concerned with the welfare of the family cat Foncho".

He goes on to refer to some of her literary output and concludes:

> "But... who am I to pontificate when we are privileged to have with us the poet and her poetry, the singer and the song. All I can do – and in all humility – is to exhort you to listen to both of them with your heart and your mind because in every line which Blaga Dimitrova has written in

her flowering maturity, ethics exudes the warmth of aesthetics and aesthetics shines with the nobility of ethics".

The session was extremely well attended and, after Blaga had read some of her poems, Brenda Walker read the English translations she had made.

She also spoke to the students at the School of Slavonic and East European Studies at London University. There she presented her essay entitled *Politics and Poetry* which was received with rapturous applause. This meeting with the staff and students gave rise later to a very interesting proposal: on October 28th Dr. Henninger, Head of the Bulgarian Department at SSEES, wrote to Pierre asking him to add his signature, and his undoubted authority, to an 'Open Letter' which the Faculty had drafted and which was to be sent to President Zhelev:

"Your Excellency
    We, the undersigned, British university teachers, writers, poets and other intellectuals, appeal to you in connection with the appointment of a new Ambassador from your country to the United Kingdom... Blaga Dimitrova's visit to the United Kingdom has helped to promote friendly relations between our two countries.
    ... In our opinion Blaga Dimitrova would be the best possible Ambassador of the Republic of Bulgaria to the United Kingdom".

This fascinating suggestion was, of course, not to be acted upon: Blaga was to join President Zhelev's team as Vice-President of the Republic.

Meanwhile, in Chelsea, poetry, translations... and cats were to be the subject of conversation at a lunch we hosted for her with our friend the poet and translator Anthony Rudolf, at which it seems no small amount of champagne was drunk!

21.X.1990г. – Скъпи Петьо, прекланям се пред твоя свръхчовешки подвиг да бъдеш жрец на българския език далеч от огнището му и да разгаряш неговия огън с толкова обич, красота и словооткривателство!
Обичам те – Блага

The next, and very minor, London Bulgarian event was the reception given for the visit of the 'Cultural Commission' at the Residence by Ambassador Dimiter Zhulev – that very one, one must suppose, who was to have been replaced by Blaga Dimitrova.

Christmas saw us entertaining three Australian schoolgirls, the ones to whose homes Mila had been invited during her stay in their country. They must have been surprised at spending the festive season indoors and away from their December sunshine!

* * * * *

1991

Vulgar Bulgars

1991, after the excitement and upheavals of the previous year – many of which affected Pierre in a very personal way – was a year of "consolidating": social meetings with friends, Bulgarians coming on visits (almost always a pleasure...).

January brought us, quite literally, the visit of one of the sons of Pierre's old friend Ancheto Fadenhecht. Her sons Nikolai and 'Bondo', with their families, had already been our guests on earlier occasions. This was the time when Pierre was to enjoy long discussions about plays and productions with the third brother, the well known actor and director 'Yosko' Serchadjiev. He and his wife and daughter arrived at Heathrow on January 14th and Pierre was there to welcome them. Everything had been arranged for the three of them to stay for two weeks in the apartment, Pierre's workplace, at 46 Markham Square. Generous as ever, Pierre did everything he could to buy tickets for the best shows in town, and not even *King Lear* at the National Theatre proved beyond his string-pulling powers; but when Yosko and his wife turned down this opportunity, I began to realise, with mounting astonishment, that either Yosko was not really serious about the theatre or that, for some reason, his wife Rumiana exerted an undue influence on him. Any social contact became difficult and I limited myself to occasional talks with their daughter Anna who spoke excellent Spanish, having had the privilege accorded to some of studying in Cuba. Pierre, however, was the model of courtesy and patience and stayed talking to Yosko while Rumiana went out to see her friends in London and go shopping.

The day of their departure was the occasion for one of Pierre's and my fairly rare serious arguments: Rumiana had arranged for a car to come from the Embassy to accommodate the many suitcases and I went round to the apartment to say my farewells. However, to my amazement, I found the apartment in a terrible state: beds unmade, kitchen dirty, dishes not washed, rubbish not disposed of... I made it quite clear that, although the car was coming and that they had limited time to get to the airport, nobody was leaving until some cleaning and tidying had been done. Pierre, of course, found himself in an embarrassing position in front of his friends, but no such things worry a Brit! I took Anna into the kitchen and explained the principles of hospitality, appreciation and civilised behaviour to her – seemingly for the first time – and left her to do some cleaning. Of course her mother sat talking in the sitting room.

I think that, despite himself, Pierre must have felt a measure of disappointment, especially as it was known that Yosko had played an active part in the democratic movement.

I am happy to report that, without exception, all our other guests have behaved impeccably! A stay in the house that I recall with particular pleasure is that of *'Rector Magnificus'* Boyan Biolchev who even looked after the cat!

Pierre's notes rarely went beyond dates and times, but on February 16th we encounter an exception: "Viktor V. called. Most friendly". Pierre was obviously impressed, surprised, pleased by this. While I cannot be sure, I take this to have been Viktor Vulkov, brother of Ivaila.

At the end of the month Pierre was in Sofia for a few days and, among the many names mentioned in a small notebook of the time, indicating that he met them there are Sasha Beshkov and Marin Goleminov. Pierre was listed as one of only two foreign delegates invited to participate in the meetings at Sofia University, held to establish "a new social movement". This was, of course, the time of many meetings and social upheaval as documented in *Bulgaria – the Beginning of Change*.

March brought us the pleasure of visits from Rosa Georgieva who, by that time, was undergoing treatment for cancer in London. She had, nevertheless, set up an international wine-exporting company, '*Rosim*', together with Margarit Todorov, the now hugely successful director of '*Domain Boyar*'. Ivan Slavkov was also in London for meetings related to Bulgaria's bid for the next Winter Olympics, and many a long evening was spent discussing football at Markham Square! April, of course, was Easter holidays, two weeks at the house in Vaucottes, dealing with the huge garden, painting the shutters, weeding the terrace, all the hundreds of things that a holiday home always seems to need! That year, however, the weather was glorious. Mila took the opportunity of going up to Paris and spending a few days with Pierre-Christian and Letizia and her cousins. France was truly becoming a second home for all of us! It was also a place where, comfortably installed in his upstairs "room with a view", Pierre was able to compose so many of his articles and presentations. This year it was to be a lecture at the British-Bulgarian symposium at SSEES in May.

Back in London we had the pleasure of a visit from Ivo Hadjimishev. Ivo had made a fine name for himself as an international photographer and was in London in that connection. At the end of his week's stay he wrote in our Visitors' Book:

"Marvellous stay with you, Sonia and Petyo; it was another semester of my London University!"

Ivo was kind enough to give me a book, *The Best of Bulgarian Cuisine*, inscribed to "The best of Bulgarian wives"; an enormous compliment which I was happy to accept! In addition it allowed me to enlarge my repertoire of tasty Bulgarian dishes!

Myths and legends

May 13th was the date when Pierre was to present the lecture on which he had been working, a *Mytho-analysis of 'Koziat Rog'* (*Goat horn*), the short story by Nikolai Haitov. Pierre's intention was to challenge the "prevailing conventional analytical method" and to base his analysis on the hypothesis that:

> "...a surface literary text conceals a deep mythical and archetypal dimension which endows it with a second hidden dimension. This is precisely what I shall endeavour to do in the hope that such a mytho-analysis may also show one possible way of evaluating the talent of writers...
>
> Bulgarian prose is rich in surface splendours and poor in depth prospection. Nikolai Haitov has given it this missing vertical dimension which may be found in Latin American writings where myths naturally blend with reality... If the wealth of mythological evocation is the measure of true talent, Haitov is to be rated exceedingly high...".

It was in May that Pierre made the acquaintance of a "new arrival" in London, Dr. Simeon Davidoff who was to become one of his devoted "fans". Probably the most noteworthy thing about Davidoff was that, in the early 1990s, he regularly mounted the soapbox on Sunday mornings at Hyde Park's "Speakers' Corner".

June 9th was the occasion for us all to celebrate Mila's 18th birthday and this was spread over two days with theatre, a meal out with friends at a hotel and a party at home. As she had already passed her driving test we passed on to her our Ford Escort thus making her much more independent! She was also to spend the summer holidays working at the prestigious Savoy Hotel in London.

Paranoia

An important Bulgarian cultural event was to take place in July when, during London's International Theatre Festival, there was a performance of Stefan Tsanev's play *Paranoia* given at the Royal Court Theatre in a translation by Rosa Hayes and Valeri Tchukov. As Tchukov wrote in his introduction:

> "In Sofia Tsanev has been playing to full houses. Things weren't always quite that rosy. Before the demise of the communist regime Tsanev was banned and banished, spending seven years in internal exile... only a few of his plays ever reached the stage... Tsanev never failed, however,... to enjoy the reputation of being a leading poet and playwright in Bulgaria."

After a relaxing holiday in Normandy, Pierre went to Paris, staying with Dora and Luben but taking the opportunity of spending time with Svetlin Roussev, who was having an exhibition at a major gallery. The story goes that the two of them spent hours talking in the gallery but, at the same time, checking until late in the night that the pictures were correctly hung. What better than to do the work with a friend!

This was a year when Pierre was, like all his fellow countrymen, taking stock of the new situation in Bulgaria; listening, meeting, talking, observing the changes. The following year was to prove a rewarding one, when he was to be justly recognised by his many friends, admirers and colleagues.

* * * * *

1992

The time of honour and acknowledgement

The year began, as it so often did, with a delightful week in Tenerife. Pierre was able to catch up with Mitko Grantcharov, who was setting up film projects with his German colleagues and Pierre was obviously able to be helpful with this. We spent time talking, sunbathing and swimming in the gardens of the elegant Hotel San Felipe or at Mitko's villa in the village of San Nicolás.

All too soon, however, we were back in chilly London, just in time to arrange a birthday dinner for Pierre. One gift, very much appreciated albeit arriving a month or so later, was a letter dated 11th March from the Vice President of the Republic, Blaga Dimitrova, inviting Pierre to be the guest of the Presidency on the occasion of the Day of Bulgarian Culture, 24th May, and to arrange for him such meetings and visits as he should wish to have. She goes on to say what an honour it will be not only for her but also for Bulgarian culture since Pierre was, during the forty or so years of the country's isolation, one of the great spirits who kept hope alive.

Pierre responded with alacrity and enthusiasm, confirming his willingness to participate in the Maytime ceremonies. This led to the proposal from Sofia University that the award be made to him of *'Doctor Honoris Causa'* at the same time. Both his presence and his speech would be a mark of recognition of the language, art and culture which he himself had so long been supporting, through his writings and his broadcasts, from beyond Bulgaria's frontiers.

> РЕПУБЛИКА БЪЛГАРИЯ
>
> КАНЦЕЛАРИЯ НА ПРЕЗИДЕНТА
>
> №
>
> СОФИЯ 11 март 199 2 г.
>
> Уважаеми господин Увалиев,
>
> След дългото Ви отсъствие от родината Вашето гостуване ще бъде не само скъпа среща на приятели лично за мен, но и чест за българската култура, защото през десетилетията на изолация, които преживяхме, Вие бяхте един от големите просветени духове на нацията ни, непоклатимо отстоявали истинските стойности на хуманността, нравствеността и интелектуалната извисеност. Вашите книги за изкуство, Вашите есета и Вашите радиоемисии, както и енергията и очарованието на Вашата личност, щедро даваха на поколения български интелектуалци утеха, надежда и сила. А любовта, с която опазвате чистотата на българския език, Ви е спечелила признателността на вярващите в животворната способност на словото.
>
> Приемете, господин Увалиев, моите топли чувства и дълбоките ми почитания.
>
> Блага Димитрова
> ВИЦЕПРЕЗИДЕНТ НА РЕПУБЛИКА БЪЛГАРИЯ

The second gift which was to come his way was the visit to Madrid which we both undertook at the end of March: while I joined my colleagues on the ERASMUS programme, he spent time with Simeon Saxe-Coburg at his villa. I have no doubt that politics, history, monarchy, government, literature and much else occupied the two men, each in his own way passionate about his country, perhaps especially at this delicate stage in the development of the "new democracy". Each later expressed himself delighted with this opportunity to talk at length and in relaxed surroundings. Pierre, it will be remembered, declared: "I am not a monarchist, but I am a Simeonist". No doubt with this in mind, Pierre prepared a translation into Bulgarian of the *Song for Simeon* by T.S. Eliot.

THE NINETIES – BULGARIA REDIVIVA

Friends and music were not forgotten either as Aldo Ceccato was in Madrid to conduct the 50th founding concert of the Spanish National Orchestra. To Aldo's astonishment, we turned up for the rehearsal, having seen the posters announcing the concert! He organised tickets for us for the following day. We celebrated my birthday with Spanish friends and flew back to London to meet Mila at the beginning of the school holidays.

Pierre was working on his lecture for the University ceremony during the ten days we spent in Vaucottes over Easter, and it was not long before we were to return to London and, on May 17th, he flew to Sofia. These few remaining pages

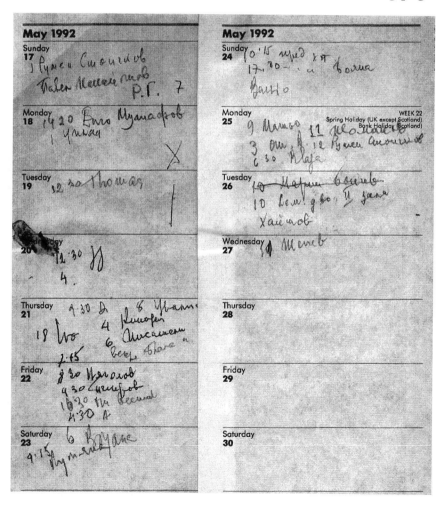

of his diary for the period give an idea of the number of people wanting to see him, the meetings and phone calls (there is also still in the "archive" a whole pack of pink "message" cards taken by the telephonist at Grand Hotel Sofia!).

The ceremony for the award of *'Doctor Honoris Causa'* was to take place on 20th May but, prior to that, on May 19th Pierre was invited to lunch by the British Ambassador, Richard Thomas, and his wife, a very proper recognition of a British citizen now returning with honour to the country of his birth, crowned with metaphorical laurels.

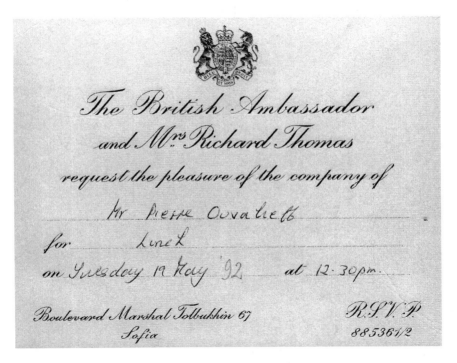

On May 20th, before the university ceremony, Pierre had an invitation to lunch with the President Dr. Zhelyu Zhelev at Restaurant *'Krim'*.

While this must have been both a pleasure and an honour, one cannot help wondering if Pierre was not too nervous to eat much! The Aula began admitting people, as it says on the invitation card, "from 15h45". By 16h., when the ceremony

> ПРЕЗИДЕНТЪТ НА РЕПУБЛИКА БЪЛГАРИЯ
> Д-р ЖЕЛЮ ЖЕЛЕВ
> има удоволствието да покани
> г-н Пьотър Увалиев
> на обяд
> от 12,30 часа, на 20.05.1992 г., сряда
> Ресторант „Крим"

was due to begin, the Aula was more crowded than anyone could remember. The reception that he and his speech *Usporednata Evropa (Parallel Europe)* received were certainly overwhelming. The theme, as we know, is one about which he felt very strongly.

The following days the pages of his diary are littered with the names of friends with whom he had meetings: "Haitov, Zhechev, Blaga, Ivo…". On the 24th of May, "Day of

Bulgarian Education and Culture and of the Cyrillic Alphabet", Pierre had an invitation to the "Boyana Residence, Building 1, at 18h" from "the Vice President, Blaga Dimitrova".

On the 26th he was invited by the University Council to give a lecture and, on this occasion, his subject was language, his title *Mnogolog (Much Language)* was a clever play on the word 'Monologue', his plea being a move from the 'single' to the 'many'. He again enthralled the huge crowd of staff, students, friends and intellectuals who attended. Bulgaria was both ready and eager to welcome "the prodigal son". Among the many eulogies appearing in the press, a long and detailed article by his good friend the art and cultural historian Dimiter Avramov was published at the beginning of June in the weekly edition of *Democrazia*. Dimiter Avramov was also one of a group of intellectuals whom Toma Tomov was able to bring together for a filmed discussion on current trends in art, culture and criticism which was shown on television while Pierre was still in Sofia. The other members of the panel were Lubomir Tenev and Ivan Slavov.

On his return to London Pierre sent news of the event to Professor Michael Branch, Director of the School of Slavonic and Eastern European Studies, who replied:

> "Allow me to offer you my warmest congratulations on the decision of the Academic Council of the St. Kliment Ohridski University of Sofia to award you an honorary doctorate and its medal. High time too, I should say!
>
> I note the reasons cited for the awards. I believe there is also a third reason: that of keeping alight the beacon of honesty, decency and good taste through so many dark decades.
>
> It is generous of you to link the School to these distinctions and I thank you. It will bring great pleasure to my colleagues to know that you have thought of us at this moment."

Nothing in the rest of the year could really match these heights!

The year did, of course, progress through summer (in France and, for me, attending a conference in Varna) and on into December when, once again, we all three made for the warmth of the south of Spain, renting a house in Mijas, as before, and enjoying the warm hospitality of the Dimitroffs for a short period over Christmas! Back in London for the year's end we marked both a very happy and a sad date: the 29th of December was our 30th wedding anniversary but also the fifth anniversary of the death of Karl Ognyanov, an occasion for Pierre to telephone to Lina and exchange memories of this charming man. The next day Svetlin Roussev telephoned Pierre from Sofia to talk about the plans for his forthcoming exhibition in London. This was something they were both to enjoy: being together, talking art and arranging the exhibition and coverage. But that is for the following year!

* * * * *

1993

More honours, more invitations

The power of the airwaves

It is perhaps difficult to imagine how, after the awards and the speaking triumphs of 1992, this year could be even richer in personal rewards for Pierre, and indeed for those about whom he was to speak during the year!

1993 started with Pierre making out a list of probable topics for his BBC broadcasts. One of his themes was notable events that had taken place in years ending in a '3': *1813 Sofroni Vrachanski, 1913 Svetulka, 1773 Paisii, 1913 BSP, 1923 Radoi Ralin.* Many other subjects were progressively to be developed in accordance with his interests, events and the places where he found himself during this equally busy year, and it was not, in fact, until April that Pierre went for a whole month to Bulgaria. His frequent travels meant that the day when he made his recording at Bush House, normally a Monday, was sometimes changed, although the broadcast always went out on a Sunday. It was during this year, and for several years after, that Stefan Prodev, the editor of *Duma* newspaper, published certain broadcasts, thus giving Pierre a deservedly wider audience.

At this point it is well worthwhile quoting from a report concerning the BBC and its Bulgarian language output written by Dimitri Ivanov:

"The interest in Bulgarian broadcasts was stronger in

totalitarian times. We could learn then from BBC the things passed over in silence by the Bulgarian censorship... Since 1990, however, things have very much changed.

Speaking of the comparatively lower language culture of our colleagues outside Bulgaria as a rule, I must also add that this rule has exceptions. The name of the exception is Mr. Ouvaliev. He is equally superior to his colleagues in London and to his colleagues in Bulgaria. Besides, one can hear from him things which could be told by him alone. In addition to his original viewpoint and wide erudition, he has never succumbed either to the linguistic cliché, or to the patterns of Bulgarian journalese. That is why for Bulgaria Mr. Ouvaliev is something more than Alistair Cook. This is an opinion of people who like Alistair Cook very much and I am one of them.

The strong personal presence of Mr. Ouvaliev, however, has a weak side: compared to him the other voices from London seem pale and cheap. Pale when they comment; cheap when they read something translated from English into Bulgarian because, without being poor, their linguistic and translating abilities are inferior to his".

This is certainly a true and very widely held opinion of the value and the continuously high standard of Pierre's broadcasts. Perhaps the criticisms of his colleagues are a little unfair?

I, meanwhile, was in Paris for a week in January for project meetings and managed to catch a concert that Raina Kabaivanska gave in the Grand Amphitheatre at the Sorbonne. The following day she was booked to sign disks at FNAC but we seem to have missed each other and I had to satisfy myself with leaving her a note. I had the pleasure of meeting up with an ex-student of mine who was then a member of the staff at the British Embassy. It was particularly good to catch up with Fiona Paterson who, since her student days, has gone on to do exceptionally well in the Foreign Office. We even once overlapped in Rousse when she was doing an inspection tour of our embassies in Romania and Bulgaria, and she claimed that she recognised my voice across a very crowded room; for good or ill, teachers' voices must be imprinted on students' minds!

Theatrical memories

Pierre left for his stay in Bulgaria on April 24th; there were several invitations and commitments, all very pleasant and satisfying. The first was his response to a letter he had received earlier in April from Yordan Radichkov, writing as the Chairman of the Committee charged with organising a programme of commemorative events for Professor Lubomir Tenev, the famous theatre historian and Professor of Theatre Studies at the National Academy of Theatre and Film Arts.

Lubomir Tenev, who had died on March 10th, had been a lifelong friend of Pierre's and he naturally accepted this invitation with pleasure. He was to give the opening lecture at the Academy on April 26th. Before leaving London he had done a broadcast about Lubomir as "an expert on English theatre... writing about George Bernard Shaw, Oscar Wilde and Richard Brinsley Sheridan", but his eulogy at NATFIZ was to be more wide ranging.

Every single one of the many cuttings from newspapers which I have in front of me tells how well Pierre spoke of his friend and of his commitment to the theatre. It was also noted that the 'Krustyo Sarafov' lecture theatre had probably never before been so crowded! Professor Tenev's widow, the actress Blagovesta ('Beba') Kabaivanova, expressed herself very grateful to Pierre for the words he had spoken. The interest that the event generated resulted in plans for an annual memorial lecture on a theatrical topic and Pierre has always been spoken of as the person who sparked this idea.

Poetic memories

One might well imagine that, after such a magnificent event, Pierre might have been able to enjoy some quiet time... This, however, would be to misunderstand the extent of his commitment to celebrating not only the people he much admired but also Bulgarian culture. He was "ready to go" when, on 29th April, he was to give the commemorative speech in honour of 100 years since the birth of the poetess Elisaveta Bagryana. The shape of this memorial was, in one sense, to be

ИНИЦИАТИВЕН КОМИТЕТ

Ви кани на

Тържествена вечер - спектакъл,

посветен на 100-годишнината от

рождението на поетесата

ЕЛИСАВЕТА БАГРЯНА
1893 - 1993

Слово: г-н Петър Увалиев

29 април 1993 г (четвъртък)   Народен театър „Иван Вазов"
Начало 19.00 часа   ул. „Васил Левски" 5

equally "theatrical": the venue was the National Theatre 'Ivan Vazov' and, in addition to a speech, there were to be readings of Bagryana's poems and extracts from *Bagryana's Youth* and *Black and White Days* by Blaga Dimitrova and Yordan Vassiliev. Poems by Bagryana had also been set to music.

Pierre had demands for the script of his speech which, as with the one for Lubomir Tenev, he had broadcast on the BBC Bulgarian service before going to Sofia. He also gave permission for it to be published in full in the literary press. It is good to reflect on the fact that Pierre's commitment to culture over the many years of his living in London was now richly acknowledged and appreciated. What he himself entitled *Skromno slovo…(modest speech…)* was obviously anything but.

During Pierre's fairly long stay in Bulgaria there were many calls upon his time and presence. One thing which he always did with the greatest pleasure was to talk to groups of students, including those of Professor Vesselin Dimitrov, who booked Pierre for a series of sessions in the Faculty of Journalism at Sofia University. Pierre was also very pleased to be invited to address students at Plovdiv University.

He was also happy to spend time with Lina Ognyanova. She had just published a memoir of her late husband, *Dnevnik za Karli (Diary for Karl),* which had been well reviewed. As was often pointed out, almost every member of the younger generation owed their safe birth to Professor Ognyanov!

I'll succeed for you!

Being in Sofia enabled Pierre to start on the important business of making his claim for restitution of his property. He had been recommended a lawyer who, having promised to undertake the long process involved, proved too busy with other matters, possibly more lucrative than a family property claim, despite his having offered his services to what must have seemed a very prestigious client... The "restitution saga" and the search for competent lawyers were to take an inordinate amount of time. Nor were the several "payments" negligible.

Returning to England after his stay, Pierre was, of course, full of marvellous stories. These had, of course, to be shared with Dora, and so he went off at the end of May to Paris for a short stay, In June he marked Svetlin Roussev's 60th birthday with a broadcast.

In July we had the pleasure of dining Ivan Boudinov, previously Bulgarian Ambassador in Paris. This was a great opportunity for Pierre to discuss movements in the art world as Boudinov, himself a passionate collector, had arranged for Bulgarian artists to spend time in Paris during his mandate. I was to see his personal collection when I was in Sofia later in the month and he very kindly escorted me around several galleries

That was a period during which, in the absence of an efficient postal service, I would be asked by Pierre to pay visits to some shady "Lawyers' Office" in the centre of Sofia, with requests for updates on progress and usually with brown envelopes stuffed with dollar bills! Despite always checking the "working hours" and making sure to observe same, I never managed to find anyone in! On a sheet of paper, dated by Pierre "July 1993", there is a whole list (office, Ministry, home…) of phone numbers for a certain lawyer.

On the 28th of July Svetlin Roussev opened a major exhibition of his work at the National Palace of Culture (NDK); this was attended by many of our friends and serenaded by Mincho Minchev on the violin. For me the month was filled with lovely times spent with Pierre's (and now my) friends, visits to the country and all this on top of the work that we project members were to complete! This was also the summer that Rosa Georgieva was completing the building which was to be the headquarters for the wine business; the building in Pavlovo district which was to be described as an "English church". I think Rosa must have been impressed by that style of architecture. She certainly had the idea that it would represent an "English pub", for she asked me to get a book of *Names of English Pubs* and I recall that she particularly favoured calling it the "Rose and Crown"!

After our usual summer holiday in Normandy, Rosa contacted us in London as she had been diagnosed with cancer and was to have treatment at a private clinic. During this time she stayed in a nearby hotel and Pierre and I were often able to visit her. He was a great comfort to her, knowing how she must be feeling in what was, after all a foreign country, even though she had worked for many years here. On my subsequent visits to Sofia, Rosa was always kind enough to invite me to stay in her flat in Lozenetz.

In September Pierre was in touch with the 'Sweet Waters' Gallery in central London where, to open the autumn season, Svetlin Roussev was to have an exhibition. Pierre happily said a few words about his good friend's works to those who attended the opening on 15th. He stressed the importance of this artist who, while his artistic education had been in Bulgaria, spoke with an authentically pan-European artistic voice.

Bulgarian artists were to have their day in London, for

Andrei Daniel had an opening at the same gallery in mid-November.

I went to Bulgaria in October to make visits on behalf of the European Programmes Committee and to arrange academic exchanges at different universities. I took with me yet another list of lawyers' phone numbers... Sadly, Rosa was back for treatment in London in late October and we tried to spend as much time as possible with her.

Winter warmth

The year's end was, for us, a stay in Tenerife, and we visited all our usual haunts: villages, restaurants, concerts. Before leaving however, Pierre had already recorded four broadcasts: for the "end of the year", for the "New Year" and two more until mid-January. I cannot think of anything that would ever have persuaded him to let his listeners or readers down.

And so, in the warm equatorial sunshine, another busy and exciting year for Pierre drew to a close.

* * * * *

1994

Yet another lawyer!

The first few days of the New Year brought us back to London, well refreshed and somewhat suntanned!

Some notes by Pierre indicate that Christo Ognyanov visited us from Salzburg, and that on January 11th he spoke by phone with "Svetlin about Japan". Might this have been regarding a visit that Svetlin was to make, or had made, to Japan? Or might it have been in connection with the collection "Japanese Woodblock Print" held in the Gallery of Foreign Art in Sofia? Looking at the catalogue and the text translated, as so often, into atrocious English (or 'Bulglish', as I prefer to call such versions...), I note a supreme irony in that a lady is described as "Editor and Profreader of the English Translation"! Enough said.

On January 14th Pierre notes that he spoke to "MG re interview and photo for *Standart*". 'MG' stands for the indefatigable and ever helpful Maria Georgieva, 'Chef de Cabinet' to Blaga Dimitrova when Vice President of the Republic, and with whom Pierre had long telephone conversations which he always assured me were his means of keeping himself informed about everything that was happening in Bulgaria. One may well ask why he should need to "assure me" but this is in relation to another subject: that of the enormous telephone bills he received and of which I took a very dim view. An example: "27th January Paid BT £622". Later in the year this grew to: "Paid BT £802.79". Large sums indeed! All in the interest of "information gathering"!

Towards the end of the month, when Rosa Georgieva was in London, Pierre and I accompanied her to buy furniture for the flat that her company '*Rosim*' was to use as the London headquarters. On this visit Rosa was accompanied by her lawyer, Reni Tsanova, and I recall an evening when we had dinner in the flat and Pierre was entranced by Reni's recounting her legal stories and successes on behalf of a range of important people, including the deposed President, Todor Zhivkov. Not only was his legal mind fascinated by Reni's stories but, of course, it gave him the idea that she might very well be able to do for him what, until that point, none of the previous lawyers had.

"As I said to the President"

March brought Zhelyu Zhelev, President of the Republic, on an official visit to the United Kingdom and, on the 28th, at a reception given in his honour at the Bulgarian Embassy, he and Pierre spent a long time in conversation.

The photo would seem to indicate that I am attempting to keep an eye on both of them! The following day, after the official business, President Zhelev and Pierre visited the British Museum where, I am sure, a lot more fascinating talk took place.

April passed pleasantly, my birthday, Rosa back for more treatment in London, I to Normandy for the Easter holiday and, all the while, Pierre preparing for an important visit he was to make to Sofia.

Rendezvous of Intellectuals

He flew to Sofia on April 23rd, arriving in the early evening. His aim was to attend the second of the Memorial Lectures for Professor Lubomir Tenev, scheduled for the 25th. The day after his arrival, however, he was plunged into meetings: "12h Katy Gallery, Christo and Maria Stefanov, Petar Petrov; 18h TV". The 25th was a very busy day: he was to phone one of the lawyers; at 17h he met Svetlin Roussev and then, at 19h30, presumably after the lecture, Yordan Radichkov, Antoaneta Voinikova and Beba Karaivanova.

The lecturer this year was Professor Vera Mutafchieva, Vice President of the Bulgarian Academy of Sciences, and her subject was one of particular interest to Pierre: *Ibero-Balkan Historical Parallels*. She proposed that: "while geographically far apart, the Iberian and the Balkan peninsulas share much cultural history". The lecture was attended by, among others, the writer and cultural historian Toncho Zhechev and theatre directors Leon Daniel and Krikor Azarian.

The following day a meeting was held with Alexander Angelov, President of the Union of Journalists, to prepare an interview and also to plan the series of sessions that Pierre would have with the students of the Faculty of Journalism at the University. In the evening he visited Nikolai Haitov and his wife Jenny Bozhilova at their beautiful flat on Latinka. On the

30th he was due at a more complicated address: "*Mladost*, Block 98, Entry A, 5th floor". No name of person noted. I can only hope that he went by taxi, thus avoiding the mistake I myself made all those years ago, when I went to *Drouzhba* housing estate instead!

The Horseman

The 3rd of May was the day on which Pierre was to be honoured with the award of *Madarski Konik 1ˢᵗ Class*. To mark his forthcoming 80th birthday, the President bestowed the medal on him, citing: "his contribution to Bulgarian culture and spirit".

I have in front of me a letter from Lina Ognynova, written the following day, giving another, delightfully personal, perspective:

> Dearest Sonche-baby
> After your telephone call I went to Petyo's hotel and waited for half an hour for him... When he came down, it seems he was late for somewhere, had cut his face with his razor and hardly saw me or heard my information about you. His decoration was shown on TV the same evening. There was a long interview with him in *24 Hours* and this morning on *Hristo Botev* radio, in which he said some flattering words about my booklet for Karl.
> Right now at 6p.m. he is at the official presentation of Radichkov's book about frogs. I am sorry I can't attend but I am going to the theatre to see a new play by Stefan Tsanev, but anyhow the 'Alexander' gallery is so small that only the invited prominents will be able to get in. When the radio announced the event, the speaker said: "Mr. Petar Ouvaliev will honour the author with his presence".

She continues with news of friends and concludes:

You always say we will meet soon and I hope this will come true. Your breakfast will await you every morning. Unhappily, I could not invite Petyo for one.

Love and kisses, Mamche-Lina

It was wonderful to hear, on his return, all about the many interesting events and special occasions at which Pierre had been present during his stay in Bulgaria.

Death and renewal

Towards the end of June, one life sadly ended and, in a different sense, another one was renewed.

On June 23rd we had a phone call to let us know that Rosa had died the previous day in Pirogov hospital in Sofia. We heard this with something near to disbelief for, although she had been having the treatment for cancer, she had seemed so resilient: she had "unfinished business". We had all three, been so close to Rosa. For Mila, her son Andrei had been something like an elder brother. The funeral was scheduled to take place on the 25th and so we phoned to Lina Ognyanova asking her to organise flowers and to attend the cemetery on our behalf.

On June 22nd, the very same day that Rosa died, the Bulgarian Ministry of Justice issued the decree, No. 138, whereby

> "Petar Christov Ouvaliev, born 12th January 1915, is given back his Bulgarian citizenship on 22nd June 1994 by the President of the Republic".

This had, indeed, been announced and awaited since the time in May when Pierre was in Bulgaria and had been awarded the *Madarski Konik* medal by the President:

> "It is expected that the President will soon sign the order for the restoration of his Bulgarian passport to Petar

> Ouvaliev, who had been obliged by the totalitarian regime to live in exile in London".

A "renewal" of a life; life as an official "Bulgarian citizen", that which had been so unfairly taken from him 46 years before. Ironic, in the sense that he had shown himself able to make a very good life in England from very difficult beginnings, but also because a large part of this "good life" had always been dedicated to Bulgaria, the country of his birth and for which he had never lost his love.

40 days for Rosa

During my annual Project visit to Bulgaria in July, I was able to attend the '40 days' ceremony for Rosa, organised by Andrei and held at the Central Cemetery in Sofia. This was very moving and well attended. Appropriately for the first female

Bulgarian civil airline pilot, the carved headstone features a piloted plane. I was able to talk afterwards to Monsignor Elderov. The Vatican's representative in Bulgaria, he much admired Pierre. It is interesting that Andrei had kindly suggested I spend the month in his mother's apartment. However, brought up mainly in England, he had forgotten that, following death, nothing and nobody should touch or be touched in the apartment until 40 days had elapsed, when she, her spirit, would have left this earth. At very short notice, as I heard on the way from the airport, he had arranged for me to stay with his mother's lawyer, Reni Tsanova, at her large villa in Boyana. This was at the time when only a few villas had been built in the area, now extraordinarily overdeveloped. Reni's villa was finished but not the garden. With the idea of an "English garden", I was able to thank her for her hospitality by bringing over some plants and containers on my next visit! Our spending time together should, of course, have been the opportunity for proceeding with the claims for restitution of property, but this seemed ever to elude us: non-existence of documents, disappearance of people and papers, the chase was interminable and ultimately fruitless.

At the beginning of August, Andrei collected me and we drove to Rosa's apartment where, as it happened, I was able to make myself very useful because it would have been difficult and emotional for him to sort and clear his mother's clothes and other belongings.

Andrei was in discussions with Margarit Todorov, his mother's partner in the wine business, about his own ability to continue her work. Andrei, convinced that he could succeed, rejected Margarit's extremely generous offer and suggestion that he allow an amalgamation. While one must admire his determination to try and succeed, it became obvious over the next few years, if not months, that he was never cut out for this type of business, whereas Margarit has achieved international success with 'Domaine Boyar' wines.

Andrei had lent me a car and, while I would never now drive

in Sofia on account of the amount of traffic, the potholes and the impossibility of parking, it was very useful for getting to meetings with colleagues in different parts of Sofia. One visit I made was to the office where Andrei's wife Violeta was working for the Philip Morris tobacco company. To my astonishment, this was located in the block on Tolbuhin, and in the exact apartment which Pierre and I had often visited when it belonged to Chavdar and Emi Damianov. What a transformation!

My "summer month" was spent, delightfully, between work and friends: meetings and outings. One "old friend" with whom I was able to catch up was Zhivko Popov. Released from the protracted ordeal of prison, he was living in quiet retirement in their small house in Boyana.

Pierre was the subject of conversation with all our friends: his activities and achievements, his visits to Bulgaria, his regained "citizenship". Meanwhile, he was working, writing and attending conferences and exhibitions in London, and I was to hear all his news on flying back to London at the end of August, when I for my part, as I see from my diary, described "30 days of frustration, fury and fun; marvels and magic!". That about sums it up! Lovely to spend time with good and dear friends, frustrating to get no further with Pierre's restitution claim…

A new approach at the BBC

One of the developments in Pierre's writing for the BBC, which he worked on over the summer, was, firstly, that he had been given his own, named, programme: *5 minuti sus Petar Ouvaliev*. We must remember that although all his listeners in Bulgaria now knew who was speaking, it was not many years earlier that he was referred to by his correspondents as "that interesting speaker on cultural topics". Now the BBC obviously realised that the broadcasts would attract even greater numbers of listeners after Pierre's appearances and lectures in Bulgaria. In this connection, and to relate his topics to his ideas and personality, he "invented" a new style of title for many of his topics: *Septemvriisko, Sofiisko, Nomenklaturno, Parlamentarno*… the word taking a neuter (or 'neutral') form yet in a very personalised way.

September brought Andrei to us in London, where he spent many hours in discussion with Pierre, his "adopted" father. It concerned Pierre and me that Rosa had left no will because, even though Bulgarian inheritance law is, in some ways, clearer than in England, it is always possible that an "undeclared" other child may come forward with a claim. More troubling, however, was his seeming inability to come to terms with the need to run the wine business in a correct and profitable manner. By then he was launched into an idea for a franchise to *PC World* magazine. This would have suited him admirably.

At the end of October Pierre was to return to Bulgaria, this time for three weeks, at the invitation of the Faculty of Journalism both at Sofia and Plovdiv Universities. This was not only enjoyable for him, and much appreciated by the students, but it enabled him to try, once again, to resolve the question of the property claim. While he was able to meet Reni Tsanova a few times, nothing ever seemed to advance. Would there ever be a satisfactory outcome?

Looking a gift horse in the mouth

It was at this stage that both Pierre and Dora decided that a way to resolve this dilemma would be to do something that they had always wanted to: create an annual award to honour the memory of their mother, that remarkable Primary School Headteacher, Guina Ouvalieva. The terms of the award were drawn up: "to enable a young teacher to specialise in the teaching of young children with special educational needs", and it was to be funded by the rents which the apartments at No.1 Karnigradska Street, once restituted, would bring in. The whole project was put to the Ministry of Education as a most generous proposal, on the understanding that the Ministry, and the then Minister of Education, Ilcho Dimitrov, would continue the claim in the knowledge that they and a member of the national teaching staff would be the ultimate beneficiaries.

I have beside me copies of the paperwork, all properly drawn up and legalised, but, perhaps unsurprisingly, the Ministry considered this too difficult a task and the proposal fell by the wayside. It was not until much later, after Pierre's death, that the Foundation, created in the name of the Ouvaliev family, was to dedicate a whole classroom and computer suite to the Denkoglu School, in the centre of Sofia, where their mother had served for so many years. Thus, in some measure, Pierre's and Dora's wishes were fulfilled.

We rounded off the year by going to Normandy for Christmas with our friends there, after which Pierre took the train to spend a few days with Dora in Paris, while Mila and I returned to London. I think now that, even at this earlier stage of his illness, Pierre was becoming affected by "the spirit of Bulgaria": the number of times he went there, the extent to which he was feted, the restitution of his citizenship, attempting to honour his mother, perhaps his taking on rather less work in England…anyhow, it was good for him to be able to spend time with Dora.

Another festive gift awaited him: not only was he able to spend time with his sister but, as he rang the bell and was let in to the apartment on the Rue de Babylone, he was surprised and delighted, as video footage proves, at being welcomed by none other than Toma Tomov and Dimiter Avramov! It would seem, however, that he was becoming somewhat careless when shaving: for the second time this year there is reference to his having cut himself, and Dora's first words as he came through the door were about the blood on his cheek! Once this had been cleaned up, Toma filmed the discussions on art and philosophy that took place over the next couple of days. A very warm and interesting way to conclude a busy year.

* * * *

1995

Birthday greetings to a "Grand Old Man"

Needless to say that one of the very first events of this year was the celebration on January 12th of Pierre's 80th birthday! He wanted to celebrate quietly but the phone hardly stopped ringing with greetings from friends, especially from Bulgaria where the media also covered the event in many column inches. Among the many expressions of good wishes was a telegram from Simeon Saxe-Coburg-Gotha, to which Pierre replied, thanking His Majesty and expressing his desire that Simeon should be "Tsar of all Bulgarians".

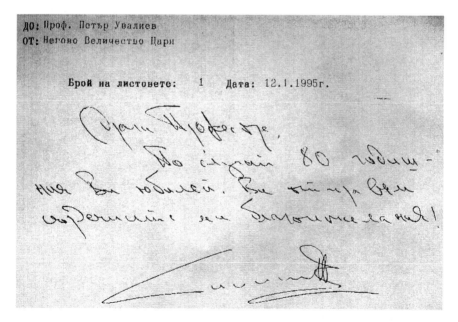

> Petar Uvaliev
>
> За Негово Величество Царя
>
> Ваше Величество,
>
> Неподатливи на вълнения са хората на моята пределна възраст, защото те са вече с един крак извън живота и затова от никого нищо не искат и нищо не очакват.
>
> Но въпреки тази календарна имунизация, неочакваното внимание което Ваше Величество ми указа наистина ме трогна: благодаря Ви от все сърдце.
>
> Тази чест ме вълнува двеж повече защото високо ценя твърдото решение на Ваше Величество да бъде Цар на всички българи. Въпреки не едно и не две разочарования, аз все още упорствувам да вярвам, че най подходящ граматичен символ на демокрацията е съединителният съюз "и" а не разединителнията "или".
>
> И друго: сигурен съм че не само аз но и мнозина по грамотни наше сънародници виждаме в безкористната привързаност на Ваше Величество към родната му страна не проява на самолюбива жажда за власт а съзнателна готовност за самжертва в името на една неувехваша рицарска "чест на рода".
>
> С потворна благодарност и отлична почит желая на Ваше Величество и на примарното Ви семейство щастие и дългоденствие.
>
> Петър Увалиев
>
> Лондон 16 януари 1995

Andrei Yanev came to visit us in London in February, accompanied by two friends who were most probably to be involved with him in the expected development of his mother Rosa's business. A great pleasure for Pierre was to spend time with Andrei's legal adviser, Malei Maleev, since his actress mother Irina Taseva had been a good friend. While all three stayed with us at the house, they spent a lot of time at Pierre's place in Markham Square, talking over old times.

It would seem that there were two receptions at the Embassy at the beginning of March. On the 2nd, I note: "Diplomatic reception at Bg. Emb. T. is so small, I missed him in the line..." This may have been a reference to the recently appointed Ambassador. Perhaps not too much of a *faux pas* for, on the following day, we attended the National Day celebration.

Teenspirit

Pierre had always insisted on attending a celebration on March 3rd, as it was a date when the Bulgaria he loved was honoured, unconnected to any passing political event or regime. With this in mind, he was only too happy to give a detailed interview to the March issue of the Bulletin *Teenspirit* of the Rousse English Language School.

> "*Teenspirit* is greatly honoured that this issue should host an interview with Petar Ouvaliev, Bulgarian émigré, polyglot, journalist and literary scholar.
>
> Q. How should one interpret the fact that you visit Bulgaria often nowadays? Is this a return to your roots? Does a cosmopolitan have roots?
>
> A. It may surprise you to learn that although for nearly half a century this faraway hospitable island has been my home, I have never left Bulgaria. This statement is much less of a paradox than it may seem. It simply means that circumstances have spurred me spiritually to break away from all bigoted territorial constraints. But Yavorov said it long ago and much better than I could: "Where are you, my homeland?...No, you are inside me, my homeland"."

The interview is fascinating in that Pierre responds to the very real interests and questions posed by these young students, assisted by their teacher Lynne Pollard. In good journalistic tradition, they submitted questions to which Pierre responded by fax.

And, indeed, towards the end of April, Pierre did make another of his more frequent visits to Bulgaria, staying for a month, meeting colleagues, giving a series of lectures and preparing in advance for the celebratory event which was to take place later in the year: the 115th anniversary of the birth of Yordan Yovkov in Dobrich.

Parliamentary questions

Pierre's absence from London meant that he was unable to attend the very interesting seminar, *The British and Bulgaria (1939–1948)*, held at the House of Commons on 18th May. Richard Crampton, University of Oxford, spoke on *British Foreign Policy towards Bulgaria (1875–1941)*; Malcolm

Mackintosh, Assistant Secretary at the Cabinet office (a charming gentleman who was a great support to Pierre in his early days at the BBC), spoke of *The Role of the Allied Control Commission in Bulgaria*, and Simon Kusseff, son of the first Bulgarian priest to minister in London, paid tribute to Frank Thompson, the British liaison officer who was killed in Bulgaria in 1944. Simon read from Thompson's poetry and, after his return to London, Pierre made a translation of a poem by Iris Murdoch, *In Memoriam Frank Thompson 1920–1944*.

While I found the whole day quite fascinating, there was another encounter which was to have lasting consequences for me: my good friend Alexandra Veleva who, at that time, was Cultural Attachée, introduced me to the newly appointed Political Attachée, (later, of course, to become Bulgaria's First Lady) Antonina Stoyanova. Knowing my long experience of London schools through my work in the Faculty of Education at London University, Antonina asked my opinion about a school placement for her son, Stefan. I was able to make recommendations and, although the Stoyanovs were not Roman Catholics, I was able to persuade my friend and colleague John Macintosh, Headmaster of the prestigious London Oratory School (later attended by the Tony and Cherie Blair children), to give Stefan a place. He did very well there, and went on to the London School of Economics. I well recall, two years after, when the results of the final exams were to be announced, that Antonina telephoned me from Exinovgrad where she was spending the summer, eager to know Stefan's marks! I also recall the Headmaster telling me that, when Stefan's father was elected to the Presidency, he congratulated him but the shy young man had replied: "I'm afraid I don't read the papers"!

Pierre let me know that, following the search for a typically English name for the 'Rosa Building' in Pavlovo, it was christened, to the sound of music and in the presence of important guests, 'The Rose and Crown'. Very appropriate!

We each celebrated the day of Bulgarian culture: Pierre in

Sofia, I in London. For him it was an official "invitation from the President of the Republic and Mrs. Maria Zheleva to the Boyana Residence for a reception at 20h30".

For me, it was a midday reception at the Bulgarian Embassy in London, accompanied, as it happened, by my future colleague and partner in a TEMPUS project, Sima Navassardian of Rousse University. She and I share many jokes and stories but the one which relates to that reception is that, after having been introduced to some of my acquaintances and starting a conversation, she happened to ask Petar Stoyanov: "And what do you do?" He was, as I have always found him, very courteous.

Pierre was back at the end of May and his teaching and broadcasting kept him occupied, as well as the major speech he had to prepare for the Yovkov meeting. We did, however, manage to make the occasional short visit to Normandy as some of the sons and daughters of our friends were to be married. In London I saw quite a lot of my two Bulgarian ladyfriends: Alexandra and Antonina. We would quite often have lunch or coffee together, either at the embassy, a local restaurant or in one of their apartments in the building (the old Embassy) in Queen's Gate Gardens.

Towards the end of July I went for a month to Bulgaria, partly to set up the new TEMPUS project with the Rousse colleagues and the Director, Stefan Dukandjiev. This summer I was staying in yet another apartment, that of Andrei's mother-in-law on the *Mladost* housing estate. I must say that, right at the end of his life, Pierre was still very upset that he and Dora had regained nothing and that neither he nor I had a place to stay which we could really call our own. One of the nicest things which I did with our friends that summer was to drive with Lina Ognyanova and Jeannie Rumenova to spend a day in Bansko. No longer can I imagine the peace and quiet of a picnic seated in the shade under one of the trees in the square: no building work, no ski lifts, no property development, no desecration of Bulgaria's beautiful landscape. While we looked at the sunlit mountains, Jeannie, having prepared a delicious picnic, quoted Bulgarian authors to us after which we wandered in the cool of the churchyard. We made a few visits to the summer houses of friends in the now overbuilt outskirts of Sofia.

As I was to present a paper on *Citizenship* at a conference organised by the 'Open Education' Foundation in Primorsko in September, I used some of the interim to research my ideas. This was to prove a most enjoyable, but also very busy, summer month. Unfortunately, however, I was seeing the last of Jeannie, though I was unaware of this at the time: she died soon afterwards. Back in London, I was met by Pierre and Mila and we had the traditional "de-briefing" lunch on the way back home. Pierre plied me with questions, not many of which I could answer in any detail, but I also told him what I thought were the interesting things I had noticed or heard about, and the people I had seen. Our notions of "important and interesting" did not, however, always coincide!

In September Pierre took as one of his themes the actress whom he had admired since his earliest days: Rouzha Delcheva. His BBC broadcast was taken up and published in *Kontinent* and one can only hope that this gave pleasure. Although he had wanted to visit her and pay homage to her theatrical achievements, she would never receive guests, fearing perhaps that they would be disappointed in how she looked in her later years.

Yovkov is

Pierre's programme for the month of November is very well documented: I have the itinerary in front of me, prepared by the most kind and efficient Boris Spassov, director of the Historical Museum in Dobrich. On the 13th he was to fly to Sofia and on the 15th there were to be four days of lectures in the Faculty of Journalism at Sofia University. This was always such a pleasure for him: imparting his knowledge and experience to students and hosted by his great friend the Dean, Professor Vesselin Dimitrov.

During these few days Blaga Dimitrova made him a delightful present of a *Speech of Thanks to Lord Peter in London from Foncho Murr-Murr in Sofia*. Some of my readers may remember that, on introducing Blaga at the Poetry Society, he referred to her devotion to her cat. *The Address*, written in verse, is full of word play and, referring to the date of his arrival: "We await you with joy, Sir, with Balkan Airlines... 13th, fateful number"

On November 19th he was driven to Dobrich. Maria Georgieva, who had been so helpful over the years (and has continued to be so, in helping me to collect and to classify

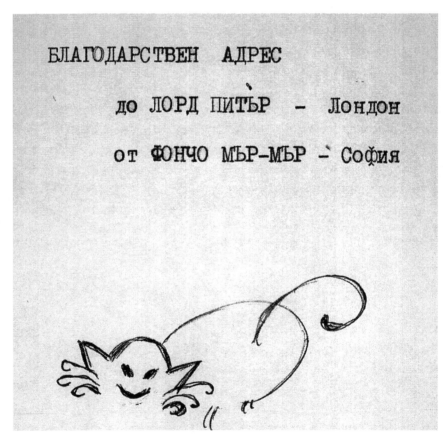

Pierre's papers after his death – such a mammoth task!), was to accompany him. The Yovkov celebrations spread over two days and Pierre's presentation *Yordan Yovkov I Sveta (Yovkov and the World)* was followed by the award of a prize to a writer "for his whole literary output". It had been judged that the recipient should be Nikolai Haitov and so it was a very pleasant duty for Pierre to congratulate one of his oldest friends!

The evening's programme concluded with a concert. I must say that, to this day, whenever Pierre's tribute to Yovkov is mentioned, the phrase that is quoted is his summary statement: "*Yovkov e*" *(Yovkov is)*.

Family reunion

By the most extraordinary of coincidences, my project team for the recently approved TEMPUS programme for *The development of multi-media materials for the teaching of English and German*, was to gather in Rousse in mid-November for our first international planning meeting. I flew to Sofia on the 16th with colleagues from the United Kingdom, meeting with others coming from Germany. This was exactly the date on which Pierre was giving his lectures in the Faculty of Journalism before going to Dobrich. We arrived in the afternoon and were to take the night train to Rousse, but I was able to "surprise" Pierre by contacting him at the Rila hotel where he was staying in the centre of town, and we had the opportunity of enjoying a meal in truly international company: my English and German colleagues, Pierre with his friends and I had, of course, made the time to go "round the corner" (I mean this literally) to ask Lina Ognyanova to join us. I am embarrassed to relate that, even though I had "European funds" for the project, it was Pierre who, with his traditional generosity, picked up the bill for a dinner for about 15 people!

Lina told me much later how, when she knew that Pierre was in Sofia but was always surrounded by colleagues and the media, she realised that the only chance she might have of spending some time with him would be to go round to the hotel and wait... One day she was in luck: he happened, unusually, to be sitting on his own in the lobby and she grasped her opportunity. They then spent a very interesting time talking over the "old days".

We left Pierre and the others at about 22h to take the train, arriving to a very warm welcome and a hearty breakfast from Sima Navassardian, the local project coordinator, at 5h30! It proved to be a most positive first meeting of the whole team of linguists and computer scientists at Rousse University, but I also had the opportunity to visit and talk with colleagues in the other contributing centres: Svishtov, Gabrovo and Varna, returning to London on November 22nd.

Meanwhile, of course, Pierre was making his much admired presentation in Dobrich, after which he returned to Sofia where, on the 29th, he was honoured with the award of the

"Ivan Vazov medal" for distinguished writers, an acknowledgement of his contribution to Bulgarian culture. Appropriately, it was the head of the Agency for Bulgarians Abroad, Guinyo Ganev, who made the presentation. Pierre made a most graceful speech of reply, saying that

> "You are the pole up which the sapling may grow. I had to think of myself as a pole and I chose language".

He later spent several days with the staff and students of Plovdiv University, returning to London in early December.

As 1995 was drawing to a close, we all went to Normandy where we spent December 30th with our friends the Watines, Guy celebrating his 50th birthday. We saw in the New Year with them.

By way of summary, I must say that the 1990s proved to be increasingly rewarding, interesting and eventful for Pierre and, it follows, for his Bulgarian friends, colleagues and admirers too. He had been welcomed back to the country that he loved, had been honoured and appreciated. In 1992 he was made *Doctor Honoris Causa* by Sofia University. Other years saw him lecturing for Professor Tenev, for Bagryana and for Yovkov. He was awarded *Madarski Konik* and the Ivan Vazov medal. In another vein, there was the restitution, in 1994, of his Bulgarian citizenship.

It is obvious that he was at the height of his powers, intellectually and personally. In retrospect, however, I notice a deterioration in his previously elegant and immaculate handwriting, there was sometimes a certain annoyance and irritation, occasional forgetfulness. An example of this is the list of dates for BBC broadcasts he prepared for the period during which he would be in Bulgaria in November and December.

These were the early signs of a tragic condition that was later to plague him.

* * * * *

1996

Bulgarians to begin the year

When I look at the pages of his 1996 "desk diary", and see the few, fairly random, notes that Pierre made, I now see the evidence of his declining powers: lists of phone numbers, especially of his doctor, medical and social services, but also of Bulgarian friends and contacts. Since first getting to know Evgenia Christova in 1994, Pierre was in regular contact with her; indeed, towards the end of his life, she was the only person whose calls he would accept. Maria Georgieva and Stefan Prodev, and their fax numbers, also figure. He made a point of writing himself "reminders" and I can detect a shakiness in his handwriting. He was also showing a tendency to misinterpret facts and events.

It is as if he were doing his very best to maintain a "normal" life. This was, of course, what he did manage to do, continuing with his BBC broadcasts until the middle of 1998. I shall illustrate this by giving, as an example, some details of the *5 Minutes...* broadcast dated '21st January 1996': Byronovo "...*na golemya angliiski poet Byron*", heroes Manfred and Childe Harold, and the links he draws with the work of Yordan Yovkov. This is as good, detailed and wide-ranging as any of Pierre's earlier articles. It was sent to Stefan Prodev with the dedication: "Here we are...from old photos...and verses!" A still brilliant mind, expressed in shaky writing.

However...after our lovely "family" New Year celebrations in Normandy, Pierre travelled to Paris to be with Dora and, as I wrote on January 1st to a friend:

> "Pierre, having spent a successful five weeks in Bulgaria, is exhausted but is, nevertheless, on his way to Paris as, since Luben's death, Dora has been in a 'suspended' state, not settling etc., and it has been found that she has a tumour on the ovary. Pierre will stay with her as she comes out of hospital and starts chemotherapy".

Mila and I returned to London, to work and study.

On the 4th Petar Stoyanov left London after the festive season, their son now well settled into the London Oratory School. With Pierre back from Paris in time for his birthday, we invited our other "Embassy friends", Alexandra Veleva and her husband Georgi Borissov, editor of the literary review *Fakel* to dinner. Pierre had the great pleasure of receiving a greetings telegram from Boris Spassov in Dobrich, wishing him:

> "Good health, a long life and to keep on encouraging us to be proud of being Bulgarians".

Towards the end of the month Andrei Yanev and his wife came to stay with us for a week. By this time Andrei appeared to be completely recovered from the nervous breakdown he had suffered a few years before and it was he who showed a great amount of care, patience and kindness in the following years when Pierre was to succumb, slowly – very slowly – but surely, to the terrible Alzheimer's disease.

Some of Pierre's notes for early March read: "1st March, 12h Embassy, 16h. Westm. Abbey 'Gladstone'"; "14th March, Maria G. to London till 21st"; "25th March, Prodev UK".

At the end of the month, I organised a grand occasion in the Senior Common Room at King's College, a party to celebrate my 60th birthday. This was great fun. Friends and colleagues came from all over the world and from across the years. There were speeches: mine reviewing my life in "academe"; Mila's, in which, among other things, she spoke of my firmness as a language teacher! Pierre enjoyed talking with my tutor, Professor Perry, himself then succumbing to Alzheimer's.

In April, three of the "Rousse TEMPUS" team arrived for a three-week stay in London, to be based with me at King's College – three charming colleagues, Milena, Mariela and Sevda, my "MM&S", with whom I have been fortunate to maintain contact over the years. We visited bookshops and examined materials, they worked with our English teacher colleague, Carys Jones, and spent time in the Computer Science Department. They also had several opportunities to meet and talk with Pierre, either at our home or in his study.

Meanwhile, Mila was writing her dissertation, taking over the table in the dining room, where she was watched over by our adorable cat, then a kitten but now a venerable elderly lady!

Pierre used to tease me and ask if there was any flat surface in the house that I had not taken over as a workspace. It is clear that Mila was following in my footsteps! She would also tease Pierre because, on one occasion, instead of buying cat food, he mistakenly bought dog food. As a matter of fact, I am sure the same food is prepared for cats and for dogs, but given different labels.

On April 29th, Pierre notes: "Phone bill £954.89 paid". As I've mentioned before, phone bills were one source of contentious discussion, Pierre claiming that the calls were his way of gathering information. While this was undoubtedly true, such use was also his way of maintaining contact with people he valued, even though the amounts were rising to stratospheric heights!

A Bulgarian inspection

In the summer it was my turn to visit the different participating Centres in North East Bulgaria and it seems that I must have given Pierre detailed information concerning my exact locations and contact phone numbers. I am sure that I would have done this anyhow but, by that time, it would have been an extra precaution. He obviously also felt the need to have this readily accessible. In Sofia I had the opportunity to talk with Lina about the changes I was noticing in Pierre; I learned of Andrei's "business problems" and that Margarit Todorov was running the wine business from the building in Pavlovo; I bought two shirts for Pierre from *Mushki Rizi 'Pierre'* (he always kept the label *Proizveden – Made in – vuv Bulgaria* stuck on his desk!). I stayed in the flat belonging to my ex-student John Lopez who was then working for the British Council. Strange to reflect that a "short course" in TEFL offered to graduate students at London University could lead to an appointment with the British Council and in Sofia!

I made my "inspection tour" of departments in Gabrovo, Svishtov, Rousse and Varna, later staying with my colleague Sima Navassardian and her family in their little country house above Varna. Sima and her husband suggested that, together with other English friends who were staying with them, we go to a performance at the Varna Opera House. Sima's husband approached the ticket office and asked for five tickets. To the shock, embarrassment and disgust of Gill, Mike and myself, we heard the employee say: "They aren't Bulgarian. The price for them will be…". Our embarrassment was born of the fact that our hosts would not be able to afford to invite us as they had intended, the "price for foreigners" being six times that for Bulgarians! Dual pricing has, supposedly, been abolished but I still encounter instances of it.

Back in London I joined Pierre and Mila for a few days before going to France. This was the time when Toma Tomov was in London on film business and he made a special point of videoing his conversations with Pierre at Markham Square. The filmed interviews that Toma made (as in Paris in 1994) are some of the best records one could have. An evening we enjoyed was with Alexandra Veleva at the Embassy, where Prime Minister Ivan Kostov's daughter, the same age as Mila, was spending some time, and the girls arranged outings. Pierre stayed in London over the summer and it was on September 10th, perhaps neatly avoiding the 9th, that there was a reception at the Embassy for Irina Bokova. She was, of course, later to be appointed Ambassador in Paris, although her name was one of several that were mentioned in relation to a successor to Valentin Dobrev in London. The workings of the Bulgarian Ministry of Foreign Affairs were to remain a mystery since it was thought that, after the elections, a prominent appointment would be made to what is, after all, an important diplomatic mission. One person who, nevertheless, felt quite sure that he would be taking up the appointment was George Ganchev. Meanwhile, Antonina Stoyanova, who was still at the Embassy, came to visit us. The talk was of Bulgaria, politics and, of course, University applications for Stefan! Could he try for Oxford or would it be the London School of Economics?

A Bulgarian wedding

Autumn brought a delightful "family affair": Pashanko and Margaret Dimitroff's second son, Brian, was getting married. Pierre, Mila and I drove to Suffolk, staying the night in a seaside hotel near the village where the bride's grandmother was arranging the ceremony. This was a real Anglo-Bulgarian event!

It is at about this time that I notice references in the "desk diary" to 'Davidoff'. Dr. Simeon Davidoff, whom I have referred to before, was a strange man, but an absolutely devoted "fan" of Pierre. For this, at least, one had to, at least try to, forgive him everything! His manner was "rough and ready", often rude, lacking tact and social grace, and his persistence was often annoying. However, his obvious devotion to Pierre brought me round and I know that he was a dogged supporter. And so he remained until his recent death.

On October 20th Pierre noted that he attended the funeral of a longstanding friend, the Polish artist Stefan Knapp, three of whose enamels we have. He was still taking an active part in the cultural and other events in London and, on November 6th, attended the lecture given by Professor Richard Crampton on *Bulgaria and the Balkans: Past, Present and Future.*

Meanwhile, I flew to Sofia and took the night train to Rousse with, as I noted, "$10,000 in cash". This was to be deposited in a bank in Rousse and used for materials development, computers and the team's visits. Unfortunately, the bank in which it was deposited then went into liquidation! It proved somewhat difficult to explain Bulgarian banking practices to the European Commission office! Such bizarre financial practices were again in evidence when, on checking out of Hotel Bulgaria in Sofia, I tried to pay my bill by credit card. According to the hotel leaflet, "You may settle your account with us by credit card". Absolute refusal at reception! This resulted in my having to run to every Exchange Bureau I knew of (no ATMs in 1996!) and try to get together sufficient local currency to pay the bill. All the while, Alexandra Veleva was anxiously waiting to drive me to the airport.

Enough of Bulgarian problems... Our plan this year was to take Dora for a winter holiday with us to the luxury Hotel Mencey in Tenerife. As it turned out, this was to be her last holiday and her last Christmas, for she was to die the following year.

Before setting off, however, there were practical things to do: the cat to be taken to the cattery, broadcast texts to be written and recorded to cover the period that we would be away. This is something quite remarkable: Pierre was certainly able to manage this side of his professional life. The list I found at the back of the diary reads as follows:

15 Dec. '*Ogledalno*'
22 Dec. '*Koledno*'
29 Dec. '*Bibliisko*'
5 Jan. '*Novogodishno*'

All set, Dora arrived by train from Paris and we set off for Gatwick, flying direct to Santa Cruz, where we enjoyed a luxurious holiday, concerts, drives into the country and a Christmas gala dinner with (what else?) a Bulgarian singer!

1997

Death ... but no renewal

For Pierre the death of his sister Dora was heart-breaking. As long as she survived there had been travel and talk, visits, meetings and friends. The relaxing Christmas holiday in Tenerife had given them both the time to be together, to reminisce. Without her, and the familiars of his past, Pierre became increasingly turned in on himself, able to write in his usual brilliant style but less able to deal with everyday concerns. Even on my return from a visit to Sofia with my usual collection of stories and gossip, his reactions would be unpredictable, often dismissive and critical. These, I am sure, were the signs of the Alzheimer's disease.

He worked assiduously at the broadcasts but went out less to receptions or the theatre. He was, however, always the generous and interested host. I particularly recall the London visit of Professor Boris Tomov, the charming Rector of Rousse University, as part of our TEMPUS Project. I took him to see Pierre at Markham Square where they talked for many hours.

Proof, if needed, of Pierre's continuing ability to construct brilliant articles and "5 Minute" broadcasts, is a script which I have with me, commissioned specially for the anniversary in February of the death of Vassil Levski: *Ritzar na Tchistota (Knight of Purity),* for a Bulgarian publication. The only indication that he might have been "slowing down" is the note: "Sorry that this is three days late. Phone me if you can't use it and I'll do it on the BBC. This will save me work, appreciated at my age".

> Прощавайте че забавих с три дни обещания текст.
> Ако по една или друга причина не ви върши работа,
> обадете ми го на лондонския ми терефон който е и факс
> в такъв случаи ще го дам на БиБиСи и ще си спестя ден
> два работа: ценен дар на моите години.
> С благодарност за вниманието
>
> РИЦАР НА ЧИСТОТАТА
>
> Покани ме един любезен приятел да драсна два реда за Васил Левски и аз
> веднага приех със самоуверената готовност на изпраксан аргат на словото.
> убеден че морето му е до колене. Но изведнъж се намерих в сляпа и глуха
> улица. Една през друга, думите ми убегваха и ме оставяха безсловесно сам,
> дори от мене си осамотен и от мене си омърсен и затова негоден да се
> докосна до непроницаемата чистота на Апостола.

Toma Tomov commented to me very recently that this piece was

> "extraordinary, in that it links Vassil Levski with St. Ivan Rilski and also brings in another of Pierre's great interests, the Bogomils".

For two weeks in April I was in Sofia, renting a flat this time. Will the Ouvalievs ever have some kind of "family home" in Sofia? One day, with Andrei giving me moral support, I went to visit the house on 6th September Street where I had so often visited Mama and the aunties. My aim, of course, was to discuss with members of the family (a niece and nephew) how Dora and Pierre might share in the property. No luck... mother and son had every intention of keeping the whole of the family inheritance for themselves. This had come about as a result of their having asked both Pierre and Dora to sign over the family property, claiming that, as non-residents, their part would be taken over by the government. Some years before "the changes", Pierre and Dora duly signed. When things did "change", retrospective claims were not accepted and they were told that they had "no rights". Perhaps I am a naive Brit, but I can't help thinking that it would have been nice if, just once, Meglena and her son had said: "Thank you, it is to you that we owe the possession of the whole house". Poverty was pleaded, but Meglena had installed a brand new kitchen, at the same time surrounding herself with the furniture which I knew from previous visits to have belonged to Pierre's mother.

On a happier note, I had meetings with the delightful Director of TEMPUS programmes, Stefan Dukandjiev; met up with John Lopez, still working for the British Council; met Antonina Stoyanova for coffee at Luciano's – she was about to become "First Lady"; attended the "Farewell to David Stokes", Director of the British Council, at NDK, with 200 or so of "the great and the good". I also spent many cosy hours chatting with Lina. In her I could confide my concerns about Pierre, his increasing distraction, forgetfulness... She and I went to a performance of the rarely performed *La Juive* by Halevy at the Opera House. As at Covent Garden, Sofia Opera always sings in the original language. It was interesting, and somewhat disconcerting, for me to attempt to understand the singing in French (difficult), or rely on the Bulgarian surtitles (surprisingly, somewhat easier!). The 9th of April was Stefan Dukandjiev's birthday and Alexandra Veleva organised a dinner party at their family home in Knyazhevo. What a lovely atmosphere: homely, relaxed, tasty food and the presence of four charming men! A lunch with Antonina Stoyanova who, accompanied by a charming blonde companion, stepped from a black Mercedes, proved yet another "change of mental gear" for me. The talk was of Stefan, his progress at school in London, Bulgarian fashion. It is certainly thanks to my many years of education and training with Pierre that I felt reasonably happy at negotiating these various social situations!

In London, the Bulgarian social scene involved a farewell reception for our friends Dimiter Georgiev, the Commercial Attaché, and his wife Galya. Late June saw the departure of the Ambassador, Stefan Tafrov. Visiting us in London was Professor Koumdjiev, Director of International Affairs at Rousse University, whom Pierre and I took out for dinner. Several of my colleagues from Rousse were also in London for a few days before going on to work at Wolverhampton University. The end of an era was marked by Alexandra Veleva's leaving London for her new appointment, again as Cultural Attachée, at the Paris Embassy. She and Stefan Tafrov had worked in tandem, first in Rome, next London and now it was to be Paris. Antonina was later to telephone me at home, from Exinovgrad, where she and Petar were spending the summer, to know the results of Stefan's Advanced Level examination. The grades he got would determine his future university studies. The results were not yet published but I was able to call my friend, the Headmaster of the London Oratory School, and he gave me the privileged information. The boy did well!

September saw me back in Bulgaria but not for long: the day after I arrived, Andrei called me during a meeting to tell me that Pierre had phoned with a message that Dora was at death's door. This meant some very quick thinking: I had to call Pierre and tell him what to do; I had to get myself back to London and contact Mila. The aim was to get us all to Paris as soon as humanly possible. Pierre was, of course, in a terrible state. I spoke to him on the phone, limiting it to the essentials: "Find your passport, your credit card, take a taxi to Waterloo and the first Eurostar to Paris". I knew that he would need this kind of "military planning" in his state of mind. Next, I went with Andrei, who explained most eloquently to British Airways that I needed to change my ticket and fly back to London as soon as possible on compassionate grounds. Why did I not fly to Paris directly? I had to be able to contact Mila, who was staying with friends in the country, a note of whose whereabouts would be somewhere in the house in Chelsea. The following day I flew to London, went home and found the address and phone number of Mila's friend, luckily no further away than Kent. I then booked two tickets for us on the Eurostar for the next morning, for myself from Waterloo, for her from Ashford. Next I phoned Mila with the news and the travel plan: she was to meet the train, to be standing on the platform, ready to board in the few minutes that the train stopped. I am still astonished to recall how perfectly the plan worked. Mila was, of course, very upset by the news; at her age she had not encountered death.

Pierre arrived in Paris just in time to be with Dora for a short while before she died. I am so pleased that he had this small comfort, to be able to say his goodbyes to his beloved sister. Mila and I did not, for we arrived two days after Pierre, but we were able to pay our last respects in the hospital chapel. Pierre-Christian arranged a hotel for us and we stayed until, a few days later, the funeral was held at the Russian Church in the Rue Daru. This was very well attended: friends, family, artists, critics and gallery owners, all came to pay their respects. In the early afternoon the hearse, with the family following in two cars, drove to Normandy. The cemetery was in the village of Criquebeuf, where Dora was to be buried in the tomb with her husband Luben. Many local friends joined us for this moving ceremony. Both Pierre-Christian and Pierre bore up very bravely. After the interment, we all drove back to Paris and, that evening, we dined with Pierre-Christian and his family, and I could sense that Pierre was incredibly affected by the loss of his sister. She was, of course, also his last link with the older generation, with earlier times, with his youth and with a certain part of Bulgaria.

The President of AICA-France, Catherine Francblin, wrote:

"We are sad to announce the death in Paris on September 12th, of our colleague Dora Vallier. Born in Sofia, Bulgaria, in 1921, she studied art history at the Sorbonne and at the Ecole du Louvre. She worked at the *Cahiers d'Art* with Christian Zervos and published many interviews with the important artists of this century, notably a profile of Georges Braque, who considered that interview with Dora Vallier as being "his testament". Basing herself on her profound knowledge, Dora Vallier published a wide-ranging and brilliant study *L'Art Abstrait*, thanks to which several generations of art lovers discovered the keys to modern painting.

President of the French section of AICA from 1978 to 1981, she was an active participant in the life of our association."

In London, during the autumn, Pierre was having fairly regular health checks, and, although from a physical point of view, he was fine, his spirits were low. It was particularly good that, during a visit I had to make to Paris, Andrei Yanev brought his second wife Tzvetana to visit London, for this was a good opportunity for him to "keep an eye" on Pierre and, of course, to engage him in conversation.

Rising to the occasion, like the well-trained diplomat that he was, Pierre was on excellent form when entertaining Professor Boyan Biolchev, who visited London in mid-November. They spent time at Markham Square and Biolchev also dined with us at the house. I was, however, becoming increasingly concerned about Pierre's depressive state, and knew that the loss of someone close aggravated it. This was definitely the case with his sister Dora. I was also to learn from his General Practitioner surgery that he would call round regularly. It is a pity that I should have discovered this in what I can only think of as a very unprofessional manner. The chief receptionist asked me to get Pierre "to stop coming round to the surgery and troubling the receptionists". I feel that this showed a serious lack of awareness of the seriousness of his condition and of sympathy with it.

At the end of the year we went over to Normandy, now bereft of family connections, but still full of good friends. We were invited to spend Christmas day with Paulette and Jean-Marie Winsback at their house in Fécamp. The day dawned badly, Pierre not really wanting to go; it was a question of persuasion. The friends and the company were very jolly but, not long after lunch, we left. My idea was that Pierre might like to take the opportunity to pay a visit to the grave in the cemetery at Criquebeuf. However, I realised that he was not feeling strong enough to do this and we simply went back to our house for him to sleep.

Aware of how much he was going through during the whole of the year and, touchingly, hoping that things would improve, Mila wrote a card to her father:

"Dear Daddy
Thank you for being a very special person. I hope that 1998 will be a lot better than 1997. Please keep healthy!
Love you loads Mila"

While we were in France for the Christmas period we had lent our house in Chelsea to our Rousse friends (soon to become "our Sheffield friends") my TEMPUS colleague, Sima Navassardian and her husband Papken. In view of Pierre's state, we cut short our stay in Normandy and returned to Chelsea. There was easily room for all of us and we spent New Year's Eve together. A photograph from the time shows the young people celebrating in a local pub!

* * * * *

1998

Decline and Fall

Two almost completely blank diaries: Pierre's through deterioration and incapacity; mine despite a concern to keep a note of more than just dates of meetings. Nonetheless I shall attempt to reconstruct a year full of worries, full of memories.

Early in the year Pierre did one of the things he enjoyed most: he entertained (in every sense of the word, with his brilliance, his warmth and his hospitality) our friends and academic colleagues from Shumen University and the Director of the Pedagogical College in his beloved Dobrich, Dr. Slavka Slavova. Photos taken at Markham Square show him much weakened physically but in eager conversation with his guests.

1998 was the year that the TEMPUS Project for which I was responsible was due to be completed. The accounts of objectives achieved, visits made and money spent had to be sent to the EC office in Brussels by October 31st. While this seemed a long way ahead, there was much to be done, visits I had to make, an international conference to be arranged... as well as my serious worries about the continuing decline in Pierre's health. It fell, quite naturally, to Mila and me to try and ensure that his appointments were remembered, kept, followed up...

In May, our German colleague arranged a meeting of the TEMPUS group in Berlin. I went somewhat unwillingly, but was pleased to have a useful meeting with my Rousse co-ordinator, Sima Navassardian. However, we were both shocked when the news dawned on us that most of our Bulgarian partners had disappeared ("collected the money and ran"). Sima was particularly cross with her fellow citizens who, it later transpired, had used the opportunity (and the *euros*...) to purchase a range of German goods, even a car! And this was long before any current "misuse" of European funds! Furious and frustrated, as I often am... with Bulgaria, I cut short my own stay and returned home.

For one week in June we had organised a conference in Varna. This was our opportunity to demonstrate to Brussels and to the many international experts who attended, the team's success in *Developing Multi-media Materials for Foreign Language Teaching*. It was also a pleasure to stay in what was still then a charming, simple hotel in St. Constantine and St. Helena. Now, I fear, I would have to make my way around the building sites and to close my eyes to the kitsch "Palace Hotels"... that have so despoiled the previously cool, green expanses of the resort. Enough of my comments...

While I was away Pierre had, noted in his diary, the dates when he was to be seen by the "Bridging Team": a group of medical, social and psychological experts who were to judge the level of care he should receive, at home and at the hospital. I telephoned to remind him of the appointments, as did his dear friend Struki Kalev. An excellent programme of care was put into place and it became easier for Mila and me once a "Community nurse" came to ensure that Pierre took his tablets. These were deemed by him to be "useless" and, I must say, with further knowledge of pharmaceutical progress and the lack of improvement in his state, I might have cause to agree... At the end of the month he was to be seen at the hospital by a specialist in the "Elderly Mental Health" unit. Meetings which I attended with him often became a source of extreme frustration for Pierre: in his lucid moments he could, and would, argue in his usual brilliant way and, occasionally, stand up and walk off, shouting at the team that they were "all idiots and understood nothing of psychiatry". I felt embarrassed at the time, but in retrospect I can only agree, that he may well have been right...

What else happened that summer? Jenny Bozhilova-Haitova came to London but this time she stayed with Bulgarian friends in Clapham and my colleagues Todor Shopov and Alexander Fedotoff visited from Sofia. This was the first time that both Pierre and I had met Alexander who, together with his lovely wife Snezhana, were to become such very good friends. Pierre was, of course, delighted to talk Russian literature with Sasha when we all had a meal together. Mila set off at the beginning of July on the long coach journey to San Sebastian in Northern Spain where she attended a summer course. Pierre and I saw her off at Victoria Coach Station and were relieved when she phoned to tell us that she had arrived and that all was going well. Free from classes and students at the end of July, I set off by car to join her for a short stay in the Basque country before we both returned to London.

Meanwhile, Pierre had been seeing his GP and, from one of the rare entries in his diary, I learn that he went, on the 8th and the 29th, to "Record BBC". On the 20th, he notes: "Medical day. Double sight, unsteadiness. 13h. Ready for Hospital". A British Telecom bill, dated July 2nd, showed an itemised record of his calls for the previous three months. When I spoke of my concerns to his consultant at the hospital, he asked if he might have a copy of the bill. Why? Because the pattern and frequency of the calls indicated a common feature of Alzheimer's. Almost without exception, the calls were to Bulgaria and, between the end of May and the end of June, to one particular number, almost every day. Whose? I have no idea.

September brought both a trial and an emotional support for Pierre. The 12th marked one year since Dora's death and, with a lot of careful organisation – of every kind (persuading, preparing...) – a ceremony was arranged with Father Simeon at the Bulgarian chapel on Sunday 13th. In the end this turned out to be very satisfactory, although I can only guess at Pierre's deepest feelings. Several friends, as well as the usual Sunday worshippers, were in attendance.

Later in the month I was invited to the 50th birthday party of Marie-Françoise Balesta, my teacher friend in Normandy. I had intended to go over for a few days and to close up our house before winter but, when I heard that "cousin Meglena" was to be in London on a "group travel" holiday and wanted to visit Pierre (what more might they want?), I changed my booking, left the party early and was back in London early the very next day. In the afternoon I went to collect Meglena from her hotel and to take her to visit Pierre at Markham Square. Before this, I had "briefed" Pierre about what needed discussing, what questions to ask, what statements and conditions to put regarding the family property. I offered tea and cakes and they did talk – certainly *he* did – but I could not follow everything. After some while I accompanied Meglena to the bus stop, reminding Pierre that I was coming back straightaway and would want to know what had been talked about. To my astonishment (I still had not grasped the extent of his "short term memory" loss), he could recall nothing of her visit or any conversation.

In October this state of affairs led to Pierre having a CT scan at the local hospital. Fortunately, Mila and I were both able to accompany him as the experience left him seriously disoriented.

Slowly, sadly... but surely, towards the end

I shall continue by giving extracts from the "journal" which I kept of the events and days which led, inexorably, to Pierre's death on 11th December.

"Tue. 13. X.
Several phoned reminders to 'be ready' because 'this afternoon we are going to see the psychiatrist at Chelsea Westminster'.

I finish at 12h30 with students and go, on time, to 46. Window open, lights on, door open, two gas burners lit... so where is he? He is NOT at 46. Has he forgotten, gone to Marks & Spencer...? I go and search there, no. Ring the hospital to say we'll be late, but have they, in fact, 'transported' him? No. (The appointment is cancelled...) Messages everywhere... BBC. 'Yes, he came. He had no text, was not well. We took him to St. Thomas' Hospital'. The community nurse comes. The daily help comes. I tell the saga... At about 16h30 he is brought back in a taxi by girl from the BBC Bulgarian service.

It becomes the BBC's fault, with a strange inversion of hospitals, going to Lambeth, across the bridge, away from King's, away from the No. 11 bus... The BBC and St. Thomas' Hospital are now the 'culprits'."

"Fr. 16. X.
The day of the Pierre-Christian visit. A late-projected (20h30) arrival becomes even later (22h15), and P., having stressed the need for money or a card for a meal out, eats in the kitchen. As ever, he is able to put together a welcome semblance of sociability and lucidity (which is good, but

enormously frustrating...). They talk (P. mostly of his youth and his parents) and at 0h. P-Chr. goes to his hotel."

"Sat. 17. X.
I to 46 at 8h45 to prepare for P-Chr. to arrive at 9h. P. had 'completely forgotten' his having been yesterday... P-Chr., cool and orderly, is unfazed. They talk and Nasco arrives re Power of Attorney. There is discussion of 'the claim' and, as ever, the logical gulfs are great... Mainly, what "my father... 'did/would do/have done'."

The days passed. My visits to Markham Square often coincided with those of social worker visits, cleaners and community nurses. The support from the Local Authority was truly wonderful. Mood swings (both Pierre's and mine!) were the order of the day. Sometimes I would be able to sit quietly (and sometimes Pierre would sleep); sometimes I would suddenly snap, shout, walk out; sometimes I would watch television, but that was often criticised: "How can you possibly be interested...?" There was talk of an "assessment" in the 'Elderly Mental Health' unit "when and if Pierre agrees, and when there is a bed available". This did seem a good idea as he was increasingly unable to cope at home. Mila and I nevertheless felt guilty, despite the practical sense it made.

When people phoned, Pierre would respond only briefly, except to the crippled Evgenia in Sofia. His delight and lucidity (which must have been an effort for him) when talking to her, was a rare pleasure to see. His erstwhile friend Emil Almor continued the childish and unhelpful practice of hanging up if I answered the phone. For a so-called "friend", his behaviour was quite simply inexplicable. I would take the time to explain to his wife Naomi, though Pierre would rightly tell me "not to waste time on them".

One day we had arranged that Brigita Yossifova (a real friend) would come to visit. I met her at Sloane Square station and we walked to Markham Square. She had specially brought fruit, the "blue plums" of his childhood that Pierre had been asking for. When we arrived we rang the bell several times but it was evident that Pierre was not there. I went to the house to get keys. At least we would be able to get in, see if he was there, see if he was all right. We sat and waited, and wondered. Some time later and, yes, it was his voice outside. Where could he have been wandering? All the way, it later transpired, to another branch of his bank. He was courteous and welcoming but it soon became obvious that the exertions had tired him and he went to lie down and sleep. It was then, I think, that Brigita realised the true extent of the decline in his state of mind and health.

The time was fast approaching for the TEMPUS documents to be sent to Brussels. October 29th had certain fixed points for me: I had to get the accounts signed off at King's, see that Pierre got to the hospital, and teach an MA class. In the afternoon, Mila and I helped Pierre to prepare some things to take with him to the Kershaw unit. He chose some books (of course!). He "checked in" – all very hotel-like – and was shown to his room. He was accepting, courteous with everyone, wearing his smart grey suit with one of his "trademark" white ties. We arranged his few belongings: a plant, photos, his books. Mila stayed with him as I had to dash off to the university, heavy-hearted, but the students were great, giving me a slight boost.

> "The days pass, friends visit. Pierre becomes very disoriented but, courteous as of old, always invites us to join him at mealtimes. The whole situation, his condition, is heart-rendingly sad... a man of such powerful and all-focussed intellect, to be so reduced. I now realise that there have been indications from a fairly long time ago... the lack of logical consistency (in talk and argument), the monomanias, the references to the past, the 'fighting in fog', the anger. Increasingly, I try to focus on, recall 'the good times'... In the chaotic disorder of papers at 46, the discovery of old photos reinforces how good it was, and... how sad it is..."

At the beginning of November, Andrei Yanev arrived to visit Pierre. We went together to see him in Kershaw.

> "Andrei is marvellous. They sit and smoke and talk. I think Pierre gets the maximum possible mental stimulation with the range of visitors he has".

Struki Kalev was also a great support; just as he always used to phone Pierre, he took to phoning us to ask about him. Lydia and the BBC, too, were helpful in arranging "repeats" of his broadcasts.

One day while Mila was visiting, the doctor told her that Pierre should have an operation for a hernia; he considered it essential and there would be no risk. Pierre's proud boast was that "I've never had an operation or anaesthetic in my life", but this one went with no problems. A few days later Andrei was to take his leave. When we got to the hospital, Pierre was getting dressed, convinced that he was in a hotel, that he needed to vacate the room, to pay... and that all this was taking place in Bulgaria. He was talking, consistently if not coherently, and had certainly got over the physical pain of the operation. We persuaded him that he "could stay one more night".

I beg of you, reader, as you come to this section of my 'memoir', to sit and reflect what a terrible affliction 'dementia' is. Literally, the mind unravelling, "de-menting". There is talk now, in the latest scientific literature, of there being "tangles" in the brain. That is exactly what it seemed like to us, confronted as we were by this phenomenon of a brilliant mind (widely acknowledged as one of the greatest of his generation), straying along paths he could not "untangle". At the same time he was relating events to past happenings: spending a night in a strange bed is somehow not unlike spending the night in a hotel.

One day, after a stimulating and amusing "catching up" lunch with Kathie Griffin, I went to Kershaw to see Pierre at about the time the evening meal was to be served. Pierre put on his jacket and tie and we sat at a "table for two"; he was attentive and responsive (requesting that we be served wine...), remembering people and places, talking in several languages. It was encouraging to see this and to participate; it was definitely a "good" moment. I felt disproportionately cheered, but I knew in my inner self that the downturns would recur. And indeed, they became more frequent.

Towards the end of November, after a three-day trip to Paris,

> "I go straight from the Eurostar to visit. Pierre's state a mixture: in his room, he responds to my telling him about Paris, my stay, meetings with people he knows, the Eurostar tag on my bag... but, tired, he soon relapses to sleep."

The staff became concerned for his physical health and Pierre was again transferred to the hospital. He had problems breathing, had a drip and was on anti-biotics. In the first week of December, Brigita visited and noted a great deterioration since her visit to him in Kershaw the previous week. On the Saturday, Father Simeon visited to perform the last rites of the Orthodox Church. He was accompanied by another true friend, Milen Lutzkanov.

As Pierre slipped in and out of consciousness and his mind wandered through the "tangled forest", there was one moment when his truly undying genius showed itself: the nurses had had no success in getting a response to their questions. I, remembering that Luben had "lost" his knowledge of French after his stroke, asked Pierre – in Bulgarian – if he knew who I was. Even after all those years I still made mistakes and, to my question: *"Koi sum as?" (Who am I?)*, his only reaction was not: *"Sonia"*, but *"Koya!"* I had not used the feminine form! Alert, a moment of lucidity, a hark back to old times!

On December 10th, Mila and I both paid a visit in the morning. Pierre was not responding to physiotherapy. Mila stayed with her father while I went and talked to the doctors. They were not optimistic about his condition.

At 3a.m. on the morning of Friday 11th December, we received the fateful phone call from the hospital: "Pierre Rouve passed away a short while ago".

Thus natural forces overtook a natural genius.

* * * * *

AFTERWORD

On receiving the news of Pierre's death, the Bulgarian media ran a whole series of articles and programmes covering the life and achievements of this exceptional Bulgarian intellectual. Anthony Rudolf's magnificent obituary was published in *The Independent* newspaper as were other tributes in the press.

Mila and I arranged for the funeral service and cremation to be held some ten days later at Mortlake and Father Simeon officiated at the Orthodox ceremony. Pierre-Christian came over from Paris, as did other friends, and were joined by a huge congregation of family, friends and colleagues. Both Mila and I read our personal tributes, and Anthony Rudolf read poems by Wallace Stevens, one of Pierre's favourite poets. Blanche Marvin spoke of Pierre as "A man of the theatre".

In mid-January 1999, Mila and I travelled to Sofia where, 40 days after Pierre's death, a service was held on the 19th at *Sveti Sedmotchislenitsi*, parish church of his youth, again attended by a large gathering of his friends, listeners and admirers.

Later, we went to place a part of his ashes in the family grave in the Sofia Central Cemetery. It is fitting that, in this way, Petar should have returned to his origins. It is interesting to recall that he had said to Rosa Georgieva that he would, ideally, have liked her to scatter his ashes over his "beloved Bulgaria" from her aeroplane. She was, however, to pre-decease him.

Although the plan that Dora and Pierre had put forward for a memorial to their mother, in the shape of a scholarship for a young teacher, was never able to materialise, Mila and I were determined that something similar should be set up. In this case, it seemed appropriate that all members of this remarkable family should be commemorated in some way. Thus it was that, with the help of Andrei Yanev and a small circle of close friends, we set up the *'Fondazia Ouvalievi'* ('Ouvaliev Family Foundation'), whose main aim is "the promotion of cultural activities in the name of the Ouvaliev family".

It is probably not surprising that many of these "cultural activities" have, in fact, commemorated Pierre. The list is truly impressive: a series of annual 'Memorial Lectures', launched by Svetlin Roussev and alternating Bulgarian and overseas speakers; the publication of several collections of Pierre's writings and broadcasts, notably on Bulgarian artists and his major work on JMW Turner; a book of "memories", contributed by his many friends. His students have not been forgotten either: a prize for "Public Speaking" at NATFIZ and, during the years of the BBC broadcasting in Bulgarian, a prize for a broadcast, lasting "5 minutes", on a topical theme. The many thousands of books from 46 Markham Square were donated – his culture and his spirit returning home – to the Library of Sofia University 'St. Kliment Ohridski' and to specially created "Petar Ouvaliev Centres" in Dobrich and at the National Institute for Library Studies in Sofia.

An occasion for general celebration was the 90th Birthday Party which we organised in January 2005, held at the Red House Centre for Culture and Debate (how that combination would have pleased Pierre!); films, talks, readings, music, eating and drinking were the order of the evening!

His mother has been commemorated by the complete refurbishment and dedication of a classroom in the name of Guina Ouvalieva at Denkoglu Primary School. More recently, a computer classroom has been equipped. His father's work is recalled by the publication, in the series "Universitetska Klassika", of his seminal work on the teaching of French, first published in Plovdiv in 1915.

It is with these thoughts and recollections that I close. Petar Ouvaliev aka Pierre Rouve, his life and his works live on. I only hope that my "story of his life" will prove of interest and awaken memories for my readers.

Sonia Rouve

London
September 2008